THE IRISH GULAG

How the State Betrayed its Innocent Children

Also by Bruce Arnold

Art History and Biography:
A Concise History of Irish Art
Orpen: Mirror to an Age
Mainie Jellett and the Modern Movement in Ireland
Jack Yeats
Art Atlas of Britain and Ireland

Politics and Political Biography:
Margaret Thatcher: A Study in Power
Haughey: His Life and Unlucky Deeds
Jack Lynch: Hero in Crisis
What Kind of Country: Irish Political Life, 1968–1983
The Fight for Democracy: The Libertas Voice in Europe

Memoirs, Essays, Literary Criticism:
The Spire and Other Essays in Irish Culture
He That Is Down Need Fear No Fall
The Scandal of Ulysses
Swift: An Illustrated Life

Novels:
A Singer at the Wedding
The Song of the Nightingale
The Muted Swan
Running to Paradise

Plays for Children:
The Wicked Woodman
Orlando's Revenge
Sean-Put-Things-Right

THE IRISH GULAG

How the State Betrayed its Innocent
Children

BRUCE ARNOLD ~

Gill & Macmillan

Gill & Macmillan Ltd
Hume Avenue, Park West, Dublin 12
with associated companies throughout the world
www.gillmacmillan.ie

© Bruce Arnold 2009
978 07171 4614 7

Index compiled by Cover to Cover
Typography design by Make Communication
Print origination by O'K Graphic Design, Dublin
Printed by ColourBooks Ltd, Dublin

This book is typeset in 10.5/13 pt Minion.

The paper used in this book comes from the wood pulp
of managed forests. For every tree felled, at least one tree
is planted, thereby renewing natural resources.

A CIP catalogue record for this book is available from the
British Library.

5 4 3 2

The Irish Gulag *is dedicated to the memory of Tommy O'Reilly and the many thousands of men and women, now dead, who suffered in the Irish industrial school system during the lifetime of the State.*

CONTENTS

A NOTE ON SOURCES

Much of the material in this book is drawn from articles originally published in the *Irish Independent* between 1998 and 2009.

Key

1. St Coleman's Industrial School for Girls, Cobh/Rushbrook, County Cork
2. Baltimore Fisheries School for Senior Boys, Baltimore, County Cork
3. Benada Abbey Industrial School for Girls, Ballymote, County Sligo
4. Mount Carmel Industrial School for Girls, Moate, County Westmeath
5. Our Lady of Mercy Industrial School for Girls, Kinsale, County Cork
6. Our Lady of Succour Industrial School for Girls, Newtownforbes, County Longford
7. Our Lady's Industrial School for Girls, Ennis, County Clare
8. Pembrook Alms (Nazareth House) Industrial School for Girls, Tralee, County Kerry
9. St Aidan's Industrial School for Girls, New Ross, County Wexford
10. St Aloysius' Industrial School for Girls, Clonakilty, County Cork
11. St Ann's Industrial School for Girls and Junior Boys, Renmore, Lenaboy, County Galway
12. St Augustine's Industrial School for Girls, Templemore, County Tipperary
13. St Bernard's Industrial School for Girls, Fethard, Dundrum, County Tipperary
14. St Brigid's Industrial School for Girls, Loughrea, County Galway
15. St Columba's Industrial School for Girls, Westport, County Mayo
16. St Columba's Industrial School for Senior Boys, Killybegs, County Donegal
17. St Conleth's Reformatory School for Boys, Daingean, County Offaly
18. St Dominick's Industrial School for Girls, Waterford
19. St Francis' Industrial School for Girls, Cashel, County Tipperary
20. St Francis Xavier's Industrial School for Girls and Junior Boys, Ballaghadereen, County Roscommon
21. St George's Industrial School for Girls, Limerick
22. St John's Industrial School for Girls, Birr, County Offaly
23. St Joseph's Industrial School for Boys, Tralee, County Kerry
24. St Joseph's Industrial School for Girls and Junior Boys, Ballinasloe, County Galway
25. St Joseph's Industrial School for Girls and Junior Boys, Clifden, County Galway
26. St Joseph's Industrial School for Girls and Junior Boys, Liosomoine, County Kerry
27. St Joseph's Industrial School for Girls, Cavan
28. St Joseph's Industrial School for Girls, Dundalk, County Louth
29. St Joseph's Industrial School for Girls, Kilkenny
30. St Joseph's Industrial School for Girls, Mallow, County Cork
31. St Joseph's Industrial School for Girls, Summerhill, Athlone, County Westmeath
32. St Joseph's Industrial School for Senior Boys, Ferryhouse, Clonmel, County Tipperary
33. St Joseph's Industrial School for Senior Boys, Glin, County Limerick
34. St Joseph's Industrial School for Senior Boys, Letterfrack, County Galway
35. St Joseph's Industrial School for Senior Boys, Salthill, County Galway
36. St Joseph's Reformatory School for Girls, Limerick
37. St Kevin's Reformatory School for Boys, Glencree, County Wicklow
38. St Kyran's Industrial School for Junior Boys, Rathdrum, County Wicklow
39. St Laurence's Industrial School for Girls, Sligo
40. St Martha's Industrial School for Girls, Bundoran, County Donegal
41. St Martha's Industrial School for Girls, Monaghan
42. St Michael's Industrial School for Girls, Wexford
43. St Michael's Industrial School for Junior Boys, Cappoquin, County Waterford
44. St Patrick's Industrial School for Boys, Upton, County Cork
45. St Patrick's Industrial School for Junior Boys, Kilkenny
46. St Vincent's (House of Charity) Industrial School for Junior Boys, Drogheda, County Louth
47. St Vincent's Industrial School for Girls, Limerick
48. St Finbarr's Industrial School for Girls, Sundays Well, Marymount, Cork
49. St Joseph's Industrial School for Boys, Passage West, County Cork
50. St Joseph's Industrial School for Senior Boys, Greenmount, Cork

Dublin

51. Artane Industrial School for Senior Boys, Dublin 5
52. Scoil Ard Mhuire, Lusk, County Dublin
53. Carriglea Park Industrial School for Senior Boys, Dun Laoghaire, County Dublin
54. St Anne's Industrial School for Girls, Booterstown, County Dublin
55. St Anne's Reformatory School for Girls, Kilmacud, County Dublin
56. St Joseph's Industrial School for Girls, Whitehall, Drumcondra, Dublin 9
57. St Laurence's Industrial School, Finglas, Dublin 11
58. St Martha's Industrial School, Merrion, Dublin 4
59. St Mary's Industrial School, Lakelands, Sandymount, Dublin 4
60. St Vincent's Industrial School, Goldenbridge, Inchicore, Dublin 8

MAP OF INDUSTRIAL SCHOOLS AND REFORMATORY SCHOOLS IN IRELAND

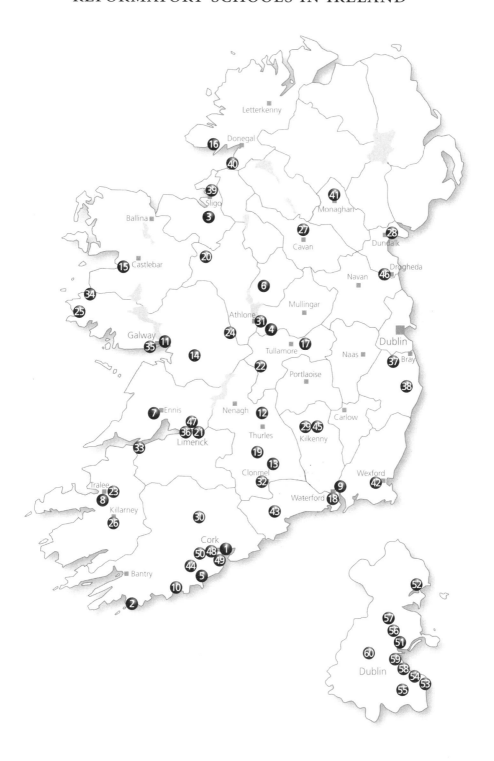

PART ONE

Institutional Child Care and Child
Abuse in Ireland—A Brief History

INTRODUCTION

During the greater part of the twentieth century the Irish State owned and managed a prison system for children spread across the whole of the Republic. The northernmost institutions were in Louth, Monaghan, Cavan and Donegal. On the Western Seaboard there were two notorious industrial schools in Clifden and Letterfrack. In the south-west there were branches of the prison system in Limerick, Ennis, Glin, Tralee and Killarney. Farther south there was an industrial school for girls in Clonakilty, another terrible place, and nearby there was the Baltimore Fisheries School, the most southerly and possibly the worst of all for its record of cruelty and neglect. Many of the towns where these places existed were beauty spots, to which countless visitors, both Irish and those from abroad, flocked during summer holidays in the simple, golden years of Irish tourism, unaware of the concealed prisons operating dreadfully punitive regimes. Across the southern midlands and in the south-east, again in beautiful, much-visited towns, were more institutions: in Lismore, Waterford, New Ross, Wexford, Cashel, Kilkenny. And so it continued up through the country to Cavan, Monaghan, Dundalk, Dunleer and Drogheda and to Dublin where more institutions were spread around the city.

They were places of shame in the communities where they were located and they were shameful places. In a country where everyone expected to know the business of other people and to know what was going on around them, there were these juvenile prisons. Enough was known about them and their inmates to make people uneasy at the thin, wan, poorly clothed boys and girls whenever they were seen. The majority of the prisons were known as industrial schools; a tiny minority of parallel institutions, run on the same lines and under similar rules, were reformatories. Together with certain other establishments for children who were euphemistically described as being 'in care', these institutions in reality constituted an 'Irish Gulag'.

The term is taken from Alexandr Solzhenitsyn, who describes, in *The Gulag Archipelago*, the network of prisons run under Stalin's rule in the Soviet Union, but for adult prisoners. As in Ireland, the Russian system was generously spread across the vast territory of Stalin's empire, from the Arctic to the Bosporus, from Europe deep into Asia. For children, such incarceration is different and the Irish system was for children. Their incarceration, introduced and carried out in the name of caring, was part of natural law; all children grow up in care and under restraint and are generally lucky if this is the natural care of their parents. But the Irish Gulag was different. It was penal: all who went through the system recall, above all else, the punitive nature of their treatment and the universal lack of kindness and affection in the way they were treated. Beaten, starved, tormented with illogical circumstance, they spent years in care that was a parody of the term.

Irish children committed to the Gulag system went through a sequence of experiences that categorised them as prisoners, and this is the way the survivors see what happened to them. It is their abiding nightmare reconstruction and has remained with the majority all their lives.

They were arrested, or taken into charge, most frequently with the flimsiest of legal justification and without normal formalities. The powers used in Ireland, mainly under the Children Act of 1908, but also under truancy legislation, were extensive and quite loosely framed. Section 58 of the Children Act was the main one used. It begins with the words, 'Any person may bring before a petty sessional court any person apparently under the age of fourteen years who — ' and it then lists a variety of supposed or actual offences, virtually all of which require clear definition. They are covered in seven paragraphs, each of which covers more than one aspect of behaviour for which the punishment of internment in an industrial school was recommended. The detail on committals is dealt with more fully later in this book. The law also required one only of the descriptions to apply and stipulated that the court should be 'satisfied on inquiry of that fact'. There is little evidence in Irish industrial school committals that this vital social and legal requirement was followed and there is considerable evidence that moral and religious circumstances, such as they could be judged, took precedence over the law and the social needs of the child. The system was well-established throughout the British Isles in the nineteenth century. The 1908 Children Act was a major legal framework for what existed. Within two years of its enactment, administrative changes were being implemented in Britain. In Ireland, after independence, the Act was unamended and the system unreformed. There followed a sustained divergence: virtually no change of the law in Ireland while in the United Kingdom the reforms and changes were considerable. Child care was steadily changed and reformed under British rule. In Ireland it was set in stone. Numbers in care in Ireland became disproportionately high. The sentences handed out by the Irish district courts were unbelievably long by comparison with those in the United Kingdom.

The Irish Gulag, though not so intended originally, became a State-run machine of draconian nature. In terms of natural justice, the State's true role should have been in *loco parentis* in the fullest meaning of the term. It was a system designed, it seems, to let the religious, who controlled and ran the institutions for the State, beat faith into children while at the same time they were starved, treated cruelly, and physically and sexually abused. The State, however, was responsible and it all began with committal by the courts.

Various recollections from former inmates refer to the presence of a guard or guards, parish priests, NSPCC inspectors, members of the Society of St Vincent de Paul and the Legion of Mary being also involved. What the children were charged with could in no sense be defined as 'crimes'; indeed the Act was there to administer a system of care. But at a time when increasingly diminished sentences—of weeks and of months—were being handed out in Britain, children in Ireland who were found guilty of the misdemeanours listed in the 1908 Act found themselves condemned to long terms of incarceration, a very large number of them for the period of their legal childhood. This is frequently the recorded term in the committal document; the age of the child, sometimes as young as 18 months, was ascertained and the sentence was then specified to end on the day before the child became 16 and could no longer be detained under the Act. On these terms the Irish Free State, and later Saorstát Éireann, summarily parted children from their parents and their families. They were deprived of their names and identities, of contact with the outside world, of their rights under the Constitution and the law of the land. In all this their fate was parallel with what happened to millions of Russians judged by the Soviet system to be enemies of the State. This parallel also applies to the many thousands of children who spent their early lives inside terrible, cruel institutions that were spread across the 26 counties of the Republic of Ireland.

The first experience these children had was their arrest. Solzhenitsyn describes such an event:

Arrest! Need it be said that it is a breaking point in your life, a bolt of lightning which has scored a direct hit on you? That it is an unassimilable spiritual earthquake not every person can cope with, as a result of which people often slip into insanity?

There are descriptions in this book of that state of mind as there are descriptions of the incomprehension and terror of being taken into custody and brought to court. There, decisions were made without reference to the child or children. They were frequently left outside the court. Questions may have been asked of the parent or parents, but their position was peripheral and weak. The main protagonists were usually the guard, who knew his job and purpose, the officer of the NSPCC, or of the ISPCC (National, or Irish, Society for the Prevention of Cruelty to Children), the District Justice on his bench and possibly the surrogate social worker, who represented the guiding hand of the Roman Catholic Church in the main decision—incarceration—that was being made. In some cases this person could be a member of the Legion of Mary or the Society of St Vincent de Paul, people who were visitors to Catholic homes and who reported to their superiors the conditions they found, the state of faith, the marital and family circumstances. They were the key to the incarceration process, who gave the evidence and made the judgments on which the District Justice and his court depended.

In December 2000 the distinguished Irish lawyer Gerard Hogan examined the Detention Orders and, in the course of a BBC Radio 5 programme entitled 'Children on Trial', he described the Detention Orders as 'patently illegal'. They were punitive as well and the sentences handed down were heavy. Kathleen Ferriter was three years and nine months old when she appeared as defendant before the District Justice at the Killaloe District Court on 20 December 1948. She was then living in New Street, Killaloe. She was 'found destitute and is not an orphan and her mother Ellen Ferriter is unable to support the said child and the mother of the said Kathleen Ferriter consenting to such order (whereas the said child is illegitimate) … and whereas the religious persuasion of the said child appears to the court to be Catholic' she was 'sent to the Certified Industrial School at Convent of Mercy Ennis Clare being a school conducted in accordance with the doctrines of the Catholic Church, the Managers whereof are willing to receive her to be there detained until, but not including the 2nd day of March 1961'.

So Kathleen, like thousands of other boys and girls, not comprehending what she had done wrong and why, at less than four years of age, she was being separated from her mother, was taken thence and transported, either by train or in a Garda vehicle, to her place of detention, there to spend the rest of her childhood.

In no educative sense were these institutions 'schools'. Not only did they not educate; they did not properly care for their inmates. Punishment was the universal rule imposed upon the tender years of these children. Even so, nothing that happened to them during their long sentences could possibly equal the horrifying abuse of their rights at the outset, when they were committed to these child prisons. Everyone involved, except the victims, had some knowledge that their actions were at best 'unsound', at worst a gross abuse of natural justice and of the constitutional protections in Ireland of children's rights.

Within the system, the reformatories were legitimately closer to being prisons for young people since those incarcerated in them were criminal offenders, ostensibly committed for crimes with sentences commensurate with what they had done. There are also distinctions among the industrial school prisoners. The full truth of quite what these young people were, indeed who they were—since identity was often taken from them and their records lost—was ultimately responsible for their blighted existence. This is a grim story involving a culpable State machinery that embraced knowledge and action by the Cabinet, including the successive Ministers for Education, Justice and Health, and of the Taoiseach himself, the Civil and Public Service, including courts of law, the police force in every town and village, the local authorities and child organisations among which, notoriously, was the NSPCC.

Much of what these servants of the State did, and allowed to be done in their name and under their ultimate control, requires close and careful examination. It should have been part of the 1999 decision to rectify the huge wrong done to thousands of men and women. The offences supposedly committed by the children or the parents were never sufficient to merit the long terms handed down by district justices. The behaviour of the children, however recalcitrant, did not merit the relentless imposition of appalling punishments, of inadequate food, clothing and health care, and finally the predatory sexual exploitation of the child inmates.

The prisons were 'secret'. They masqueraded as something else and the subterfuge of Church and State, jointly responsible for the Gulag, was widely accepted by the Irish people. It was equally well known that something quite terrible was going on. Evidence emerged regularly; it surfaced in Dáil questions and debates, in media coverage, in local authority confrontations. The episodes were never fully investigated. They were almost always dismissed by successive Ministers for Education, often as 'isolated incidents' (which of course was no excuse for not investigating), or a Department of Education inquiry was claimed as having taken place, its result invariably being the exoneration of those in charge of the relevant institutions.

Terrible physical conditions prevailed in almost all the institutions. Checking on the ones that were claimed to have been 'good', after the long lapse of time, is a task overwhelmed by the huge body of testimony from the notorious schools, one of the worst being the boys' reformatory at Daingean, County Offaly, where conditions are described that were rarely short of appalling.

There were good and reasonably well-written Rules and Regulations for the treatment of the children—though they had serious defects as well—and had they been followed, to the letter, the lives of the children might have been bearable. They covered all aspects of life, including education, clothing, diet, health, restraint and moral care and punishment. They are not without fault, particularly as regards punishment, but if they had been adhered to, the incarcerations might have been ameliorated. This would not have excused the reasons for incarcerating the children, nor the legal methods employed, but it would have given a measure of protection to their lives.

However, throughout this juvenile prison system, the rules were widely ignored. The inmates of the child prisons were ill-fed, often to the point of starvation; yet the rule on diet clearly imposes balanced and adequate feeding. They were improperly clothed; yet the rule on clothing is a carefully worded direction for physical protection. Their health was neglected; yet the stipulation is entirely contrary to this often irreversible neglect of dental care, protection of eyesight and other protections. They suffered from the illnesses associated with poverty, which was inexcusable and a clear indication of the neglect that was a breach of the rules. They developed diseases leading in many cases to abnormalities of sight, dental defects, stunted physical growth and many psychological handicaps.

Above all, they were cruelly punished. The punishment regimes in all the institutions were put into operation without regard to the rule on punishment. They were chronically excessive, cruel and perverse. The children were flogged, they were assaulted, they were physically disabled by extreme forms of physical oppression. Limbs were broken, eyes were poked out, hands were rendered unusable, children were made deaf by beatings to the head, jaws were broken. Furthermore, and much more broadly, the mental impact of punishment and the threat of punishment, all the time, created a level of fear and terror that made it impossible for the children to pursue any kind of normal existence. Its later effects were a lifelong imposition of personal lack of worth and confidence, sustained nightmares, breakdowns and deeper traumatic problems.

The history of this prison system dates from the foundation of the State. Much of it was in place from the mid-nineteenth century, but under the Westminster administration, through the Chief Secretary for Ireland, it has to be inferred that it was reasonably controlled. After 1922 it certainly changed, and evidence is contained in various sources mentioned in this book of the cruel and oppressive regimes that different victims suffered during the period dealt with here.

There were certain chronological watersheds that have been noted by writers on the subject. These include the Cussen Report, published in 1936, the Kennedy Report, published in 1970, the series of television documentaries made by Mary Raftery, *States of Fear*, the 'Apology' by Bertie Ahern, and the process that followed that apology and which led to the Commission to Inquire into Child Abuse and, subsequently, the Redress Board.

States of Fear was a significant moment in this process of a supposed self-discovery of the widespread abuse of children in the industrial schools and the three reformatories that had existed during the time covered by the findings of the programmes. While I have great respect for the quality of research and revelation, and for the testimony of the brave men and women who took part in the three programmes in the spring of 1999, they created a misleading and unbalanced public response. Their main burden was the telling of the story of abuse within the prison system for children from which came the relentless testimony that went to the hearts and minds of so many people who saw the series.

It was as if, within the institutions, the priests, brothers and nuns who serviced or ran them took upon themselves a licence to be cruel, ignorant and sexually exploitive of their human charges. The relentless nature of the record set aside the State's responsibility, not deliberately, but as a result of the vast testimony from the victims and the failure of the State, through the Department of Education, to acknowledge or be honest about its own shortcomings. The religious flogged the children mercilessly, for the slightest misdemeanour, sometimes for no misdemeanour at all, and in ways that were entirely outside the system of rules, itself defective, that had been in place, at least since the 1880s. They failed to educate them. They used them as slave labour on their land, in their laundries, bakeries, tailoring shops, shoe-making workshops, wherever they could deploy human help. Boys and girls strung rosary beads that were sold on behalf of convents. Boys worked through the year tending the farmlands owned by the Christian Brothers at Letterfrack and Artane, and by the Oblate Fathers, who had charge of the reformatory at Daingean.

The quantity and standard of food, in almost all the institutions, was inadequate and the children were permanently starving. The boys at Daingean had no underclothing. Their clothes were shared in common. The infrequent collection of clothing for washing led to a redistribution that was haphazard. They suffered from infestations, of body lice and, worse still, of the mites that cause scabies.

The catalogue is a horrendous one, and the brave men and women, in the media and in political life, who brought it to public notice are rightly commended for their courage. There is an element of pornography attached to the revelations, particularly when these are sustained and horrific. It does not have to refer to sexual abuse; it is relevant in any obscene behaviour, including the cruelties that were manifest throughout this prison system. In all this the parallel is again close, between the Russian Gulag and its Irish equivalent.

The testimony of sexual abuse was high-profile during the period of the *States of Fear* revelations and those giving their accounts have exercised a compulsion by becoming public witnesses to the shame and grief that they suffered. This has generated a general belief that it was fairly widespread in the institutions ostensibly caring for boys and was certainly present in convents, in a psycho-sexual form for which the testimony is often more difficult to understand. It was, by its nature, covert. Boys were summoned to the private apartments of Brothers and sexually abused and this was witnessed by others, and explained in detail by innumerable victims.

The issue of this widespread abuse, and the existence of the Gulag of child prisons, quite incorrectly called 'industrial schools', became more widely known during the 1980s as a result of research and investigation for books and articles and also because of police investigations and the prosecutions of abusers. There was a growing threat to the State of legal actions by men and women who had been inside the prison system, often for many of their childhood years. The implications for the new Government led by Bertie Ahern became a matter of concern during 1998 and was an issue before the Cabinet for which a special committee was established.

Mary Raftery, with the backing of RTÉ, began her researches at this time and was met with a positive response from the Department of Education. Parts of its archives were opened to her and this made possible a much fuller treatment of the subject than had previously been the case. The abiding impact of the programmes concerned abuse, with an inevitable emphasis on the cruel punishment regimes that prevailed in the institutions, and on the sexual abuse, mainly of young boys.

As far as the State was concerned, this emphasis on the revelations of the horrors of industrial school life and the cruelties and oppression of reformatories, and indeed of all the institutions, was a welcome distortion of the reality. It placed the burden of blame on the religious orders who ran the institutions, it placed the emphasis on the abuse of rights; inevitably, the emphasis was further concentrated on physical and sexual abuse. All this reflected very badly on the religious orders, less so on the Church as a whole which was able to distance itself and plead lack of knowledge.

A much harder severance was involved in respect of the role and responsibilities of the State. The State was responsible in law for the system, for its funding, inspection and control. Whether or not the Department of Education, in order to lessen the attention paid to the source of this wholly corrupt and iniquitous prison system by distorting the presentation of material through the selective release of documentation, is a matter for speculation. What is not a matter for speculation is the resolute determination of the State to block all investigation of the most crucial issue of all, the committal through the courts of tens of thousands of children without proper investigation of the complaints about them and the domestic circumstances used to justify what then followed. This ignored what was required by law.

Nothing in the lives of the victims of the industrial school system had quite the compelling trauma of their being arrested and then brought before the courts where generally they faced summary conviction. They all remembered being torn from their threadbare lives and imperfect family situations where a ragged form of love and protection had been given to them, often in poverty-stricken circumstances. Worse, of course, followed, as these pages will relate. But the key to it all, an unjust and painful State system of incarceration, was the moment that changed their lives for ever.

In his Speech of Apology, Bertie Ahern, on 11 May 1999, said:

> The Government considers that the interests of justice and the common good require the provision of such a forum [allowing the victims to relate their experiences], and to that end it has decided to establish a Commission to Inquire into Childhood Abuse. The Commission's terms of reference have deliberately been drawn quite broadly, and have a number of different elements. The primary focus of the Commission will be to provide victims with an opportunity to tell of the abuse they suffered, in a sympathetic and experienced forum. In addition the Commission will establish as complete a picture as possible of the causes, nature and extent of physical and sexual abuse of children in institutions and other places. It will make such recommendations as it sees fit.

This undertaking, which included the word 'causes', was strengthened in the terms of reference the Government gave to the Commission. These stipulated that the Commission would:

> ... establish as complete a picture as possible of the causes, nature and extent of physical and sexual abuse of children in institutions ... including the antecedents, circumstances, factors and context of such abuse.

'Causes', 'antecedents', these were at the heart of the experiences of the men and women who had been through the system. It could be said that they represented the most important part. The system was there from the middle of the nineteenth century. The abuse of it crept in later. It remained unreformed in Ireland, whereas hugely significant changes in the law and the Rules and Regulations took place in the United Kingdom.

Reference to antecedents was dropped when the Bill was drafted. It does not occur in the Act. At all stages of progress in the legislation, attempts to reintroduce investigation of the role of the courts into the remit of the Commission were blocked by Michael Woods, who was Minister for Education at the time and steered the Bill through all its stages. He gave a reason that bordered on the absurd: he said that because of the constitutional separation of powers he doubted that the Parliament could legislate for such a provision. Though this was not the point, he consistently used the argument to block its investigation.

> I am legally advised that it is constitutionally unacceptable that the Commission should seek to review the decisions of courts in individual cases. I am satisfied, however that the Commission can consider the general system which led to the placing of children in care. The Bill, as amended by the Dáil, adequately meets the concerns underlying [the] amendments.

Apart from the travesty this was of the constitutional provisions covering the issue, there were several more complex problems. The first of these, huge in its implications and only partly understood by politicians, concerned the many thousands of victims of abuse in the industrial school system. Their anxieties ranged from the worry with which they had lived throughout their lives, that they carried the stain of a criminal conviction in the Irish courts, to the much broader issue, concerning the actual legality of what they had done. In the first category there were many who had fled the country after their release from imprisonment and felt they could not return, could not work in Ireland and might well be further pursued, as they had been when they were children, by an unpredictable and unintelligible legal system. Then there were those who knew that the convictions in the courts were wrong and unjustified and suspected that they were also illegal. This illegality, substantiated more fully later, concerns the statements made by Michael Woods, one of which is quoted above.

He was using a not uncommon ploy by Government: to raise constitutional doubts, however tenuous, as an excuse for not doing things.

The court judgments themselves, in the case of all children committed to industrial schools and reformatories, were final. They could not be set aside retrospectively by anyone, Government included, and certainly not by a judicial or non-judicial tribunal, nor by legislation. But that was confined to the decision itself. In no sense did it prevent a Commission from investigating what was done and, if it was the case, finding that due process of law had not been followed in the vast majority of these committals since there had been no inquiries held—as the Children Act of 1908 required—no representation in court on behalf of the defendants, no appeal possible, and for many other reasons as well. Nor did it preclude the victims from bringing such views and doubts as they had before the Investigative Committee of the Commission to Inquire into Child Abuse. Ruling this out, as Michael Woods did, was to act duplicitously.

It was also improper to do this in view of the fact that, if only theoretically, it prevented an examination in the correct framework of questions about possible reform. Woods, by blocking the whole matter of court committals, was impeding fresh legislation designed to ensure that similar decisions would not be reached on the same facts in the future. There were reasons for investigation on this matter by the Commission. But they were blocked and this meant they would not be able to make a recommendation for change.

In other words, fault would have to be found. It was not sufficient to rely on the broader, less investigative, consideration that 'the general system which led to the placing of children in care' might come before the Commission, as, in theory, it had done before the seriously defective Kennedy Committee, more than 30 years earlier.

Undoubtedly wrong had been done, and it was traceable directly to the State, not to the Church. Michael Woods, a highly intelligent man, must have known this. He must also have known that the Constitution requires only that the decision stands for the parties involved, not that the desirability of such a decision should be above review or criticism.

Macabre though it may sound, when *States of Fear* was shown, in 1999, the reaction of shock and horror manifested by the Taoiseach, Bertie Ahern, and his Minister for Education, Micheál Martin, was clearly, and misleadingly, designed to emulate, in a despicable way, the genuine and well-researched lead given in the three RTÉ documentaries: what was really being revealed was not a malfunctioning State operation but a private, covert and improper sequence of events which, if the State had known of them, it might have acted upon.

The State did know of them and it did not act. The State was content to control the system of management, administer the laws affecting the children, even amending the Children Acts, and exercise comprehensive responsibility for a truly dreadful child prison system. The component parts masqueraded as industrial schools and reformatories under the charge of members of religious orders. It was a system that in theory was governed by the law, but in practice this was not just perverted by those in charge, but was also based on laws that were not properly observed, in the court committals of the children and then simply not implemented in what happened to the children thereafter. The prison system comprehended a vast incarceration of children and that system was allowed to run out of control and remain out of control for decades. During that time the lives of tens of thousands of boys and girls were ruined. They were prisoners and they were in prisons. They had less protection than adult prisoners and they faced vastly more cruel and damaging punishments. And when it came time to investigate it all, following a supposedly 'heartfelt' apology, the heart of the investigation was excised from the terms of reference for the bodies carrying out the work, and the work itself was corrupted in the interests of State protection.

It was a Gulag Archipelago, to use Solzhenytsin's phrase about the Stalinist labour camps. And no one reading that terrible account will fail to see the acutely felt parallel of the Russian writer's account of the unjust arrest, incarceration and trial through which millions of Russian men and women went. The system of schools stretched from Donegal to Cork, from Dublin to Galway. In no positive sense were they schools. As anyone who has attended boarding school will attest: children do not go as a result of being dragged before a court, publicly disgraced, 'charged' with an offence of vagrancy or moral turpitude or poverty, and then committed with a sentence, in some cases of several years. They do not serve out their time under a perpetual regime of punishment. They are not cut off from their parents, deprived of their names and given numbers instead, criminalised in their general treatment and consigned to forced labour.

The children sent to Ireland's industrial schools were generally not charged with custodial offences, if they were charged at all; yet they were deemed guilty and sentenced to detention. This is not how people go to school. If they ran away and escaped from their euphemistically named 'boarding' school, they were made subject to penalties that were entirely outside the law. They were mercilessly flogged, their hair was shaved off, and they were made to eat off the floor. They were then handed over to their peers—who had suffered as a result of their escape—to receive a second wave of punishment. This is not even a criminal law possibility. It was organised sadism. Schools are not prisons; prisons are not schools. The industrial school system was a prison network and nothing less.

Yet this fact, and the closely related issue of how the children were gathered in thousands each year and consigned to the industrial school system were largely overlooked in the waves of astonishment and horror at the revelations of abuse. The men and women brave enough to come forward and be interviewed for television by Mary Raftery's team were not able to analyse the legal abuse to which they had been subjected, nor could they remember, in detail, the court appearances which they made at the beginning of their ordeal. In due course many of them obtained the details; yet even then they did not know what to do about them. The main issue was abuse, rather than the State's involvement in an illegal system of committal without which the industrial school system could not have survived.

A school is a place of learning. Yet the principal learning in the industrial school was learning to fear and it was learnt rapidly and unforgettably. Artane Industrial School, arguably the most famous of them all, deliberately, and as a matter of policy, restricted the education of its inmates to bare literacy at best. The 1936 Cussen Report, one of the watershed documents mentioned above, says:

> We note with regret that in Artane industrial school, with over 700 pupils, only the minimum standard of literary education required by the regulations is provided, and pupils, however promising, cannot, as a rule, proceed beyond the sixth standard.

This view is echoed powerfully in Father Henry Moore's Report to Archbishop John Charles McQuaid about Artane, written when he was chaplain there in 1962. One of his themes runs through all abuse testimony: this is how work on the land, and work on behalf of the religious order, took precedence over the educational life that should have been paramount.

During the first 10 years of the State's independence, the 'Rules and Regulations for Industrial Schools' were those of the pre-1922 British administration. Britain had already moved on to a greatly reformed system, with short sentences, reduced corporal punishment, strict inspection and accountability.

But the 1933 Rules and Regulations, issued by the Minister for Education of the first Fianna Fáil Government, whose name was Tomás Derrig[1], effectively re-certified the institutions according to the same rules, unamended. These rules, which had to be duly signed by the Minister and the prison manager, after which they constituted the certificate or licence for the 'certified' school, designated them as fit places to hold children detained by the State.

The timing of Derrig's recertification is significant. It demonstrates a State takeover, with a clear understanding of what it was that was being taken over: places of detention for children that were under State control. It was clear at that time, also, that sufficient unease was felt about the system for the Minister to seek an inquiry. A 1933 Department of Education memorandum says:

> The Department of Education [has] had under consideration for a considerable time the need for an inquiry into the present reformatory and industrial school system with a view to introducing reforms and improvements. Many circumstances combined make such an inquiry a matter of urgency and importance. The statutory provisions relating to these institutions and the treatment of juvenile offenders and delinquent children are based principally on the Children Act 1908. These provisions have been amended more than once in Great Britain and at present the Free State [is] behind most European countries in its arrangements for dealing with this

---

[1] There are variations of Tomás Derrig's name. The form Tomás Derrig has been used throughout this book.

important social question. Before introducing reforms, the Minister for
Education wishes to have the whole position enquired into and reported on.
He proposes to set up a Commission for that purpose.

This led to Cussen. G.P. Cussen was the Senior Justice in the Dublin District
Court and its chairperson, with some powers in the monitoring of committals of
children to the industrial schools and reformatories. His Commission was
charged with investigating the plight of 'juvenile offenders and delinquent
children'. This deeply prejudicial phrase—since the children, in the main, were
not offenders nor were they *delinquent*—is not from Cussen but from the
Department of Education memorandum and is consistent with the general view
in such documents on the children. The Commission was given good terms of
reference. They included looking into the committal procedures and the other
statutory provisions and regulations, as well as the care of the children, both
generally and when they were suffering from physical and mental defects. Cussen
was also to look into staffing and financing.

He was aware of the prison context surrounding the industrial schools and
reformatories. They were, after all, established under the Westminster Home
Office Prisons Department. They were prisons; the real nature of the institutions
was always known to anyone who wished to see this. The Cussen Commission
confirms this when it says, 'From the establishment of the Reformatory system in
1858, to 1927, with the exception of the period 1890 to 1906, the Inspector of
Reformatory and Industrial Schools held, in addition, an appointment in the
Prisons Service' (Cussen p. 9). Yet the Commission's solution to this was
hypocritical. The report laments the 'false perception in the public mind that the
places were prisons' and it proposed enhancing the deception about the nature of
the institutions by renaming them! 'Industrial Schools' were to be called 'National
Boarding Schools' and the 'Detention Order' was to be called an 'Admission
Order'. In due course, more than 30 years later, the Kennedy Commission
followed the same course.

None of this was done. There were no reforms following the Cussen Report.
The system continued unchanged. Though a central issue was the widespread use
of savage regimes of corporal punishment, the issue of punishment is not debated
at all in Cussen nor in Kennedy, and the Kennedy Report actually excises, without
explanation, the 'Rule' on punishment from the set of rules published as an
appendix. The truth is that corporal punishment went unregulated in the Irish
child prisons. The Derrig rules—unchanged and unreformed, despite huge
changes and reforms in the United Kingdom—permitted almost any type and
degree of violence. Slaps and punches to the head and body were permitted, as
was naked flogging on the buttocks with a strap, cane, birch or indeed
instruments of worse invention. There was no upper limit on the punishment
that a child prisoner could receive. The violence—or physical abuse of which the
former Irish inmates complain—was within the Derrig rules. And the

misrepresentation of this situation went on through the period 2000–2009 during which time an accurate grasp of the true picture eluded Ms Justice Mary Lafoy and Mr Justice Seán Ryan in their periods chairing the Commission to Inquire into Child Abuse.

In 1911, the then British Home Secretary, Winston Churchill, recognised that if the Government was going to permit grown men to flog little boy prisoners then they had to regulate tightly what could and could not be done. There always loomed the possible result: that of a child being beaten to death. Tomás Derrig saw fit, in 1933, not to regulate the violence of the Christian Brothers, notwithstanding the Brotherhood's 'unenviable reputation' for violence. This was underlined by the fact that two of the Brotherhood's members had, in the early 1930s, been executed in Canada for child murder.[2]

Tomás Derrig didn't even have to go to the trouble of devising a set of safeguards. He could simply have lifted the English rules of 1923 or 1933. They were there for the taking. This shows beyond doubt that Minister Derrig in 1933 wilfully chose to introduce rules that allowed Irish child prisoners to be whipped without limit or safeguard by men of violence one of whose principal objectives, in maintaining discipline, was the whipping of little boys.

This, then, is the context for the opening of the story contained in the following pages. This was signalled by Bertie Ahern's speech on Tuesday, 11 May 1999. Two of the three *States of Fear* documentaries had been shown (on 27 April and 4 May, the third was due for broadcast that evening). The Apology could not have been better timed. 'We must start by apologising,' Ahern said, and he continued:

> On behalf of the State and of all citizens of the State, the Government wishes to make a sincere and long overdue apology to the victims of childhood abuse for our collective failure to intervene, to detect their pain, to come to their rescue … Too many of our children were denied this love, care and security. Abuse ruined their childhoods and has been an ever present part of their adult lives, reminding them of a time when they were helpless. I want to say to them that we believe that they were gravely wronged, and that we must do all we can now to overcome the lasting effects of their ordeals.

---

2   The Brotherhood operated two institutions similar to Artane in Ontario: St Joseph's at Alfred, and St John's at Uxbridge. In her report, *Institutional Child Abuse in Canada*, Ronda Bessner of the Canadian Law Commission describes a catalogue of abuse that was inflicted on the inmates of these two prisons in the 1960s. Flogging on the bare backside was the norm, even after the practice was banned by the Provincial authorities. Bessner says: 'The Ontario government policy prohibited corporal punishment. Staff were not permitted to strike, handcuff or kick the boys. In 1957 and 1958, the Ontario Department of Reform Institutions ordered staff at St Joseph's and St John's to read and sign directives banning the strapping of residents on the bare buttocks. A prohibition against strapping the hands was introduced in 1960. These policies were ignored.'

In what turned out to be a master-stroke, Bertie Ahern had completely side-stepped the main issue: that the State had run a Gulag of prisons for children, and focused instead on a revealed pattern of abuse in those prisons that was being laid at the door of the religious who had run them. He failed, in his full statement, to acknowledge at all any wrongdoing on the part of the State. He was apologising for 'a failure to detect pain' and to intervene. The State had run the institutions—through willing agents who made money out of doing so—and was now side-stepping that responsibility. The State had authorised the terms under which the children were managed, including how they were starved, clothed in rags and punished to extreme degrees. But there was no apology for this. The State had not ensured, as was its duty, that the strictly defined terms of incarceration were followed or observed, nor that they were properly checked.

The apology is for the derelictions of unknown criminals who breached Government rules. The known criminals, ministers and public servants, who presided over the system and the rules and who allowed the law of the land to be subverted, are not mentioned. The State authorised the inflicting of unlimited amounts of pain upon inmates. Successive Ministers for Education were aware that such pain was being inflicted since they had laid down, signed and agreed the well-defined punishment rules and they dealt, in the Dáil, with the intermittent complaints about excessive punishment, always asserting that the incidents were 'isolated'. They knew how open to abuse those rules were and they knew they were being abused. They were aware of the shortcomings of almost every procedure of industrial school management, of all the supposed services for the children, and of the principle of care which should have been followed and was not. In every instance the State did nothing to rectify these shortcomings. It failed to implement the Cussen proposals. It failed to follow the advice in the Kennedy Report. Instead, the State, through Bertie Ahern, was apologising for a 'failure to detect pain'.

Two days later, on 13 May, the Minister for Education at the time, Micheál Martin, claimed that Ireland, when all of this happened, was ignorant of children's rights. He did this in a Statement on Industrial Schools delivered to the Dáil on that day in 1999 as part of the collective Government response to the revelations about child abuse. He said, 'The concept of the child as a separate individual with rights came late to this country.' This was complete nonsense, and Martin, who elsewhere had claimed to be a historian, ought to have known better.

As well as delivering the Apology, Bertie Ahern reinforced the emphasis on the abuse that had taken place—without accepting that any blame at all devolved upon earlier governments—and he put in place a number of remedies for abuse and for people who had suffered this abuse: 'a new, comprehensive approach is required to deal with the effects of previous abuse, to detect the children caught in frightful isolation, and to put proper structures in place'. This, of course, was worthwhile as an initiative but had nothing to do with the child prison system that had housed the innumerable acts that were in defiance of the laws of the land, the Rules and Regulations, the rights of the children, the common humanity that was not applied to them and the ill-health, disease and starvation they faced.

Ahern took pride in announcing a Commission to Inquire into Child Abuse but had no recompense mechanism in his mind at that stage; that came much later. Indeed, it did not come at his behest but at the insistence of Ms Justice Mary Lafoy, after she had begun work as chairperson of the Commission to Inquire into Child Abuse. Ahern was vague in what he sought. He thought victims might like a forum where they could tell their story.

> This would give them assurance that the wrongs which have been done to them are recognised publicly in a responsible manner, and that lessons are properly learned … The primary focus of the Commission will be to provide victims with an opportunity to tell of the abuse they suffered, in a sympathetic and experienced forum. In addition the Commission will establish as complete a picture as possible of the causes, nature and extent of physical and sexual abuse of children in institutions and other places. It will make such recommendations as it sees fit.

How it was allowed to happen, who were responsible, what abuses of the law were involved: these were not considered.

Ahern offered the setting up of counselling services for the abused. This would 'help them to overcome the effect of the abuse'. This, of course, was 30, 40 or 50 years afterwards. Five years on from the Taoiseach's Apology, in May 2004, the new incumbent as chairperson of the Commission to Inquire into Child Abuse, Mr Justice Seán Ryan, made a statement.

At the time there had been investigation by the Attorney General of the Investigation Committee within the Commission. Ryan, who had been announced in September 2003 as the person who would replace Mary Lafoy and who had taken up his duties in January 2004, referred to research done into 'what lessons could be learned for this inquiry'. He went on:

> The function of the inquiry at its most basic is as we see it to find out whether child abuse took place; if so what was the nature of the abuse; where did it happen; why did it happen; why was it not discovered and stopped; how widespread was it in any institution and how many institutions were contaminated by child abuse. Another vital function of this or any inquiry into child abuse is to look at the present and the future to see what steps can be taken to reduce the risk of abuse of children in care taking place in the future … In other words, it is part of the healing process for victims to know that measures are being recommended to prevent what happened to them being done to children in the future.

He also implied that there would be no attempt to name individual abusers unless they were people who had been convicted in criminal cases.

> If somebody has either pleaded guilty or been convicted in a Court of a crime
> of abuse of a child or children then it seems to me to be legitimate to take
> those facts as established and to proceed accordingly. That would mean
> inquiring where appropriate as to how the person got away with the conduct
> that constituted the crime and whatever other related issues appeared to arise.
> We have to decide this question before we begin hearings into institutions. We
> plan to begin our inquiry work proper with a hearing into the emergence of
> child abuse as an issue in Ireland.

It was an astonishing statement. Here we all were, five years into the consideration
of a known and revealed set of circumstances, and yet we were being invited to
start all over again, with the basic question: did child abuse take place in the
industrial schools? This was particularly odd since Seán Ryan, two and a half
years earlier, had chaired a Compensation Advisory Committee that had
produced a report called *Towards Redress and Recovery*. Not alone did this report
provide the tables of compensation for those abused in the institutions, it readily
accepted that the abuse had taken place. It acknowledged 'the State's response to
the tragedy of institutional child abuse' and summarised all the work that had
been done, including the setting up of the Commission to Inquire into Child
Abuse, the National Counselling Service giving support to 'any adult who had
suffered abuse in childhood', the setting up of 'a National Office for Victims of
Abuse' as far back as November 2000 to help representatives of the abused, and it
went on:

> It is unquestionably true that no amount of money can 'compensate' for a
> body which has been battered and a mind which has been shattered; but the
> award of appropriate financial redress can at least provide some tangible
> recognition of the seriousness of the hurt and injury which has been caused
> to the victims of institutional child abuse.

Could the author of these words be the same man who was now, four years later,
making a decision to question whether abuse had actually taken place? In any
case, was he not compromised? He told in his report of the wide number of
submissions, some of which came from victims. They in turn have told me of
their experience. They had no reason to believe that Seán Ryan did not accept
their testimony. They said later that they did have good reason for questioning his
appointment, since he had already been involved with victims and with
compensation for victims. How could he have been questioning, in 2004, whether
or not abuse took place?

But it was far worse than that. Within the broad remit of the new chairperson
of the Commission, the key issue—of Government responsibility for allowing the

system to run and for allowing a non-stop supply line of children to troop into their places of misery and damage—was not to be investigated. Nor was it. The shame of what we have seen, in 10 years, is the exclusion of this fundamental and inexcusable act of State avoidance of a collective crime that cries to Heaven for vengeance.

Judge Ryan's work of investigation has been over for more than a year. His final report is now published. His investigation never touched on the most important question of all, that of the criminal negligence of the Department of Education and the responsibility of successive governments for sustaining the Gulag of child prisons.

I have supped on political horrors and have confronted political chicanery and duplicity in my time. Nothing I have experienced comes near to challenging the deep dishonesty of the supposed recompense that was offered by the State— and, sadly, made, to those gullible enough to accept the Redress Board's work and intentions—which were then covertly implemented, with grave legal threats against the recipients if they divulged details. The Irish State bathed its hands in the blood of generations of innocent children tormented by the prison warders who took charge of them and who were, in the main, nuns and brothers of different religious orders. The State imprisoned the children. They were not imprisoned by the religious orders, who did not have the power in law to do so. The State constructed the regime of committal, punishment and privation that ruined the lives of those incarcerated in the industrial schools and reformatories. The Catholic Church did not have the power to do that, either. It did have the power to abuse what was regulated by the State and it clearly did so, in many dreadful ways. But the State, which had the power to impose restraint and protect the children, failed to do so, and that was far worse than anything the religious orders did. The State knew; even with the poor performances of the inspectors, the Department of Education knew what was happening in the industrial schools and reformatories. And because it knew, it was also aware of the unfeeling and cruel treatment of children meted out by religious orders. The State's failure to do anything was what Bertie Ahern should have made the centre of his Apology. Why he did not do so is the material out of which the following pages have been fashioned.

Chapter 1 ∾

A PRISON SYSTEM FOR CHILDREN

The first industrial school for children in Ireland was erected in the Coombe in Dublin in 1805. It was part of the Erasmus Smith Foundation and was designed for boys and girls. No distinction was made in respect of the religious faith of the pupils, but within 10 years of its foundation it had become exclusively Protestant, with more than 300 pupils, evenly balanced between girls and boys. They were taught in large classrooms at either end of the building. In the centre were apartments for the male and female staff. The school had on one floor apartments intended for factories where the children would be employed on alternate days 'in some system of industry', but this plan was not pursued and, writing about it in an 1818 general account of the Erasmus Smith schools, these 'fine apartments' were described as 'unoccupied and useless'.[1] As with other Erasmus Smith establishments, the policy of no religious distinction generally failed. This first industrial school, like others that followed, was not penal.

A penitentiary for children was established earlier than the Coombe School but did not include instruction. It was started in Smithfield in 1801 in association with the Dublin House of Industry.[2] According to Joseph Robins,[3] this was the first time that special provision was made for young offenders but it was essentially a prison for them. Initially there was no attempt made to achieve their reform and certainly no regular programme of training. This changed in the early years of the nineteenth century. An 1810 report from a visiting governor on conditions in the Smithfield prison referred to boys being 'usefully instructed and industriously employed', but the regime was in general harsh and punitive and many of the prisoners were there prior to transportation. Girl prisoners were held

1   J. Warburton, Rev J. Whitelaw and Rev Robert Walsh, *History of the City of Dublin*, VOL. II, T. Cadell and W. Davies, London, 1818, p. 860.
2   The Dublin House of Industry was set up in 1773 to combat the growing numbers of impoverished people moving to Dublin and begging on the streets. An appeal was made to them to enter voluntarily; when this failed, the onus passed to the parochial authorities.
3   Joseph Robins, *The Lost Children: A Study of Charity Children in Ireland, 1700–1900*, Institute of Public Administration, Dublin, 1980, p. 108.

in the House of Industry but sometimes were sent to the Smithfield penitentiary as a punishment and confined in dark cells. Those sent to the Smithfield prison had often committed offences while in one of the Charter Schools, or had run away from this form of charitable schooling, started in the eighteenth century.

During these years, early in the nineteenth century, the school system contributed significantly to the welfare of orphaned and destitute children. Endowment was disproportionately favourable to Protestant establishments. In 1816 it was reckoned that £44,000 covered the cost of 29 Protestant schools in the city, educating 3,194 children, while £8,000 paid for 32 Roman Catholic schools, educating 5,095 children. A further 5,500 children of other faiths, including dissenters, were educated, at a cost of £5,000. The disproportion led to a much earlier end to destitution among Protestant juveniles than among those of the majority religion and this general tendency always prevailed in respect of child care.

In 1838 the Irish Poor Relief Act introduced the workhouse system and the institutions, set up around the country under the Irish Poor Law Commissioners and then under the Local Government Board for Ireland, became the main refuge for abandoned children and the children of impoverished families. It was a harsh system, the control essentially punitive, yet the concept was humane and there was concern over the welfare of workhouse children. The Famine years, which represented an unprecedented crisis, undermined the operation of the poor law and brought various additional problems of want and disease within the workhouse walls. In 1862 a notable step forward was achieved by the introduction of boarding out for children.

Up to and including this period, in spite of these solitary exceptions, children guilty of vagrancy and law-breaking were generally treated as adults. It took a further half-century, leading up to the legislation that brought into existence the institutions specifically for children, for a new concept to develop and then inspire change. This was essentially that child criminals were often the victims of circumstance beyond their own control. These child criminals were widely believed to be cursed with an inherited taint. The view was still expressed, during recent inquiries in Ireland into child abuse in the second half of the twentieth century, that the inmates of the industrial schools, though not in fact guilty of crimes, had suffered from the neglect of uncaring or vicious parents and had been the victims of evil surroundings, bad example and 'pernicious promptings'. Charles Dickens had dealt with these ideas, in both early and late novels, as had many other commentators on children; yet the general idea persisted that class and background could make children potential, if not actual, criminals. The slow change that took place was a movement away from punitive measures and towards rescue and regeneration.

Dickens played a significant role in this alteration of public perception and in inspiring the legislation that led to the first industrial schools. His portrait of the training of child criminals under Fagin's guidance, in *Oliver Twist*, represented an extraordinary reality. This was the existence at one time of more than 200 'flash houses' where up to 6,000 boys were being trained in thieving and depredation. Dickens also, in what he had to say in *David Copperfield* about Salem House school and the dreadful figure of Creakle, who 'handsomely flogged for disorderly conduct', gives the essential condemnation of violence in schools. Creakle, ironically, ends up a magistrate and a prison commissioner, inviting David Copperfield, now a famous writer, to visit Maidstone Gaol where he and his friend, Traddles, find Uriah Heep, fawning and being humble all over again, this time about the prison system, where solitary confinement is 'the only unchallengeable way of making sincere and lasting converts and penitents'. The following brief but telling passage relates directly to Christian Brother discipline in Ireland in the twentieth century. This was disproportionate to a huge degree in its dependence on flogging and whipping, very little of which was carried out within the laws and regulations laid down:

> In a school carried on by sheer cruelty, whether it is presided over by a dunce or not, there is not likely to be much learnt. I believe our boys were generally as ignorant a set as any boys in existence; they were too much troubled and knocked about to learn; they could no more do that to advantage, than anyone can do anything to advantage in a life of constant misfortune, torment and worry.[4]

Towards the end of the first half of the nineteenth century—*Oliver Twist* was published in 1838, *David Copperfield* in 1849–50—it was reckoned that between 11,000 and 12,000 juveniles passed through prisons in England and Wales, a third of them in London alone. Both the level of incarceration and the parallel emphasis on Dublin, compared with the rest of Ireland, may be assumed. It is not surprising that Dickens took a benign view of the industrial school alternative. In the light of his wisdom, experience and compassion, Dickens saw good in the then nascent idea of the industrial school, seeing it as a better investment than the massive structure of Maidstone Gaol. That the idea behind such schools should have been so comprehensively corrupted in Ireland has less to do with the system than it has with those who took it over.

Before the passage of the laws that established a reformatory school system followed by an industrial school system for England and Wales there was intense debate. There was also debate in Ireland, where the setting up of reformatories was impeded. This was because the Roman Catholic Church considered that there were insufficient protections in the legislation from possible proselytising

4   Charles Dickens, *David Copperfield*, chapter VII, 'My first half at Salem House'.

by Protestant religious groups. Irish Catholic members of the House of Commons defeated the 1856 Bill on the grounds of their insistence that young offenders should only go to reformatories run by those of their own faith. A structure divided on sectarian grounds was the result and this prevailed in Ireland, both for reformatories and for the industrial schools that followed 10 years later. It was in part responsible for another important distinction between the development of places of juvenile detention in Ireland, and those in the rest of the British Isles. Since the majority of these places were under Roman Catholic management, they were located in institutions that already existed. They were mostly run by the religious orders. Buildings were adapted or new buildings constructed as part of an existing establishment and were the property of the orders. The system of ownership and management by the State which, to a limited extent, prevailed elsewhere, was inappropriate in Ireland, where a per capita payment by the State to the Church was the funding mechanism.

A lasting defect throughout these islands was introduced into the Reformatory Schools Act when it was passed. This was the provision that children found guilty of crimes and sent to a reformatory had to serve a short period in prison as a form of deterrence. The long wrangle between those who saw this as important and those who condemned it because it inflicted an indelible prison taint and contamination, was not resolved until the preliminary prison term was eliminated by an act in 1899.

Numbers are important, in the light of the huge disparity that developed later, between England and Wales, on the one hand, and Ireland, both before and after independence. By 1907 there were 44 reformatories in England and Wales, containing 5,500 juvenile offenders. This represented a downward trend and was approved by supporters of the system.

In Ireland the number of reformatories never exceeded ten, the first one following rapidly on the passing of the legislation for Ireland; this was the Reformatory Schools Act of 1858. By 21 December of that year the High Park Reformatory School in Drumcondra, Dublin was opened. A few months later St Kevin's Reformatory School, in Glencree, County Wicklow opened. The first of these was for girls and was run by the Sisters of Our Lady of Charity. It was part of a complex around their convent; this later included the largest Magdalen laundry in the country. St Kevin's was for boys and was run by the Oblate Fathers. Ten years later, in 1870, they opened a second reformatory school, St Conleth's, at Daingean in County Offaly. For this establishment they took over a military barracks outside the small country town. This very grim establishment, entirely surrounded by massive and high walls, had been built in 1776 as a military garrison. During its first hundred years it had been used for a time for the incarceration of men condemned to transportation and awaiting passage to the colonies. It remained operational for more than 100 years, becoming the only

Oblate reformatory when St Kevin's closed, in 1940. The boys from the Glencree establishment were then transferred to Daingean.

With all the problems and defects in the system, many of which simply did not come to light as a result of the prevailing 'closed' system, these first reformatories represented a further important advance in the system of care for the young. They brought under legislative control many voluntary institutions. They opened the way for religious organisations to engage in the care of juvenile offenders. They did this at public expense and this meant that the reformatories were brought under an inspection system.

As with London, in respect of England and Wales, so in Ireland there was a heavy emphasis on Dublin as a focus for the problems of poverty, disease and crime. So extensive was the poverty that punishment was the remedy for want and the parish became a significant arm of law and authority, committing to foundling establishments or to prisons the abandoned children and those engaging in petty crime. But the legislation passed in England was held up in Ireland because of the objection of the Irish Roman Catholic members of Parliament.

The theory behind the reformatory system was good. Their aim was 'to train, not to punish'.[5] The reality was rather different. Under British administration the inspection system appears to have worked. Within a short period of the reformatory legislation being passed, ten reformatories, five for boys, five for girls, had been certified in Ireland. Only one additional reformatory was certified and the numbers of children remained in hundreds rather than thousands. This was seen as a mark of progress. It meant that juvenile offenders, those actually found guilty of crimes, were numerically on the decrease in the British Isles in the last decade of the nineteenth century and well into the twentieth. As a result, the reformatories, built for recalcitrant juveniles who appeared before the courts on criminal charges, were doing their job.

Quite a different argument had given rise to the industrial school system. The intended inmates were children who were in need of care through poverty and socially inadequate parenting. The belief was that 'many of the rising generation might some day lapse into evil ways but were still on the right side and might with proper precautions be kept there'.[6] Their origin was the Ragged Schools, an invention of John Pound, the Portsmouth shoemaker, who sought to set up charitable schools 'to educate destitute children and save them from vagrancy and crime'.

The reformatories therefore did not prosper, a fact that was seen as representing the successful reduction of juvenile crime which did indeed take

---

5   From Mary Raftery and Eoin O'Sullivan, *Suffer the Little Children: The Inside Story of Ireland's Industrial Schools*, New Island Books, Dublin, 1999, p. 61. Their own footnote source is given as L. Foley, (1923) *The Reformatory System*, Dublin, Browne and Nolan, p. 31.

6   *Encyclopaedia Britannica*, 13th edition, 1926, article on Juvenile Offenders.

place. The industrial school system certainly thrived. The provision of industrial schools in England was introduced by the Industrial Schools Act 1857. It did not extend to Ireland since there was bitter opposition from Ulster Protestant MPs fearful that the pauper children of their faith would be threatened. A similar fear was felt by Roman Catholic leaders and MPs in respect of the British legislation applied to Great Britain. Nevertheless, the industrial school system was extended to Ireland by a separate Industrial School Act in 1868.[7] The reformatory continued to perform its role circumscribed by the fact that juvenile crime was largely contained, as a phenomenon, by policing. Numbers remained stable at around 5,500 in the 44 reformatories in England and at a proportionately smaller number in the 10 or so Irish reformatories, some of which subsequently closed. During more than a century after they came into existence, in Ireland in 1858, an absolute total of 15,899 children were committed, having been found guilty of juvenile offences. Vastly more boys than girls were in the system, 13,428 boys, as compared with 2,471 girls. In the latter years of their existence, between 1930 and 1960, on average 150 children each year were sentenced to several years each in reformatories.

In contrast, the industrial schools flourished and grew steadily in number. The industrial schools were established for 'neglected, orphaned and abandoned children'. They were funded from public money and run by the religious orders, in the case of Roman Catholic schools, and otherwise by the churches of the smaller denominations or by charitable institutions. Before independence, the approach and management of the schools seems to have been fairly standard. The periods of detention were relatively short. On first admission it was, on average, 14 weeks; on readmission this went up to 17 weeks and on second readmission to 24 weeks. There were also day industrial schools, to give some kind of education and care to the large numbers of juveniles in major cities. Children who were neglected, living in degraded conditions, lacking proper food and clothing, with 'little hope of growing into healthy men and women or becoming good citizens', were the object of this day-school part of the system.

The wider system, embracing all types of industrial school—and there was a steady increase in the number of them, from 45 at the outset to 90 in 1878, 102 in 1907, and in Scotland 31 in that year—was that of 'the well-governed school', small enough for the head to know all his charges. In the larger schools, where the individual head could not know all his charges, the approach was to divide the school into houses, putting each under a subsidiary house head. It is recorded that Ireland in 1905 conformed in its industrial school system with what was done in England and Wales and in Scotland. In that year the number of reformatory schools had come down to six. There were, in contrast, 70 industrial schools.

The legislation governing both reformatories and industrial schools was

---

[7] Detailed analysis of this period and the legislation is contained in Robins, *The Lost Children*, pp 301–309.

regularly amended between the Reformatory Schools Act of 1858 and the Industrial School Act of 1868. These were then superseded by the Children Act of 1908.

The settled times at the end of the reign of Edward VII were to be seriously disrupted in Ireland by the rise of Nationalism, the counter-revolution of militant Unionism, the impact of the First World War and the struggle for independence which began militarily with the Rising in 1916, an event that had in its objectives a concern for children—and how they should all be cherished equally—that has resounded down through the remaining years of the twentieth century. The sequence of events between 1910 and 1922 was a cataclysmic watershed for Ireland.

The fate of children was an issue in the campaign for Irish independence, the famous pledge 'to cherish the children of the Nation equally' being contained in the 1916 Proclamation. The first, revolutionary Dáil, of 1919, declared: 'it shall be the first duty of the Republic to make provision for the physical, mental and spiritual well-being of the children'. There was no detail then, or for much later, of how this would be accomplished and no suggestions were made for an alternative system to the industrial schools, whose early establishment, sixty years before, had led to a steady growth in their number.

The State was founded amid these aspirations, but the judgments led to no real action or reform. In 1924 the Department of Education 'noted' that there were more children in industrial schools in the Irish Free State than there were in the whole of the United Kingdom. Yet this extraordinary disparity was accepted; five years later, with the passing of the 1929 Children Act, provision was made for the sending of children to industrial schools even if they had not committed any crimes. This inevitably widened the scope for increased numbers, worsening the comparative figures with the United Kingdom and demonstrating a lack of any inclination towards reform. A further endorsement of this broad view of the usefulness and value of the system followed in 1933 when the rules governing industrial schools were reissued but not changed, despite the reforms that had taken place in parallel institutions in the United Kingdom. However, funding for them was increased.

In the fiery transition from British rule to independence, spread over the period from the 1916 Rising through the War of Independence to the Civil War, dark clouds hang over what happened within the industrial school system. Whatever it was, there descended a pall of terror and abuse. Within it the single most persistent thread is of a disciplinary system that was harshly maintained, with cruel and at times sadistic beatings.

All the abused, both girls and boys, who have survived as witnesses to the twenty-first century State Apology, recompense and redress, recall this as the constant factor in their lives. It induced fear of a disproportionate kind, overwhelming all the other activities they were made to pursue. It dominated the work they did for the institutions, on the farms, in the workshops, in the tailoring and baking departments, in the kitchens and around the grounds.

The savage beatings they received—on the head and the face, on the back, the buttocks, the hands and the legs, with whips, rubber truncheons, stiffened leather straps, birch rods and ashplants—were not specific punishments; they were given all the time, often in a frenzy of sadistic madness, at other times in calculated acts of humiliation. The children did not know when to expect them, when to prepare for them. They were most often uncalled for and undeserved. They were not imposed to improve the child. They were not related—as widespread corporal punishment in normal schools was—to the idea of correction, often accompanied by such expressions of a form of compassion as 'this hurts me more than it hurts you' or 'this will teach you to be better' or 'this has your parents' approval' (an explanation common within the British public school system).

Irish industrial school violence was of a different order altogether. It was administered to instil fear. It was not just corporal punishment, whether within the rules, correctly followed, or outside them. It was a form of assault on the inmates by those who had absolute power over them and were not regulated or checked by the State. The State was empowered to check and regulate. This was a legal requirement and a civic duty. It was not done.

The violence, which was a common thread in the testimony of inmates over five decades, and within virtually all the institutions, seems to have been largely irrational and unfocused. Ghastly as ritual is in such circumstances, it does have the merit of regulating the level of punishment and the reasoning behind it; this gives some kind of rationale, and when it suited, this was there; yet it did not preclude the sudden, irrational and violent descent of savage beatings that underpin so much testimony.

If it had a broad purpose, then it was designed to support and sustain the unbroken reign of terror that so many inmates of industrial schools and reformatories remember. Its purpose was less directed at individual offenders as at all of the inmates, becoming a comprehensive weapon to terrorise the whole population of each institution. Behind it was the collective and parallel fear felt by members of the religious orders: fear of their charges, fear of their own systems of control, fear of a supposed inadequacy in the rules drawn up by the Department of Education, which were so comprehensively ignored and flouted and in consequence became increasingly defective. There was a fundamental ignorance in this. The oppressive physical abuse was not related to educational shortcomings, since the education itself was inadequate and superficial. It was a panacea for the management and control of all inmates.

The religious punished inmates for bed-wetting, for having worn out their clothing, for having lice or other vermin in their hair or on their bodies. Boys were beaten if they were found awake before the morning bell and beaten if they failed to get up immediately after it sounded. They boys themselves were condemned as irredeemable savages at the start of their internment and remained in that condemned state throughout periods that ran into years. This was how they were judged by their keepers; though the natural variation between the brothers and nuns at different times and in different schools meant that levels of violence varied, beating was the absolute constant remembered by all victims and experienced by the majority in a sustained and relentless way.

The legal and political circumstances surrounding industrial schools and reformatories changed in Ireland with independence. What they changed from and to is not entirely clear and the process was not immediate. The Pro-Treaty side, led by Cumann na nGaedheal, was more accepting of the British heritage, the civil service administration, the laws and the regulations. In what was at first the Irish Free State, this should have applied to the industrial schools and reformatories. There is compelling evidence, notably in Peter Tyrrell's book, *Founded on Fear*, that the 1920s were no less horrific than later periods. But his evidence is confined to one institution, the Letterfrack Industrial School. With the change of power, in 1932, there were changes and as the country became first Éire and then in due course the Irish Republic, the steady impact of Fianna Fáil made itself felt, helped in particular by the long period of unbroken power. This lasted sixteen years and embraced the Second World War.

During the 1922–32 period, under Ministers for Education Eoin MacNeill and J.M. O'Sullivan, the rules were those of the British administration. They were an expression of the principles of governance for the schools. They 'certified' the schools. They were a form of contract between the State and the school manager. The document, entitled 'Rules and Regulations for the Certified Industrial Schools in Ireland'[8] was signed on behalf of the State by the Minister himself, and before him by the Chief Secretary. The relevant statutory instrument was the 54th Section of the 1908 Children Act. The 'Corresponding Manager' signed for the school, his declaration containing the words 'These Rules have been adopted by the Managers.' Derogations were possible. One of them, dated 1955 and specific to one school, reads: 'In the case of Artane Industrial School, Co. Dublin, the foregoing Rules may be modified in accordance with Time Table attached hereto.'

The rules were set out in 30 numbered paragraphs. These dealt with all aspects of the lives of the child inmates. In 1933 Rule 11 was removed. This stated: 'The Manager shall see that the children are constantly employed, and that they are taught to consider labour as a duty, to take kindly to it, to persevere in it, and to feel a pride in their work'. Rule 17, allowing for a child to be sent out to be apprenticed 'to any trade or calling' and to go to 'a trustworthy and respectable person', was rendered obsolete by the 1941 Act, which also allowed for the payment of capitation grants to be extended to children under six. A third rule, on punishment, remained unchanged and was oppressively central to the

8   'Saorstát Éireann' was substituted for 'Ireland' in the 1933 set of rules.

management of the schools until they were all closed. Ironically, and without explanation, it was 'dropped' from the rules as later published by Eileen Kennedy in her 1970 report, which contains only 27 Rules.[9]

What is remarkable about the Rules and Regulations, in a forbidding and depressing way, since it indicates no instinct to reform, is their consistency over a period of many decades. A comparison of the rules issued for Artane in 1885, those for 1912, and the set of Rules and Regulations signed by Derrig for Artane in 1933, show basic consistency and a general character of protection and care. There are 30 numbered paragraphs in each, beginning with the name of the institution, its first certification—which in the case of Artane was on 9 July 1870—and its size, in terms of the maximum number of possible admissions. The physical care and protection of the children, their sleeping accommodation, food and clothing are defined, so are the standards of education and training.

These would all be unexceptional, in terms of protecting young people held in the State's care for extended periods of time, were it not for the fact that many of them were breached, sometimes flagrantly, and the clear picture of this is presented in Tyrrell's account of Letterfrack between 1924 and 1930.[10] They were to be given 'neat comfortable clothing in good repair, suitable to the season of the year' and they were to be fed on 'plain, wholesome food, according to a scale of Dietary to be drawn up by the Medical Officer of the School and approved by the Inspector' (1912 version). In 1933 Tomás Derrig expanded on this by adding: 'Such food shall be suitable in every respect for growing children actively employed and supplemented in the case of delicate or physically-under-developed children with such special food as individual needs require.' He also stipulated no changes should be made without prior notice to the Inspector and that the 'Dietary' should be copied to the cook with a further copy kept in the manager's office. A chronic complaint, throughout the whole period of the existence of the industrial schools concerned the inadequacy and poor quality of the food, in some cases, notably the Baltimore Fisheries School in Cork, reaching levels of starvation where the boys searched for food in people's dustbins. Universally, as a matter of record from many former inmates, the shortage of food and its poor quality is a major complaint.

There were careful regulations as between all children receiving national school education, 'not less than four and a half hours five days a week', this to be combined with the industrial training. This latter aspect was to be aimed at 'fitting the boys for the most advantageous employment procurable' and for girls, to be carried out 'in accordance with the Domestic Economy Syllabus'. All this, which was effectively denied in most of the industrial schools, was to be inspector-approved. Fire drill, recreation, parental or guardian visit, apprenticeship training, the keeping of proper timetables and the medical care

9   The full set of Rules and Regulations is to be found in Appendix 1.
10   See Chapter 3.

programme were all specified, the latter in some detail. It provided for obvious records, as well as for quarterly examinations of each child and the examination of the sanitary conditions in the schools. Dental care of the children and regular inspection of their teeth were written into the rules. None of this was observed.

Discipline and punishment were carefully spelt out, the main purpose to protect the child, or so it seemed. In fact, the Rules and Regulations permitted great licence, since they did not detail the scale of the beatings that became the universally oppressive source of fear and damage to the child in all industrial schools. Under 'Discipline' in the Rules and Regulations before independence, the manager alone was authorised to punish. In 1933 this was extended by the phrase, 'or his deputy', which, it could be argued, embraced all teachers and staff so nominated by the person in charge. This came to be interpreted—if 'interpretation' was ever the word for it—in the broadest possible way, authorising punishment by everyone in every institution. However one interprets it, this became the norm, way beyond anything originally specified in the rules. A book was to be kept in which all punishments were recorded and this was to be 'laid before the Inspector when he visits'. No records exist of this being done, noted and reported by departmental inspectors.

An addition—pious in the hope it expressed—was then inserted in the rules: 'The Manager must, however, remember that the more closely the school is modeled on a principle of judicious family government the more salutary will be its discipline'. It was expected that this would lessen the need for punishment. It was followed nowhere and had no reductive effect on the excessive scales of illegal punishment that went on everywhere.

These punishments included three categories: forfeiture of rewards and privileges, 'moderate childish punishment with the hand' and 'chastisement with the cane, strap or birch'. Girls over 15 were not to be chastised; those under were beaten only 'in cases of urgent necessity' each one to be fully reported to the inspector. The one significant record of this period, that of Peter Tyrrell, who was an inmate in Letterfrack between 1924 and 1931, indicates that virtually all the Rules and Regulations were broken or disregarded, not periodically, not from time to time, but as a constant and accepted management approach. He even includes a sad little paragraph about the highly improper chastisement of a girl of 15 by a priest.

The abuse of the system of regulation was criminal in the results it produced, including gross and perpetual physical punishment. It denied the children all the benefits laid down in legislation about education and health, while subjecting them to physical violence. It was unmitigated by any attempt to meet minimum requirements. As a result, hunger, fear, disease and ill-health were constantly part of the children's lives.

Chapter 2

TOMÁS DERRIG TAKES CHARGE

As far as the story of the industrial schools went, from then on, the central figure for the greater part of the next two decades was Tomás Derrig. He became Minister for Education, a portfolio he retained—with a short period in Posts and Telegraphs and Lands, 1939–40—until Fianna Fáil went out of office in 1948. He was born and educated in County Mayo and took his degree at University College, Galway. He there organised a corps of the Irish Volunteers. After the 1916 Rising he was arrested and imprisoned. During the War of Independence he was interned in the Curragh; while there he stood for election, winning a seat for Mayo North and West. As a republican opposed to the Treaty and to political participation in the early Dáil assemblies up to 1927, he was very much an enemy and was taken into custody by the Free State forces. In the 1927 general election he won a seat for Carlow–Kilkenny.

In the period from 1916 to the War of Independence Derrig had a job as headmaster of a technical college in Mayo. On the strength of this experience he was chosen by Eamon de Valera, when he came to power in 1932, as his Minister for Education. He was to prove a tough and unbending holder of the office. The most significant act performed by Derrig, in respect of the industrial schools and reformatories, came in his second year in office, 1933. This was when he issued the Rules and Regulations that were to apply to the industrial schools and reformatories (so-called certified schools).

What is remarkable about the Rules and Regulations is their consistency over a period of many decades. A comparison of the rules issued for Artane in 1885 and in 1912, set against the rules signed by Derrig for Artane in 1933, shows basic consistency and a general character of protection and care. There are 30 numbered paragraphs in each, beginning with the name of the institution, its first certification—which was on 9 July 1870—and its size, in terms of the maximum number of possible admissions. The physical care and protection of the children, their sleeping accommodation, food and clothing are defined, as are the standards of education and training.

Derrig, whose professional knowledge of teaching requirements and general experience of normal education—as opposed to the penal education of children within the industrial and reformatory school system—had qualified him for the ministerial portfolio he held, took almost verbatim the wording used by his predecessors. In the period before independence, this was the Chief Secretary and, in the case of the 1912 document for Artane, this was signed on 12 January by Augustine Birrell, the Chief Secretary for Ireland. Derrig's own signature in 1933 came on foot of a document largely unchanged from the one Birrell had signed.

However, the 1933 Derrig rules, which were issued to all Irish institutions in that year, indicated that he and the Government were running against the trend for reform and were reconfirming and setting in place a regime that was long outdated in the judgment of the administrations from which it had derived— those under British rule. This was simply because of the substantial reforms, dealt with below, which had taken place in Britain, both before and after independence. The facts are incontrovertible. Yet judgments have been made in respect of the child prisons in Ireland between 1922 and the Second World War, which are without due reference to the wider circumstances of reform elsewhere and notably in Britain.

The Free State had indeed kept an eye on what was happening in Britain—not in any self-informing way but with an instinct for separation and new departure—even if this followed a reactionary rather than a reformist line.

The whole set of legal and political circumstances surrounding industrial schools and reformatories had changed in Ireland with independence, though not in any benign or reformist way. It also changed fundamentally in the United Kingdom. However, the changes were in diametrically opposite directions. In the United Kingdom, following considerable public and parliamentary debate—the issue of corporal punishment being central—a more enlightened approach was adopted. The heavy threat and exercise of flogging was steadily reduced, with greater controls, all of them spelt out in detail. This is analysed more fully later in the chapter. In Ireland, there seemed, under Derrig, to be a deliberate attempt to turn the country away from these reforms, to give broader licence to the orders running the institutions and to ignore lapses when these came to public attention. This divergence is dealt with at greater length below. The process of change, in Ireland, was not immediate in the legal sense. Nevertheless, as will be seen in the next chapter, the experiences of Peter Tyrrell indicate that the regime applied in industrial schools and reformatories remained unreformed and became progressively more brutal.

The Pro-Treaty side, led by Cumann na nGaedheal, were outwardly more accepting of the British heritage, the civil service administration, the laws and the regulations. But it was a loosely regulated acceptance and, in what was at first the Irish Free State, it clearly did not apply within the industrial schools and reformatories. But the situation in fact was far worse. What was accepted by Government in the 26 Counties in the first decade of independence, in terms of child care, took little or no notice of changes elsewhere in Europe, notably within the United Kingdom. Ireland had no programme at all aimed at reforming conditions for children in detention but remained at odds with what was being changed elsewhere.

Progress in the United Kingdom, in the period before 1922, when the legal structure included the whole of Ireland, was responsive to growing recognition that the situation for children in penal institutions had long been seen as unsatisfactory and in need of reform; and indeed much reform was initiated from 1910, when Winston Churchill became Home Secretary, and again during the period after the First World War. In the Irish Free State and later, in Éire, the lack of reform continued as a result of the emphatic divergence of approach. In looking at what happened in those critical early years of independence, which were to shape in a very negative way indeed the lives of children within the juvenile prison system, it is important to understand this process of reform in Britain and to question why it was not followed in Ireland.

The Children Act 1908 (cited in the certification preamble to the 'Rules and Regulations for the Certified Industrial Schools in Ireland' as '8 Edw., VII., Ch. 67') was ostensibly applied, with minor variations, to Ireland. This was the Act (at Sections 45 and 54), that empowered an institution, either to make rules of its own, or follow those in the certification document, provided in either case that all such rules were approved by the Chief Secretary for Ireland, and, after 1924, by the Minister for Education. The seriousness of this rules document cannot be overstressed. It is emphasised by the signature of Chief Secretary Augustine Birrell on the 1912 rules and is reconfirmed by the fact that the Education Minister, Tomás Derrig, is the signatory for the 1933 rules. No fresh version of the rules was issued between these two dates. Yet in the United Kingdom significant changes took place at this time, substantially reducing dependence on corporal punishment and imposing stricter regulations.

The move in favour of reform derived from a Home Office report of 1896, known as the Mahoney Report. This revealed truly dreadful conditions in the child prisons throughout the United Kingdom. There had been earlier agitation for reform from the leaders of the philanthropic Reformatory Movement. They had declared, many years earlier, that if children were sent to the philanthropists' child prisons (the reformatories and industrial schools) instead of to adult prisons then the children would be treated more humanely. Mary Carpenter (1807–1877), her friend, Octavia Hill (1838–1912) and Matthew Davenport Hill (1792–1872), were all notable reformers in the field of child protection. This may well have been the case in some places in the United Kingdom, which then included Ireland, but the 1896 report revealed that the child prisoners were in fact being treated far worse than adult prisoners. Conditions in the adult prisons were gradually improving while those in the child prisons were deteriorating. The report criticised the institutions for following the pattern of prison discipline, for enforcing silence during meals, for forcing the children to work an eight-hour day to the profit of the institutions, and for inflicting beatings in excess of what was permitted by the 1890 Home Office Rules. These rules permitted a maximum of 18 strokes to be given with the cane or birch. One priest, the Rev. Sidney Turner, who was the superintendent at the Philanthropic Society's Redhill Reformatory, boasted to the 1896 Committee that he regularly dispensed whippings of 'three dozen' strokes, in clear defiance of the Home Office Rules.

By the early 1900s the Home Office was in the position that it had given too much power to the private child prison owners. It spent the next half-century trying to claw back those powers, consolidating its control over all locally controlled and private adult prisons. By such means, the worst excesses of cruelty and exploitation were rectified. Adult prisoners had organised pressure groups and these campaigned for prison reform. No such organisations campaigned on behalf of child prisoners. This may well have been because the child prisons masqueraded as 'schools', a fiction readily penetrated by anyone taking the trouble to investigate, either with the objective of reform agitation, or with the more direct purpose of changing the legislation.

Successive governments were slow to implement the 1896 Committee's recommendations. As a result, the 1908 Children Act, by no means a satisfactory or up-to-date piece of law when passed, was but a piecemeal measure resulting from widespread concern. It did not deserve the term, 'Children's Charter'. In fact it actually extended the categories of children who could be imprisoned. It did nothing to improve conditions in the child prisons. By 1913 child prison numbers exceeded those in the adult prisons in England. Corresponding figures for Ireland are worse. The Act rendered children powerless. It was a child prison owner's charter. In the wrong hands it could be used as an instrument of tyranny. In 1922, in Ireland, it undoubtedly fell into the wrong hands. Just how wrong they were is central to the story of what follows.

As a result of reports of horrendous ill-treatment in the English reformatory schools and industrial schools, the British Home Secretary, Winston Churchill, established in 1911 an inquiry (the Griffith Committee, of which his wife, Clementine Churchill, was a member). Churchill is often forgotten for his reformist work at this time, noted with approval by the *Manchester Guardian* in a number of different social situations, including his handling of riots, strikes and disturbances. The penal institutions for children were a minor embattlement for him. The Griffith Committee was to investigate 'the methods of maintaining discipline' and 'encouraging good conduct, and the extent to which further regulations with regard to punishment are desirable'. Addressing the Commons at the time, Churchill said, 'There is far too much flogging in these institutions for anybody's good.'

The Griffith Committee condemned in round terms the unnecessary use of corporal punishment. Its report, published in 1913, had recommendations on corporal punishment which were implemented in 1915 when the Home Office issued new Model Rules (replacing those of 1890) and reducing considerably the amount of corporal punishment permitted in the child prisons. Further reforms followed.

The Home Office Children Department was established in 1920. New Home Office Model Rules were issued in 1923. These regulated strictly the use of corporal punishment. They replaced the capitation grant system with annual budgets (as recommended in a 1913 report, 10 years earlier). This removed the prison managers' incentive to maximise numbers. In addition, the Home Office took the power to appoint or veto up to one-quarter of the management committees of the industrial reformatories.

Following the First World War detainee numbers fell rapidly. A Home Office report of 1927 comments approvingly on the closure of about 40 institutions. This should be compared with the reaction of Irish Department of Education officials as late as the 1960s. Departmental officials and prison managers expressed themselves as 'perturbed' at the decline in the numbers of children in industrial schools and took measures to check this decline. This was a time when there had been virtually no fundamental reforms in the system for 20 years and when Irish economic improvements were changing the social circumstances and definitions of poverty.

In 1925 the British Home Secretary, William Joynson-Hicks, appointed another inquiry into English reformatories and industrial schools. This focused on treatment of inmates. The Maloney Committee, as it became known, was 'to inquire into the treatment of young offenders and young people who, owing to bad associations or surroundings, require protection and training; and to report what changes, if any, are desirable in the present law or its administration'. The recommendations contained in the Maloney Report of 1927 were implemented in the Children and Young Persons Act 1933. This largely repealed and replaced the 1908 Children Act, not before time, and amalgamated industrial schools and reformatories, renaming them 'Approved Schools'.

The Home Office also placed further restrictions on the use of corporal punishment. The Approved School Rules of 1933 spell out in detail what is and is not permitted by way of corporal punishment. In view of past abuses, numerous safeguards against the misuse of corporal punishment were put in place. After the abolition of judicial corporal punishment (the sentence of whipping) by the Criminal Justice Act of 1948, concern was raised about the corporal punishment of prisoners. This included the punishment of child prisoners. The Franklin Committee's report of 1951 (*Review of Punishment in Prisons, Borstal Institutions, Approved Schools and Remand Homes*) made recommendations that sought to reduce corporal punishment in the approved schools.

Corporal punishment in adult prisons was regulated by statute (the Criminal Justice Act 1948 and subsequently the Prison Act 1952), by the Prison Rules and by an enormous body of regulations designed to safeguard against improper use. The qualifying prison offence had to be very serious (mutiny or serious assault on a prison officer) and even after a lengthy quasi-judicial process, including a right of appeal, each incidence of punishment had to be approved by the Home Secretary. Indeed the process was so onerous on the authorities as to limit the infliction of prison corporal punishment, and by the mid-1950s the incidence was falling steeply.

Between 1955 and 1962, only 37 corporal punishment sentences were carried out in English prisons. A typical sentence was 10 strokes (in excess of 12 strokes was common in Artane). The last whippings were given in 1962 and the practice was abolished altogether by the Criminal Justice Act 1967. A child prisoner incarcerated in Artane between 1961 and 1963 has told me that he endured more than 37 floggings. This means that he suffered more floggings himself in those two years than were given to all the convicts in all England's convict prisons in the seven years from 1955 to 1962. The victim was legally an innocent child—one of only about 420 such children in Artane—and Artane was only one such prison. The statistic gives some indication of the scale of the violence in the Irish child prisons. It illustrates the gross injustice inflicted on the imprisoned children.

Ireland ignored these changes made in the United Kingdom. They included the Home Office Model Rules of 1923 and the Approved School Rules 1933, the latter coinciding with Derrig's own rules, which accorded no protection against the improper use of corporal punishment. The English rules applied to the whole of the United Kingdom. They were followed by further reforms which set an upper limit on the number of strokes that a child prisoner could be given. The Derrig rules set no upper limit. The Home Office regulated the size of the cane that could be used. Ireland, as is already clear from the weapons used at Letterfrack, did no such thing; even if it had made restrictions, clearly they would have been ignored. The United Nations was also ignored. Standard Minimum Rules for the Treatment of Prisoners, 1955 (Note Rule 5(1)):

> The rules do not seek to regulate the management of institutions set aside for young persons such as Borstal institutions or correctional schools, but in general part I would be equally applicable in such institutions.

Ireland became a member of the UN in 1955. The Department of External Affairs, according to the UN, received copies of the UN Standard Minimum Rules on the use of corporal punishment. Member countries were obliged to observe those rules. Ireland knew what was what and did nothing to conform. The fact that Ireland possessed these rules in 1955 makes a nonsense of the claim by Micheál Martin, already cited, that the concept of children's rights was little understood in Ireland. In other respects, of course, Ireland claimed to be a model member of the UN. This was particularly so when it came to human rights. The country formed a habit of criticising other countries (the United Kingdom, the Soviet Union, China) for human rights abuses.

Every properly conducted prison, for obvious reasons, must have rules that apply to the inmates as well as the managers and prison staff. The rules need to be known to the prisoners. They have to be enforced by appropriate procedures such as those that have applied to any prisoner entering an institution like

Pentonville Prison. The prisoner was given a card bearing the main prison rules written in his own language. The rules were read to any prisoner who could not read and copies of the full Prison Rules were posted up in every wing of the prison. Nobody could be expected to observe rules of which they were unaware, hence the need to publicise them. Rules held people to account—both prisoners and staff. In their absence—universal within the industrial school and reformatory system in Ireland—nobody could be held accountable for breaches of the rules. Prisoners—and the boys and girls were nothing else but prisoners—could be abused without means of redress.

The 1923 Home Office Model Rules (at number 31) say:

> A copy of these Rules shall be given to each member of staff of the school who shall sign a written undertaking that he has read and will observe the Rules and will maintain the discipline of the school and arrange for the instruction and training of the children in conformity with the Rules.

Tomás Derrig's rules made no such provision, nor did they follow another significant imposition in the Home Office Model Rules, that

> … no person employed in the school shall inflict any kind of corporal punishment and the term 'corporal punishment' includes any form of striking, cuffing, shaking or physical violence. If any person commits a breach of this rule, he shall be liable to instant dismissal.

There is constant irony in the contrast between what existed, what reforms might have been adopted, and what was actually happening in the schools. Rules are essential to the proper operation of such places just as they are in the broader society. When applied to that society, this doctrine of the Rule of Law holds that society must be governed by law and that no one is above the law. This simply did not apply to the boys and girls in the child prison system.

There are particular reasons why the observance of rules by the staff is important in child prisons. The inmates of Artane were incarcerated, according to the Education Minister, because of their unruliness—they were delinquents. The child prisoners were there to observe rules and it was incumbent on the State, having put them there, that prison operators should set an example by strict adherence to rules, as well as by making the rules available to the inmates and understood by everyone.

The reforms in the United Kingdom that followed the 1927 Maloney Report were well-known in Ireland; well-known also was the impending repeal of the 1908 Children Act, leaving Ireland with a piece of 'orphan legislation'. Nevertheless, this Act was the one on which the Minister for Education depended for certification, and therefore management, of industrial schools and reformatories.

If the Peter Tyrrell testimony, together with other reports and evidence, is anything to go by, the situation in Ireland remained as it had been, without reform or even the notion of protecting and making better the lives of the boys and girls in the institutions. Nor did this change when, in 1932, Fianna Fáil came to power.

Speaking generally, the new de Valera Government was determined to dismantle the remaining constitutional links with the United Kingdom. Speaking specifically about the Irish children in penal care, the net effect of political separation was to allow the creation of cruel and unbending regimes in the industrial schools and reformatories, accompanied by inadequate State inspection and control.

The timing of Tomás Derrig's recertification procedure, clearly credited to Section 54 of 'the Act, 8 Edw., vii., Ch.67', is significant. An internal Department of Education memorandum at the time says the following:

> The Department of Education [has] had under consideration for a considerable time the need for an inquiry into the present reformatory and industrial school system with a view to introducing reforms and improvements. Many circumstances combined make such an inquiry a matter of urgency and importance. The statutory provisions relating to these institutions and the treatment of juvenile offenders and delinquent children are based principally on the Children Act 1908. These provisions have been amended more than once in Great Britain and at present the Free State [is] behind most European countries in its arrangements for dealing with this important social question.

It went on:

> Before introducing reforms, the Minister for Education wishes to have the whole position enquired into and reported on. He proposes to set up a Commission for that purpose'.[1]

It is worth making the point that Irish detainees, at least the vast majority in the industrial schools, were not 'juvenile offenders', nor were they 'delinquent' in any legal meaning of the term. It was quite usual, in internal Irish Government documents, so to refer to them, both at this time and later. But it was an inaccurate and, seemingly with intent, a pejorative use of language.

There is no doubt that Tomás Derrig was aware of events in Britain and probably keenly aware that the widely hated figure of Winston Churchill, as Home Secretary, had been responsible for initiating change. Ireland was deeply involved with the League of Nations at the time, and was rather fond of signing human rights instruments, particularly those relating to the rights of children. In

---

[1]   Transcript of Ryan Public Hearings, 21 June 2004, p. 94.

the pages that follow we shall find it widely claimed that Ireland was largely ignorant of children's rights, already noted in respect of Micheál Martin. This is simply not true. The claim made in the 1916 Proclamation, about cherishing the nation's children equally, and repeated in the 1919 Dáil, was sacred in Irish political texts. It was offered up as a verbal sacrifice on the altar of independence whenever the public vindications of such social charges and obligations were being aired. It meant nothing at all. It was just 'air'. No constructive purpose was served by the repetitious hypocrisy of the child-cherishing mantra. Those who fought for Irish freedom knew that such rhetoric would attract public support for their campaign of violence. Their true intentions were revealed when they came to power. As soon as the last British administrator departed from Dublin, the notion of children's rights—when the children were seen as wrongdoers, rather than criminals—was comprehensively dismissed. The industrial schools remained prisons in the same way as the reformatories. Having been established under the Home Office Prisons Department, they remained unchanged in material terms for a further 40 years, the only change being their administration by the Department of Education. This administration repeatedly let down the inmates, failing them at every level and on all issues material to their welfare, care and growth as children.

What had been parallel systems continued to diverge. The details of this are embarrassing to Ireland. In Britain, in the renamed 'Approved Schools' offenders had a trial before an Approved School Order was made against them, leading to their committal. In Ireland they were not, in general, 'offenders' and there was no 'trial' in any accepted meaning of the word. In the United Kingdom every child was assessed before being assigned to an approved school institution. There were no such assessments in Ireland. The United Kingdom rules, together with the provisions made for inmates, were age-related. There were three groups: Juniors, aged 10 to 13 years on detention; Intermediates, 14 to 15 years; Seniors, 16 to 17 years. Artane held boys aged from 7 to 17 with no differentiation as to rules or provision. The English approved schools held mainly offenders, whereas the Irish industrial schools principally held non-offenders. In Artane, the largest industrial school in Ireland, of the 413 inmates in 1962, five were offenders. In 1967, Court Lees, the largest approved school in England, held 121 inmates, 118 of whom were offenders.

A child could spend up to 16 years in an Irish industrial school. No child could spend anything like that long in an English approved school. A child had to be over 8, or more usually 10, to be detained in an English approved school. In 1949 the average periods of detention in English approved schools were as follows. Senior boys: 1 year 9 months; intermediate boys: 2 years 1 month; junior boys: 3 years 2 months. For girls the figures were: Senior girls: 1 year 11 months; intermediate girls: 1 year 10 months; junior girls: 3 years. The average time for which Irish children were incarcerated was probably in excess of 10 years.

The United Kingdom was operating a child prison system for offenders. A child was often only sent to an approved school after having committed two or three offences. Ireland was operating an ideologically inspired mass incarceration system for non-offenders.

Tomás Derrig set up the Cussen Committee in 1934 under the chairmanship of G.P. Cussen, a senior Dublin District Court Justice. It was charged with an investigation of the conditions in the country's industrial schools and reformatories. The decision may have owed something to the reforms that had taken place in Britain, and to remedy the fact that, in marked contrast to the concerns at Westminster and the changes in the law made there, the position of the Irish State was to rely on the imperfect legislation surrounding child prisons and simply to go on using the existing administrative laws and regulations.

The findings of the Cussen Committee were very negative. The Cussen Report of 1936 contained reservations about the numbers held in the institutions and the long sentences they were serving. It also judged the education given as inadequate. Located, as the institutions were, throughout the country, the report suggests that there was a lack of local support. For a number of reasons, including the closed nature of the 'child prisons' and the secretive attitude of the religious orders in their operation, this was understandable. The report also condemned the stigma attached to those who had been through the system. Nevertheless, Cussen concluded that 'the schools should remain under the management of the religious orders'. This meant no change and Derrig adopted a 'no change' approach. The procedures for management and inspection remained as they were. The recertification of the schools remained unchanged for the rest of the 1930s. The rules, duly signed by the Minister and the prison manager, constituted the 'licence' to go on.

The Cussen Committee painted a dismal picture of the industrial school system in Ireland. Cussen laments what he considers to have been 'the false perception' in the public mind that the places he was investigating were prisons; nevertheless he had to admit that 'From the establishment of the Reformatory system in 1858, to 1927, with the exception of the period 1890 to 1906, the Inspector of Reformatory and Industrial Schools held, in addition, an appointment in the Prisons Service'.[2]

Cussen sought to enhance the deception about the nature of the institutions by renaming them. 'Industrial Schools' were to be called 'National Boarding Schools' and the 'Detention Order' was to be called an 'Admission Order'. These changes were not pursued. The idea of an admission order was a seriously deceptive proposal since, for the vast majority of men and women who had been consigned as children, this was the event that haunted them as much as any of the other abuses, with the possible exception of the floggings. The same change alluded to by Cussen was repeated, as an argument, by District Justice Eileen Kennedy in 1970.

In examining the impact of Tomás Derrig's early period as Minister for

[2]   See Commission of Inquiry Report into Reformatory and Industrial School System, 1934–1936, p. 9.

Education, we have dealt so far with the processes by which he came to judgment of the country's needs. They indicate a hard-line approach to the commitment of children to the institutions—this of course is not part of the Rules and Regulations—and a hard-line approach to the reformist lead given by the United Kingdom Government. Among de Valera's ministers Derrig had the advantage of his studies as a university student and then as headmaster of a technical school in County Mayo. It seems not to have helped him to understanding or compassion. The sternness of attitude may well have been reinforced by a negative view of the United Kingdom as a place from which the new State might seek guidance in its social and educational policy. It may also have been related to a view, then common in Ireland, that Britain—particularly in the decade of the 1920s with its dances, parties, and post-war exuberance—was a long way from the Celtic purity and religious fervour espoused in Ireland. Whatever the reasoning inspiring or shaping the beliefs and principles of this quite complex and rather rigid person, his actions were the primary cause of the dark shadows that overhung several generations of young people who then went through the industrial school system.

Of the many points that can be made about the soulless circumstances that surrounded the lives of those boys and girls sent to the industrial schools, the most telling of all are those that are to be made about the categories of perpetual discipline and punishment contained in the Rules and Regulations published by Derrig in his first period in office. When the day of retribution eventually comes, it will be remembered that the single biggest issue in the memories of those who suffered relates to physical abuse. This, rather than any other form of abuse, produced most of the complaints made to the Lafoy/Ryan Commission. The system of punishment that existed in the schools went far beyond the Rules and Regulations.

In conclusion, there was a reign of terror and it was constantly imposed on the inmates. The punishment was effectively unregulated. The Derrig rules permitted just about any type and degree of violence. Slaps and punches to the head and body were permitted. Naked flogging on the buttocks with a strap, cane or birch was permitted. The Derrig rules placed no upper limit on the amount or degree of punishment that a child prisoner could receive. Most of the violence ('physical abuse') of which the former Irish inmates complain was within the Derrig rules. And his own record, in response to cases that became the source of widespread public concern and at times horror, is one of wooden and inflexible denial. Several such cases are recorded below.

Having made his new set of rules, modelled on the more extreme restrictions observed under the Westminster Government, Derrig saw fit not to regulate the violence of the Christian Brothers. He did not have the proper inspections carried out. He did not punish, nor did he dismiss or sanction, the many criminal assaults carried out against juveniles.

Notwithstanding the Brotherhood's 'unenviable reputation' for violence towards children, nor the very public fact that two Christian Brothers had recently (in the early 1930s) been executed in Canada for child murder, Derrig allowed a free range approach in the industrial schools run by them and by other religious orders. He did not even go to the trouble of devising a set of safeguards. As has been said, he could simply have lifted the English rules of 1923 or 1933.

Chapter 3 ∾

PETER TYRRELL AND LETTERFRACK'S REIGN OF TERROR

W e are fortunate to have an account of one boy's experiences in an industrial school between 1924 and 1931. *Founded on Fear*, by Peter Tyrrell, was first published in 2006 and has since been republished.[1] The book is testimony of the utmost importance, covering industrial school life during the first decade of the Irish State, a period not otherwise well documented. It may be taken as a guidebook to the life experienced by inmates in one of the Christian Brother establishments. St Joseph's Industrial School for Senior Boys, at Letterfrack in County Galway, was arguably the worst of these and vied with Daingean for the title of 'worst of all'. It was certified for 165 children and was closed in 1973. (Its status was an indeterminate one, half industrial school and half reformatory.)

Its brutal regime, which Peter Tyrrell tells in great detail, is confirmed by endless additional testimony throughout the whole period in which the schools existed up to their closure in the early 1970s. But *Founded on Fear* is unique for its complete narrative of a period and for the coverage of the early years of the State's management of the industrial school system. The Department of Education was responsible for what happened to Peter Tyrrell. The Ministers for Education at the time were Eoin MacNeill for the first two years, up to the end of 1925, and for the rest of the period J.M. O'Sullivan.

Peter Tyrrell was admitted to Letterfrack at the age of eight in the company of his three older brothers, Joe, Paddy and Jack. Two younger brothers, Martin and Larry, were 'sent to the nuns in Kilkenny' because they were too young. There were nine others in the family, eight brothers and one sister. They had all lived on a small farm near Cappagh in County Galway. Their father was well-liked in the community and helped others with their problems, but he was slow to work on his own farm and managed things badly. The family was often short of food.

1   Peter Tyrrell, *Founded on Fear*, Irish Academic Press, Dublin and New York, 2006.

Tyrrell's mother, from a better social background, borrowed or begged for money, and this led to the court orders affecting half the children.

> We lived in the village of Cappa, near Ahascragh, Co. Galway. We had just one room and kitchen and four acres of land with several acres of bogland a mile away. There were no windows in our house and I think it was really a stable we occupied when the old house fell down. The room and the kitchen were separated by a wall about four feet high and my older brothers would stand on the table and climb over the wall at bedtime. There was a door in the room leading on to the street, but the lads did not like going out in the dark to go to bed because one of them always saw a ghost!

When Peter Tyrrell started going to school in 1923, he used to wear his sister's long coat. On the first day the teacher told him to take off this coat and hang it on the back of the door. When he removed it, the other children laughed because he had nothing on underneath. He liked school. The teacher gave them a sweet on most days and bread and butter from her own home. Each day there was a small brown paper parcel on the window ledge; this was lunch for his brothers and himself. They ran through the fields in their bare feet after school. They would find potatoes and turnips in the fields and bring them to their mother to cook. From time to time Tyrrell's father got employment breaking stones on the roadside. He was paid 15s a week. Otherwise he had no income. The family depended on money sent by relatives in Boston. His father once had a letter from the United States with the suggestion that he should till the land instead of begging and praying. The family had a horse and donkey, a goat and kid and a few chickens and ducks. The eggs were bartered for tea and sugar. At times the children went for several days without eating, getting pains in their stomach. Their mother would make them lie face down until the pain eased.

Peter Tyrrell remembered no court case prior to his committal to Letterfrack Industrial School. But early one morning towards the end of January 1924 the Ballinasloe police took him and his three brothers away.

> We had a good breakfast, which was an event in itself, while the police waited outside or wandered in the fields. Then we travelled in a police car, an old Ford, to the police station, where we had dinner and tea and, in the late afternoon, we were put on the train for Galway.

Letterfrack Industrial School stood at that time on about 150 acres of its own land. It was wild, barren and desolate country, and the roads were very poor. Nevertheless, the farm made money and the boys had to work hard on the land. Letterfrack village had two shops, a public house and a post office. The sea, in the form of an inlet or bay, was a mile or so to the west and Kylemore Abbey a mile to the north. The main buildings of the school were in three sections, the ball alley and terrace completing a square which was called the yard of playground. East of the terrace was the monastery and beyond it the infirmary where the Tyrrell brothers slept on their first night.

Peter Tyrrell's life from this time on was dominated by fear of physical assault. It pervaded life at Letterfrack. Virtually from the first day, when he watched a Christian Brother chasing a group of the younger children and lashing the backs of their legs with a long stick, the sustained torment of beatings was central to all their lives. Some of the boys were only six years old.

The boys formed 'divisions' of 14 at each table. They went there after the breakfast 'whistle' and stood until Grace was said. There was then a rush for the bread and margarine. Tyrrell says the bigger boys got all the food. The division monitors got gallon tins of cocoa and filled the small white mugs. Talking was forbidden until the order 'talk away' was given. After breakfast they were marched in single file across the yard to the lavatory. There were about 12 toilets and the boys lined up in front of them. Each boy was required to spend three or four minutes sitting down. 'When the monitor in charge sounded the whistle, we sat down, and when the whistle sounded again, we stood up and dressed.' The practice, which applied to the small boys, was discontinued about a year later.

Tyrrell and his youngest brother were in Infants' Class. The young boys did not have desks. They all stood round the blackboard. Their teacher was an ex-pupil from Artane Industrial School. He was 17 years old and was also the bandmaster.

The brother in charge of the junior school, including Infants' Class, used a leather strap to beat the pupils on the hands and face. When asked a question, a pupil was required to stand and answer without thinking. 'Shoot the answer!' the boys were told. The brother would put boys across his knees in the classroom and give them about six blows on the bottom. This would be for looking at the clock, scratching, yawning, looking round when the door was opened or writing with the left hand. The brother also beat the Infants' Class teacher—the ex-Artane pupil—for not beating the younger children.

The many sad stories contained in *Founded on Fear,* which are told in a calm, restrained way, include one with a particularly haunting character about a shy and timid boy called John Coyne. Coyne's father murdered his mother. The son was sent to Letterfrack. Tyrrell describes him as 'a really handsome boy with a lovely round face, dark hair and brown eyes. There was that searching look in his face. He seemed to be asking "Do you really know the dreadful experience I have had? Do you really mind very much? Do you condemn me for what has happened? Will you hold it against me?"'

Tyrrell befriended him, shared with him what his mother sent him from home and never questioned him. 'I was extremely fond of this little lad.' He witnessed the first beating Coyne had at the school. Coyne fell under the cruel punishments of Brother Vale, who flogged boys without mercy, using the rim of a motor car tyre reinforced with steel.

Vale has beaten this unfortunate boy terribly during the last year. His lovely face seems to have changed an awful lot, that roundness has vanished, instead his face is long, his cheek bones stick out, his eyes just glare (or stare) and there are dark shadows underneath. His cheeks were once rosy but now they are chalk white, with several spots.

We learn nothing more. The image is one of many cameos of mental and physical destruction at Letterfrack. They are clearly delivered in Peter Tyrrell's essentially restrained narrative about a truly terrible place.

Two individuals are singled out in Tyrrell's book for the extreme beatings they gave. Brother Walsh was the first to beat him. He claimed that Walsh beat everyone on the head and ears with the strap. A boy called Dick Hunt was nicknamed 'cauliflower ears', not because of natural causes, but because his ears were badly swollen and festering. They almost healed, then deteriorated and 'now look awful'.

It's now Sunday morning and about twelve of us are lined up to be beaten in the washroom at the end of St Michael's dormitory. We are ordered to take off our pants. Walsh now goes away to his room and returns with a stick. It's a new stick he cut a few days ago. I am at the very end and I have to see all the others flogged before me. The Murtaugh boy is now being beaten and he is screaming loudly it's frightening to hear this almost daily. It's my turn next, after about six blows I manage to run away, down the stairs and into the bathroom. Walsh now follows me down, he is now hitting me on the head and face and back, as I put up my right arm to ward off a blow he hits me a heavy blow on the arm. My arm is broken. I spend two weeks in the infirmary. A doctor called Lavelle is now in Letterfrack. Old Doctor John who lived on the hill is now dead. Lavelle comes to the school once a month. Walsh now comes to tell me to say I fell down the stairs. There is only one other boy in the infirmary, Caleba. He is suffering from sleeping sickness.

Dr Lavelle visited the infirmary the next day to see Tyrrell and Caleba, who were in the same ward. He was a long time with Caleba and then inspected Tyrrell. Brother Keegan was with him. The doctor asked Tyrrell how he had fallen down the stairs. Tyrrell gave the answer Brother Walsh had told him to give, saying the stairs were slippery because they were polished each day. Tyrrell was then examined and marks were found on his head, ears and back. Further inspection revealed that the backs of his legs still had the marks from the stick. Nothing was said.

Caleba died that night. He had not eaten at all but had always asked for water, which Tyrrell got for him. On his last night there was only one request for water.

Worse was to come for Tyrrell and the other boys. This was the arrival of Brother Vale, who had worked for seven years in a school for children who were deaf and dumb. He wore dark glasses so that no one could see his eyes and was about the same age as Walsh. Vale supervised meals. A week after his arrival, boys started talking in Division Three.

> Like a flash brother Vale rushed to the table and beat everyone across the back and the head with something which was neither a stick nor a strap. We couldn't see him carry any weapon. He struck everyone about six blows at terrific speed. The screams and shouts were most frightening … my brother Joe discovered what it was the boys were beaten with. It was eighteen inch long piece of rubber that had been cut from a solid rubber tyre. … It was the rim of the tyre with steel wire running through it.

Brother Vale's beatings became constant and savage, making Tyrrell 'terribly lonely and homesick, a lot worse than when I first came to the school'. He had a bad accident, falling down in the bathroom. He was terrified of being beaten naked. On this occasion he was beaten on the floor. The boys were given a signal by Vale hitting the wall with his rubber truncheon, and they would all run up to bed with Brother Vale following them. Tyrrell's hurt leg meant he could not run and Vale hit him again and again. He could not sleep and was trembling all night. The next day he was moved to the infirmary.

Tyrrell deteriorated seriously during 1929 when, he says, Vale beat him several times daily for weeks.

> When I go to the refectory for meals my hands are sweating. My sight is getting blurred and I am unsteady on my feet. I feel hungry but when I eat the food will not stay down. I am now weak, and as I walk along find it difficult to keep my balance.

Tyrrell, unsurprisingly, had dreadful nightmares which he recounts. But his daytime recollections, appalling though they are, give a measured, even a calm view of the dreadful regime at Letterfrack. It is a chronological account; the passing years are dealt with in a reflective way, the few good times are remembered, as are the people he came to like or respect. It was, for Tyrrell, a maturing process, not because of any thoughtful or caring attitude by those in whose charge he suffered, but because of his own growing wisdom and acceptance. He loses his faith, not completely, but in a series of conversations with brothers; in his own reflections on their attitudes and actions he finds he cannot equate the ordeals he passes through with any sustained belief in the tenets of the Catholic faith. As late as Christmas 1931 he receives from the leader of a mission at Letterfrack 'new rosary beads, which are blessed by the missioner personally'. The following January the superior, a man called Kelly, offered to let him stay on after his release date and Tyrrell's response is to wonder if he knew what was going on. If he did, surely he would stop it.

I am sure that Keegan [the first superior] did not know that Walsh and Vale simply tortured the children. Keegan himself was a hard and cruel man. He beat the boys sometimes severely, but there was always a reason. He beat them for having lice and sores on their heads. What he really beat them for was for not going sick, when they had sores or skin diseases. He said lice were due to laziness and dirt. The most terrible law in Letterfrack was we must not complain. In the words of Brother Kelly, 'it is sinful in the eyes of God to complain'.

Tyrrell admired Kelly but held against him one mistake. This he could not forget. It related to a lay teacher in the school called Tom Griffin. He was present in the yard every day. He worked from six in the morning until nine at night, never took a holiday, never missed a day, looking after the boys during holidays, taking them to the sea. He was good to the children; he would read and write their letters for them. Griffin had started at Letterfrack in 1882 and in Tyrrell's time was paid 8s a week. He was dutiful and polite towards the brothers, always lifting his torn cap to them, addressing them correctly. They treated him with disdain. He had a dog called Toby which the boys loved, but Brother Keegan, who had a dog called Spot, and knew it would always win against the smaller Toby, set it on the other dog which it used to hurt, making the boys cry and Keegan laugh. Griffin carried the dog away afterwards to the warm glasshouse. Griffen could not afford a shirt or socks and on one occasion Tyrrell helped in the making of a suit in the tailors' shop for him. At the time his weekly wage had risen to £1, but was then reduced by 4s as part of Letterfrack 'economies'.

It was Brother Kelly who reduced Griffin's wages and Tyrrell found this deeply shocking.

On his departure, Tyrrell summarised the worst of Letterfrack, claiming that the religious were savage and brutal, mean, cunning and ferocious. And he named the key offenders: Fahy, Vale, Walsh, Blake, Reardon and to a slightly lesser degree Keegan, the superior. He claimed these to be the brothers who had turned the school into 'a terrible prison' where life was made unbearable for innocent and defenceless children. They were aged between 38 and 50. 'What damage have they already done, how much more destruction will they be permitted to do? The amount of pain and suffering perpetuated by such evil creatures must be enormous.'

Brother Fahy merits a postscript. He came to Letterfrack from Artane, arriving in Tyrrell's second year there. He was an erratic character who led a Jekyll and Hyde existence, keeping a girlfriend called Lydon O'Neill who lived in Clifden. She had some influence over him, took a dismal view of the Letterfrack boys, saying 'they looked like a bunch of convicts with their bald heads' (their hair had been cut by Fahy) so he changed to a 'fancy' haircut. He had clothes made for him in Dublin, including a suit of herringbone (at that time all the brothers wore black). He used to bring his girlfriend into the school, but only when the superior was on holiday. Her presence meant that Fahy did not beat the boys, so they were always pleased to see her.

Brother Fahy knew the priest from Kylemore Abbey, a Benedictine establishment with a school attached to it. It was run by an order of Belgian nuns. The two men used to play handball together at Letterfrack for money, usually £1 a game, high stakes at the time, but sometimes it was more. The priest, a man aged between 28 and 30 during Tyrrell's fourth year (1928), when first he became aware of him, did a tour of the school, arriving in Tyrrell's class during catechism and asked a number of questions, not all of which were correctly answered. He said to the teacher, Brother Conway, 'You are not using the cane enough.' Tyrrell comments that this 'was the first time I heard a priest speak of beating. Until then I imagined that a priest would not hurt anyone.' Tyrrell was in for a further shock. In the summer of 1931, his last at Letterfrack, he went on a school walk with other boys to Kylemore Abbey:

> As I was walking with Matt Feerick we make conversation with one of the convent girls. She is fifteen and is a very pretty girl. We sit on the grass and ask each other questions about our respective schools and I am horrified to learn that this beautiful girl is beaten in the same manner as the boys in our school. I could not believe her story when she said she was often beaten by the priest and the beatings were often severe, so to prove her story she showed marks on her arms and legs. I know this priest well as he often comes to our school. I now know that she did not lie to me as she looked me straight in the face. When I tell a lie I have to drop my eyes. Besides why should she want to tell a lie about the priest, of all people? I am now very upset, because, whatever doubts I had about religion, I still had a great respect for a priest. I always believed he would be the very last one to hurt anyone, least of all a girl. I could never have the same respect for a priest again, and whenever I see one I am reminded of what the girl told me.[2]

This episode involving the priest at Kylemore Abbey occurred under the 1912 rules which forbade the corporal punishment of girls over 15, a regulation that was kept, two years later, in the Tomás Derrig rules. At that stage, in the United Kingdom, the corporal punishment of girls, other than on the hand, had been abolished.

There was a surprising degree of quality and order in the teaching in the 1920s at Letterfrack. School was from 9 a.m. to 12.30 p.m. and from 6 p.m. to 7 p.m. The subjects taught were catechism, Irish, English, reading, writing and mathematics, and in the senior classes, geography, scale-drawing, geometry and Irish history as well as the Old Testament. Compared with later experiences in other industrial schools, this was a full curriculum. The time allowed for each subject varied

2   Tyrrell, *Founded on Fear*, pp 94–5.

greatly, from half an hour to several hours, days or even weeks. For example, for three weeks or a month before a catechism examination, the subject all day and every day would be catechism only.

Dinner was at 1 p.m. On Sunday, Tuesday and Thursday they had boiled or roast beef, potatoes and cabbage, peas or turnips. On other days, except Fridays, they had a bowl of soup, with half a slice of bread and boiled potatoes. On Fridays they had fish, usually mackerel. Puddings were rice boiled with raisins, and on some Fridays rhubarb and rice. Supper was a slice of bread and dripping and a mug of cocoa.

At 2 p.m. all the pupils reported to their workshops. Shoe-making, tailoring, baking, farming and knitting were taught. There was a garage for motor mechanics, a powerhouse and a smithy. Young boys did the darning and knitting or polished the floors or worked in the greenhouse. In the farmyard there was a slaughterhouse where cattle, sheep and pigs were killed. Letterfrack was almost entirely self-supporting.

There was recreation time from 5.30 to 6 p.m. After supper the boys drilled in the yard. Boys who made mistakes at drill were beaten on the back and legs by Brother Walsh, who used a cane walking stick. Drill was also done on Sundays.

On Saturdays boys attended workshops in the morning, and in the afternoon went to confession. On Sundays there was Mass and sometimes football in the afternoons. On one day a week they all went to the hall, undressed and picked the lice off their clothing.

There were three dormitories, St Patrick's for the senior boys, St Michael's for the boys aged from 9 to 13 and a small dormitory for the very young children in the new building. The two big dormitories had six rows of beds, three each side, with a brown carpet in the centre. Outside there were shelves and very small pigeon holes where Sunday suits, blue serge jackets and short trousers, were kept, with each set of clothes being numbered. Beds were also numbered with white paint. Peter Tyrrell's was number 151.

In each dormitory there were three electric lights. The centre light was very dim and it burned all night. Boys who wet the bed had a towel knotted round the rail at the head of the bed. This was for the benefit of the night man, who would call the boys every two hours to use the toilet. The night man was often drunk and he would fall asleep sitting on one of the beds and when he woke he would beat the children by putting them across the bed and using a whip made of leather laces. Those who had wet the bed were beaten on the bare bottom.

Boys were called at 6 a.m. and went immediately to the washhouse after collecting a piece of red carbolic soap and a stopper for the basin. After being washed and dried, they lined up to be examined.

We held out both our hands showing backs and fronts, leaned forward to show the back of our necks, and turned the head slowly in a clockwise motion to show our throat, ears and face. If not washed clean, we would be beaten, sometimes on the hands and other times on the bare back or face, usually six blows. Then we would be handed over to a monitor to be washed in a bathroom with a scrubber.

At the back of the school was an avenue to the main road. This avenue was infested with rats. They lived well on fish heads and other garbage thrown out a little distance from the back of the kitchen. Older boys would catch the rats in wire cages and take them to the yard and poke out their eyes with wire before releasing them to be killed by the school manager's cocker spaniel. The brothers said it was sinful to be cruel to any of God's creatures, including rats, which were put on this earth for a very special reason.

A few of the boys had visits from their parents from time to time, but they would dread these visits and hide in the lavatories when the parents arrived. The reason was that the parents would be ragged and badly dressed and the children were ashamed to be reminded that they were paupers. The boys were always being told that their parents were no good because they couldn't look after them and that the boys themselves were no good either.

Tyrrell's parents, to his relief, were unable to afford a visit. He hated being reminded of his father and stopped opening his letters. His mother once sent half a crown which the teacher divided equally between the four brothers.

Tyrrell's book is crowded with images, most of them truly terrible. The savagery of Brother Vale has an insane fury behind it, with indiscriminate floggings, on the body, around the head, while the boys worked, while they ate; the punishments have no logic or reason behind them. They often resulted in boys going to the infirmary, damaged by the attacks. There is a compulsion in the way Peter Tyrrell tells his story. His memory is remarkable. His treatment of each episode is calm and measured. One never doubts the facts; it is all too realistic in presentation.

In *Founded on Fear* Tyrrell demolishes the whole representation of what happened in Christian Brother industrial schools during the period of their operation. There were not just 'bad times', or 'bad people'; the savage, unrelenting cruelty was systematic, constant and comprehensive. The public thrashings were designed to create fear, even terror. The neglect of the boys reflected the utter worthlessness in which they were held. On one occasion Tyrrell was made to stand up before the other boys in his class and hear a withering account of what a useless and miserable member of the human race he was.

There was no attention to the children's health. Those with eye defects simply became more blind. Those with dental problems became chronically diseased. There is a pitiful description of one boy with blood and pus coming from his mouth. They had septic discharges from their ears. Their chilblains, which were chronic, went septic also.

The name Peter Tyrrell first became known as the result of an article originally published in *Hibernia* in 1964. The piece was carefully written. The brothers, many of whom were still alive, indicated by letters thus: 'Brother J.', 'Brother P.' Its publication coincided with the work done by Senator Owen Sheehy Skeffington, a Trinity professor who campaigned against corporal punishment in schools, including the industrial schools, and who befriended Tyrrell. Another person who campaigned was the architect Martin Reynolds, who later proposed designs for the rebuilding of parts of Daingean reformatory.

Attempts have been made to lessen what happened in Letterfrack, Artane and elsewhere by claiming that they did not differ much from ordinary schools, and that the poverty was a common distress shared by the population. *Founded on Fear* silences that argument. It has the compelling strength of Solzhenitsyn's *One Day in the Life of Ivan Denisovich*, only with Tyrrell one day stretches out into years. He was in a system where his incarceration was really not much different from the Stalinist Gulag. Lost, fearful, in despair, physically and mentally neglected, he came to hate his own home, to throw away letters unread and unanswered, and in the end to take his own life. He has articulated the grief and fear of something like 30,000 men and women who will never forget the experiences they had. They have badly needed this unforgettable testimony. But we should all welcome it, and read it.

Chapter 4 ∾

THE CHRISTIAN BROTHERS AND THE INDUSTRIAL SCHOOLS

Artane Industrial School was the largest industrial school in the country, certified under the legislation to cater for 825 boys. It features largely in this book because the religious order that controlled and ran it also managed several others, among them the notorious industrial school at Letterfrack. The Christian Brothers have been aggressive and resourceful in defending their good name in the course of public inquiry into the industrial school system over the past decade. This is understandable, since they still maintain schools and other institutions worldwide. These are now run by a Trust.

The background to their work is of central importance in understanding the development of education in Ireland, though this includes the major blot on their work in respect of Artane, Letterfrack, Glin and others.

The Christian Brothers achieved their central role in education in Ireland, particularly of poorer children, because of the dedicated initiative of Edmund Rice from the time he founded his first school in Waterford, in 1803, when he also founded, with two other men, the Society of the Presentation. He was following in the footsteps of Nano Nagle, who had set up the Presentation Sisters with the same purpose, to provide a Roman Catholic education for the poor.

Rice died in 1844, by which time the original Presentation Brothers had become the Christian Brothers and had 11 communities in Ireland, 12 in the United Kingdom and one in Sydney, Australia. They had educated 8,000 boys and the Order had 100 Brothers. The Order had negotiated independence from diocesan control with a constitution that placed it directly under the control of Rome. As has already been made clear, there was widespread fear among Irish Roman Catholics of Protestant attempts to proselytise, aimed directly at poor children who could be enticed by free schooling in Protestant schools or orphanages. Some of Rice's earliest associates did not accept this change and remained as the Presentation Brothers; the rest took their vows as Christian Brothers in 1822.

Edmund Rice had founded the schools at his own expense, and the development of Christian Brother schools, isolated not only from the Hierarchy but from the country's developing national school system, which was welcomed by the Hierarchy as a means of education at State expense, cost him dearly. But he valued highly the independence of the Order, even to the point of insisting on it having its own school textbooks written to conform with the Order's religious and patriotic ethos, one that combined 'Faith and Fatherland', necessarily to the disadvantage of a wider, English ethos, which could be said to have represented mixed faiths and a belief in 'Empire' rather than 'Fatherland'. The thread of this divergence, which runs through Irish history and historical study for much of the past 200 years, is a notable aspect of Irish intellectual and political thinking.

Inevitably, Christian Brother involvement in the control of industrial schools, though not reformatories, followed when they were established. And this became significant, making them symbolic of the harsh regimes that were applied in the closed environment of such institutions. Side by side there existed an education system widely admired by the many generations of Irish boys who went through it, and who acknowledged the sometimes heavy recourse to corporal punishment, and the quite different punishment regimes applied within the child prisons, peopled, as far as the Order was concerned, with 'criminals'.

Of course, making regulations was an important part of this regime, but it was singularly one thing, a book of rules; enforcing such regulations, or not enforcing them, was quite another. There can be little doubt that the Christian Brothers, founded in a strict independence of domestic rule in Ireland, whether from the Church or the State, would have sought to ignore any regulation of their power to inflict whipping. By the time the industrial school system was introduced in the British Isles—Ireland being then still part of Britain, and governed from Westminster by means of a Chief Secretary—the Christian Brothers had grown in strength and size and had expanded to other member Dominions, States and Colonies of the British Empire.

One of these was Canada, where it operated two institutions similar to Artane in Ontario: St Joseph's at Alfred, and St John's at Uxbridge. In her report, *Institutional Child Abuse in Canada*, Ronda Bessner of the Canadian Law Commission has described a catalogue of abuse that was inflicted on the inmates of these two 'prisons' in the 1960s. Flogging on the bare backside was the norm, even after the practice was banned by the Provincial authorities. Bessner says:

> The Ontario government policy prohibited corporal punishment. Staff were not permitted to strike, handcuff or kick the boys. In 1957 and 1958, the Ontario Department of Reform Institutions ordered staff at St Joseph's and St John's to read and sign directives banning the strapping of residents on the bare buttocks. A prohibition against strapping the hands was introduced in 1960. These policies were ignored.

What was required was strict regulation backed up by effective inspection. The Rules and Regulations signed into force by Derrig in 1933 provided for both. Neither was delivered. Ireland failed to implement the regulations by making no proper provision for the inspections. Even District Justice Eileen Kennedy, in other respects so pathetically inadequate, pointed out some of the inspection defects. As stated above, by the Edwardian era the British Home Office had realised that strict regulation of corporal punishment was required.

A year later, when industrial schools throughout the United Kingdom were abolished, no similar action was taken by the Irish Free State. In the same year, the Commission to Inquire into Widows' and Orphans' Pensions found that only 350 of the children in industrial schools were orphans. This was 5.3 per cent of the total number of inmates.

In 1937 the Irish State enacted a Constitution that was relevant to the care of children in various articles, a clutch of which were concerned with the family, whose 'inalienable and imprescriptible rights' were guaranteed. There were, and still are, grounds for serious questioning about the lack of change in the industrial school system in the light of the constitutional requirements. It was as if it did not apply, was not known, was even irrelevant as far as these imprisoned children were concerned. Families were being consistently broken up, many of them for the maximum duration of internment in the industrial schools, which could keep inmates until their sixteenth year and to which children as young as eighteen months were committed. In fact, what happened was that the Children Act of 1941 increased State funding for the industrial schools and largely maintained the established administration, the system of inspection and the overriding authority of the Church, through the religious orders that were widely in control, over how they would carry out their responsibilities.

In 1943 a terrible fire occurred at St Joseph's Industrial School for Girls, in Cavan town. Thirty-five girls and one elderly lay helper lost their lives. There was a public inquiry; the nuns, who belonged to the Order of the Poor Clares, were exonerated from all blame. In *Children of the Poor Clares*, a pioneering work on what happened at St Joseph's and the fate of its inmates in the succeeding years up to the time the school was closed, the public investigation was shown to be a travesty and the fate of the generations of girls generally who were committed there was exposed as one of deprivation.[1] A chilling footnote is provided in the Annual Report of the Department of Education, which simply states: 'A serious outbreak of fire which unfortunately resulted in the deaths of 36 persons (including 30 children under detention) took place at St Joseph's Industrial School, Cavan, in the early morning of 24 February 1943.'[2]

St Joseph's Orphanage, in Cavan town, was certified as an industrial school for female children in 1869 and was to operate as such for close on 100 years. The Poor Clares was the only closed order to be given the care of children. It is indicative of the extent of Roman Catholic control over the whole system of

---

[1] Mavis Arnold and Heather Laskey, *Children of the Poor Clares: The Story of an Irish Orphanage*, Appletree Press, Belfast, 1983.

[2] Department of Education, Annual Report for 1942/3, p. 70.

institutional care of deprived children that a contemplative order of nuns, their lives shut off from the world, their concepts of love focused on Christ and Our Lady, should have been allowed by the State to have absolute charge of children taken from normal family life.

The fact that the Poor Clares was a closed order aggravated the rescue operation. On the night of 23 February 1943, at 2 a.m., a card player in a house near the convent, looked out of her window to see what the weather was like. What she saw, billowing out of the vent in the orphanage, was smoke. For the first time in its history, the doors of the Poor Clare convent were burst open by the outside world. Breaking locks and forcing doors, men intruded into the silent orderly life of the nuns. Within 40 minutes, the fire had taken the lives of 35 girls and an old woman who had made her life in the convent. Research into the treatment of the inmates, then and later, revealed a way of life that was quite different from the benign picture of care and sacrifice by the nuns on behalf of the children in their charge.

Children of the Poor Clares was the first full exposure of the administration and funding of such institutions. It revealed a punitive regime, harsh, brutal and vindictive. The children were denied proper physical and mental care. Their education was rudimentary, a fact that showed in the very limited opportunities they were able to achieve after departure. There was no proper 'after-care' and the girls generally fell into low-paid and unsafe employment. Many drifted from job to job, without any self-regard or confidence, and had children out of wedlock.

The following year, the Irish State's Inspector of Industrial and Reformatory Schools, P. Ó Muircheartaigh, in his report of the previous year's work inspecting the schools, stated that in general 'the children are not properly fed'. He found 'semi-starvation and a lack of proper care and attention'. This was a serious indictment of a system, which, he said, 'should not be tolerated in a Christian community'.

As a result of his findings that year, two Sisters of Mercy, who were the resident managers of the industrial schools in Lenaboy in County Galway and Cappoquin in County Waterford were dismissed for negligence and for misappropriating funds. The Church resisted this action. No other changes to the administration of the industrial schools were made. A year later the Department of Education agreed to pay industrial school teachers at the same rate as national school teachers and the Secretary of the Department wrote to his opposite number in the Department of Finance denouncing conditions in the industrial schools. He blamed 'parsimony and criminal negligence' for the poor feeding and clothing of the children. The implication seems not to have been against the parsimony and criminal negligence deriving from the management of the schools by the religious orders, but the State's, since that same year funding for the industrial schools, under the per capita arrangement, was tripled. A further increase followed in 1946 when the industrial school rules were supposedly updated. What in fact appears to have happened was the following.

The Department of Education allegedly issued a circular to all industrial school and reformatory managers (circular 11/1946). It was entitled 'Discipline and Punishment in Certified Schools', 'certified schools' being both industrial schools and reformatories. The circular was advisory. It did not amend the 1933 rules.

There is no clarity about which institutions received the circular. It was not sent by registered post or delivered and signed for, so that negative evidence, in the form of denial, has emerged from various investigations. Some at least of the institutions did not receive the circular. Ms Justice Mary Lafoy, in her Baltimore Report, says ' ... the Committee has no proof that the Resident Manager of Baltimore School actually received the 1946 circular'.[3] At Seán Ryan's public hearings, the Rosminians asserted categorically that they had never received the 1946 circular and to this day do not have a copy of it in their archives.

The indications are that the 1946 circular was a red herring. It appears that references to it were introduced, or reintroduced, at a recent date by the Department in an attempt to deny that it had authorised the flogging of child prisoners in the post-1946 era. In 1970 District Justice Eileen Kennedy's report sought to conceal the fact of departmental authorisation. It seems doubtful that the 1946 circular—whatever its actual circulation—had any legal or regulatory force. No evidence has come to light that its applicability was ever tested in the courts, or that its supposed superseding of the standard set of rules took place. There is very substantial evidence from the most reliable sources—the thousands of child prisoners who went through the system and have survived—that the circular was ignored by industrial school staff and by all subsequent ministers. The 1933 rules remained in force until the 1990s and beyond. In 1960 the Department approved supplementary rules for Daingean reformatory. The Department has refused to disclose those rules.

Something of the true state of affairs in the industrial schools emerged in 1946, with the Gerard Fogarty case in Limerick. Fogarty was in Glin Industrial School in the town of that name west of Limerick on the banks of the River Shannon. He was 14 years old. He ran away from the industrial school to his mother, in the city of Limerick, but was found there by the police and returned to Glin. He was flogged naked with a leather cat-o'-nine tails by one of the brothers and then made to swim in the salt water of the Shannon estuary. He slipped out of the industrial school and walked home again, through the fields. When his mother saw the injuries on his back and arms, she went to a local councillor, Martin McGuire, who took up the issue with the Minister for Education. There was a public outcry but the State's response was to refuse any public inquiry and refuse also to explain how such punishments were possible in a State-funded institution. McGuire engaged the help of Father Flanagan, the founder of the Boystown Schools in the United States, who visited Ireland in 1946 to see for himself. He described the Irish industrial schools as 'a national disgrace'.

3   Baltimore Report, Third Interim Report of the Commission to Inquire into Child Abuse, 2003, p.133.

There were debates in the Dáil and coverage in the newspapers, but under Department of Education and Catholic Church pressure Father Flanagan was forced to leave Ireland. His death, two years later, terminated the debate started by his visit.

Criminal negligence was found in another case, in St Kyran's Industrial School, Rathdrum, where a three-year-old inmate, Michael McQualter, was scalded to death in a hot bath. The case was not pursued by the Department of Education. With the change of Government in 1948, Ireland had a new Minister for Education, General Richard Mulcahy, who was faced the following year with complaints about Greenmount Industrial School, Cork. Again, the action taken was a prearranged visit of inspection when the circumstances of the complaint were found to be unwarranted and no action was taken.

The Church at this time ran as a parallel form of government, presiding over the sexual lives of citizens, setting conditions on inter-Church marriages, precluding the State from involvement in social and health reforms, one of which—'The Mother and Child Scheme'—caused a major rift between the 1951 inter-party Government, led by John A. Costello, and the Hierarchy, in which the Archbishop of Dublin, John Charles McQuaid, played an important part. The scheme provided direct State funding to expectant mothers for their children and was presided over by Noel Browne, the newly elected and newly appointed Minister for Health. The Government caved in before Church pressure, the scheme was abandoned and Browne resigned.

There was further Church–State conflict that year when the religious orders refused to provide financial records of their funding of the industrial schools. They were asked for this as a condition for increases in the per capita payments for the schools, a request no doubt reinforced by the incidents of cruelty, want and death which had occurred during the latter half of the 1940s. In spite of the Church's refusal to co-operate, State funding for industrial schools continued.

There were further grim revelations during the 1950s. Incidents occurred, were investigated, and the school administrations exonerated. In 1955 the Secretary of the Department of Education himself, T. R. Ó Raifeartaigh, visited Daingean reformatory and found that 'the cows were better fed than the boys'. Nothing was done. Two years later Marlborough House, a reformatory in Dublin, was condemned by the Office of Public Works as a building judged to be 'a grave risk of loss of life'. No alterations were made.

In 1959, when Jack Lynch was Minister for Education, Gus Healy, Mayor of Cork, and, like Lynch, a Fianna Fáil representative for the city, complained about Upton Industrial School. Again, a visit was arranged with prior notification and the allegations about the school were set aside.

The 1960s saw a marked change in life in the Republic of Ireland, with more open challenging of social circumstances. A leading figure in this work of revealing and criticising the dark side of the Roman Catholic Church's authoritarian and oppressive attitude towards Irish social and sexual life manifested itself through the courage and hard work of individuals such as Senator Owen Sheehy Skeffington and of groups like Tuarim. This was a social ginger-group which held meetings and, perhaps more importantly, published pamphlets which were left-wing and reformist in the main. Leading figures included the Labour Party TD David Thornley and the barrister Donal Barrington, who later became a Supreme Court judge. Throughout this period, however, the industrial schools remained closed from public view and monitored very strictly as far as inspection and regulation were concerned.

One priest was able to make pornographic films of children in his care at Our Lady's Hospital for Sick Children in Dublin and develop them for sale in England. The Garda Síochána followed this up and reported it to Archbishop McQuaid. His response was to arrange for the offender, Father Paul McGennis, to have treatment. The Archbishop claimed 'this was successful at the time'. McGennis's abuse of children at the hospital in the 1960s was not brought to court until 1997 when he was convicted.

Archbishop McQuaid was concerned about stories involving Artane Industrial School. He appointed Father Henry Moore to be chaplain there and asked him to make a report on conditions at Artane. This report was suppressed. The Department of Education, made aware of it, carried out an inspection which exonerated the administration at the school. It was not until 2007 that the Moore Report was made public, adding to the dismal catalogue of abusive institutions Artane, the pride of them all, this home to the world-famous Boys' Band, many of its performers victims of the band-leader's abusive nature.[4]

In conclusion, it is perhaps worth dealing with certain general questions about the historical period up to the mid-1960s when a major shift in thinking emerged as a result of OECD interest in Ireland's education system as part of Europe's investigation of Ireland's suitability for EEC membership.

The first of these is specifically directed at educational legislation that was passed and which some have seen as reformist. This concerns the drafting and enactment of the 1941 Children Bill. For some reason, never satisfactorily explained, Eamon de Valera, when he reshuffled his Cabinet in September 1939, transferred Tomás Derrig out of Education, taking over the portfolio himself. He was already head of government as well as Minister for External (later, Foreign) Affairs and he kept a close control over all ministries, exercising an authority that was, by that stage, supreme. No decisions of any significance were taken without his knowledge. His move into Education coincided with the drafting of the Children Bill. This piece of legislation was in preparation from the time when de Valera took over the Department and it seems that a sensitive issue was vocational education. At the time it was under secular control and there were Church fears about this, reflected in correspondence between de Valera and McQuaid. In the event, no transfer of control over vocational education to a religious order was made.

[4]   The full text of the Moore Report appears as Appendix 6.

The 1941 Children Act was a complex Bill amending the Children Acts 1908–1929. The Taoiseach's role, as responsible minister, was limited. He allowed Tomás Derrig to introduce it, probably because he was too busy himself. This was in November 1940. It was enacted in June 1941 as the Children Act 1941. Before dealing with its content, it is worth recalling that, according to Archbishop McQuaid's biographer John Cooney, 'the McQuaid factor' was behind this move, that is the part of the Cabinet shuffle putting de Valera into Education.[5]

The Bill contained provisions making it easier for a child to be imprisoned in an industrial school. It also made it more difficult for the parents to recover the child from State custody. Dáil deputies objected that the provisions were unconstitutional, but Derrig ignored all objections. The provision that required the consent of both parents to recover a child from an industrial school was subsequently ruled to be repugnant to the Constitution by the Supreme Court in a 1955 case, *Doyle* v. *the Minister for Education*. The same provision was used to deny parental petitions from a parent whose partner was absent from the family home. And it was used to ensure that children of Irish servicemen in the British forces were not released to their mothers. This had a profound impact on the children of Irishmen who decided to join the British armed services, some of whose fathers were not able to return until well after the war had ended. One instance of this has been given, that of a woman, now in her seventies, who was one of these children. She and her sisters were placed in an industrial school when their father crossed the border and joined the British Army. Their mother tried to recover the children, but without success. The father wrote to his children from Northern Ireland and then from army bases farther afield. His letters were intercepted, read, but not passed on. The woman received no letters and assumed her father had forgotten her; the father thought his daughters did not want to reply to his letters.

The father's letters (or in some cases handwritten transcriptions of them) bearing his army address were sent to the Department of Education. Notes on the letters show that the Irish Government was tracking the man's whereabouts. He was also sending money to support his children. He survived the war but the bond between the woman and her father had been destroyed. She never met him again.

Considerable numbers of the children of Irishmen serving with British forces were incarcerated in Ireland's industrial schools during the Second World War. Beginning in 1943, the Department of Education and the Department of External Affairs were in correspondence with the UK War Office, the Dominions Office and the UK Representative to Éire's Office demanding maintenance payments for the imprisoned children of Irish HM servicemen. It was an extensive correspondence and went on up to D-Day.

The Department of External Affairs notified the War Office with a list of named children of serving soldiers who were in industrial schools or reformatories. In a letter sent by Freddie Boland to Norman Archer, a British

5   John Cooney, *John Charles McQuaid, Ruler of Catholic Ireland*, O'Brien Press, Dublin, 1999, p. 112.

diplomat serving in the Dublin offices in Lower Mount Street of Sir John Maffey, United Kingdom Representative to Éire, and dated 1 May 1944, it was stated:

> ... in not a few of these cases the lack of parental control to which the committal of the children is due is attributable to the absence of the fathers with your Forces.

The British dragged out the issue, finally agreeing restitution but the war was by then over. The theory, by no means clear but evident, is that de Valera took the Education portfolio in 1939 for certain sensitive reasons of Church–State politics while at the same time seeking to both penalise and profit from the fact that Irish people, mainly men, were employed in military service outside the country. Restitution was sought in order to pay for the children of these men serving with the British forces. His actions, if this was the reason, would have been justified on the grounds of the children of such servicemen being an expense to Irish taxpayers.

The second general question about this period, during and after the war, concerns the established power of the Roman Catholic Church and the widespread view that its work was generous and beneficial. This was what gave public consent to the Church, directly and through a wide number of religious orders, including the Christian Brothers, to establish and regulate the management of these child prisons, including control over education. That it was done in such abysmally terrible and frightening ways is a separate issue.

The answer lies in the latter part of the question, the control over education. Within Catholic society—the society of the vast majority of the Irish population—this control was accepted, almost without question. Equally accepted, in broad terms, was the fact that the State could not deal with its own poverty. This was endemic, chronic, in many cases extreme and country-wide.

Thirdly, there was the authoritarian nature of the impoverished society. The Church offered a panacea combining faith and good works. The good works may have included the awful regimes in the industrial schools, but at least the children were being contained and provided for away from family circumstances that failed so to provide.

Church control itself was generally a product of Irish independence. It had come about at a time of international debate about the nature of society generally. This was set against the background of political beliefs such as fascism and communism being in conflict at a time of widespread poverty and social unrest. For the new Irish Free State, liberated at last from the overwhelming weight of British rule, the creation of a pure form of a Catholic State was an enticing prospect and attracted many minds discussing various theories. One example is Father Edward Cahill, S.J., the author of *The Framework of a Christian State*, a lengthy, detailed and comprehensive introduction to social science as it might be implemented in Ireland.[6] Basing his arguments on Catholic Christian

6   Father Edward Cahill, s.j., *The Framework of a Christian State*, M.H. Gill, Dublin, 1932.

teaching, and leaning heavily on the teachings of Pope Pius xi, Cahill goes in great detail into the relationship of the secular State with Christian dogma and theory, defining parallel duties and expressing in firm and unmitigated terms the prior claims of the Church over the State. In respect of education—to which he devotes a substantial chapter—he claims:

> The rights and duties of the State in education, not being founded upon a title of fatherhood, are on a completely different plane from those of the Church and family. The State, unlike the Church, is in no sense the parent of its members, who exist before it and whose rights are prior to those of the State.

This view would be seriously at odds with the approach to the State's duties upheld within the United Kingdom. This broad approach is relevant to the relationship between State and Church in respect of the industrial school system. Though not referred to directly, Cahill puts forward the argument that the State can assume direct control of the child's education 'taking care, however, that the religious and moral training of the child be carried out under the direction and guidance of the Church'. And Cahill quotes Pope Pius xi:

> It also belongs to the State to protect the rights of the child itself, when the parents are found wanting … whether by default, incapacity or misconduct … in such cases, exceptional no doubt, the State does not put itself in the place of the family, but merely supplies deficiencies, and provides suitable means, always, however, in conformity with the natural rights of the child, and the supernatural rights of the Church.

It will be no great surprise that Cahill had some small influence over Eamon de Valera in the drafting of the 1937 Constitution and, among other things, was responsible for a draft article on religion, Church and State. This was circulated as part of the document well before its enactment, for the purpose of discussion. It defined 'the Church of Christ' as the Catholic Church and required the State to acknowledge this as 'the true religion'. The proposed article also contained an interesting section dealing with Church–State agreements, such as the one that many years later was made in respect of Church–State relations over the abused in industrial schools.

In cases where the jurisdiction of Church and State requires to be harmoniously coordinated, the State may come to a special agreement with the Church and other religious bodies, upon particular matters, civil, political and religious.

Undoubtedly, from an early stage in the development of legislation and of the constitutions, of which there were two, the Catholic Church demanded and got a special position within the State. The good side of this has shaped Irish thought and belief to an enormous degree. The bad side, part of which is outlined in this book, is at times too awful to contemplate.

| THE IMPACT OF THE OECD

An entirely new and formidably powerful force entered the picture early in 1962. Ireland at this time applied for membership of the European Economic Community (EEC). It did so in the company of other European states, including Britain, Denmark and Norway. Part of the required process for accession involved an audit of the country's democratic structure. This also involved investigation of Irish education at all levels by the OECD (Organisation for Economic Co-operation and Development). An audit of the country's education policy and of State institutions was done jointly at Ireland's request, in October 1962 . It was organised in co-operation with the OECD as a project under the Educational Investment and Planning Programme of the Organisation. This covered similar surveys in other countries on which information was supplied, together with funding and technical support. The competence of Irish education was an essential prerequisite to EEC membership and the levels of proficiency had to meet OECD standards. Though the 'invitation' came from Ireland, the requirement for such an audit was reinforced by the EEC demands in the wake of the country's application.

The Minister for Education at the time was P.J. Hillery, who had succeeded Jack Lynch in the job in June 1959, when Seán Lemass took over from Eamon de Valera. He was the man primarily responsible for the early period of the OECD team's investigation in Ireland, at least until the publication of its report, in 1965, an election year. On returning to power, George Colley was made Minister for Education. Seán Lemass resigned as Taoiseach the following year, 1966, and Donogh O'Malley took Colley's place. He was there for the further investigations of the OECD, fully aware of the great importance the Government attached to satisfying the EEC that the country was ready for entry. O'Malley's time was short-lived. He died of a heart attack on 10 March 1967. He was succeeded by Brian Lenihan. The Government was seriously engaged in this whole process. Apart from the country's preparation for entry to the EEC, there was a need to get Ireland's educational 'house in order' and this included the seriously defective industrial school system. Indeed, all four men had dealings with the powerful European organisations. They all understood what was at stake for Ireland's future, specifically in respect of the country's entry into the EEC, whether this happened then or later.

The eminent OECD team included a former Belgian Minister for Education, a Canadian minister from Quebec Province called Rassmussen, an educationalist from Copenhagen and others. They met Colley and Hillery, and, presumably in the early stages, O'Malley and, after his death, Lenihan.

Part of the process included 'confrontation meetings'. These were high-powered and essentially investigative of the Irish situation. A report was published in 1965 and debated in the Dáil at that time. A final OECD document—under the general title, 'Reviews of National Policies for Education', dealing with Ireland—was published in Paris in 1969.

This contained general remarks by the head of the Irish delegation, Dr T.R. Ó Raifeartaigh, who was then Secretary of the Department of Education. He spoke of Ireland's economy having no frontiers and being open in particular to Great Britain and the United States. He claimed as a fundamental objective 'to establish as rapidly as possible real equality of educational opportunity for young people from all areas and all social classes'. Because of the wide decentralisation of resources, close co-operation of local educational authorities with teachers and the Department was necessary. This of course applied particularly with the large number of industrial schools, spread widely in many counties in Ireland. There was to be 'ample room for continental languages'.

The OECD team worked from a Department of Education document called *Investment in Education*. This had been prepared by a departmental survey team set up in 1962. The report was published in 1965. It contained an appendix on 'Reformatory and Industrial Schools'. Much of the information given in this key document is seriously open to question. It claims, for example, that 'a course of continuation education provided by the local education committee' was provided for the 29 boys in the boys' reformatory (this was Daingean, the only surviving boys' reformatory at the time); it was not provided for the girls' reformatory. It was not, in fact, provided in either. The same spurious information is not provided for the 48 industrial schools then operating in Ireland (13 for boys, 35 for girls, of which eight were also certified to receive a limited number of boys of tender years). The reasons for committal are, however, given. Taking boys (364) and girls (247) together—an overall total of 611 committed in that year (1962/3)—45 were committed for 'poor school attendance', 483 for 'lack of proper guardianship', 15 for being 'uncontrollable' and 68 for indictable offences.[1]

Investment in Education: Annexes and Appendices claims, wrongly, that 'in practice, very many of the committals are made at the request of the parent(s). In such cases, if at some future date an application is made by the parent(s) to have a child released, the child must in accordance with the Constitution, be granted absolute release irrespective of the home conditions.' In a footnote to Appendix B, the writer tritely says that 'this was not always the position' and then refers to the

---

[1]   These statistics are taken from the Annual Report of the Department of Education, 1962/3. They are quoted on p. 27 of *Investment in Education: Annexes and Appendices*.

1955 Supreme Court action which sought and obtained the release of a girl. The court did so on the basis that holding her under provisions in the Children Acts was unconstitutional. But the practice of refusing such releases continued. Cases are documented among abused people of parental requests simply being turned down. Even in the wake of the 1955 judgment, Paddy Hillery, as Minister for Education, turned down a parental request for the release of a child. The Supreme Court's constitutional judgment of 1955 was, in this and other cases known to me, ignored or deliberately flouted.

No data were collected or offered by the Department of Education on 'the educational level of children on committal to industrial schools'. The only available information—on reformatories—came from an earlier Department of Education Annual Report. But the low levels of educational attainment was extrapolated from the findings in the 1965 report that a clear majority of boys who went from school to employment went into 'farm work' or 'hotel work' and a majority of girls went into 'domestic work'.

This accounted for only a small percentage of the numbers leaving the industrial schools, and they would have been the unluckiest. The vast majority, totalling more than 80 per cent, returned to their parents, having served a full sentence, up to the legal age limit. The age limit under the Children Act 1908 was 14, a 'child' being defined as a person under that age; a 'young person' was aged 14 to 16. The Children Act 1941 extended the age threshold for a child to 15 years. Under this provision children were discharged on the day before their sixteenth birthday. A 'young person' was redefined as being between 15 and 17 years of age. The report clearly expresses only a qualified satisfaction with the statistic on those, mainly boys, going to 'hotel work'; knowing the circumstances at the time of hotel training organised by Bord Fáilte and of educational requirements for this, the report states: 'one would like to know more about the kinds of hotels these children are going into and the positions they occupy in them'.

The report on the industrial schools was critical, but not confrontational. By careful implication the low level of employment competence attained generally by inmates of the industrial schools was used to question the educational programme in such establishments. So, too, was the issue of low competence generally by inmates. They went, as is outlined above, essentially to labouring jobs. All these jobs were essentially unskilled. The unluckiest of all were the boys and girls who went to work on farms or for families.

The Department of Education knew well that the kind of penal containment of children in institutions was no longer regarded as appropriate for a country joining the EEC. The Department of Education tried to ameliorate this by claiming, dishonestly, that children could be withdrawn by parents, but only in cases where the parents had requested the committals. These cases were rare. Though it was strictly true, as a result of the 1955 constitutional case restricting the circumstances where the Minister was holding children, there were cases in this category where this constitutional right was flouted.[2]

The Department also knew of the shortfall in education in the same establishments. Of all the various forms of abuse, the worst is probably abuse of a fundamental right to education. It makes totally cynical the remarks of Dr T.R. Ó Raifeartaigh, Secretary of the Department of Education, quoted above.

The OECD Committee was lied to by the Department of Education. All its heads of department were seen for interview. The head of the industrial school section in the Department told the Committee that all children so interned were there 'at the request of their parents' and that 'the parents could have their children out at any time, irrespective of the home conditions'. This was in no sense true, neither in the first claim nor the second. (Reference to it was contained in the report.)

Confrontation meetings between the OECD Committee and senior civil servants and others *followed* the report. The final such confrontation meeting was in November 1966. It is hardly a coincidence that the Kennedy Commission into Industrial Schools and Reformatories was set up in January 1967. Though it was printed and published, and then debated in the Dáil, the OECD Report was then effectively 'buried' by the Government. It is extraordinary that, in the immensely long and eccentric list of publications consulted by Eileen Kennedy and her team, the OECD Report is not included.

The report's lessons were stark enough in respect of the industrial schools system. The schools themselves were contrary to the educational policies in the EEC and it was clear to any up-to-date educationalist that they would have to be closed down.

Closing down the industrial schools and reformatories would have been too obvious a response. Such a decision, indicting the Church's tarnished role in this shabby side of Irish education, just would not do. It needed an Irish vehicle and this was the primary reason for the Kennedy Committee. This was set up in the immediate wake of the OECD investigation. We do not know what happened at the confrontation meetings. All documentation about them has disappeared, as has an enormous body of archive material dealing with the reformatory and industrial school system.

Our Common Market application, which at the time proved unsuccessful, was done in alignment with Britain. This was blocked by General de Gaulle's veto but remained thereafter an actively pursued objective, ultimately achieved on 1 January 1973. By then much had happened to change the face of Irish education, including the dismantling of the reformatory and industrial school system.

This whole aspect of industrial school management is not well recorded. Non-attendance at school, shortcomings in completing educational programmes and failure to sit proper examinations are hardly likely to be recorded when

2   There is no reference to the selective respect for this constitutional judgment. The relevant sections in *Investment in Education: Annexes and Appendices* to the report of the ministerial survey team, p. 27, are very carefully worded with the added and distorting implication that 'the duration of a child's stay in a school might then be relatively short'. Short stays were not an option.

absenteeism and child labour are imposed by the educational institution in defiance of the law of the land and of the Constitution. Indeed, even the solemn Proclamation of Easter 1916 is made into a travesty by what was done in this area.

This chapter, which might be seen as an extended preamble to the Kennedy Committee, must in fairness be furnished with an alternative construction of the reasoning that led to its setting up, based on a rather slight file of evidence that has survived in what otherwise can only be described as a holocaust of destruction or loss of Department of Education archive material.

The source for this direct reference to the setting up of the Kennedy Committee has survived in a file from the Office of the Taoiseach and is in the National Archives rather than in the Department of Education. There it would undoubtedly have disappeared, as have also disappeared, in addition to all the Kennedy Committee documentation, the files dealing with the earlier Cussen Report. The Kennedy-related file is entitled 'Children—General File' and was brought to the attention of the Commission to Inquire into Child Abuse by Dr Eoin O'Sullivan, Statutory Lecturer in Social Policy in the Department of Social Studies in Trinity College Dublin. This was during lengthy testimony of his researches into industrial school and reformatory child abuse on 21 June 2004. The full text of the day's proceedings is of extraordinary value, since O'Sullivan, who collaborated with Mary Raftery on the *States of Fear* documentaries and was the joint author, with her, of *Suffer the Little Children*, spent the greater part of the day giving evidence.

He gives detail of the memoranda contained in the file, which he refers to as 'the only original information that we have on that report or certainly that is available in the archives'. In January 1966 the then Taoiseach, Jack Lynch, wrote to Donogh O'Malley expressing concern about comments made on television by the Vicar General of the Irish Christian Brothers, Brother N.C. Normoyle, who had claimed that the lack of grants from the Government was a factor in the closing of a number of industrial schools. Lynch suggested that Normoyle might be right, but, if not, 'much as I admire the Brothers, I would not wish to let the matter go without some comment. On the other hand, if there is something in what Brother Normoyle had said you might look into it'. O'Malley responded with the stock Department of Education answer: the primary problem with the schools was the inadequacy of the capitation grant. O'Malley said it was 'a constant cry with them that the grant is only about one third that given in the six counties'. This issue itself has always been a contentious one, when funding is mentioned, since there is a difference in kind between such institutions in the United Kingdom, including Northern Ireland, and those in the Republic. O'Malley then went on:

> There is, of course, something in this. It is not so easy for them to provide a building, maintain it, provide staffing, clothe and feed the pupils, take them on annual holiday, provide medical and other care for them at 2 pounds 7 shillings and 6 pence per head per week. In fact, while the 40 or so industrial

schools generally are well run, there are some marked deficiencies, particularly in relation to the provision for the psychiatric treatment of children.

Eoin O'Sullivan gave as his opinion that O'Malley was then rather condescending in dismissing the comments made by Brother Normoyle, 'effectively suggesting that he did not quite know what he was talking about. Anyway, we find an agreement to set up a Committee in 1967.' There is an additional memo announcing the proposed Committee of Inquiry into Reformatory and Industrial Schools; this became the Kennedy Committee. It might well have become the Hurley Committee, since the first nominee to chair it was John Hurley, 'a cinema manager with wide social interests' who was joined in a list that included Declan Lennon and Margaret McGovern, who were members of the Dublin Junior Chamber of Commerce. The Chamber had interested itself in seeking improvements in the facilities and amenities provided in Artane Industrial School. Kenneth McCabe, a Jesuit priest working in Middlesex, England, who had done 'a great deal of work in the field of juvenile delinquency and neglected children', and was especially recommended by Declan Costello, a Fine Gael deputy who later became Attorney General in the Liam Cosgrave-led administration of 1973–7. For many years Costello had interested himself in the problems of children with physical and intellectual disabilities. Other names put forward included Caoimhin Ó Caoimhe of the Little Sisters of the Assumption, in Corbally, Limerick, Brother Francis O'Reilly, Resident Manager of Artane and Secretary of the Resident Managers of Reformatory and Industrial Schools, and finally, Dr John Ryan, Medical Director of St John of God's Services for the Mentally Handicapped.

The proposal for the establishment of the Committee was submitted to Cabinet and approved on 5 October 1967. It was approved subject to certain membership changes being made: Father McCabe's name was deleted and Hurley was demoted to become an ordinary member. The Cabinet decided to appoint District Justice Eileen Kennedy as chairperson. There were also to be nominees from the Departments of Education, Justice and Health. That was virtually all the documentation seen by Eoin O'Sullivan, though he added:

> I think there is a short file I saw in the Department of Education that related to the very first meeting, but I think it mainly continues the menu for the dinner that was being had that Friday.

Eoin O'Sullivan gives a good summary of the report, but his outline of the reasoning for setting up the Kennedy Committee, though based on authentic exchanges, makes little sense since it refers to no other motive beyond assuaging the deeply flawed reasons given on television by a Christian Brother, whose remarks do not really make sense. That the serious indictment of the educational output of industrial schools and reformatories is ignored—as were the OECD reports and responses to them—is simply not credible.

Chapter 6 ❧

| THE KENNEDY REPORT

The reality, whatever about the motivations, was that within three months of the final encounter between the OECD team and senior civil servants, which took place in November 1966, the Kennedy Commission into Industrial Schools and Reformatories was set up. It sat for three years, reporting in 1970. The Kennedy Committee was chaired by District Justice Eileen Kennedy, the first woman in Ireland to be appointed to the Bench. It included the manager of Artane Industrial School, Brother P.A. Ó Raghallaigh (to give him his name in Irish), who would have had first-hand knowledge of the OECD team, which visited the school. The secretary to the Committee, Richard O'Donovan, came from the Department of Education, as did a psychologist on the staff of that Department, Antoin Ó Gormain. Other Departments of State represented on the Committee included Justice and Health. The senior medical officer of the latter department, Dr J.G. O'Hagan, was appointed, as was Risteárd Mac Conchradha, an assistant principal officer in Justice. It is not unreasonable to assume that a sufficient number of State and Church representatives on the Committee knew a good deal of the deficiencies of the system and were also aware of the investigate work done by the OECD. Yet one of the more extraordinary facts regarding the Kennedy Report is that there is no mention of the OECD-backed report *Investment in Education*. This had appeared at the time of the Committee's appointment, its findings widely covered in the press. Some 113 documents are listed as having been consulted, including *Yugoslavia—A New Look at Crime* and *Denmark—A New Look at Crime* as well as booklets and pamphlets, among them *Protection de la Mère et de l'Enfant*, but nothing at all with the crucial OECD imprimatur. All subsequent references about the industrial school system, by the Government and by the Department of Education, have since been related back to District Justice Eileen Kennedy and her committee. The publication of it has been treated as a watershed in the industrial school history. Eileen Kennedy and her committee have acquired an undeserved legendary status and her report is a sacred text.

It was nothing of the sort. Its main merit was in looking forward. It attempted to construct and recommend future improvements. Worthy—indeed, necessary and overdue—though this objective clearly was, it could not be achieved without a full and detailed investigation of what existed at the time. This problem of truthful penetration of the existing circumstances was not confronted. To all intents and purposes the findings of the Kennedy Report were essentially dishonest. The text is largely a whitewash and Eileen Kennedy was the architect of a cover-up. To start with, the OECD visit, its detailed investigations and the subsequent reports were ignored. Even their existence was covered up, the bibliography in the Kennedy Report making no reference to a crucial series of documents bearing on educational shortcomings throughout the industrial school system. Put simply, the events of that crucial period, when Ireland was under examination to see whether the country qualified for EEC entry, testing out education within the industrial school system, were treated as though they had not taken place.

This process of cover-up was much wider than simply the effective concealment of an educational survey by a European organisation. Guided, no doubt, by the Department of Education, its newly appointed Minister, Donogh O'Malley, set up the Kennedy Committee but was dead before it held its inaugural meeting on 20 October 1967.

O'Malley's terms of reference were very general: 'To survey the Reformatory and Industrial Schools systems and to make a report and recommendations to the Minister for Education'. The Kennedy Committee felt free to interpret the dead Minister's thinking in a paragraph that is superficial:

> The late Mr Donogh O'Malley, then Minister for Education, realised not only the limited nature of the powers vested in him by the 1908 Act, but also that the Act was not suitable to an era of changing conditions. He felt that the Community was not doing all it should to help underprivileged children, particularly those who had to be placed in these schools and, consequently, he advised the Government to set up this Committee to examine the problem and to suggest alterations and improvements in the system, which would bring it into line with modern thinking in the matter.

Having been responsible, as Minister for Education, for the next important stage in EEC accession, which included further meetings in Paris, to which officials and ministers were summoned, the Committee's explanations of what it thought had led him to its setting up are perverse. The powers vested in the Minister by the 1908 Children Act were vast and allowed for much of the abuse, yet there is no mention of this. Nor is there mention of the 1941 Children Act and no general examination is proposed at this point, nor does it arise later, of the shortcomings of the legislation. Manifestly, the interpretation moves away from the terms of reference—but in the wrong direction.

In the whole documentation of the Kennedy Report, both material—much of it now lost—and judgments emerged which then led to an inadequate if not fraudulent presentation of the circumstances surrounding the whole industrial school system. The report gives a false view of what was actually happening in the industrial schools and reformatories. It resolves very few of the problems and it gives misleading information. Those who framed it—and all participants share equally in responsibility for this—are guilty of excising from the Rules and Regulations the paragraph on punishment. Moreover, at no point in the document was the issue of punishment—absolutely crucial to the experiences of inmates—reported on. Punishment was the pernicious lubricant on which the wheels of the industrial school movement relied. It was the foundation on which control of the children rested. To pretend it was not there, neither in the rules nor in the reasons for the closure, for example of Daingean, is a piece of bureaucratic madness.

Under the rules, as has already been made clear, punishment was a graded process, beginning with forfeiture of rewards and privileges, confinement in a room or cell, moderate childish punishment with the hand and then chastisement. In reality, this grading was telescoped into one remedy: corporal punishment. The exercise of discipline was physical tyranny, no more, no less. And the Kennedy Committee skirted around this fact completely, comprehensively.

Widespread evidence, implied rather than specific, but running through the whole Kennedy Report, clearly suggests that punishment was not there at all. The reality was the opposite, and the rules failed to impose any restraint. Under the key heading, 'Chastisement'—in the rule that was left out of the report—graded restraints should have been spelt out. However, they were neither defined nor controlled.

As we have seen in previous chapters, quite the opposite prevailed in the United Kingdom. There, new Rules and Regulations designed to reduce physical punishment and control it in exact ways were introduced during the second and third decades of the century. No parallel action was taken in Ireland. Recourse to heavy flogging was used initially, and was then carried out comprehensively in most of the institutions on all ages of both boys and girls. This punishment system, unrestrained by the State in accordance with its own rules, left an indelible mark on the minds of the boys and girls, making assaults on their bodies central to the waking hours of their lives and disturbing them psychologically in ways that led to lasting damage, both physical and mental. For the Kennedy Committee to ignore this and to edit out of the rules the key entry on the subject undermines Eileen Kennedy's fitness to chair such a body and renders the report itself—which has for so long been offered by the State as the starting point for modern reform—profoundly flawed in its approach to the problem it was set up to investigate and remedy. To ignore punishment was to bypass the most fundamental problem of all.

The second important issue, central to the dreadful nature of the system, and not examined at all in the Kennedy Report, was the committal procedure used by the courts. District Justice Eileen Kennedy knew more about this than any other judge sitting on the Bench in Ireland. She herself had committed many boys and girls to the industrial schools. She had done the same, though to a lesser number, in sending them to the reformatories. She knew that the system used was not only dreaded by the victims of it and by their parents, but was also more widely feared by the public. She also knew that it was being administered illegally. No proper investigation of each case brought before the courts, involving pleadings or statements on behalf of the children—as was required by the Children Act of 1908, the legislation used for committal—was being carried out. Such investigations were widespread in the United Kingdom and increasingly carried out by trained professionals with an understanding of child psychology and the principles on which child care operated. Such professionalism was in its early infancy in Ireland in the late 1960s when the Kennedy Committee was appointed; moreover, those who trained, in university social sciences departments, knowing how limited the system was in the Republic and how poorly paid the work was, looked for employment in Britain.

Thirdly, District Justice Eileen Kennedy and her committee failed to examine the character, training and psychological capacities of those who did work within the industrial school system; these were the nuns, brothers and priests involved in the supervision and control of inmates. Their training in the subtleties of child care was effectively non-existent, yet this was supposed to be an important part of the system she had been asked to investigate and it was certainly in her mind if one is to believe the trite introductory remarks at the beginning of the Kennedy Report. In fact those who should have cared were a major part of the problem—with little or no understanding of what care meant. Another part of the problem is that the Kennedy Report collectively exonerated them.

The Kennedy Committee, as the report conscientiously claims, met 69 times and visited all the country's industrial schools and reformatories, 'some more than once'; these visits included 'informal discussion with many of the children'. None of these visits is referred to in the report and none of the evidence supposedly gleaned from the 'informal discussions' is included.

The Kennedy Committee received 42 written submissions and 14 oral submissions. The substance of very few of these is recorded in the report and the documentation has now been 'lost'.

The Kennedy Committee saw 113 publications and documents, some of them of the most abstruse kind. Apart from formal summaries of legislative instruments, such as the Children Acts and certain other regulations, there is no precise relationship between the Committee's reading matter and what appears in the report.

The Kennedy Committee has been 'credited' with percipience over Daingean reformatory, which it said 'should be closed at the earliest possible opportunity'. Yet its report on it (p. 42) lays stress on the old and neglected buildings, their poor layout, the lack of hot water, and its location in the Irish midlands, many miles from the home background of most of the inmates, who came from Dublin. Nothing is said about the lack of teaching, the ignorance of the supposed 'educators', the farm labour in which the boys were employed, the punitive regime with constant and brutal floggings, many of them in public, as well as other intentional cruelties and deliberate humiliations.

The Kennedy Committee knew about them. Two doctors on the Committee, John Ryan and J.G. O'Hagan, questioned Father McGonagle, who was the manager of Daingean, responsible for the implementation of the Rules and Regulations with special responsibility for all episodes of punishment. On the subject of corporal punishment, he gave an open and unembarrassed explanation that 'ordinarily the boys were called out of the dormitories after they had retired, and that they were punished here on one of the stairway landings. The boys wore nightshirts as sleeping attire when they were called for punishments. Punishment was applied to the buttocks with a leather.' One of the doctors put the question:

> I asked if the boys were undressed of their nightshirts when they were punished. Fr McGonagle replied that at times they were. He elaborated some further remarks to the effect that the nightshirts were pulled up when this was done. This remark was subsequently commented upon by the Committee members in private discussion. The point was made that when boys were punished with the leather they could hardly be expected to remain still and his struggles were likely to enlarge the state of his undress, and the likelihood that a struggling boy could be struck anywhere on the naked body could not be excluded. Some other Committee members asked why he allowed boys to be stripped naked for punishment, and Fr McGonagle replied, in a matter of a fact manner, that he considered punishment to be more humiliating when it was administered in that way.[1]

This encounter, one of many made on behalf of the Kennedy Committee, took place at the end of February 1968. On 4 April 1968, District Justice Eileen Kennedy wrote to the Department of Education seeking details of all complaints about the industrial schools and reformatories received over the previous five years. She wanted to know how the complaints had been dealt with. The Department did not reply. A year later, on 5 May 1969, she sent a reminder: 'My Committee is concerned at the failure to obtain replies to enquiries made to your Department affecting your Reformatory and Industrial Schools Branch.' She referred to the previous letter and also to one sent in June 1968, with a reminder the following March about St Conleth's in Daingean. Two other points exercised her: one was a complaint made by the ISPCC about an incident of excessive corporal punishment at Artane Industrial School which a representative of the society had raised before the Committee; the other was an incident at Marlborough House, Glasnevin.

The above makes clear that visits, and possibly 'informal discussions' with the inmates, did take place. Even if the beatings—under threat from the Oblate Fathers—were not mentioned, there were other good justifications for the key

---

[1] Kennedy Report 1970 (Private papers of Kennedy Committee, 28 February 1968).

Kennedy recommendation—to close the Daingean reformatory. Why, then, is the entry about Daingean, together with the summary recommendation to have it closed, given with no reference at all to the punishments carried out there? These were of an obscene brutality, the evidence given directly to committee members. The punishments were within the Rules and Regulations fully designated and authorised by successive Ministers for Education. Yet they were sufficiently outrageous to prompt written record by John Ryan and J.G. O'Hagan.

Daingean reformatory was a disgrace. It remains a memorial to a hideous regime. Yet what the Kennedy Committee meant by saying that it 'was not in line with modern thought on Reformatories' is hard to work out when set against the perfunctory and superficial paragraphs on it. The Kennedy Committee carried out its deliberations on Daingean well before the report was published, sending inquiries to the Department of Education, obviously of an urgent nature, in both 1968 and 1969, and culminating with the Committee sending 'a request to the Minister for Education asking that immediate specific steps be taken to ameliorate conditions there'. These steps were not taken. The entry about the Daingean reformatory ends with the words: 'It is recommended that St Conleth's be closed at the earliest possible moment'. This was not done. It did not close until 1973, four years later, and after Ireland had signed the EEC Accession Agreement.

Correctly, the Kennedy Committee recommended the closure of the only reformatory and also the closure, 'forthwith', of Marlborough House, and then said nothing when this did not happen. Having said that use of the industrial schools 'should be considered only when there is no satisfactory alternative', the Committee then suggested changing the basis of payment from the capitation system to grants based on budgets 'and agreed to by the Central Authority'. There was no Central Authority. The words have no clear meaning unless they refer to the Department of Education, which was in authority over all the institutions. But if the Department is meant, why is this not made clear?

The Kennedy Report, like the Cussen Report in 1936, found fault with the system generally, yet failed to make any recommendation about changing the collective band of 'pilots' who were guiding this immense vessel of national shame and punishment ever nearer the rocks. The religious orders are neither analysed nor blamed for what they did or failed to do. The buildings are blamed for not being warmer, lighter, equipped with proper heating. The dismal educational record of the inmates collectively, as revealed by the OECD, is not investigated nor assessed. Clearly, ability to deliver proper education was not a capacity to be found among brothers and nuns. Yet this is not examined and the recommendations do not sufficiently call for reform.

The adverse judgments made about St Conleth's in Daingean are also made about Marlborough House and St Patrick's Institution or Borstal, in Dublin, both of which are condemned and their urgent closure recommended. Yet the reasoning is faulty. It is mainly based on the physical structure of both places and not on the punitive regimes and inadequate moral, mental and social care of the inmates. Throughout the Kennedy Report there is this imbalance. St Patrick's Institution housed young male offenders, including those on remand, and it therefore came under the Department of Justice, one of whose assistant principal officers, Risteárd Mac Conchradha, sat on the Kennedy Committee and added reservations to the final report. At the end of the second of these he comments on the inmates as 'educationally backward and where a significant proportion are below average intelligence'. This judgment, for which there is no recorded evidence supported by specific testing, is a factor that enraged inmates who felt they had been characterised, without proof, as 'subnormal'.

Another feature of the Kennedy Report is the absence of any written or oral submissions from the Department of Education. There were 42 written submissions listed, without reference to their content, many of them from individuals representing organisations involved in the industrial school system or actually sent in by the organisation. For example, the Industrial and Reformatory School Resident Managers' Association made a submission, the Knights of Columbanus made two. Others that took part with written papers included the Dublin Institute for Adult Education, which had been involved with the OECD survey of Irish education and would have known of the criticisms of the educational standards achieved by the schools, as would the Institute of Professional Civil Servants and the Economic and Social Research Institute. In the light of the cases cited above, of cruelty, malnourishment and the death of a very young child—all of which were the subject of reports to the Department of Education—it is astonishing that no one from the Department made any submissions, written or oral.

It is true, Tomás Derrig, who had been Minister for Education from 1932 until the Fianna Fáil Government went out of office in 1948, had died in 1956. But his officials, who had dealt with the various high-profile cases—like the flogging of Gerard Fogarty in Glin Industrial School or the dismissals from Lenaboy and Cappoquin of the sisters guilty of negligence and misappropriation of funds—were in many instances still working for the Department. Despite this shocking lacuna in the report, the Kennedy Committee profusely thanked two of the Ministers for Education and various other departmental officials.

The Kennedy Committee's own account of the history of the reformatory and industrial school system, going back to the middle of the nineteenth century, makes no mention of specific incidents, or of Dáil and other debates provoked by public outcry or the publication of details of neglect and crime within the institutions.

Given the serious flaws in the Kennedy Committee's understanding of its job and in respect of knowledge about many appalling circumstances that had come to light in the previous two and a half decades, any detailed analysis of its findings—were this possible, in the absence of the Committee's documentation—would serve little purpose. The Kennedy Report does not make clear what was known, or not known, to the Committee. The Committee's main recommendations are of very mixed value or relevance to the actual circumstances.

As to the proposal, more or less coming out of the blue, that grants should replace capitation, but based on budgets, how could this work without Church collaboration in budgetary transparency? Yet throughout the preceding period, back to the end of the Second World War, the religious orders had stubbornly obstructed the State's attempt to extract audited accounts from them and had accepted per capita payments with frequent applications for increased amounts. So Kennedy condemned the system, suggested it should be funded differently, recommended some closures and also suggested 'the highest standards of Child Care [in the institutions] to be attained and maintained', all without full logical argument or reasoning.

The issue of capitation payments as against grants for the institutions will never be known. Like everything connected with District Justice Eileen Kennedy and her committee, the full story will never be known because the Department of Education has 'lost' all its documentation. Even so, from the internal reasoning offered or implied by statement without supporting data, the work of the Kennedy Committee appears to have been a deliberate and comprehensive fraud.

There is evidence of confusion about the future. This would be consistent with the private purpose of the Kennedy Committee and its report, which, it is here suggested, was aimed at bringing Ireland into line with the educational requirements of the EEC as they had been indicated by the OECD in its report. The evidence in other chapters in the Kennedy Report, particularly on the key issue—education—seems to suggest that this confusion of purpose runs throughout the document. Chapter 7, 'Education', cries out for the detail contained in the OECD Report, none of which is given.

The Church fought strenuously against the supposed intrusions of the Kennedy Report and the institutions knew well the real purpose of the investigation. The Department of Education had alerted them in just the same ways in which they warned of forthcoming inspections. An inmate of Artane Industrial School at the time, who worked there in the shoe shop under a man called Noble with whom he got on very well, gives a flavour from 1969 of what went on. Noble told him that he had been summoned to the Christian Brothers' head office and told he was being made redundant. He told his apprentice worker, who remembered the occasion, and also his words: 'Places like Artane have to close down. It's to do with Europe. Places like Artane won't be allowed.' In his time as an inmate, Kennedy Committee representatives visited Artane and carried out aptitude tests. The brothers had Kennedy documents at the time. They were annoyed by the very word 'Kennedy', disparaging it. It reflected on their educational capacities and the way they had performed their duties as teachers.

The annual Bishops' Conference, held in Kilkenny in the year following publication of the report, made the 'money' argument, expressed by a nun from the Good Shepherd Order: 'Just how could any body, voluntary or statutory, be expected to provide a skilled and humane service on the pittance granted by the State?' Yet this was most misleading. Details of the per capita payments to the institutions are given in the report, at least for the period during which it was engaged in deliberations. These record that in October 1967 the per capita rate was £3 7s 6d per week. In July 1968 it was £3 11s 6d and was raised at that time to £4 6s 6d. A year later the per capita amount was doubled, to £8 13s. Against the cost of living indices of those years, these sums were more than adequate to provide proper food and clothing and to pay for other benefits, including lay teachers brought in, provision for entertainment and hobbies. Of course, none of this could be measured, since the religious orders refused to make their accounts available to the Inspectorate of Reformatories and Industrial Schools.

The Church's delaying action worked for a time. The closing date for Artane was postponed as were those of many other institutions. The closure in 1972 of Marlborough House, recommended by the Kennedy Report, was the first to take place. It was followed by the closure of Letterfrack, arguably the worst industrial school, in 1974, and by the reformatory at Daingean in the same year. Belatedly, in 1980, a task force on child care services called for child care staff training, care for children after they had left the institutions (those still open), and family support. Four years later the per capita system of funding children in care was abolished and a scheme for fostering children in need of care was introduced.

Some long overdue legislation followed, including the Children Act of 1989 and the Child Care Act of 1991. A trickle of literature, which had begun with *Children of the Poor Clares*, continued with Paddy Doyle's *The God Squad* and *Fear of the Collar* by Patrick Touher, a book that went through various updated editions. Abuse continued in certain institutions and was detailed in The Madonna House Report of 1996. The Government suppressed parts of this, including two chapters which were completely removed. One of these dealt fully with the sexual abuse at Madonna House. The second detailed management incompetence.[2]

In 1997 Irish television began showing documentary programmes about abuse, the first of them, *Dear Daughter*, causing major public concern and a debate on the industrial schools. This was followed in 1999 by *States of Fear*, presented by Mary Raftery and researched by Eoin O'Sullivan. In the same year they published *Suffer the Little Children: The Inside Story of Ireland's Industrial Schools*. With the Apology by the Taoiseach, Bertie Ahern, in 1999, following the RTÉ broadcasting of the final episode of *States of Fear*, it seemed that the long travail of victims of institutional abuse in Ireland, stretching back 70 years, was coming to an end and that true retribution, recompense and recovery would follow.

It was not to be. The real abuse story, that of the continued troubling of the hearts and minds of men and women who had suffered from childhood at the hands of Church and State, was really beginning all over again in the worst possible form of all: that of a second betrayal by the State.

---

2   See Raftery and O'Sullivan, *Suffer the Little Children*, p. 386.

PART TWO

The Modern Era

Chapter 7 ∾

| *STATES OF FEAR*

The RTÉ documentary series *States of Fear*, on abuse in the industrial schools, was shown in the spring of 1999. The transmission dates were 27 April, 4 May and 11 May. The series had a huge impact, far exceeding anything that could be achieved by books or articles, though articles followed in their hundreds. Mary Raftery, who produced and directed the series of three documentaries, later said that the 'absolutely voluminous surrounding literature was best described as a kind of tidal wave'. Eoin O'Sullivan, who is recognised as the foremost expert on the Irish industrial schools system, was the consultant to the programmes and responsible, with Mary Raftery, for a considerable amount of research.

The programmes were made in collaboration with the Department of Education, almost certainly directed to release material on the orders of the Minister. Without the willing participation of Government and the release, by the Department, of an unprecedented amount of documentary evidence made available to the RTÉ team, the programmes could not have been made with any real credibility. While the Department of Education co-operated willingly with what was done, the Church and the religious orders that had run the industrial schools did not co-operate. The Christian Brothers and the Sisters of Mercy, who had charge of the greater number of male and female inmates of the schools, declined to participate. This resulted in the telling of a distorted story, one that was heavily weighted against the orders responsible for running the industrial schools, far less so against the Government.

From a Government point of view, the heavy emphasis on abuse, sexual and physical, though a product of State neglect and indifference, nevertheless directed much of the retrospective criticism against the Roman Catholic Church. The essential message of the programmes concerned the widespread physical and sexual abuse, together with deprivation, in health care and education, and with some emphasis on the blighted lives that this comprehensive cruelty produced.

What the programmes seemed less concerned to deal with was the structured and State-funded prison system into which thousands of young people were consigned, often with the entirely illegal support of the State, backed by the courts, the police, the judiciary, organisations like the NSPCC, whose operations were regulated by law, and by Irish society generally. People knew about the industrial schools, they knew of the involvement of the Roman Catholic Church and they followed a natural Irish instinct to say nothing.

But the real impact of most of the filmed interviews was the primary evidence they gave of countrywide abuse on an astonishing scale and at a level of brutality that justified the comparisons, made by some of the victims, with the Nazi system of concentration camps. It fully justifies the title of this book. The industrial schools, as revealed by men and women who had spent years inside them, were places deprived of protective laws for the inmates. Irish law, essentially protective of those living in the State, offered no such care inside the industrial school system. A primary purpose of law, which is to withstand tyranny, protecting people from physical assault and mental oppression, did not so operate. Barney O'Connell, who was in Artane, saw his name taken away from him and replaced with a number, 12,847. It was, he said, on his boots, his bed, his blankets. 'It was on my brain. It was cold, it was damp, you were alone. Nobody cared about you.' He came from a big inner city family and the shock must have been enormous. John Pryor was in St Joseph's, Tralee. He had a number, 892. 'Just dare you forget it.'

In rapid succession men and women appeared, the truthfulness of their statements so clearly apparent in their demeanour and in the fidelity of the extraordinary detail contained in their statements. Mary Norris went to St Joseph's in Killarney. Her father died of cancer when she was 12 years old. Her youngest sister was only six months. Her mother, left caring for eight children, was befriended by a local man who visited her. She is quoted in *Suffer the Little Children*, from a much fuller interview, as saying, 'I think maybe on some occasions he stayed the night. It didn't interfere with me or my siblings. We saw nothing that we shouldn't see. He used to bring us a few sweets, and we saw our mother a bit happy.' But the local priest imagined a good deal that he neither knew nor saw and he engineered the children's incarceration. A car with a guard and an NSPCC inspector (one of 'the Cruelty men') took them to court where they were ordered into detention. Mary Norris was later sent to work in Tralee. She earned 2s 6d a week, milking, cooking, washing and cleaning. She had one night off when she went to the pictures. When she once went out on a second night, she was dismissed and the NSPCC inspector took her back to the convent in Killarney. The nuns there sent her to the Magdalene laundry run by the Good Shepherd nuns in Cork. Since she was already 16, this was illegal, but she worked there unpaid for two years before getting out and going to England.

More than 1,000 children a year in the 1950s were 'farmed' or 'harvested' for the industrial schools, where the fruit of their presence was a double grant, part of it from the State, part from the local authority. More than 50 industrial schools, many of them quite openly and dishonestly trading under the title of 'orphanage', were spread across the country, always ready to take in more candidates for the register, which meant more per capita payments. As Eoin O'Sullivan explained, as part of his careful, accurate testimony throughout the three documentaries, 'the more children there were, the more money was received'. The religious orders were 'touting for children' and a compliant national child protection organisation, supported by the Garda Síochána and with an equally compliant Bench to complete the process, fed a steady stream of children into a system that destroyed their lives.

Gross deprivation is a common theme in the testimony. Sharon Murphy, who became a singer and songwriter, was sent to St Joseph's Industrial School in Clifden. She remembers stealing from the buckets of pig food, she was so hungry. In Artane there was an occasion when the sacristy was raided and the wafers for mass were stolen and eaten. The boys were all paraded and ordered to turn out their pockets. If wafer fragments were found, very severe floggings were immediately administered.

Mannix Flynn, who was Number 2,612 at St Joseph's Industrial School in Letterfrack, said the place was 'just a penal colony and we were slaves'. He describes weeding carrots and sorting out potatoes on extensive land managed by the brothers. Standing, as he does, in the yard at Letterfrack, a grim and dismal area surrounded by buildings, he describes it as always being 'a bloody and savage place'.

Don Baker was in Daingean reformatory for two years and describes a dish of maggoty potatoes for dinner, the terrible physical punishments, the shaving of the heads of runaways. There were runaways from Letterfrack, as remote as any industrial school, buried as it was in the wasteland of what is now the Connemara National Park. One group of five boys who ran away were beaten for two weeks. According to Mannix Flynn, 'it turned them into simpletons, talking gibberish'.

Although the impressive starting point for her three documentaries was historical, with the recollections of men and women who had experienced the horrors of the industrial schools during an era that people liked to imagine was dead and gone, Mary Raftery extended her coverage to include current institutions for the care, education and medical treatment of children. These included schools for the deaf and dumb, where unimaginable cruelties operated, closely analogous to those pursued in the 'normal' industrial school settings. Blind children were beaten for bed-wetting, and were force-fed and deprived of proper care. Deaf children were expected to conform to strict discipline.

Christy McEvoy was an inmate of St Joseph's School for the Blind in Drumcondra, Dublin. He had been blind from birth and was one of a family of seven. He was allowed home once a month. 'I can't understand why they were so cruel,' he said. For bed-wetting he was given a cold bath and then flogged. He remembers others receiving the same punishment, the impact of the leather and the screams affecting him years afterwards. Clearly troubled by the memory, he said to camera: 'It had a very bad effect on me.' A poor learner among the blind boys was beaten for this from behind and propelled forward, crashing into the desks with his disciplinarian screaming at him, 'Mind the furniture!' He remembered the swish of the leather in the air. 'The stick is saying *fuill* [blood] and it means there will be loads of flogging tomorrow!' It seemed to him and to others that the only method of teaching was by way of perpetual beatings. As in the industrial schools, the boys in special schools, despite their disability, had to work—one short piece of old film shows a group of boys at a table, their sight clearly impaired, trying to thread beads onto rosaries; undoubtedly, their education was neglected. It was 1980 before a boy in the school took the Leaving Certificate. One boy, called 'John', barely learnt to read or write. On one occasion he was flogged by three brothers at the same time. 'I don't forgive them for what they did to me. I still have nightmares.'

States of Fear was not the only documentary made by RTÉ, but it was the first to tell the truth. In the early days of RTÉ documentaries, several were made on industrial schools. The pictures painted were benign and wholesome. Since then, at least some of the children who took part have tried to set the record straight.

The impact of the first of the *States of Fear* programmes was raised in the Dáil on 28 April 1999 by Joe Higgins, the Dublin West representative and sole elected member of the Socialist Workers' Party. He said: 'The broadcast last night by RTÉ of *States of Fear* showed the most appalling, widespread and systematic cruelty of children in industrial schools. The new information that emerged was that it resulted from a systematic perversion of the courts and the justice system.' His intervention was ruled out of order, but he persisted in calling on the Taoiseach, Bertie Ahern, to introduce legislation. Higgins wanted 'a commission of compensation and support for the innocent victims of the systematic perversion of justice inflicted on little children in this State over many decades'. Ahern responded by saying that a Cabinet subcommittee had been working on the matter since the previous year. 'Irish society still has to face up to many of the problems of child abuse in the past. That subcommittee will, hopefully, bring forward recommendations shortly which may or may not require legislation.'[1]

There were calls for an apology by the State, and Labour TD Breeda Moynihan-Cronin asked for a reply 'because, as we saw last night, those children were in the care of the State and forgotten about. The least they can be given now is an apology.' Another Labour Party deputy supported this and said it should be the Dáil that would make the gesture, 'on behalf of previous and successive Administrations, to offer the minimum of an apology and to give an undertaking that, in so far as we have any control over the situation, it will not happen in the future'.

'Society owes a considerable debt of gratitude to Mary Raftery, producer of the television series *States of Fear*, and to researcher Sheila Ahern, and to RTÉ, for jolting the conscience of the nation,' said Jim Higgins TD, Fine Gael spokesperson

[1]   Dáil Éireann Report, Volume 503, 28 April 1999.

on Justice, speaking in the Dáil, on 27 May 1999.

Bertie Ahern again referred to the Cabinet subcommittee but made no explicit commitment along the lines asked for. He did say that 'what went on in these institutions over the years was inhuman and degrading. All those children were isolated and without help', which was what everyone else in the country was saying. Beyond it, he seemed uncertain, as though guided more by the sub-committee than by any political instinct.

Ahern was not well briefed. John Bruton had suggested that abuse of children was still going on and Ahern said, in reply, that 'the late Donogh O'Malley closed those institutions based on the Kennedy report in 1970'. Donogh O'Malley had been dead for three years when the Kennedy Committee reported. Ahern admitted:

> As a society, however, we have not dealt with these matters. These programmes [*States of Fear* on RTÉ] are based on facts made available by the Minister for Education and Science. I have had many discussions with him regarding their contents, about which he is greatly concerned. My colleagues and I are anxious to find a mechanism to deal with the issue properly. It is a job which remains to be done and it cannot be left undone. These people were isolated and treated in an unbelievable manner. I know times were different then, but that does not excuse child abuse. These matters have to be dealt with and I hope our recommendations will help to do so.

Ruairi Quinn then cut to the heart of the matter:

> If this is left to legal advice, we will be told not to say a word for fear we might incur compensation claims. For my part and that of my party, I simply want to apologise—no more, no less—and I believe that is true for every other Member of the House. I ask the Taoiseach to kill the argument about compensation, ignore it for once, and let the House give a public apology for things that should not have happened and which will never happen again.

And Quinn's party colleague, Jan O'Sullivan, raised a second critical point:

> Will the Government consider amending the statute of limitations which currently means victims of child sexual abuse who are three years beyond the age of 18 are prohibited from taking action, unless they were of unsound mind at the time? This is a prohibiting factor with regard to people who have been sexually abused taking action. Does the Government intend to amend the statute of limitations in this regard?

Again, there was uncertainty in Ahern's reply. He merely said that the statute of limitation 'will have to be looked at as part of the overall process'. As he was later to claim, the Government had first discussed 'the need for a formal response to the needs of victims of childhood abuse'. The previous December a Cabinet subcommittee had been appointed, under the chairmanship of Micheál Martin, the Minister for Education, and including his own deputy leader of the Government, Mary Harney. It had held a number of meetings, including ones that considered 'best international practice'; the subcommittee was in the process of bringing forward 'a comprehensive package' and this would be presented to Government, with its recommendations within a fortnight. Yet Ahern was unable to answer the two key questions, concerning compensation and the statute of limitation. It was a decidedly poor performance. *States of Fear* provided an invaluable and lasting service, dealing comprehensively with the whole industrial school system and doing so with a great deal of primary research, much of it contained in the testimony of the former inmates. As in a court of law, one judges the truthfulness of their evidence on their demeanour, on the unique character of what they described, on the evident anguish and pain suffered years before and still causing them distress, and on the internal, collaborative consistency of their several accounts.

The programmes were rightly acclaimed. Kathryn Holmquist, writing in the *Irish Times* said, '*States of Fear* was more than a TV documentary series—it was a cultural event.'[2] Liam Fay wrote in the *Sunday Times*: 'After one searing instalment of this three part series—produced, directed and written by Mary Raftery—it already looks as if *States of Fear* will become a milestone in Irish documentary making.'[3] The *Star* reported, 'The flood gates have opened and the shame of our past has poured out ... RTÉ's *States of Fear* series produced by Mary Raftery was one of the most important TV programmes ever screened.'[4] Fintan O'Toole wrote of 'the brilliant ... ground-breaking *States of Fear* series'.[5] Declan Moroney, in *Ireland on Sunday* wrote: 'It isn't recommended viewing—it's compulsive ... this series is, in every respect, quite astonishing, appalling, credible and incredible ... a magnificent production from RTÉ.'[6] John Boland, in the *Sunday Independent* wrote: 'Once in a long time something does come along that, if not actually watched by everyone, should be watched by everyone ... *States of Fear* is so shockingly important that it shamed the Government into response.'[7]

The Taoiseach was more muted: 'I would like to acknowledge the work undertaken in the *States of Fear* series,' he said. His Minister for Education, Micheál Martin, was more forthright: he said the series of programmes 'has had a major impact. I acknowledge the incredible work of Mary Raftery and her production team for the *States of Fear* series. They have performed a major public service and have shown us all the compelling power of top quality documentary work' (speech in the Dáil, 13 May 1999). What he and the Government did next

---

2   *Irish Times*, 15 May 1999.
3   *Sunday Times*, 2 May 1999.
4   *Star*, 17 May 1999.

5   *Irish Times*, 21 May 1999.
6   *Ireland on Sunday*, 2 May 1999.
7   *Sunday Independent*, 15 May 1999.

represents the great test. The response was to last for the next decade and to leave everyone in doubt, with the former inmates feeling that, yet again, they had been betrayed and punished.[8]

8   *States of Fear* was shown internationally and received many awards. These included: Irish Film and Television Academy Award (IFTA) for Best Documentary (October 1999), Justice Media Television Award (September 1999), World Medal Winner at the New York Festivals (January 2000), Special Jury Gold Award at the Houston WorldFest (April 2000), Silver Screen Award at the US International Film and Video Festival, Chicago (June 2000) and it was judged as one of the Top 10 European Documentaries for 1999 by the Prix Europa, Berlin (October 1999). It was screened in Canada at the Montreal World Film Festival, at the Vermont International Film Festival, USA, at the 2000 Festival Internationale des Programmes Audiovisuelles, in Biarritz, France, the INPUT festival 2000, in Halifax, Nova Scotia, at the Banff International Television Festival, Canada, in the summer of 2000, at a special screening by the New York Film Council at New York University and in November 2000 at the Festival International du Film d'Amiens in France.

Chapter 8 ⌁

POLITICAL RESPONSE BY TAOISEACH BERTIE AHERN

A fortnight later, on 11 May 1999, at 5 p.m. in the Dáil, Bertie Ahern, on behalf of the Government, made his 'sincere and long overdue apology to the victims of childhood abuse for our collective failure to intervene, to detect their pain, to come to their rescue'. It was seen as a pivotal, defining moment. It seemed it would change everything; that was the purpose. In reality it was no apology at all. It did not deal with the culpability of the Irish State. Coming, as it did, on the day of the final RTÉ *States of Fear* programme, it had the desired effect of appearing generous and responsive. In reality it dealt—rather fumblingly—with the fallout from *States of Fear.*

He claimed that what he offered was a major contribution in acknowledging and dealing with 'the more uncomfortable elements of our past' in respect of institutional abuse. Yet what he really offered was quite limited, and how he described it—given the explicit testimony contained in the RTÉ programmes— was far from adequate. To begin with there was no mention whatever of the role of the Roman Catholic Church. All the institutions covered by *States of Fear* had been run by Roman Catholic religious orders. They had been indicted repeatedly in the testimony given in the programmes. The whole structure of Church–State relationships, in respect of the care of these children, had been shown up as guilty of neglect. Religious orders and individual men and women had been exposed throughout the documentaries, as had the evasive responses on behalf of Church organisations.

Ahern referred to the 1970 Kennedy Report, though not by name, drawing from it the conclusion that abuse ruined the inmates' childhoods and continued to be an ever-present part of their adult lives. Yet the Apology, like the Kennedy Report itself, made no reference to those men and women in the religious orders shown as responsible for abusing the children in their care.

Following outspoken Dáil criticism, Micheál Martin, Minister for Education, made a speech two days later, on 13 May 1999. This included the clear view that, 'contrary to statements made by certain deputies last week, we were not driven by a concern to find legal ways out of taking action.' In due course evidence to the contrary would be offered and would increase in magnitude in the months ahead.

The source of this evidence was Government documentation of meetings of the Cabinet subcommittee, of which Martin was chairperson. This was sought and got by individual abused people and, later, by the organisations they set up. It was published in due course, revealing an entirely different set of objectives and contradicting what Martin had said in his speech. The most important matter that emerged was that the legal issue was central and paramount. Equally it was clear that, neither then nor later, was the primary objective 'to assist victims of child sexual abuse'. The clear motive throughout was to protect the State.

For the members of the subcommittee there were three key issues, all of them of a legal nature. The first was to discover 'the projected scale of cases against the State'. Views on this were given by Senior Counsel, Gerry Durcan. There was also advice from the Attorney General. Legal privilege has been persistently invoked to protect the parts of any documentation covering this issue. The importance of what has been suppressed may be gauged, however, by the fact that Mr Durcan's report fills 30 pages, almost half the total text of the main Government report.

Ministers on the subcommittee secondly sought advice on 'the establishment of a commission and the implications of this for State liability in litigation'. One way or the other, there had to be public confrontation of the threat of legal action. Inspired in part by the processes being followed in South Africa in ameliorating the anger of black Africans who had been wronged by the State, the setting up of a 'peace' or 'reconciliation' commission was seen as an important option. With the exception of one sentence, this advice is present in the released document, and is dealt with below.

In December 1998, the Cabinet subcommittee had a meeting which made even more pointed the legalistic nature of their objectives. It identified 'the projected scale of cases against the State' as needing a report, and it asked the Secretaries General of the Departments of Justice, Health and Education to ascertain what impact a commission might have on State liability in litigation.

Within the various discussion papers prepared and circulated there were quite revealing language differences; children who were 'incarcerated' in the memorandum, were 'placed' in institutions in the report. A good deal of loose allegation about abused people was cut out, some of it extremely damaging to them. Personalised and opinionated expressions were changed. Emphasis on the Commission was reduced.

A third important aspect of consultation, of compelling relevance to victims, was 'the effect of the Statute of Limitations and the implication of amendment of it'. On this the State's legal position was invoked; again, legal privilege was used to block access. A section of the report, pages 12–15, headed 'Legal Issues', was withheld.

Nevertheless, what is clear from the report is that, far from being a *Report on Measures to Assist Victims of Childhood Sexual Abuse*, it is overwhelmingly concerned with 'measures to assist' the State. The arguments deal with the huge legal problems of State neglect of the abused.

One would expect any State report on victims of abuse to deal with the Roman Catholic Church. Leaving aside institutional abuse, members of the Church had been responsible for widespread abuse leading to many prosecutions and many substantial cash settlements to avoid court judgments. It was evident throughout this process that the Church acted illegally in protecting clerics who had been guilty of serious criminal assaults on children. Such protection is itself a criminal act.

None of the implications of this for the Government is considered in the document. Nowhere are key questions raised as to how the Church could be brought to answer for abuse. Such a course would involve legal reforms directed against the Church's refusal to acknowledge properly its responsibilities for reporting crimes. The absence of this is an indication of the narrow focus of the report as well as emphasising the lack of balance in the Government's approach.

This and much else seems to confirm that the sole purpose of the Cabinet subcommittee and the committee of Secretaries General was protection of the State. Then and later there was considerable public support for this position and it embraced many significant arguments about the poverty and distress in Irish society which the industrial schools were used to alleviate. In terms of Government responsibility to the taxpayer, and the responsibilities of those heading the public service in the country, this was an entirely legitimate focus for the actions that were being discussed, together with the remedies being formulated. Part of the scandal is the pretence otherwise; another part is the hypocrisy of still seeing the industrial schools Gulag as having achieved any of the social objectives. Its performance was a mockery of these.

From the Taoiseach down, the public picture that was presented was a meretricious one: that this was on behalf of the abused. It would take many years for truth to emerge, and even now the detail continues to be hotly argued.

Those following these events knew, from watching the process itself, hearing the speeches, witnessing the compassionate and caring reflections on the plight of the abused, that the Department of Education, over a long period, was guilty of neglecting its responsibilities for the welfare and integrity of the inmates of the institutions. At the time, in 1998, when the special group was organised, awareness of the abuse story was beginning to be exposed through television programmes, cases in the courts, cases pending, innumerable articles and books about the sexual abuse of children. Though facts continued to be held back under legal privilege, legal advice on the growing tide of cases was increasingly negative from the State's point of view. It became clear, as the facts emerged, that the State had been involved in incontrovertible and enormous damage to a high percentage of the 42,000 children committed to industrial schools. As the report states, 23,520 had been born since January 1940, making them under 60 years old at the time that the first Ahern Government took up the task of resolving the legal threats to the State.

These abused people were likely to take action as their rights became known to them. Legal actions on behalf of 145 individuals had been initiated at the time of the report. These are described as 'only a vanguard of a much larger number of claims which might emerge'. Unfortunately, key paragraphs on 'the scale of the problem' have been suppressed under legal privilege, in the same way in which the whole section on 'Legal Issues' is protected under State secrecy.

The South African Truth and Reconciliation Commission is identified as the inspiration for the Commission to Inquire into Child Abuse, which became known as the Lafoy Commmission. This turned out to be a travesty. The South African attempt, largely successful, was based on the basic concept that people brought before it would tell the truth. On the whole, that is what happened. The process benefited from the chronology of events in South Africa where there had been continuity up to the time of the transfer of power and where witnesses had almost all been adults with good recall of what had happened to them. This was not the case in Ireland where, from a quite early stage, Ms Justice Mary Lafoy, a High Court judge and the first chairperson appointed ahead of the enactment of the legislation, was beset by a quite different motivation, in respect of truth, than the one that supposedly inspired the Cabinet subcommittee.

It derived from the Conference of Religious of Ireland (CORI). They represented the religious orders. Their stated position was that they would refuse to be categorised as the sexual or physical abusers of the young. Unlike the Department of Education and the Minister directly involved, including the Taoiseach, CORI had no intention of admitting abuse. Without conceding this key point, which appeared initially to have been accepted 'in principle', Ms Justice Mary Lafoy's work was hampered from the outset. Choosing this road of reconciliation was an Irish solution to an Irish problem and probably unique in the known world: skip the truth, indemnify the Church institutions, and make it as difficult as possible for the abused.

It seemed clear enough that the State was now under obligation to publish in full the internal advice that produced Bertie Ahern's Apology, gave birth to the Lafoy Commission—precariously based on Pontius Pilate's version of truth— and in due course saw the Redress Board set up. Anything less would further undermine confidence in the processes begun publicly in May 1999. Yet the Government did no such thing. It stuck with the web of deceit and growing burden of lies and misrepresentations and it fumbled on. It was to continue fumbling for several more years. The flawed process, leaching evidence on a weekly basis, continued to be bolstered up in order that it might pursue its crippled way.

The so-called 'comprehensive package', on which the Government sub-committee had laboured for more than a year and which had been approved at that morning's Cabinet meeting on 11 May, had in fact only one major proposal: the setting up of a Commission to Inquire into Child Abuse. Older victims of institutional abuse had sought a forum, Ahern said, in which they could tell their story. It has never been very clear that this was in fact the case. Who were these 'older victims'? What did the younger ones want? Who counted them, recorded them, knew them? Difficult to rely on the Department of Education, which was responsible, at this time and later for the process and which controlled all aspects of back-up material.

Ahern claimed, quite wrongly, since the Commission would hear their stories in private, that this new Commission would give to the abused 'assurance that the wrongs which have been done to them are recognised publicly in a responsible manner, and that lessons are properly learned'. As well as hearing the stories of individuals, the Commission would 'establish as complete a picture as possible of the causes, nature and extent of physical and sexual abuse of children in institutions and other places'.

The Commission was non-statutory to begin with, would have three members, broad terms of reference and would make 'such recommendations as it sees fit'. It would begin by working out whether or not these 'terms of reference' needed to be altered and what powers and protections this would require. The looseness of this reference frame, when compared with normal Government requirements about State investigations—and the country was already engaged in several significant and long-lasting tribunals which had been clearly defined—represented an extraordinary approach by Ahern. Over a relatively short period of time, the Commission was made statutory and legislation followed. But at the outset it was quite clear that nothing specific had been thought out, despite the 14 months in which the Cabinet subcommittee had been considering 'best international practice'. Nevertheless, Ahern's expectation of the Commission inspiring confidence among the past victims of abuse was well received.

He proposed also a counselling service funded at a rate of £4 million a year. There would be problems about getting this started. The same would be so with work directed through the Health Boards which then ran the country's health system, including psychiatric social services.

Ahern undertook to introduce legislation 'during this Dáil session' to extend the Statute of Limitation in respect of child sex abuse cases and to refer to the Law Reform Commission non-sexual childhood abuse. There were other measures, including mandatory reporting and the introduction of a register of sex offenders; these did not directly affect the main issue, which was to give reality to the apology offered to those who had been abused in institutions in the past. The same could be said about Ahern's promises to amend the Child Care Act 1991, in respect of still existing residential institutions and centres, as well as work on the promised further childcare legislation. This would offer a new juvenile justice system.

There was no intent expressed in the important area of compensation. Yet, as will be shown, this was a major issue facing the subcommittee in its 14-month deliberations. There was no mention whatever of the Church's real or potential role in dealing with the long catalogue of abuse during its involvement in the running of the industrial schools and reformatories.

The public's response was positive. The details of what was offered alongside the Apology were not carefully examined. Ahern's own good intentions were taken at face value. As a result, victims began an important process for themselves: the formation of representative groups.

On 22 May 1999 the Government announced the names of three people to form the Commission to Inquire into Child Abuse. They would be appointed when the legislation came to be enacted. Ms Justice Mary Lafoy was to be the chairperson. Dr Imelda Ryan, a consultant child and adolescent psychiatrist specialising in child abuse, and Bob Lewis, a former Director of Social Services in Stockport, England, were also named. The Minister for Education, Micheál Martin, who announced this, described the members as 'eminent' and said they would have the full support of the Government. (There were three later additions, bringing the number of members to six.)

These necessary—if preliminary—moves were followed on 4 February 2000 by the publication of the Commission to Inquire into Child Abuse Bill, followed by the announcement of details of witness expenses for those seeking to appear before the Commission.

The Commission's relationship with the Government was through the Department of Education, 'the sponsoring department'. It was funded through a subhead in the departmental vote. The Commission to Inquire into Child Abuse Act was passed on 26 April 2000, with the establishment day for the Commission set on 23 May 2000.

The principal functions of the Commission were to hear evidence of abuse from those alleging that it had happened during their time in the institutions 'from 1940 or earlier to the present day'. The Commission was to determine causes, nature, circumstances and extent of such abuse. It was to publish reports on its findings and recommendations on how to deal with the effects of such abuse.

The Commission had two committees. The first of these, the Confidential Committee, provided a forum for people who had suffered abuse in childhood, in the designated institutions. As its name implied, it was entirely confidential. Nothing from the Committee would identify or lead to the identification of witnesses or those against whom the witnesses were making allegations. It did not allow anyone connected with the named institutions to challenge the truth of statements.

The Investigation Committee held both public and private sessions. The early work was interrupted by a number of delays, some of them through quite inexcusable behaviour by the Department of Education, leading in the end to the resignation of the chairperson, Ms Justice Lafoy. During its first three years of operation, as she reported in December 2003, the Investigation Committee conducted so few hearings that it constrained what she could sensibly report. But she did reveal that most hearings had been in private despite the discretion of this

Committee to hold public hearings, an objective reinforced by the Act, which indicates the desirability of public hearings. In due course those public hearings, which became protracted and extensive in the matters covered, constituted the most widely known activities of the Commission. The five-volume record of the committees' work and the findings, which were set to be published in May 2009, together with the earlier, three interim reports published by Mary Lafoy in December 2003, upon which concluding act her own resignation came into force, will constitute the full published work of the Commission.[1]

The Commission's first public sitting, which sought submissions from members of the public affected by its work, took place on 29 June 2000, followed by a more significant second public sitting on 20 July at which 'the Survivors' Solicitors' asked that the Commission would sort out with the Government 'an appropriate scheme of compensation'. Without this, it would be of no value for the solicitors to advise potential clients to participate in what was proposed.

In July 2000 Bob Lewis resigned from the Commission and was replaced in November of that year by Dr Kevin McCoy, who worked in Social Services in Northern Ireland and had been a consultant with the Department of Health and Children in the Republic when it was setting up its Social Services Inspectorate. He also helped to draw up the 'Children First Guidelines on Child Abuse'.

The Government dragged its feet over the demand for a compensation structure so that the next public sitting consisted of an announcement of this. Then, on 3 October 2000, the Government agreed in principle to compensate people who, as children, had been victims of abuse 'while in the care of institutions in which they were resident and in respect of which State bodies had regulatory or supervisory functions'.

On 22 November 2000 CORI agreed 'in principle' to participate in the Child Abuse Compensation Scheme. This was in advance of the Government's approval of this scheme, decided on 27 February 2001. It was an adroit move but one lacking in practical terms or specific undertakings. To all appearances, it seemed that Church and State in Ireland were moving towards some kind of common ground in respect of abuse, and this represented a serious danger to the third and most damaged party in the circumstances of industrial school abuse: those people who had been incarcerated.

These broad decisions were of questionable value. It became reasonably clear that some kind of conspiracy of self-protective silence and obfuscation was already emerging in the early stages of the Commission's work. The progress of this within the Church was well advanced. As far as the State was concerned, it seemed to be less focused and less well developed. It could have been argued at this stage, long after the Apology and well into the period in which the Commission—had it not been held up over compensation—might have been engaged in its primary work, that the State was enmeshed in legal incompetence

---

[1]   Bruce Arnold's analysis of the report may be read online at www.irishgulag.ie.

rather than in conspiracy. If so, then the incompetence was of a threatening kind which needed urgent reddress.

The Government announced the main elements of the compensation scheme on 27 February 2001. The Residential Institutions Redress Bill was introduced on 11 June 2001. It was not sufficient or precise enough—and of course was not yet law—for the solicitors to bring their clients into the Commission. What Ms Justice Lafoy was able to do was to introduce the terms and conditions for legal fees. This was begun the previous July. It was notified to the Minister for Education, who was asked 'to make the scheme'. He did not do so until 9 May 2001. The solicitors found it 'seriously flawed' and the Minister had to think again. He reported back to the Commission in November 2001. All this impacted on the proper work of the Commission where, by 30 April 2001, 1,238 witnesses had indicated their intention to participate.

The system set out in the legislation and followed by the Commission, involving two committees, meant that Commission members were assigned to one or the other of these but not to both. The guarantee of total confidentiality, including the fact that their allegations are not investigated, renders the Confidential Committee's work difficult to analyse or pursue other than through Ms Justice Lafoy's eventual report. And this will be the case with the further reporting under Mr Justice Seán Ryan. With the Investigation Committee, which did investigate and hold hearings in accordance with fair procedures, considerable public interest in those hearings and much media reporting did take place. The Investigation Committee was to reach conclusions on the evidence and report on the proceedings, saying that abuse had occurred in a particular institution at a particular time or period and naming the institution and person responsible. This meant that all the people or institutions had to have the opportunity of defence.

As for the Roman Catholic Church, its general response was reflected in its own 'language of abuse', a curiously vague generalisation, of regret rather than apology, and accompanied by emphasis on the passage of time that had elapsed between alleged examples of abuse and the present. 'Hurt' and 'pain' were substituted for 'crime' and 'sexual abuse' or 'sexual assault'. A particular method of address was employed, which, somewhat unctuously, embraced the almost complacent admission that something terrible had happened, but that the Church was now distanced from this. In respect of the alleged acts or abusive behaviour of individuals, this emphasis implied a personal rather than an institutional 'straying from the straight and narrow', devolving responsibility from the Church. Questions of inappropriate action, or no action at all, by those responsible for the abusers were not dealt with. Church spokesmen habitually said that, if there had been hurt, then the Church regretted it. What they did not say was: 'Here are allegations of crime. We acknowledge our part and accept responsibility.'

This approach by the Church was comprehensive and deliberately constructed as self-protection. My own judgment, expressed in a lengthy article on the subject in the *Irish Independent*, was that it had been carefully refined over the previous five years. It seemed that its purpose was motivated by understandable concern over the potential financial costs involved.

Three important objectives were being pursued by the Church in its strategy. The first was to leave open the question of whether or not a crime as such was being considered at all. The second was for the Church to distance itself, in time, from whatever happened when young and vulnerable children were abused. The third, and perhaps most questionable of all, was to separate, as far as possible, the Church as an institution from the individual, usually though not exclusively a priest, a brother, a nun or sister, who was either being charged for abusive or sexual offences, had been found guilty of them, or had confessed.

Institutions, of themselves, do not commit crimes. And if the individual who does commit crimes can be separated from his Church and floated away as an 'errant' or 'delinquent' human being, this helps to absolve the institution from the complicity that needed to be established and proved.

It will be obvious that the most serious danger threatening the Church was where, as an institution, it could be implicated alongside the offender, thus shifting the onus of civil action and recompense onto the Church itself, which could afford to pay for the dreadful and usually permanent damage which sustained sexual and physical abuse causes to young girls and boys.

Where institutional abuse happened, and the institution was comprehensively responsible for the care of young people, the guilt was more easily placed on the religious order within the Church. Where a parish priest commits a crime, it becomes more difficult. But where he commits it having himself acted in his Church role, using the institution and ritual of the Church as a means of persuasion, entrapment or enforcement, then the responsibility and therefore the guilt of the Church become part of any civil action. A legal strategy to fight these and other points of argument about where the guilt shifts from individual to institution or from institution to individual was behind the often disturbing language that was used, turning sustained, serial crimes into a 'hurt', and rendering lasting and profound emotional and psychological disorder into what was becoming at the time a widespread, ill-defined 'pain'.

Reinforced by its protective strategy, the Church was looking with close interest at the progress of legislation designed to amend the Statute of Limitation Act. This was part of the Government's response. It was made more complicated by the danger already explicit in the actions of the Minister for Justice in trying to draw a line between sexual and physical abuse. The two, in terms of many of the cases which have already been through the courts, and many of the examples which have come up in articles, documentaries and books about individual and institutional oppression, were not amenable to the division the Minister proposed.

At the time, the Statute of Limitation imposed on the adult the need to bring a case within three years, or within six years if there had been a failure of statutory duty. With a child, the period of statutory limitation began at the age of majority, 18. The High Court and the Supreme Court—though initially unenlightened in this field—came to recognise that in abuse cases there were good arguments to the effect that victims buried, psychologically, the damage done to them through terrible criminal acts, and that many years could pass before these events surfaced and were confronted, often through psychotherapy and other treatments. There was beginning to emerge, in the context of institutional abuse, general acceptance that cases should be heard on merit, rather than under statutory limitation conditions.

Nevertheless, through the very act of confronting their experiences and speaking out, it was becoming clear that those people who had been victims, for example, of Brendan Smyth or Father Payne,[2] now found themselves outside the remit of legal recompense because their 'coming to terms' with what had happened occurred outside the statutory period. Many of these people had faced trauma and deep embarrassment in order to help in bringing to justice the 300 or so child abusers who at that stage had been successfully prosecuted. A substantial number of these involved the Church. Yet the courage of these damaged people in doing this had rendered them victims a second time, by placing them outside the statutory limitation period in making such claims as they now considered appropriate.

At this time, well before the abuse investigatory mechanism had been put in place, the Minister for Education, after an initially bullish performance, became confused. It was the Opposition in the Dáil, led in particular by Alan Shatter, a brilliant lawyer on the Fine Gael Front Bench, and Jan O'Sullivan, a trenchant spokesperson for the Labour Party, who put the Minister right on his duties. Special provision had to be made for the victims under the legislation, and a special timeframe established.

Though this was suggested, there was no need for the Law Reform Commission to look into it. It was purely a political decision, and it needed to lean in favour of victims and their rights, putting the onus on the courts to establish the true facts. This was obviously preferable to placing a debarring structure within the legislation. It was inherently wrong to use the law to limit the application for recompense of people, now adults, who were damaged as children, frequently by the actions of the Church, and often because of the failures of the State to honour its legal responsibilities in the care of children. It was *always* the State which regulated care, and made the decisions, often requiring or involving the courts, and which led so frequently to so much of the abuse.

2   The arrest of Father Brendan Smyth, who was charged with sexual abuse, led to the fall in 1994 of the Fianna Fáil/Labour Coalition led by Albert Reynolds. Father Ivan Payne was convicted in 1998 for child abuse. Between 1968 and 1987 he abused an unknown number of boys.

The danger of a conspiracy between Church and State was evident enough. They shared a mutual interest in damage-limitation, which meant cost-limitation. The State was in a position to narrow the gates through which actions by victims of State neglect and Church exploitation could arrive at court settlements. At the time, the courageous assault on the Government by Alan Shatter and Jan O'Sullivan was the only thing to confront and block this danger.

Chapter 9 ∾

| MS JUSTICE MARY LAFOY

M s Justice Mary Lafoy presided over the Commission to Inquire into Child Abuse from her appointment as chairperson on 23 May 2000 until her resignation. This was notified in September 2003 but took effect only on 12 December of that year, when her Third Interim Report was published. She therefore served for three and a half years.

Her chairing of the Commission was fraught with difficulties. Most of them derived from obstructions by the Department of Education. From the outset there was a fundamental and, in my view, deliberate flaw in the legal structuring of her work. This was to vest in the Department of Education the role of sponsoring department and this meant that among the significant issues that arose was the fact that the funding of the Commission came through a subhead of the Vote for the Department. Many of Ms Justice Mary Lafoy's problems derived from lack of clarity about how she was to proceed and lack of the wherewithal, a properly costed and funded budget. The Department, either deliberately, or through incompetence, failed to prepare the ground for the implementation of the legislation it had put before the Oireachtas. This led to delays and prevarications from the outset in furthering the Commission's work, initially in getting a decision on payments to be made to lawyers. But in reality it affected every cost aspect.

It did much more. The Department of Education was a pernicious presiding force over the whole abuse issue, not just from the Taoiseach's political Apology, in 1999, but from the much earlier stages, when the State's strategy was largely planned by a special group of senior civil servants within the Department. Some of the details of these early stages are contained in the previous chapter, while others will emerge later.

It was simply wrong in every way for the Department of State that had been responsible for the protection of generations of children in Irish industrial schools and reformatories to be sponsoring the investigation of its own past performance. The control of the investigation should have been vested in one or other of the two key departments dealing with the abuse, but not responsible historically. These departments are Health and Children, and Justice, Equality and Law Reform. They, too, would have faced difficulties over many aspects of what went on in the institutions; they would not have faced, however, the nonsensical situation in which the Department of Education operated.

Historically, as a Government department, it has been the guardian of the Irish Roman Catholic ethos in the upbringing of generations of children and was so in its operation of the industrial school system. It handed over control to the Church. It did not regulate or inspect properly. It did not supervise management or look after its human charges. The main strategy that led to the Taoiseach's 1999 Apology, led to the formation of the Commission and the Redress Board, came from the Department of Education. The provision of grants to survivor organisations, the supply of psychotherapy services, in Ireland and Britain and the funding of pro-survivor groups and Irish clubs in the United Kingdom were all controlled by the Department of Education. There appears to have been reporting back of the views and opinions of former victims in order to guide and direct Government in dealing with the growing unrest and dissatisfaction felt by abused people as the process of hearing them, recompensing them and setting their minds at rest became snarled up in departmental inadequacies. It was wrong at every level that this Department continued to have a controlling role in any of the work undertaken after 1999. It should have been transferred out of its hands. The Department, its records and its personnel should have been made answerable. The fact that they remained in control, the extraordinary fact that they drafted and put through the legislation, is a clear indication of the hypocrisy behind the whole operation of State 'healing'.

At the time of the Second Stage debate of the Commission to Inquire into Child Abuse Bill, on 9 March 2000, Ms Justice Mary Lafoy was already associated with its prospective programme of work, having accepted the position as its chairperson in advance of the relevant legislation. She was working in a preparatory capacity as chairperson.

During the Dáil debate, Richard Bruton, Fine Gael's spokesperson at the time on education, commended what Judge Lafoy had done while at the same time sounding several warning notes:

> A recent meeting of the Organisation of Survivors of Child Abuse voted unanimously to veto co-operation with the commission we are considering today. The obstacle to its participation is the Government's refusal to lift its exclusion of childhood victims of physical abuse from claiming civil damages under the new Statute of Limitations Bill. It is cynical for the Government to profess sorrow for the abuse and then deny the opportunity for redress.[1]

At that stage only sexual abuse was covered in the Bill. Bruton described it as 'discriminatory and unworkable' and pointed out that it was a critical issue for the abused, and one not mentioned by Michael Woods introducing the Bill. Woods tried to amend his statement and was roundly criticised for not attending the meeting of the abused and not having any departmental officials present.

---

[1]   Dáil Éireann, Volume 516, 9 March 2000. Second Stage debate on the Commission to Inquire into Child Abuse Bill 2000.

Woods then tried to make it a point of order, which it manifestly was not, and said:

> May I explain for the information of the House that the commission can and will consider physical abuse. The matter to which the Deputy is referring is a separate matter of civil law.

Bruton replied:

> The Minister's Department was not represented at a recent meeting of survivors of child abuse. The key issue on which they voted unanimously was that they would not co-operate with the commission because the Government had not addressed the matter [of including physical abuse]. It is misleading to come into the House and state this is a separate issue … If the Minister had been represented at the meetings of survivors of child abuse, he might understand why this issue is of such concern.

Bruton also pointed out that Ms Justice Mary Lafoy had envisaged comprehensive support to the survivors going through the process. The Bill, he said, was anything but comprehensive and its integrity potentially undermined:

> The Bill envisages the use of staff seconded from the Department of Education and Science to act as the administration for this inquiry. This is the Department which had responsibility for funding and regulating many of the institutions which will come under scrutiny in the inquiry. Surely this is insensitive at the very least and may also raise the issue of a conflict of interest.

The problem with this and other critical comments was that they were made under the benign shadow of the Apology at a time when the good intentions apparent in that statement were being widely taken at face value, thus muting the doubts that many politicians felt. Nevertheless, members of the Opposition came out with significant reservations which unnerved Michael Woods during the debate and led him to say things that clearly indicated how limited the preparations by the Department of Education had been. He exaggerated the benefits. This was not to become evident for several years, but his opening statement was not borne out by the experiences of abused people in subsequent hearings:

> This Bill will enable the Oireachtas to put in place one of the key measures relating to abuse of children in institutions announced last May by the Taoiseach. Through the Commission individual victims will be given an opportunity to overcome the lasting effects of abuse. The past failures of our society in allowing child abuse in institutions will be acknowledged. The facts

of abuse, however unpalatable, will be brought into the open so that we can confront the truth, and the lessons taught by past failures will be well learned to protect the children of the future.

Very tellingly, in reply Richard Bruton, at the end of his speech, raised the point that is at the heart of this book and remains the most offensive and long-lasting of all the shortcomings that followed Ahern's Apology. Bruton said:

> It is impossible to understand why the terms of reference of the commission have made no explicit reference to inquiring into the role of the State in the abuse that occurred. It is the State which is responsible for the legal frameworks which snatched children from their families and for the systems of regulation and inspection. It is the State which must answer as to whether this abuse could have been discovered at an earlier stage, or as to whether complaints were acted upon.
>
> The record of the Department of Education and Science, documented in *Suffer the Little Children,* makes stark reading. There was no action on reports of criminal negligence where a child died from exposure to boiling water in a bath. Records were apparently destroyed and there was repeated insistence by the Department on institutionalization so that the Minister might not be embroiled in inquiries if boarding out went badly. There was no regular inspection and there was rejection of the proposed visiting committees as a 'grave nuisance'. The reality of what occurred for so many years is astonishing. There were more than 1,000 children committed to industrial schools or institutions of different sorts each year. They were not orphans or offenders. That book shows that less than 5% were orphans and less than 5% were offenders. The book describes how the majority were taken from their families by the cruelty man and put into these institutions, supposedly for their own benefit, but the reality was very different. This was a highly interventionist State policy that went badly wrong. Apologies are necessary and I hope they are met with the same commitment to reform for the future.

In retrospect, the debate, muted by compassion and by an undeserved trust in the Government's stated position involving apology and reconciliation, was insufficiently aggressive in getting the proposed legislation right at the outset. It touched on the key issues but did not insist on them becoming fully integrated in the Bill. Most significantly of all, the idea of investigating the State's established culpability was insufficiently incorporated in the new Commission to Inquire into Child Abuse Act.

The point was made that individuals who perpetrated abuse could not, and should not, shoulder the whole responsibility for what happened. Some measure of responsibility had to be taken by those who did not act on complaints, did not put safeguards in place, turned a blind eye and did not provide sufficient funding for children entrusted to the care of the State.

Richard Bruton felt that Ms Justice Lafoy was the right person for the job and had shown her commitment. He looked forward to the Committee Stage of the Bill, which would cover how the Commission would work in practice. It did not turn out like that.

Bruton's criticisms of how the legislation dealt with the responsibility and possible culpability of the State in crimes against children were reiterated by the Labour Party spokesperson, Roisin Shortall:

> It is easy for the State to point the finger at institutions and religious orders. They acted in *loco parentis* and on behalf of the State in regard to children whom the State deemed to be in danger of neglect, for example, where the mother was a lone parent or was poverty stricken … The State is absolutely culpable for the neglect of children and its failure to provide the services which vulnerable and marginalized children needed. It was only too happy over many years to allow the religious orders, in particular, to take responsibility for the welfare and care of children. It cannot now avoid its responsibility and should not attempt to do so in this legislation. The State has a clear role in providing for the care, welfare and protection of children, a responsibility that was overlooked in the past.
>
> However, equally, complaints were made about the role of the State when abuse was reported to State agencies. The State had access to records and information and was seen as the authority to arbitrate in cases involving allegations of abuse, yet it failed to respond to such allegations. Officials did not reply to or lost letters, did not return telephone calls or told direct lies about their involvement in particular cases. All this activity needs to be addressed by the commission. A number of people were culpable in terms of neglect in the past and some may even still be in the State's employ.

Roisin Shortall also made the point—borne out by circumstance—that the Commission would be working for much longer than the two years suggested in the Bill and she wanted regular reporting in order that this issue could be kept to the fore, encouraging greater public awareness of the issue. She raised the issue of compensation and cited the members of the Army who had received compensation from the State for hearing loss.

> If the State is prepared to pay compensation to soldiers whose hearing may have been marginally affected in some cases, the very least that should be done is to pay compensation to those people whose childhood were robbed from them due to State neglect. Equally, the Government's approach to the Statute of Limitations issue, the fact that people are statute barred and that physical abuse is not included, makes the need for a proper compensation tribunal or mechanism all the more urgent.

Fine Gael's Alan Shatter also referred in scathing terms to the fact that the Department of Education was an inappropriate arm of the State to be in central control of the administration investigating the past record of that same Department. Everyone knew it had a record that did not bear scrutiny. He was forthright in condemning this: 'Worthy of a Franz Kafka creation' was how he put it. Quite rapidly, such mistakes—and they appear gross and insensitive—can lose the trust and support of the people whose suffering should be at the heart of the investigations and whose welfare depended on the legislative remit under which this appalling history of gross abuse of children, and deliberate and cowardly neglect by the State's protective machinery, was being investigated.

These fundamental flaws in the Government's approach, inexcusable in the most obvious of ways, were severely aggravated by incompetence over the implementation of the plans decided on in 1998–9. They were half-baked. There was no clear definition of the Commission's full role. There was no anticipation of the position that would emerge over legal fees. There was no intention to recompense the abused. The Redress Board was given birth as a result of Mary Lafoy's insistence. To begin with, physical abuse was not given the benefit of an extended Statute of Limitation in the same way as sexual abuse and the Minister, Michael Woods, tried to promise this during the Second Stage debate.

As a result of this seriously deficient legislative start, where the Minister made vague promises on the Second Stage debate and then inexcusably rushed through the vital Committee Stage, Ms Justice Lafoy found herself working her way through a minefield of incompetence and obstruction. She responded well, her language always polite but her message damning. And when she eventually resigned, she left the Department of Education and the Minister stripped of all credibility and self-respect. Politely and in terms that were legally impeccable, she humiliated Irish politicians and public servants, exposing—for those who had the wit to see it—what an utter sham the whole recompense of the victims of abuse had been, from its initiation to its end.

Long before the end of Ms Justice Lafoy's term, the children whose care was placed in her hands had long since tried to let their painful childhoods pass from their memories. This had not happened. Though they were children no longer, some of the periods of distance from childhood being as much as 70 or more years, the memories had left indelible stains. Though they had long since moved on from the wretched and at times savage and abusive childhoods, they remembered all too clearly the detail. Many of them had later led bleak adult existences. A very large number of them had moved away from Ireland. The years had not healed many of them.

Those who were abused, not just sexually, but in a number of other gross and terrifying ways, were angry at their blighted lives and bewildered by what had happened. But they were increasingly well-informed about what was now going on. Some could not voice what it was they wanted. It included as many demonstrations of remorse, compassion, guilt and compensation as there were individual men and women to receive the overdue tribute of a country that had wronged them. They had some faith in her, and for good reason: she did identify and tackle the problems. But she was manifestly hindered by the State.

Mary Lafoy confronted two powerful institutions: the Roman Catholic Church and the Irish State. They were primarily culpable. Both had shown clear evidence of wriggling and squirming in the face of past guilt. Both were engaging in prevarication and, most important of all, the failure to surrender—in the spirit of apology—the evidence about what had happened.

In brief, what had happened was that the State—on which Mary Lafoy was dependent for the operation of her Commission—was itself the primary culprit. Furthermore, it was sheltering the Church, responsible in a multitude of ways for the people, both men and women within the religious orders, who had perpetrated the innumerable crimes of abuse against imprisoned children. It was because of the failure of the most dismal and irresponsible section of the Department of Education—its Inspectorate of Reformatories and Industrial Schools—that Ms Justice Lafoy had become involved. That inspectorate effectively had sanctioned the exploitation of children, their deprivation of food, their inadequate clothing, their subnormal education, their piecemeal subjection to terrible sexual abuse and the constant beatings that characterised every institution now being investigated. Because of this, the State was open to legal process by the victims, and answerable for an unimaginable tide of expenditure.

Ms Justice Lafoy was conscious of this; conscious also of the failure of the Department of Education to come up with proper proposals on a compensation body. The correspondence with the Department, in the Third Interim Report of the Commission (which reprints the two earlier interim reports), covers the various public sittings up to that time, and it makes dismal reading. It gives the impression that, despite the introduction of legislation and the discussions on departmental interests and the interests of the Church organisations, the Government had been very slow to get round to considering the central, key issue—the establishment of a compensation body.

Not surprisingly, Ms Justice Lafoy referred to her work being impeded, and this was of particular concern for two reasons. She was acting under a time constraint of two years, set by the Oireachtas. Not to have everything she needed in place from the beginning of her work was an inexcusable handicap. Secondly, the work of discovery could not forecast the numbers of men and women who might come forward, which would affect the amount of work, since the solicitors were not able to give assurance to witnesses that appearing before her Commission, or making application for compensation, would be worthwhile.

The slow pace of progress by the Commission, the central and first organisation set up to help the abused, seems, from the record, to have been the direct result of deliberate delays and failures resulting from the slow pace of Government responses. These, in the end, were to contribute to Ms Justice Lafoy's dramatic resignation, in September 2003. It was evident that the State, not directly represented by the Government though clearly advised by the Government, failed to back her work appropriately. The evidence suggests that this was deliberate. Much was to happen elsewhere. But as interim reports made clear, progress in the Commission dealing with the abused was ponderously slow and it was evident by November 2001 that Government targets for completion of witness appearances had been hopelessly misjudged. Mary Lafoy's report at that time predicted dates in 2004 and 2005 'at the earliest' for a final report. This would later be extended to 2008 and to 2009 by the new chairperson, Mr Justice Seán Ryan.

Justifying this review requires a brief chronology of events which initially show that the first 18 months of the Commission's working life saw its statutory mandate hindered 'due primarily to factors outside its control'. The first of these was that the Government had failed to put in place 'an appropriate scheme of compensation'. The point was made by the 'Survivors' Solicitors', noted for Government action at the second public sitting on 20 July 2000. It was not until 3 October 2000 that the Minister announced Government agreement 'in principle'. 'Principle' did not become 'firm intention' until 27 February 2001, with the Residential Institutions Reddress Bill being introduced on 11 June 2001. The Bill did not satisfy the Survivors' Solicitors, who could not advise their clients 'with confidence' because of the exclusion of categories from the Statute. The Commission did make a ruling, on 20 July 2000, about legal representation before the Investigation Committee on behalf of complainant or respondent, and invited the Minister, the following day, to 'make the scheme'; the Minister did so, almost a year later. The Survivors' Solicitors found the Bill 'seriously flawed'.

By 31 July 2001, the final date for 'the submission of requests to participate in the Commission's inquiry', 3,149 had lodged requests, 1,192 for the Confidential Committee and 1,957 for the Investigation Committee. By the end of November of that year, 254 hearings before the Confidential Committee had been concluded. There were inordinate delays in the preparatory or preliminary inquiries, stipulated by the Act for the Investigation Committee, and only five cases were scheduled by November 2001. Though the Commission could predict June 2004 for completion of the Confidential Committee hearings, no such timeframe was possible for the Investigation Committee. One of the obvious implications of this rate of progress involved Commission staff and the need, also obvious, of changing to a panel of professionals. It was clear that the original target date for the completion of the Commission's work—23 May 2001—could not possibly be met. By Government Order—but not until 17 April 2002—the remit was extended until 22 May 2005.

None of this had been thought through during the crucial year that preceded the Taoiseach's Apology, in May 1999. Yet the single substantive intention announced in that Apology was the setting up of the Commission. The Department of Education had not fallen down on the job; it had simply not done its job at all. Nor did it now respond properly to the publication of the changed timetable. What followed, between June 2002, when the Commission, faced with the changed timetable of work, requested additional resources, until September 2003, when Ms Justice Mary Lafoy announced her resignation, constituted further serious delays. As late as November 2002 the Department was asking the Commission to furnish clarification 'regarding the comparison between the Commission continuing as presently constituted' and the alternative for which new State funding was deemed necessary.

Ms Justice Lafoy decided to publish 'the letters which it is considered are of seminal importance in defining the relationship between the Commission and its sponsoring Department'. These were then set out in the Third Interim Report. When, finally, extra resources were sanctioned, they were made conditional on a review of the Commission's terms of reference. The Commission was to proceed 'in a gradual fashion', employing additional people on 'a short contract basis'; if the mandate were to change, this would be reflected in the final amount of additional resources.

All this, apart from the protracted destabilising of the Commission's work, was grossly unfair to the abused; their age profile, which Ms Justice Lafoy mentioned in her account of the truly astonishing behaviour of the Department of Education towards the Commission, was a significant imperative. These were middle-aged or elderly people, many of whom had fled from Ireland after release from the child Gulag, and were living in England. The hopes raised by Ahern were as ash now on their lips. Whom could they blame but Ms Justice Lafoy?

Rhetorically, there was no clear answer to this until Ms Justice Lafoy published the full story, at the end of 2003. Ironically, one of the causes of delay was the stance taken by the abused's own representatives, the Survivors' Solicitors; but this was a minor factor when set against the enormities of the changing positions and the manifest—and, apparently, deliberate—uncertainties of the Department of Education, combined with the greater threat of a Government retaining the right to review the workings of this statutory body and then telling the Commission, on 4 July 2003, that it would engage in such further review.

There is a direct political context to this series of changes, initiated in the summer of 2002 and announced in September of that year by the Minister for Education, Noel Dempsey, of 'a second review of the Commission's remit' and this was the fact of a general election earlier that summer in which Ahern secured a second term in office. Politically, he was no longer under threat of the abuse issue undermining his position.

The pivotal date in the life of the Commission to Inquire into Child Abuse was 1 September 2003. On that day the Department of Education released a press statement announcing the July decision of the Government that it was going to 'engage in a second phase of a review relating to the Commission'. The Government had already announced (the previous December) that it was 'initiating a review of the remit of the Commission'. Both processes were being done to shorten the timeframe and save money; a further reason given was that legal challenges would be facilitated. Between the two dates—December 2002 and

September 2003—the Government had drafted legislation. The Government also said it was 'prudent' to await the High Court judgment in respect of the case taken by the Christian Brothers which is described in Chapter 13. In making the announcement Noel Dempsey clearly saw no problem and was quoted as saying, 'the Commission is performing a vital task in providing survivors of abuse with an opportunity to recount the abuse they have suffered, to inquire into the widespread abuse that occurred and to report to the public'. He saw no interference in the Commission's work resulting from this significant legal change.

Ms Justice Mary Lafoy viewed it entirely differently. The Commission issued a statement the following day saying 'these changes will affect the workings of the Investigation Committee' making evidence irrelevant or redundant, and that this process would be stopped. Complainants and respondents were advised to prepare no further material.

That same day, 2 September 2003, Ms Justice Lafoy announced her resignation to the Secretary General of the Government, Dermot McCarthy, bypassing—as was proper—the Department of Education, but referring to its press release. Her resignation, she said, would take effect 'as soon as the Interim Report on the work of the Commission under its current mandate … is published'. She promised that she would give an outline of the 'factual circumstances which have given rise to the members of the Commission being in the wholly invidious situation in which they now find themselves'.

Not alone had the Commission been rendered powerless, according to Ms Justice Lafoy; it had also had its completed work to date, covering several years, undermined:

A Commission which works first to one mandate, and then to a substantially different mandate, would leave itself open to legal challenge on the grounds that, in the course of exercising its first mandate, it obtained information or formed impressions which would affect its capacity to exercise the second mandate with a fully open mind. While, on the basis of independent legal advice which I have obtained, I believe that this risk is a slight one, nonetheless, even a slight risk may be unacceptable in a matter of this importance.

She appended all the related material for the Government's benefit. When she published her Interim Report in December, she also published correspondence with the Department of Education. It makes sorry reading and, together with her letter, represents one of the sternest indictments of State behaviour by any Government appointee to a statutory body. Ms Justice Lafoy nevertheless undertook to take all necessary measures to protect the public interest.

In her letter she said that this move by the Government, undertaking a change in the law in order to speed things up and save cash, was,

... merely the latest in a series of events which have, since the inception of the statutory Commission over three years ago, impeded the completion by the Commission of its statutory mandates as set out in the Act of 2000 in a timely fashion. A range of factors over which the Commission has had no control have together produced a real and pervasive sense of powerlessness. In retrospect, it appears to me that since its establishment, the Commission has never been properly enabled by the Government to fulfil satisfactorily the functions conferred on it by the Oireachtas.

She included among these factors the two years it took the Government to introduce the Redress Board, allowing for compensation; the same delay in providing a fee structure for the lawyers representing abused men and women; the proper funding of the Commission in the face of the unexpectedly high tide of allegations; the delay between the decision to review the mandate (3 December 2002, to be completed February 2003) and the date of her resignation, by which stage it had still not been published; finally, the absurdity of the Government agreeing in principle to increase resources, but making this contingent on the outcome of the review which it had not, until that point, published.

These matters, Ms Justice Lafoy said, not without a hint of irony, were 'matters of policy', quite a different thing from her statutory task, governed by the 2000 Act. Her summary of the implicit meaning of these handicaps to her work, affecting long periods of the Commission's operation,

... has effectively negatived the guarantee of independence in the performance of its functions conferred on the Commission by section 3(3) of the Act of 2000 and has militated against the Commission being able to perform its statutory functions as envisaged by the Oireachtas with reasonable expedition.

She listed several of the problems made intractable by the Government's position and expressed as her conclusion that the only clear inference to be drawn from the recent correspondence sent to the Commission by the Department of Education was that:

The Government has decided that the Commission will not implement its current statutory mandate ... the Commission is still fixed with an unqualified mandate from the Oireachtas as set out in the Act of 2000, as amended by the Act of 2002.

Despite the clear and precise terms in which Ms Justice Lafoy had presented the full story of how the Government had frustrated her work and brought about her resignation, the public reaction was one of confusion and misjudgment. Media reaction fell far short of the reality when the charge amounted only to incompetence and incapacity. The *Sunday Tribune* said that the Government's handling had been 'nothing short of plain incompetent' and its political correspondent, Stephen Collins, called it 'chaos' and then went on to say that the great institutions of the State—including Government, Oireachtas and courts—'have been utterly incapable of dealing with the serious and fundamental issues as they arise'. This was not at all what Mary Lafoy had said. She was not dealing, in her correspondence, with chaos or incompetence. She was dealing with the deliberate undermining of her work and of the legislation passed by the Houses of the Oireachtas, which should have governed that work. She was saying that the Government had decided to block her mandate, which came from the Oireachtas, and bring her work to a stop.

This reading of the case, made public with her letter, was not the one adopted by the general public, but it was broadly the way the victims of abuse saw her fate. It completed the long drawn-out process of defining and hardening their attitude. Many had already lost faith in Mary Lafoy on the basis of her poor achievement to date. Now, as a result of her resignation, it became clear that she had been undermined and blocked in her work. In a very clear and precise way the focus of blame switched back to the Government.

Chapter 10 ❧

GROWING DOUBTS ABOUT THE STATE'S INTENTIONS

For many people, the resignation of Ms Justice Mary Lafoy was an intense and sustained period of political drama. For those who had been in the industrial schools and other institutions of care, where they had been abused, it represented confirmation of a stalled and dishonest process. That was how many of them saw it, and this view grew steadily. In their eyes, the process had been corrupted in its operation by the State, apparently deliberately. Their attention was refocused on the culpability of the Government. It was not a new outcome for them. Suspicion had grown, during both 2002 and 2003, and several events had caused increasing doubt over the real intent of Government, as well as deeper questions about the pernicious behaviour of the Department of Education.

The performance of the Department seemed fully to justify the views of Ms Justice Lafoy and others, that the Department should not have had responsibility vested in it to control and monitor what was being done for the victims of the Gulag. But the Government's changing position was a far greater threat. Collectively, these events added to the dismay of the abused. What was happening now began to take on the true character of perfidy and treachery masquerading as a programme of recovery for those wronged by the State.

In this and following chapters some of the parallel manifestations of trouble, uncertainty and dishonesty will be dealt with in a backtrack of events during the period that might sensibly be called the Lafoy Era, from her appointment, in advance of the passing of the Commission to Inquire into Child Abuse Act 2000, to her resignation at the end of 2003.

One telling event to emerge was the probable, and then established, fact of a private deal done between the Government and the Church. There was a deal, of course, made public in June 2002. This was claimed by the interim Minister for Education, Michael Woods, as:

... the commitment of the government and the congregations, together, to help people who have been hurt as children to find some peace and comfort in their lives.

But was this the whole truth of what had been agreed between the Church and the Government? Woods made various claims about the achievement, the money being donated by the religious orders, the land and property being transferred, and he mentioned 'an indemnity from the State to the congregations concerned'. He also claimed that the State would have full control over any case to which the indemnity extends and that the Agreement provided for a process of independent arbitration if an irreconcilable disagreement arose between the parties. The claims he made might have been seen as beneficial, in the light of the Church's ongoing embarrassments about abuse. However, the full terms of the deal were not released until much later. When this happened, a different set of perceptions was applied; the 'Secret Deal's' existence, raised further questions about the State's integrity. It is dealt with fully in the next chapter.

There was also growing evidence of activities by the Department of Education designed to penetrate and infiltrate the organisations working with and for the abused. The majority of such organisations readily accepted funding from the Government through the Department from an early stage in their existence and there were fears that this money was awarded in some cases without adequate surveys of membership, together with the audit of expenditure. Other concerns were about the prospects of any continuing process towards reconciliation in the face of the comprehensive resistance by the Church about being made answerable to the law of the land over child abuse.

It had for long been obvious to many that not alone did the interests of the State coincide with the interests of the Church, but that this was a motivating force in the actions being taken by both institutions. The two most powerful organisations in the country needed to settle the haunting historical spectre of child abuse in institutions they had jointly run. There was the need to minimise the expense of compensation and there was the need to formalise the process to allow for the smooth resolution of claims without costly and embarrassing court actions.

But there was a price to be paid. The Department of Education funded the programmes for helping the victims of institutional abuse with adult education. It also funded the societies, clubs and social organisations in Britain frequented by many of the victims. It funded some of the psychiatric help that was offered. And it was no surprise to victims to discover that psychiatric help was coming from members of the religious orders, including orders that had been indicted for offences against the inmates. These factors represented a clear conflict of interest and created a lack of trust. Where it did not, the offers of Irish State funding for representative organisations acted as a mechanism to choke criticism from such groupings.

By early 2002 it began to look as if there had been some kind of deal done between Church and State. Growing evidence of real crime of a peculiarly dismal, disgusting and horrific kind had earlier emerged in pioneering investigative work, then in the large-scale survey by Mary Raftery and Eoin O'Sullivan, then in a growing number of court cases. This evidence grew in magnitude, rendering denials increasingly unsustainable and changing the burden of guilt in a form in which it was unevenly shared by Church and State.

Individual cases in institutions of care were mirrored and corroborated, compelling the revelations forward as a clear pattern of deliberate cruelty, neglect and abuse. What was recorded had resulted on occasion in the near-murdering of innocent children, and occasionally in the actual deaths of children. It had created a widespread and horrifying environment of fear, even terror, among girls and boys who were in the care, legally, of the State, and mentally and physically of the Church. Crimes of an appalling kind had been committed widely, and with impunity. Lives had been ruined and the people concerned had gone on suffering from criminal acts, often in the distant past, which had not been recognised or punished.

At the end of 1999,[1] the focus of attention in this real world of crime was on a priest in County Donegal who pleaded guilty to dreadful cases of sexual abuse over a period of years between 1966 and 1982. It was clear then that the Church had a three-pronged strategy. I wrote of those three objectives then:

> The first is to leave open the question of whether or not a crime as such is being considered at all. The second is for the Church to distance itself, in time, from whatever happened when young and vulnerable children were abused. The third, and the most sinister of all, is to separate, as far as possible, the Church as an institution from the individual, usually though not exclusively a priest, who is either being charged for sexual offences, has been found guilty of them, or has confessed.
>
> It will be obvious that the most serious danger threatening the Church is where it, as an institution, can be implicated alongside the offender, thus shifting the onus of civil action and recompense to the Church, which can afford to pay for the dreadful and usually permanent damage which sustained sexual and physical abuse causes to young girls and boys. A legal strategy to fight these and other points of argument . . . is behind the nauseating language which is being used, and which turns a horrendous crime into a 'hurt', and turns lasting and profound emotional and psychological disorder into 'pain'.

---

[1]   At the time, the controversial issue of abortion was being hotly debated, the Roman Catholic Church being particularly vociferous in its opposition. The reason was simple enough: it had an academic argument that could be readily stated and debated largely in abstract terms. Totally different was the issue of child abuse. This was far from abstract. It may have relied on evidence of abuse of one kind or another going back four or five decades or even more; but it was, at the same time, painfully real for the victims. The Church had no wish to debate with them.

The Church was facing a hideous and all too real worst-case scenario involving an unending saga of crime and recrimination, and of its own members being brought to book. Not surprisingly, when the details of the deal emerged, the sense of a secret deal having been struck came forcibly home with the announcement of the lop-sided arrangements for compensating victims of clerical child abuse. For it soon emerged that the State had placed on the shoulders of the country's burdened taxpayers the lion's share of compensation payments. The State had cut people out. It had accepted as 'payments' cash and kind that were extraneous.

Mary Raftery came out against any form of deal or contract between Church and State. She thought the deal that actually emerged was suspect. The exclusions from it were unacceptable. The details were being misrepresented. The burden borne by the Church was not enough. Yet again, it was getting away with murder. And the Minister for Education, whose first duty is to the people and to the law, had sided with the Church in unjustly furthering its protection and exoneration.

The issues became matters for the ballot box, involving as they did State deception and misrepresentation; but the role of the ballot box had been played out in the 2002 general election. By this time the suspicion of a deal, reinforced by the sequence of events, rendered public compliance in either amending the Constitution or in accepting the wholesale exoneration of the Church from past crimes, and at public expense, unacceptable.

Then came the bombshell of Father Seán Fortune, interrupting the painful unpicking of historical abuse, and the way Church and State were dealing with it, and substituting an all-too-contemporary example which exposed brazen Church behaviour and the pusillanimous arguments of the State.

Seán Fortune was a serial abuser of young boys who attended his church in Ferns, Wexford, and helped him to serve Mass. The sequence of events came to light as a result of a BBC programme, *Suing the Pope*. The programme was broadcast on 19 March 2002 and concerned allegations of clerical child abuse in Ferns. The details do not have a place in this account, which is of industrial school abuse over a much longer period of time and covering a much wider territory.

What was important in respect of this particular example of clerical sexual abuse was that it was handled by the State in an effective way and led to an unprecedented level of co-operation from the Roman Catholic Church despite an unnecessary and overcautious stipulation by the Senior Counsel, George Birmingham, who was chairperson of the initial and preliminary inquiry. He said that 'responses or lack of responses to allegations' should be seen 'in the context of the time'. It might have been more truthful and direct to have said that everything should have been seen in the context of the law, though this might also have closed off Church co-operation. All abuse inquiries have been hampered by imprecise and at times misguided contextual approaches. This is of relevance to the victims of industrial school abuse since the harsh punishment regimes they faced, together with the acute shortages of proper food, appropriate clothing and health care were all put down repeatedly to 'the context of the time' when such shortages of food and clothing, as well as a climate of almost relentless corporal punishment were the norm, in Christian Brother schools in particular. General deprivation was also normal, through the country's endemic poverty, within the domestic environment.

George Birmingham was appointed by the Minister for Health and Children, Mícheál Martin, to make a preliminary investigation following the *Suing the Pope* documentary. He was to 'identify the central issues for any Inquiry and make recommendations as to its form and structure'. Birmingham consulted with victims and with the Catholic Church 'to ascertain the level of cooperation'. In the event, the Church opened up its files, as did the State agencies. He also consulted with those involved in the Commission to Inquire into Child Abuse, chaired by Ms Justice Lafoy, to ascertain how that Commission or its experience might be suitable or useful.

Also after the broadcast, Bishop Brendan Comiskey, Bishop of Ferns, was asked to make a statement, which he did. It made chilling reading at the time. The main reason he gave for not participating in the programme was the superficial and marginal one of how the media might perceive his actions. Comiskey expressed abhorrence and regret. He said that he had learnt 'painful lessons' and had 'not always got it right'. He then fell back on Church and State guidelines and the idea that a multi-disciplinary approach was the way forward.

It was patently clear that the so-called 'open-door policy to survivors of child sexual abuse' which the Bishop followed had not worked and was not working, nor was it supported by any professional monitoring or research. The open door policy had no clear mechanism. The Bishop's stated reliance on it indicated how far out of touch he was and what a failure there had been to investigate in any logical and comprehensive way the trail of desolation left by Father Fortune. The Church had followed no multi-disciplinary approach. There had been no co-operation of Church, State, voluntary agencies, Health Board, local authority or the Guards in the Ferns Diocese. He used a formula of 'caring' and 'concern' without either term producing anything of value at all to the victims who were unidentified at that stage.

Bishop Comiskey resigned at the beginning of April 2002. It was an admission of defeat and deserved and got a measure of compassion. He was not alone among the leaders of the Church in having found himself increasingly out of his depth, inadequate for the challenges of the habitual and criminal molesters of children, and embarrassed by the Catholic Church's collective confusion. He was governed by unclear and muddled beliefs.

The Church claimed at the time to have put its house in order. This was on account of its 'Framework document' and its Child Protection Office. Neither the practical Church on the ground nor the Church that expressed itself through the Conference of Religious of Ireland or the Irish Episcopal Conference had any clear code of behaviour in the face of a not uncommon set of circumstances along the lines of those created by Father Fortune. Bishop Comiskey was a victim of this.

Bishop Comiskey himself was simply not adequate for the challenges facing him. He moved in several different directions; he adopted different approaches; he says that he tried compassion and he says that he tried firmness. The abuse went on. It was sustained and brutal. And at every level the Bishop lost while abuse won. He was not supported by the Primate, Archbishop (now Cardinal) Seán Brady. He was not supported by Cardinal Desmond Connell, who was Archbishop of Dublin. Cardinal Connell, as Comiskey's Metropolitan, made clear his limited knowledge and his wish not to be associated with the Ferns Diocese. He washed his hands of responsibility. Archbishop Brady, in an interview with RTÉ, expressed a similar distancing. They claimed instead that their organisation was firmly rooted in an established structure unaffected by events. They set the resignation aside as 'a personal matter'. They then offered to the public the Church's document 'Child Sexual Abuse: Framework for a Church Response'. Yet Comiskey's failure to act had already discredited the guidelines contained in the document. It had worked neither before nor after the BBC documentary. The Bishop knew neither the names nor the addresses of the victims of Father Fortune's abuses, nor had he done anything to fulfil the requirements of the Church's policy guidelines. There was no evidence that it was working as George Birmingham began his investigation.

Archbishop Brady and Cardinal Connell issued a press statement. This was to coincide with Bishop Comiskey's resignation. The Archbishop and Cardinal were then President and Vice-President respectively of the Irish Episcopal Conference:

> The sexual abuse of children by priests is an especially grave and repugnant evil. To all victims of such abuse, to their families and to their parish communities, we again offer our profound apologies.
>
> We offer this statement on behalf of all the bishops because we realise that the whole Church in Ireland is suffering at this time from the scandal caused by this evil and the manner in which it was dealt with at times. It is a scandal which has evoked entirely justified outrage. The sexual abuse of children by priests is totally in conflict with the Church's mission and with Christ's compassion and care for the young.
>
> We believe that the protection of children is of paramount importance. The document 'Child Sexual Abuse: Framework for a Church Response', was adopted jointly by the Conference of Religious of Ireland (CORI) and the Irish Bishops' Conference in January 1996 to ensure correct procedures for handling complaints or allegations of Child Sexual Abuse by priests and religious. These guidelines, which include procedures for reporting to the civil authorities and outreach to victims, are still being followed throughout this island and are reinforced by the services of the Child Protection Office established by the Irish Bishops' Conference in 2001.

We are greatly saddened by the circumstances surrounding Bishop Comiskey's resignation. It is his own personal decision and comes out of a context of deep human suffering, both of victims of abuse and of himself. May the memory of all the good he has done in the service of his people and clergy be a source of consolation to him in the future.

We realise that the events of recent weeks have also caused great distress and anxiety to the faithful throughout Ireland, particularly those of the diocese of Ferns and the parishes affected. Not only has trust in the Catholic Church been damaged, but so too has the faith of the people and the morale of clergy.

In this Easter Season we pray that the Risen Lord will inspire all of us to bring new life and healing to victims of child sexual abuse and that He will give us the courage to renew our efforts to bring about reconciliation and peace regarding this painful issue.

There was a political motive in the setting up of the Ferns Inquiry. It was in keeping with the political strategy then being adopted by Fianna Fáil for the forthcoming general election in May 2002. It fitted in with the huge package of legislative promises, actual Bills, and the climate of optimistic anticipation of a return to the 'Peace, Prosperity and Progress', which, with some justification only, anticipated the party forming the major element in the next administration. The inference, like Iarnród Éireann advertising, is 'We're not there yet, but we're getting there.'

The decision by the Minister, Micheál Martin, to set up an inquiry provoked, in the face of its broad terms, calls from many different directions for a more urgent response. It was in fact a very soft and loose response, hardly meriting the term 'urgent', but possibly appeased the sense of outrage about clerical abuse in the Ferns Diocese and the Church's absolute failure to deal properly with this. Given that both Fine Gael and Labour had called for such an inquiry, the Minister's decision took the specific issue off the election agenda.

Among the victims of industrial school abuse, this side-lining of the issue of child sexual abuse and the role of the Church generally—issues which should have been part of the election in view of the Church's pervasive and damaging intrusion into the State's running of the country—was seen as one of an increasing number of betrayals. The Church had repeatedly demonstrated its capacity not to be answerable and had shown its power in withstanding State intrusion into its affairs. It could clearly sustain this invulnerability even in the realm of criminal actions. And this was an issue that would soon grow in importance. At the time, however, it simplified the electoral contest not to have abuse as part of the campaign.

For the present this invulnerability, which was a form of Church self-rule outside the State's Constitution, would go on. The Church, when it saw fit or needed to protect itself, operated according to canon law rather than according to the laws of the State. It had frequently and consistently flouted the laws of the State by ignoring them. Legal cases, some successful, others not, were clearly indicating that this was going on regularly. The State tolerated this because the politicians were weak to the point of feebleness, and the institutions—Health Boards, police, inspectorates—were often undermined by the climate of political collusion and timidity towards the Church.

To many it seemed that it was neither the intention, nor would it be the result, of Minister Martin's inquiry, to resolve any of this. His was a facile response, meeting neither the scale of the problem nor its countrywide extent. Ferns was not the only territory where there had been clerical child abuse. Minister Martin's approach was potentially flawed from the start by its 'voluntary' nature. Only by Bishop Willie Walsh of Killaloe laying open the Church files was this averted.

Bit by bit, a view was emerging: that of making the Church and its members exactly the same as other citizens, just as the Constitution requires. They would pay the same taxes, submit to the same civil and criminal law, be investigated by the Guards in exactly the same way as secular abusers are. This was only theory, however; it has not happened.

The Church's canon law would be confined to a remit within the organisation of the Church and not having any relevance outside it. Elsewhere the Church should be made amenable, in every respect, to the law of the land. This would mean the kinds of conformity over reporting crimes that can make civil failure to do so a criminal offence. We are in marked contrast with the actions in America, where bishops of the Roman Catholic Church have handed over full details of all abuse cases. This is not the result of divine instruction, but has resulted from legal advice, that the Federal and State law would be applied if the Church did not co-operate.

Such legal advice would be different in Ireland. Lawyers give their advice on the basis of case law rather than theory. Until a wider range of crimes—those of being accessory to crimes, of concealing criminal acts, of claiming extra-territorial authority—are addressed by the State in the courts, it seems we are unlikely to follow the American lead on child sexual abuse by clerics, or the general lead of countries such as Britain.

At the time of Bishop Comiskey's humiliation and the subsequent Ferns Inquiry—and it has not changed much since then—virtually all our political parties were as dynamic as wet dishcloths on the issue of Church–State relations, where crime was involved, and on the supposed supremacy of law and Ireland's Constitution. Shocked horror greets the event but there is no legislative follow-up.

Brave leadership was given at the time by Colm O'Gorman[2] and Marie Collins[3], specifically in respect of two quite different areas of abuse. But too much optimism seemed misplaced on the issue of Minister Martin's proposal. In the

[2]   Founder of One in Four and a victim of Father Séan Fortune.
[3]   A victim of clerical sex abuse.

event, the Church's response was slightly better than expected. It later became much better, as we shall see, with the appointment by the Vatican of Archbishop Diarmuid Martin to the Diocese of Dublin.

The general election, in the summer of 2002, did not cover any of the abuse issues. By the autumn it was clear enough that the State, meaning both the Government and the law as expressed through the police and the Director of Public Prosecutions, did not know how to proceed against the Church in respect of child abuse. It had done less than the minimum required by the circumstances so far discovered in the past. It was doing less than required regarding present revelations. And it was likely to go on in the same way into future abuse cases unless changes were to be made.

At the same time, many individual cases against those religious who had been found guilty of abuse, in some cases of a gross and extensive kind over periods of years—as in the case of Father Fortune—were taken. Prosecutions had been successful and prison terms resulted. Yet this use of criminal law, in a precise and focused way—usually as a result of a complaint by a parent or a victim—seems to have absolved those senior members of the Church guilty of wider criminal actions; they had a duty to police the territories over which they exercised power and responsibility and to report all such crimes and not to protect anyone from pursuit and prosecution. They generally did the opposite, protecting those accused of abuse, 'moving on' recalcitrant priests to places where they continued to abuse, and ignoring the fact that such people were guilty of serious criminal offences.

In October 2002 Bishop Walsh said: 'Each of us has to be subject to the law of the land.' And he added, 'I should be subject to the law.' The Vatican did not then agree with him, and even today seems ambivalent on the issue of duty to the law. Nor does the Vatican agree with the American bishops who are now working along the same lines, that the criminal law of the United States takes precedence for them and for their Church over the canon law of the Church of Rome.

Ireland should of course have been the same, at that time, only more so. And that was the meaning of what Bishop Walsh said. He should have been joined in that statement by every bishop in the Irish Hierarchy. Any who found in the making of it a conflict of interest or a clear case where they had flouted that legal priority of the State over the Church should no longer be in charge of other clerics.

The State did not recognise this, did not assert its primacy. It had not then called on the Church to make itself fully subject to the law of the land, nor has it done so explicitly since. It may arguably have reason for respecting certain things within the Church, such as the confidentiality of the confessional. But in respect of crime, and particularly of serious crime, there are no two ways in which citizens can travel. They may not board a train protected by canon law and behave differently from the way other people behave while on it. They must abide by the law.

The Government's record was particularly derelict in respect of the agreement it reached with the Church on a compensation package, which is the subject of the next chapter. It was to prove a breaking point in the confidence of the abused in the Government's actions supposedly on their behalf. After it became public, the numbers of victims rose steadily.

Their cry for help and justice, especially after the showing of the RTÉ documentary *States of Fear*, came out of a grim silence on the part of the State and the Church; the resultant anguish of their suffering was all the more poignant because of this. Those who suffer abuse suffer it lifelong. This is not just the case with sexual abuse; it also applies to the neglect of education, health and physical integrity—and wrongful criminal committal. They wanted a hearing. Many wanted vengeance for what was done to them by both the abuser and their protectors. During 2002 they saw a new expression of concern for the abused even if they had received a measure of compensation. And they were right.

Meanwhile, the Church continued to fumble behind closed doors, to deliver inadequate and confused messages, to deal in pity and apology. 'Mea culpa's' of a pathetic kind continued to be expressed without the Church confronting the central issue of criminal culpability. Cardinal Connell, in deference to the Judge Gillian Hussey Commission[4], hid behind inadequate and confined terms of reference. When these were announced, in April 2003, the narrow focus was clearly evident. The emphasis was on investigating the past and on confining Judge Hussey's investigation to 'complaints'.

We had already moved on. The baleful Church desire to explore 'pain' and 'feel it', as though it could possibly do any such thing, was moving into a different realm of criminal culpability. An RTÉ documentary programme at the time reminded us of this central fact. We were dealing—or should have been—with something that was way out in the sea of criminal distrust and not concerned any more with discovering how much pain was caused and how deep the damage may have been.

---

4   Judge Gillian Hussey chaired a Catholic Church Commission to Inquire into Child Sexual Abuse, mainly in diocesan settings.

PART THREE

Exposing State and Church

Chapter 11 ∾

| THE SECRET DEAL

The handling of the devastation caused by Father Seán Fortune should have strengthened the hands of those trying to sort out the shattered lives of the men and women who had suffered in the industrial schools and reformatories of Ireland. The general tone of the questions being asked by the State and its fair and open response to the shocking events should have reinforced the case made by Ms Justice Mary Lafoy against obstruction and prevarication by the Department of Education. The publication of the Secret Deal, early in 2003, should have further altered the circumstances surrounding the investigation of institutional abuse out of which a more transparent and realistic justice for the abused could emerge. Sadly, neither event had such a beneficial result. In each case the opposite transpired.

Michael Woods signed the Secret Deal—the indemnity agreement between Church and State—in his capacity as Minister for Education on 5 June 2002. This was after the general election, but before the appointment of the new administration, led by Bertie Ahern. Woods continued to hold his appointment as Minister for Education during that brief period after the 2002 general election result was declared. He was to lose the Education portfolio when the new Government was appointed. He had no moral authority to take so momentous a decision; he did so without debate at Cabinet which from a legal perspective may very well have been a constitutional impropriety. He also did it without the Cabinet being made aware of any adjudication by the Attorney General. It was wrong, but it clearly indicated that the State's attitude to the Church was an unchanged subservience. As for the abused: they were being treated as callously as they had been from the start. When in due course they learnt the full facts, they were no longer in a mood to settle for the miserable deal done between Church and State at that time. Yet what could they do about it?

The deal between the Irish State and the 'Contributing Congregations' was followed by a statement in which Michael Woods, the sole Government signatory, claimed that it marked 'the commitment of the government and the congregations, together, to help people who have been hurt as children to find some peace and comfort in their lives'.

On the Church's side, 14 representatives of religious organisations signed.

They represented the reformatories, industrial schools and children's homes among the various institutions listed in an appendix at the end of the Residential Institutions Redress Act 2002. This had been passed in the outgoing Dáil.

The Department of Education consistently blocked attempts to get the full Agreement, under the Freedom of Information Act on the grounds of 'legal privilege'. The worries were numerous. The Church donation was fixed. The claims from abused people were an unknown quantity, with a cost that no one had measured.

On behalf of the *Irish Independent*, I obtained the Agreement and published the details. The picture that emerged was one of a seriously flawed set of commitments by the State, an impregnable position given to the Church, and the concealment of a number of very serious clauses which were in conflict with the legislation passed by the Oireachtas, with the spirit of the Apology given by the Taoiseach in May 1999, and clearly at odds with virtually everything said by the Minister in putting through the relevant legislation in the Dáil between 2000 and 2002.

Two things stood out above all else. The first was that the cost, to the taxpayer, was open-ended. No one had any clear idea of how much would be involved and where it would lead. No one saw how the truly dreadful levels and types of abuse perpetrated in the prison-like institutions covered by this Agreement would emerge in monetary terms. Yet the deal that was struck established a finite payment by the Church, whereas that of the State was infinite.

The second was that the Agreement, in much of its material detail, was a pact designed to involve the State in the protection of the Church, and of itself, against the abused. That this was the view, anyway, of Michael Woods is evident in the drafting of the legislation during the previous two years. The Residential Institutions Redress Act, for example, has many clauses protective of the individuals from religious communities together with their institutions, while it imposes penalties on the abused if they give wrong information, or if they disclose details of claims made by them.

What was not made at all clear was the fact that the Agreement contained detailed Church covenants to help the State 'in the defence of claims'. This was not revealed until the *Irish Independent* published that aspect of the Secret Deal. This Clause, number six, simply ran against the spirit of what was publicly claimed when the Agreement was signed.

The Minister, in his press release, claimed 'a process of independent arbitration'. There were two processes for dealing with differences outlined in the document. Neither was by arbitration. In fact the term 'arbitrator' is specifically ruled out in favour of an 'expert' whose decision will be 'final and binding'.

In broad summary, the deal struck the previous summer, between the Government and the Roman Catholic Church, over child sex abuse, was demonstrably contrary to the interests of abuse victims. It contained the clear intention of defending the State against claims by people who had been abused.

The Church comprehensively committed itself to 'assist the State' in the defence of claims in any legal proceedings, currently and into the future. It did not embrace abuse cases that had occurred after the introduction of the scheme. The document was a form of covenant between the Ministers for Education and Finance and the signatories of different orders involved in residential care. There were clauses indicating unity of resistance against the claims for redress under the Residential Institutions Redress Act.

The covenant gave details of the Church's modest financial contribution to the State. Some of these figures had already been released and were widely criticised. The cash contribution was €41.14 million. Of this sum, €12.7 million was ostensibly for 'education'. Parts of this sum had been either disbursed or promised to organisations that had no professional involvement in education. The balance of the Church's contribution was in land. The ownership of and rights to some of the property were disputed. These figures, represented by cash and kind, were trivial when compared with the huge sums involved in the Redress Act. These are conservatively estimated to run to €500 million, but could easily exceed €1,000 million and perhaps much more. This would depend on the fairness of the redress process and its compatibility or otherwise with court settlements. Though the covenant was made by the Ministers for both Finance and Education, the administrative control was with the Department of Education.

The Agreement materially qualified the terms of that Act and was contrary to the public interpretation of the Act's purposes given by Michael Woods, who as Minister for Education steered the legislation through the Houses of the Oireachtas and subjected it to unacceptable guillotine measures. He was principally responsible for negotiating the deal with the Church, and with what are called 'the Contributing Congregations' drawn from the Conference of Religious of Ireland, (CORI).

In the Agreement, the State covenanted and agreed 'to fully and completely indemnify each of the Contributing Congregations'. This included redress awards and court awards that were related to redress appeals. It also included current court proceedings which might become applications for redress. The blanket indemnity covered threats of litigation and requests for records or information.

In all these circumstances the State took over responsibility for the legal defence of the Contributing Congregations. There was conflict of interest between this legal undertaking to the Church and the purpose and intent of the Residential Institutions Redress Act as it had been presented for enactment. Publicly the State, through the former Minister for Education as well as in the declared purpose of the Act, undertook to care for those who had been abused. Privately, through the covenant contained in the Secret Deal, the State undertook to throw all its resources behind the Church and defend its position against claims.

The indemnity covered all the relevant institutions that are listed in the schedule to the Redress Act.[1] These were the institutions of so-called 'care' likely to be indicted by the abuse victims in their evidence generally, whether publicly or privately to the Commission or in individual submissions to the Redress Board. Also included were institutions and places that might, at some future date, be added to the list by ministerial order. Blanket provision for this was given authority in the Act. There were lawyers at the time who considered that this provision, along with many others, greatly exceeded the constitutional powers normal to Oireachtas legislation.

The indemnity extended to 'each and every member, and former or deceased member, of any religious body or congregation of the Contributing Congregations'. The State undertook, when requested, to take over defence in any legal action taken against the indemnified individuals and institutions.

The Church signatories included the Congregation of Our Lady of Charity of the Good Shepherd, responsible for the Magdalen laundries, the Rosminians, who ran the Drumcondra Homes for Blind and Deaf Children, the Congregation of Oblates of Mary Immaculate, responsible for the Daingean reformatory and for ministries among young men in London, the Christian Brothers and several orders involved in running children's homes.

The abuse victims, who were assured of help and sympathetic hearings, were undoubtedly faced with a deal prejudicial to their interests, a stalemate comparable to that faced by the Lafoy Commission. The general terms of this and their impact on the abused men and women were fully recognised by Ms Justice Lafoy at the time.

Further grim details of the implications of the Michael Woods–CORI Agreement later emerged. Most significantly, the terms of the signed covenant acknowledged no liability at all for abuse. The State and the Church were mutually excused responsibility. Payments made to abused victims, of both Church and State, represented no admission of liability or of responsibility for the damage concerned. On this broad but highly important issue alone, the contrast between this deal and the procedures that were covered by the Ferns Inquiry and the Report, when it was published, are striking.

The indemnity deal covered the religious congregations, the institutions they ran, the places where they ran them, and all the people involved. This applied whether they were living or dead. All were indemnified against making any defence whatever against claims lodged by victims. The only exception to this is when a religious organisation sought to vindicate its reputation, or that of an individual, when it could repossess itself of the proceedings.

The first four pages, consisting of six main paragraphs out of the 12-page Agreement, between Church and State, are concerned with this process of legal and mutual self-protection. They conclude with the covenant made by the Church 'to undertake to assist the State Party in the defence of claims which come within the Scheme made in any legal proceedings that are now in being or may be issued in the future'.

1   The Redress Act 2002 also lists some institutions that are relevant for legal reasons but were not institutions with children in their care.

Though strenuously opposed by the Church, the State insisted in this final paragraph that clerical institutions would bear the cost of record retrieval. Though this was a trifle within the main financial burden, it is worth stating that it was in part written off, since record retrieval remained inadequate, incomplete, as well as lacking transparency and answerability. Ms Justice Mary Lafoy did insist on widespread record delivery to the Commission, but the abused continued throughout the whole process to have difficulty obtaining records of their lives as State prisoners. Neither the State nor the Church, at any point in the Agreement, where it was concerned with claims by abused people, made any reference to their protection, in administrative or legal terms. The balance of the Agreement was about money and property.

There was one serious issue on which the secret Agreement between the Church and State was in conflict with the Residential Institutions Redress Act. In Regulations for this Act it is stated that religious representatives 'who wish' to co-operate with the Redress Board have the choice to do so. The Woods–CORI Agreement, in exchange for the various indemnities it contains, imposes on all religious communities the clear and inescapable obligation 'to assist the State Party in the defence of claims'. It seemed to those men and women who had been abused that a wall of stone had been constructed and they were waking up to the reality that they would have to prepare to hurl themselves against it in pursuit of the supposed settlement of their long-standing and legitimate grievance against the State.

In his Second Stage speech to the Dáil, introducing the Residential Institutions Redress Act at the beginning of 2002, Michael Woods had given a bland and generalised picture of the climate in which abuse had developed in the institutions of residential care. He suggested official neglect, with the Churches and charities stepping in to help. It was, he said, 'difficult and largely unrewarded work'. He claimed it had been improved a bit by the Children Act of 1908. As late as 1970, however,

> … the Kennedy Committee found that the industrial and reformatory schools were housed in old and often unsuitable buildings, the institutions were under staffed by under trained or untrained personnel, the emotional needs of the children were not catered for even though they came from backgrounds of deprivation, an institutional approach prevailed, and financial provision made by public bodies was inadequate as was the system of inspection.

Woods claimed that this litany of deficiencies was as much the fault of contemporary Irish society and its leaders, as it was the fault of managers of the schools who, in many cases, were making do with the few resources they got.

> Should it surprise us then that many children suffered emotional neglect, were hungry and poorly clothed, that corporal punishment was frequent and that

the regime in most of the institutions could best be described as harsh?

That was his version, and it was designed to spread the blame over us all, embracing the Church, but identifying no real culprits. The true picture, much of which has been referred to in different contexts in earlier chapters, was quite different. Abuse was not the fault of Irish society, it was the fault of Government, and, more specifically, of successive Ministers for Education and the Department of Education.

Chapter 12 ❧

| THE MONEY TRAIL

T
he managers of the industrial schools, despite their constant claims for more money, never had to 'make do'. There had always been sufficient funding. In the harsh economic climate of the 1920s and 1930s, in the difficult period of the Second World War and its aftermath, conditions generally had been Spartan. But the industrial schools had been sensibly funded. In part the funding process was a macabre one. It depended on a high level of internees. The more children there were in the industrial schools, the more money they got. On the arithmetic of scale alone, this made good sense. But, as Frank Duff, the founder of the Legion of Mary, wrote to Archbishop McQuaid in 1941, the State 'simply shovelled children into Industrial Schools'.[1] They were regularly 'shovelled in' for the full period allowable under the law, the end of their sentence being the statutory date—the day before their sixteenth birthday. The court committal documents have this as a common feature.

It was what happened then that mattered. Those who managed the institutions had, quite simply, perverted the law and misused the funding. There can be no other explanation for the impoverishment, the starvation, the lack of medical care, proper diet, education on the scale maintained elsewhere in the Irish education system. Nor is there any alternative explanation than this for the fact that no accounting took place, no accounts were submitted to the Department; expenditure on the children was a private and secret matter, directly related to the widespread testimony from the abused about their constant and abject impoverishment. The issue of funding was regularly raised by the religious orders or managers running the institutions. This came in the form of requests for increases. Yet the per capita grant for the boys and girls was roughly equal to an agricultural labourer's wage for much of the period of Irish independence. The Department less regularly raised the issue of accounting. It appears that, on behalf of the State, they sought more information and the industrial school inspectorate may or may not have prompted it.

A good example of how this relationship over funding operated is given in the Third Interim Report of the Lafoy Commission, in respect of the Baltimore

---

[1]   I am indebted to Finola Kennedy for this information. Further detail on Frank Duff and the Legion of Mary appears below, Chapter 15.

Fisheries School. Between 1939 and 1947 Dr Anna McCabe, who had been appointed the Department of Education's medical inspector for industrial schools in 1938, filed reports. Those that have survived are of irregular dates during that period. The documentation for the school is not complete. An affidavit of discovery was obtained from the Department of Education by the Commission which declared itself satisfied that it had obtained all surviving material and that 'there is little point in trying to trace the missing documents'. A wider examination of the conditions in the Baltimore Fisheries School will be found in Chapter 15. Here it is sufficient just to dwell on the evidence from Dr McCabe's reports indicating that no material improvements in the school, no evidence of the expenditure of money on necessary improvements, was ever found during her series of visits. The building needed repair, the sanitary arrangements were inadequate, the children drank their tea from chipped mugs and jam jars, the salt at mealtimes was scattered loose on the tables, the boards of which were not washed down after meals, the crockery was badly cracked or broken, clothing was 'too patched', children did not have individual toothbrushes and there were cases of gingivitis, inflamation of the gums, one of many poverty-associated infections or illnesses common in the industrial school system. Dr McCabe found, during her visits, that bread on the tables was 'really mouldy'—the result, she was told, of the baker providing the school having 'a monopoly for bread in Skibbereen'.

The account of Dr McCabe's reporting suggests confusion in her own mind about what she found and about how it should be dealt with. Notwithstanding the conditions, the boys 'looked well, clean and happy'. Despite all her criticisms between 1939 and 1945, she reported in July of the latter year that 'nothing had been done' and that 'general slackness prevailed'. In 1946 she said 'to see the boys washing there has to be seen to be believed!' Dr McCabe's exclamatory but not very informative reporting was frequently demonstrated; she clearly could not believe what she was seeing on each visit, but it did not include the expenditure of money. Nevertheless, side by side with these grim details, from 1937, well before her first visit, Bishop Patrick Casey, chairman of the governors, was making constant representations to the Department, in writing and in person, for more boys. He specified that Baltimore 'was not getting its fair share of transfers'. (This was the transfer of pupils from junior industrial schools.)

This was the actual record, despite the fact that the financial provisions were adequate, and the feeding and clothing of inmates could have been properly organised, as could their education and training. The system of inspection could have been a good one, and had previously, under British administration, worked well, as far as can be ascertained. However, its inadequacy and feebleness is clearly indicated in the muddled responses, year by year, of Dr McCabe and in the failure of the inspectorate, and of the Department as a whole, to effect real change. The overwhelming, unanswered question remains: what happened to the money?

The sufferings of the children that Michael Woods refers to should surprise us, since they were neither necessary nor ordained. It was a regime imposed both deliberately and arbitrarily and it did untold damage. No one within the system tried to stop it. The strange position adopted by Dr McCabe, as revealed in her surviving reports on the Baltimore Fisheries School, seemed to consist of a mixture of cajolery and mild ticking off. And while the weighty figure of the Inspector of Industrial and Reformatory Schools, a statutory officer, was more authoritative, he seems to have dealt in minor matters like the scattering of the salt on the bare boards of the dining tables.

In most cases, those who held positions of responsibility or authority turned a blind eye. The Kennedy Report, praised vastly beyond what it merits, as we have seen, was also wrong in its analysis, and reprehensively so because it knew, and ignored, the valuable contribution made by the OECD Report of 1965 which dealt with reformatory and industrial schools, and gave the lead to Kennedy, a lead not properly followed.

The State on its foundation in 1922 inherited what was regarded as an effective piece of legislation, the Children Act of 1908, controlling institutional care and covering the administration of all institutions for children, including industrial schools, orphanages, homes for disabled children and ordinary children's homes. The Act, as far as parallel care in the United Kingdom was concerned, had been superseded, through the widespread introduction of reforms and changes in administrative procedures. Again detrimentally, these were largely ignored in Ireland after independence, and, since the main Act governing the industrial schools was a different Act from the one for the United Kingdom, this also remained largely intact in the Irish Free State. It was this Act that governed the 'Rules and Regulations for Industrial Schools and Reformatories'.

The State inherited sound rules of conduct and management in the institutions, but failed to update them or regulate the details. The new Redress Act of 2002 listed more than 100 institutions, most of which were in existence or came into existence during the early life of the State.

The administration was the responsibility of the Department of Education. The Children Act of 1908, bringing in what were largely retrospective reforms designed to update a creaking and outdated system, was a dedicated legislative instrument, but a crude and blunt one. It does not deserve all the praise it gets. Within the United Kingdom it was superseded piecemeal during the following three decades. In Ireland it was kept, like the Tablets brought down by Moses. Its administration as law had to be in conjunction with the Rules and Regulations. These laid down standards for clothing, food, education, training and discipline. There was a countrywide inspectorate. This group of public servants was required to carry out annual inspections and file reports. The institutions had to have a manager who was answerable to the State. In all these component parts there was malfunction and indiscriminate disregard.

The inspectorate reports, when they are not missing, are still in the

Department. They are an intermittent record. As with Baltimore and Dr McCabe, they were confused. There seems to be some evidence of the concealment of what at times was a collapse of the system in individual schools. A notable case was Daingean reformatory, the subject of an adverse judgment in the Kennedy Report. It is an example of the way the inspectors and the State, intimidated by the Church, failed totally to carry out their assignment required by law under the 1908 Act. The system had been designed to ensure the proper upbringing of the inmates, boys and girls. Instead, those administering it sanctioned the almost complete abrogation of control and protection. This led to educational neglect and the climate or culture of uncontrolled cruelty caused by neglect, indifference and brutality. The culture extended to sexual exploitation, and in some cases led to the maiming and deaths of children. For years the majority of these children were underfed, and suffered disablement as a result. There was adequate money to feed them, provided by the State; clearly, it was widely sequestered and used for other things by the managers. The disciplinary regimes were appalling. The institutions were far worse than the most brutal of prisons, and lacked any of the restrictive controls that the State exercises within its prison system.

When the issue of child abuse became the great shame faced by the country, it was realised by many people, and certainly by Michael Woods well before he became Minister for Education, that there was some benefit to the State—and in a sense to the Church—if the burden of blame were somehow to be shared, blurred and diluted. It was always seen that the Church had compensating factors in its favour. It could claim good works, and it could rely on the faith of many of its supporters. The enormities were presented at first as isolated ones, or as the crimes of individuals. Admissions of wholesale abuse, neglect or cruelty were very slow to emerge, as were apologies and recompense.

But whatever might have been the problems facing the Church, it was recognised from an early stage that the Department of Education had no such sympathy in its favour. As a consequence, the neglect and indifference of the Department and its inspectors had been protected. It was essential to recognise that, while the widespread abuse was taking place in Artane and other institutions, the reports that went to the Department can have given no expression at all of unease over what was happening, since the Annual Reports are regularly anodyne and uncritical. The general situation throughout the system was known. It was known to inspectors. It was known to the Cussen Committee and the Kennedy Committee. This was true, not just occasionally, but year on year and decade on decade.

The law, represented by a sound but loosely-worded administrative weapon, the Children Act, and by additional legislation, was almost completely ignored, save in one respect—the comprehensive and widespread committal of children for long terms of childhood imprisonment. The State did not deal openly and fairly with the problem of abuse when it was happening. It has not dealt openly and fairly with it since the Taoiseach's Apology. The Secret Deal is further proof of this. The State chose to see nothing of what went on. No action was taken on foot of any report. No prosecutions were pursued. With one or two exceptions, already referred to, no managers were rebuked, removed or imprisoned.

At this midway stage—2002 to 2003—in the increasingly alarming evolution of the story of institutional abuse, there was still a view that the number of abused was modestly estimated at around 2,500. The global, average figure for Redress Board compensation was expressed as €50,000. The real figure for the number of abused men and women was rather different. The organisations that had come into existence during the early years following the Ahern Apology were presenting the total number at around 20,000.

Michael Woods was in charge during much of the work of setting up this falsely persuasive answer to abuse. He joined the Cabinet subcommittee on Abuse when he was Minister for—of all things—the Marine. He took overall charge of legislation and negotiations from 2000 until the passage of the Residential Institutions Redress Act in 2002. After the election, he went to the backbenches.

Michael McDowell was one influential lawyer who was involved in much of the preparatory discussion of the issue of abuse in the industrial schools and reformatories. His voice is important in the context of what had happened under the previous administration and also after the change of Government, in the summer of 2002. Michael McDowell had become Minister for Justice in the new 2002 Coalition Government led by Ahern, in which McDowell's party, the Progressive Democrats, was an important partner. He had been Attorney General from 1999 to 2002. He made clear, in a radio interview, that he was involved in what he called 'the discussion stage' of the controversial deal between Church and State on the abused. This was not strictly true; he took over a process that predated his appointment. 'The Attorney General,' he is reported as saying, 'was involved in discussions of legal principles and all the implications involved.' In the interview he went further than other members of that Government in accepting wide State responsibility, saying that the State 'caused the children to be lodged there [in the institutions]', and that the State had been 'derelict in its duty'. He made one other important point, which is dealt with below, when he said: 'The State Redress Scheme won't need strict proof, adversarial justice or courtroom procedures.'

There were serious questions attaching to McDowell's more general remarks about the State's culpability in respect of the abused. This admission, with all that it implied, had been long awaited by the vast majority of people who were abused while in institutional care or custody—mostly custody. Michael McDowell, as a talented advocate, was always precise in his use of language, and when he said 'the State caused the children to be lodged there', he must have known what he was talking about. This was not just in the general sense, but as a legally loaded interpretation of events. We are dealing with a story of denial and this is a further dimension of it. Essentially, the children were denied their legal and constitutional rights in many of the instances where they were 'lodged' in institutions. McDowell must also have been aware—as the legal officer of the Government when it was considering the 'principles and all the implications'— of the many letters and other appeals made by victims of abuse other than sexual abuse. Finally, he must have been aware of the significant differences there are between the abuse of legal and constitutional rights, and the fundamentally different, covert and secretive sexual abuse that went on, mainly in hidden places, in the reformatories and industrial schools.

As far as can be ascertained, the inspectors, throughout the whole period in which the Irish Gulag operated, simply failed to do their job properly. They failed in respect of ensuring proper education. They overlooked children being used as slave labour when they should have been at their desks being properly taught. They failed to guarantee housing, warmth, clothing and adequate food. They failed to protect children from a bewildering array of punishments. They failed to ensure the fulfilment of a fundamental family right, by separating children from the same families. In some cases, brothers and sisters, who may have been committed as infants, were together in institutions without being told of their siblings' existence, let alone their presence near to them. The greater part of these failures belonged in a territory quite different from that of sexual abuse.

In accepting blame on behalf of the State for dereliction of duty, what was Michael McDowell really doing? Few lawyers know better than he does the constitutional rights and the legal rights that were thrown over in so many cases. Making the blanket *mea culpa* that he does, and by implication dividing two different types of wrong, he seemed to me, at the time, to have been suggesting or inviting a fresh approach. Could it be that he envisaged a two-tier system of recompense and reconciliation? Only this would cater for the widely different emotional, psychological and legal approaches demanded by the circumstances.

At one level, that of the State's broad failure to protect the educational rights, the freedom, the justified appeals for release that were never made on behalf of children, never heard by the courts, and never acted on, Michael McDowell was responding more generously than any former minister. What he was really saying was the following: we, the State, were wrong; they, the abused, were wronged. And he arguably invited the charting of a mechanism whereby the State could rectify this in a way that did not, and should not, require the complex establishment of the material case of the abused.

If the State so chose, it could simply have paid a basic initial sum of between €10,000 and €20,000 to the 20,000–25,000 men and women whom, by everyone's acknowledgment, it had treated so unfairly. Such a payment could have been based on one simple and overwhelming event, one that deserved such an initial financial recompense. This was the single, colossal indignity and legal enormity of committing them for excessive terms in prison when they were guilty of no crime. The conditions that followed such committal, in respect of what should have been 'child care', had been widely revealed and were as widely acknowledged by the State, from the Taoiseach down. There should have been redress for that and it could have been made without conceding the potential claims of abuse in individual cases.

The powers for this were put into the Redress Act but could have preceded that legislation in a simple and comprehensive response in line with the Apology. The cost of it would have been between €250 million and €500 million. Access to it should have been uncomplicated and ameliorative. We were not talking about forgiveness; we were talking about rights. Such a payment should have been accompanied by an expanded apology, indemnifying those people, many of whom, as children, were stigmatised as criminals. And this would have lifted from them the burden of shame that their past had laid against them.

They had never merited the punishing and exacting process the State has created for redress, nor does this particular deprivation have much to do with the religious orders. This State process of committal does not fall into the Secret Deal in the way that those who were sexually abused do. In this sense, such a recompense—and we, as a State, have always owed it to them—would not need to be related to that other, quite different matter, of the various forms of abuse, including sexual abuse.

When Michael McDowell made that other remark, that the 'State Redress Scheme won't need strict proof, adversarial justice or courtroom procedures', he was right only in respect of the non-sexual abuse dimension.

Another important contributor to the debate during the highly charged exchanges in early 2003 was Helena O'Donoghue. She signed the State–CORI Secret Deal on behalf of the Congregation of the Sisters of Mercy. She appeared on RTÉ radio and answered a question about the response to abuse claims. She said: 'We will not be contesting the evidence except in very exceptional circumstances.' She did not expand on this and the meaning was obscure. Is there any case of the sexual abuse of a child that is unexceptional? Educational abuse? Physical abuse? Health abuse? When children's teeth rotted in their heads or their eyesight was irreversibly damaged, was this 'unexceptional'?

It was becoming increasingly clear that the religious orders and the Church had a different interpretation of how to deal with sexual and physical abuse of children in their care from the views taken by the general public, by the abused themselves and by the law of the land. Yet here was a participant in the Secret Deal giving notice of legal contest in matters that had not been prescribed in any way. Sexual abuse cases would be contested. The preliminaries were already being contested by the religious. The Christian Brothers were blocking the Lafoy Commission's progress. They would do the same when the Redress Board started its hearings. In that same RTÉ interview, Helena O'Donoghue went on to say: 'We cannot as congregations be indicted as abusers.' This was not a healing approach. It was an adversarial one. The tone was conciliatory only in her general remarks; when it came to specifics, it was a declaration of future conflict and the message was a stark one. From her own point of view Sister O'Donoghue was right to say the congregations could not be indicted as abusers. The same view was held by the Dublin Diocese. What Sister O'Donoghue was giving publicly was just another indication of the rough times facing plaintiffs.

These views and positions adopted by people involved in, or privy to, the negotiations and the deals that had peppered the previous years were carefully noted by Opposition deputies, including the Fine Gael spokesperson on education and science, Olwyn Enright, who had identified the key issues surrounding the constitutional rights of the abused and was attempting to raise them in the Dáil. Joan Burton, Pat Rabbitte, Phil Hogan, Roisin Shortall and Jan O'Sullivan also pursued the issue of rights. They were among the politicians who stood up to the Church and saw its iniquities clearly and bravely.

Fianna Fáil politicians had a different view of things. A notable example was Michael Woods's successor in the Department of Education, Noel Dempsey. There was a view at the time that Dempsey would not be happy with certain provisions of the Act, some of which were extreme and inexplicable. Nor was he perceived as a politician favourably disposed towards any secret deal. Whatever he might do, however, the victims of abuse, alerted to the new situation, which seemed to be little short of a deliberate betrayal, were looking at everything with new eyes. Dempsey would need to tread carefully.

He was not all that careful, but he was determined. He agreed to an interview with Pat Kenny the following Monday. He did so in order to reply to the *Irish Independent* stories on child abuse in Irish institutions. He circumvented questions of secrecy by an adroit move. Kenny explored the secrecy issue, asking him, 'You say it's not a secret deal?' The Minister handed the document over the table and said: 'There's a copy of it.' He also expressed himself to be 'happy'. He was satisfied with the arrangements. Thus he closed off the kind of loophole politicians are often quite glad to be offered by saying that they would look into the issues that had been raised. Shortly afterwards Dempsey did the opposite with Ms Justice Mary Lafoy, whose public statements had challenged him and the Government. On her interventions, he said, on 20 December, that he would look into them again.

Despite Dempsey's gesture, the document was, both legally and in practice, a secret deal. Senior journalists who had been trying to obtain the Michael Woods–CORI Agreement under the Freedom of Information Act were still being denied it on grounds of 'legal privilege'. They were being denied all related files.[2]

At the very least the Minister was operating eccentrically when he calmly handed across the microphones to Kenny a seriously restricted document on which his department has claimed 'legal privilege'. It raised questions as to whether Dempsey himself was in breach of the terms of the Freedom of Information Act where it protects documents. Was he engaging in *lèse majesté*? Or was it just theatre, designed to pretend that, in the Irish jurisdiction, 'secret' means 'public'?

2   The journalists technically had to go to the Information Commissioner, who then had to seek from the Department reasons for the refusal before making a report. They had been overtaken by the events.

Would the Minister next tell us that the law does not mean what it says, it means what he says it does, depending on the context? This was roughly what he did say in the course of the interview with Pat Kenny. He suggested that the *Irish Independent* was taking a narrow view. What was required was 'the overall package'.

By this he meant the Redress Board, the Lafoy Commission to Inquire into Child Abuse and the Confidential Committee within that Lafoy Commission. Surprisingly, he did not add the Ryan Report and Bertie Ahern's speech as well. The law, with which he seemed to be playing, was at this stage represented by the Residential Institutions Redress Act, of 2002. But it was also represented by the Secret Agreement between the Government and CORI. He seemed reluctant, to the point of being cavalier, about the fact that in the end we are governed by the law, and not by the findings of commissions and committees, however important and valuable these may be. And if the law was wrong, or failed to embrace particular evils visited in the past on defenceless children, then 'the context', recommended by Dempsey, would rescue no one.

The Taoiseach's 1999 speech had contained vague and unsatisfactory undertakings and was very short on specifics. It should subsequently have gained precision and direction from Lafoy and from the Ryan Report. The Ryan Committee, chaired by Mr Justice Seán Ryan, was set up following publication of the Redress Bill—a quite different document from the Act that was passed two years later. It was a good committee, and its report—not followed—was a valuable contribution to the system that should then have constituted the legislation. It contained many useful aspects, including recommendations on payments, and on how to analyse abuse. These *were* recommendations for use by the Redress Board under the Act. But its precise relationship to the Redress Act, always tenuous, and contained in the Act's small print, is made even more so by the revelations of the Secret Deal so generously 'made public'—dare one say 'published'?—by the Minister when he handed it over to Pat Kenny. Where does the Redress Board lie when the Church and State have made a mutual defence covenant?

The Ryan Report, wrongly in my view, made an extraordinary exclusion order over a whole fact of abuse which was also missed by the legislation. A programme of legitimate and long-overdue assistance to those who had been abused was needed. It should have included counselling and was also meant to include education. On foot of its so-called 'outreach' structure, however, the Ryan Report made the extraordinary statement that 'some of the support services which might otherwise have to be taken into account in assessing the appropriate level of redress are already being provided by the State'. How could this possibly compensate for the past?

The abused had been deprived of a proper education for their whole term in detention. They had also been deprived of proper food, the clothing specified in the rules, as well as human and medical care. Was 'outreach' also 'backreach', solving those past indignities and acts of criminal neglect?

One abused victim described to me at the time working at lifting potatoes at 11 o'clock at night, by tractor lights, and being out in the daytime doing profitable manual, gardening or workshop tasks for which he got no pay and when he should have been at his books. He subsequently demonstrated, in his career, as many others did, his intellectual brightness. But the State and the Church rubbished that talent. Was that not abuse?

The Ryan Report also referred to how this and other elements in the programme of assistance, including the provision of counselling, psychiatric care, help for the groups that work for the abused survivors, had been put in place. But this had been done under the auspices of the Department of Education, potentially the key defendant, and arguably the most blameworthy single institution in the State dealing with abuse. It was a black and unfeeling place throughout the long and awful history of its perpetrations upon generations of young people.

Officials of the Department of Education were crawling all over the structures that had been set up to manage the whole abuse recovery regime. To its credit, the Ryan Report refers to this in critical, if oblique terms. It says:

> In July 2000 a firm of solicitors, on behalf of a number of solicitors who represent many—but not all—survivors of institutional child abuse, contended that 'the significant role to be played in the work of the [Lafoy] Commission by the Department of Education, its personnel and resources' constituted an unacceptable conflict of interest, particularly in the light of a denial of liability by that Department in civil proceedings brought by survivors.

This was now 10 times worse. The Department of Education had done everything in its power to eliminate independence on the part of those who should have been aiding the abused men and women in their search, not just for justice but for peace of mind as well.

There was clearly much to put right. Dempsey's first action should have been to make the covenant into a regulation within the Redress Act. He could have done this by ministerial order. This was a legally binding covenant and should have been an annexe or a regulation within the Redress Act. Opposition deputies should have been calling for that as a starting point to a reassessment of this legislation. Dempsey had the power to do this under Section 36 of the Act. It could then have been reconsidered by the Dáil and changed if the elected representatives so wished.

Unsurprisingly, none of this took place. The covenant had already been immunised from rewriting because of the mutual interests of the contracting parties. The Church, for very obvious reasons, had got out of the problem of dealing with the history and the cost of intolerable and persistent abuse for many decades. It had achieved this by a modest grant of cash to the State and the transfer of buildings. Some of these, it must be said, the State had handed back to the religious.

The State had also gained control of virtually the whole operation of dealing with abused people and their claims. It was funding the supposedly independent organisations representing the abused. It was helping to run NOVA, the umbrella organisation for abused people's groups. The Redress Act had placed the Redress Board directly under the Minister for Education. He had ultimate control over its operation. The State also controlled the Lafoy Commission.

Thus, in summary, the people whose lives were being allegedly helped had been abused in institutions in this State. These institutions had been run by the Church. They should have been inspected and controlled by the Department of Education. The many thousands of damaged and disturbed men and women whose lives have been wrecked were now even more confused by what was happening to them.

At the time, having written many articles, I was receiving individual testimonies to these disturbed and terrible lives. I never ceased to find them shocking and grotesque. They told a sad and shameful story of Irish social attitudes, supposedly of Christian behaviour, and of highly questionable principles of care over a long number of years. At this mid-point in the process of healing and recompense, the evidence was that we were *still* not being fair to the abused. We were prolonging their agony and confronting them with obstruction and illusion.

The central issue in the Church–State Secret Agreement signed on 5 June 2002 was the question of indemnity. In return for the paltry and disputed sum, either paid or to be paid, in cash and kind by the various congregations of the Church, the State was offering them indemnity funded by the taxpayer. It was increasingly clear that Irish taxpayers faced an unknown and growing burden. An estimate of €1 billion, published early in 2003 by the *Irish Independent*, was widely accepted. It was publicly accepted by the Labour Party. It was already beginning to look conservative in the light of new applications.

Department of Education attempts to ascertain the numbers of potential abuse cases had come up with approximately 23,500 inmates of industrial schools and reformatories born since January 1940 who were the most likely to take action against the State. Moreover, this figure applied only to those committed by court order. A further substantial number were committed under Department of Health legislation. Coming from dysfunctional families, or being the children of unmarried mothers, or other desertion cases, these were the most vulnerable, and often suffered the worst treatment. They entered industrial schools as young as one year and ten months. Their number is not recorded by the Department of Education.

The public attitude of the State was to wait and see, and was expressed in the quite unacceptable public response from the Minister for Education, Noel

Dempsey, which he made in answer to a parliamentary question asked by Phil Hogan. The question concerned three industrial schools or reformatories, in Cappoquin, Kilkenny and Clonmel, and covered the years from 1976 to 1996, a period in which abuse appeals would be concentrated. It is the period for which records were clearly in reasonable order and more accessible than those from the early years of the State, though increasingly the comprehensiveness of all these records—so long as no one is burning them—is indicated by private memoranda in the departments.

In view of this, the answer by the Minister was an extraordinary one. Referring to 'the extent to which officials of the Department of Education between 1976 and 1996 were aware of child sex abuse in three institutions', he told the deputy that

> ... to establish precisely what Departmental officials did or did not know in that period would require a thorough examination of a very significant number of documents. In addition it would be necessary to interview those members of staff who worked in the administration of the industrial and reformatory schools at the time and are still available for interview.

This work, he said, was being done by the Lafoy Commission. 'It is in that forum that the kind of inquiry which the Deputy seeks can best be carried out.' However, there was no mechanism for Deputy Hogan to get the information from Ms Justice Lafoy. He was precluded by legislation from asking questions in the Commission: he would not be answered. Commission matters were confidential. He had tried asking questions in the Dáil, and that is where they should have been answered. That is what the place was there for. And it was an insult by the Minister when he added: 'It would be neither effective nor appropriate for my Department to try to parallel the inquiries of the Commission.'

Yet his department had already paralleled the work of the Commission. Moreover, his department had assembled the information, or a great deal of it, and was holding it as part of the Secret Deal between Church and State. Held in Four Folders, called in the Secret Agreement 'Folder 1, 2, etc.', they were part of that deal. They were the only annexes to the legal covenant between CORI and the Government acting in the name of the taxpayers of the State. Where the Folders applied was in respect of other categories and it was in them that we were more likely to find the key to the answers to Phil Hogan's questions. Folder One contained material where court proceedings were issued before the date of the Secret Agreement. Folder Two contained material that referred to existing threats of litigation, either oral or written. Folder Three contained details of where people—presumably the abuse victims or their legal representatives—had requested records or information. Such requests were presumably to pursue a claim. Most extraordinarily of all, Folder Four contained the record number of 'each and every matter which is the subject matter of evidence to the Commission to Inquire into Child Abuse [the Lafoy Commission]'.

One other outcome of the CORI deal with the Government concerned the educational fund provided by the Church. The idea of making any provision to rectify the 'lost' education of those who had been institutionalised was not an element in the Taoiseach's speech of May 1999, but a sum of €12.7 million was included in the terms of the CORI Agreement. Just over a year after the signing of that deal, in mid-summer 2003, all was business on the education front. Advertisements in the newspapers, application forms, educational 'facilitators' and a vast committee were busy preparing how to spend the cash.

Almost every aspect of the process for this was wrong. What should have happened first, if the Department of Education and the Taoiseach were truly honouring the pledges made to the survivors of abuse in institutions, was the establishment of a proper statutory remedy for those seeking some replacement for the education of which they were deprived when in the institutions. This required a statutory provision, in the first instance backing up the €12.7 million with State funding; in the second, creating a grant application structure. This would make the approach not unlike the statutory provision the disabled enjoy, and about which they became so angry over Government concealment of cutbacks in advance of the Special Olympics in 2003.

The problem with the survivors of institutional abuse—including, of course, the serious deprivation of their education—is that they were far more numerous, and a very high percentage of them lived in the United Kingdom. Nevertheless, their right to recompense on the educational front was of significant importance, even at this late stage, and should have been arranged.

What in fact happened bordered on the ridiculous. The €12.7 million was handed over to the National Office for Victims of Abuse (NOVA), which itself is a potential recipient of part of the funding, creating an immediate conflict of interest. It is also the co-ordinating body for survivor groups. These offered generally low-grade educational opportunities. When the NOVA manager, Kevin Brady, spoke at a meeting of the Irish Survivors of Child Abuse (SOCA) in London at the end of March 2003, he listed 'basic literacy, self-development, computers, drama, art and music therapy' as educational options. And he quoted 'feedback' from lucky learners: 'Computers made me aware of classes. Now I am able to do anything I want. I am hungry for anything that is going.' 'At long last, I am learning how to shape a jumper that I can wear, all my own work.'

The audience Brady addressed—intelligent, alert, angry, demanding—was generally appalled that this was the educational level at which the Government's appointed disbursement of funding was aimed. It was so low-grade as to be absurd. And what followed was absurd also. A single education facilitator, operating from the NOVA offices in Dublin, was there to grapple with the vast complexities of providing some form of third-level education throughout the United Kingdom and in the Republic. It was a cipher for the act, not the act itself.

Realistically, the survivors needed access to funds that were denied them when young, when they should have had the full range of educational opportunity. This could be properly administered only by the same skills and resources that young people, mature students, intellectually disabled students, had the right to call on.

What was also made clear, and repeated to me on a visit to NOVA when I met Kevin Brady and the education facilitator, Eithne Doherty, was that the €12.7 million was unsupported by the broad range of State educational resources; when it ran out, that was it.

SOCA expressed grave misgivings at the time about the non-statutory basis of the NOVA operation, the failure to establish a proper Trust to control and monitor the money and its use, and the irresponsibility of allowing its provision on a finite basis without knowing whether or not the demand for educational help might exceed the available amount.

Clearly no proper research was carried out, either in Ireland or in the United Kingdom. No one knew, then or later, the level or extent of demand for education by those who spent their days lifting potatoes or being the equivalent of farmyard machinery like hay rakes, their fingers torn and blistered by stubble because they were softer and more vulnerable than the tines in forks.

The same SOCA spokespersons were filled with misgivings about other circumscribing constraints. Applicants for help had to have registered a complaint with the Redress Board. Spouses, who were not incarcerated, might apply. 'Funding may be made available for groups of survivors who come together.' How was that to be assessed? What would happen if they were refused? It was clear that specifically, according to the NOVA manager, Kevin Brady, in his speech in London in the spring of 2003, four survivor groups were put on the committee dealing with the money. Inevitably this meant others were excluded, while those on the committee were in a position to award money to their own survivor groups.

There were further serious questions as to how what was, in the short term, a huge sum of money transferred from CORI to the State was to be handed over without legal responsibility, either by the donor or the recipient. Self-styled 'Administrators of the Fund', NOVA did not accept that the Agreement—and the educational funding that was part of it—should have been annexed in some way to the Redress Act, which is the central piece of legislation covering the educational project.

Disbursement of the funding was another matter of potential confusion or worse. The obvious difficulty of finding those who had been abused and needed educational help was in part solved through the representative organisations. These included NOVA—already referred to above—which had various roles, one of them being liaison with representative bodies. Then there was SOCA UK, run by Michael Waters, IRISH SOCA, run in Dublin by John Kelly, with its English executives, Jim Beresford and Patrick Walsh, One in Four Ireland, the Aislinn Centre for Healing, run by Christine Buckley, Right of Place, Cork, and Right to Peace, Clonmel, run by Michael O'Brien.

There were many questions surrounding every aspect of this education fund, from its poorly controlled creation on. In the early stages, NOVA published discussion papers in which administrative procedures were examined. The idea of the fund being on a non-statutory basis was favoured. A further proposal was that a legal Trust of some kind would be too expensive to operate. This put the money and its control mechanisms into a kind of free fall, with its administration not having educational or financial controls or accounting.

The fund was given birth by means of the Secret Deal involving the Indemnity Agreement of 5 June 2002 between the State and 18 religious congregations. This supposedly gave it legal status. It was therefore not annexed to the Redress Act or to any other legal instrument.

Under the terms of the Agreement, there is provision for a sum of €12.7 million to be used for former residents and their families to facilitate them in accessing programmes.

Almost four years later, on 17 February 2006, the Minister for Education, Mary Hanafin, formally established the statutory body, the Education Finance Board (An Bord Airgeadais Oideachais). This different approach was provided for in the Commission to Inquire into Child Abuse (Amendment) Act 2005.

The statement about this claimed that 'prior to the establishment of the Board some expenditure from the fund was undertaken by an ad hoc committee which oversaw a parallel administrative scheme pending the enactment of the legislation'. This was not in fact the case. The enactment of legislation was not considered at the outset and it is reasonable to infer—though never publicly claimed—that it became subject to legislation because of the yawning gaps in which abuse of the fund could occur.

The Board was to pay grants to former residents of institutions and their relatives. This was to assist them with educational services. Very belatedly the Board was to publish criteria for the payment of such grants. The Board was appointed by the Minister. It was independent. Of its eight ordinary members, four were former residents of the institutions. The chairperson was Richard Langford. The members were Inez Bailey, John Brennan, Christine Buckley, Jacqui Kavanagh, Brian Mooney, Michael O'Brien, Jacinta Stewart and Patrick Walsh. Walsh was a leading figure in Irish SOCA and had been highly critical of the haphazard earlier administration of this fund.

The issue of the Folders was never properly investigated. The questions that were raised included the following: how did Lafoy Commission material, whether documents or records of documents, names or other details, get into Folder Four? Who controlled the Folders and where were they held? Were there dual versions kept separately, for Church and State?

Such transfers as were implicit here were not specifically authorised by the Commission to Inquire into Child Abuse Act of 2000. Quite the reverse; such material was covered by confidentiality clauses in the Act. The Secret Deal was not in place when the Act was passed, nor were the Folders in existence.

One of the implications was that the Church was running an effective intelligence service and could well have internal knowledge of everything going before the Lafoy Commission. What could not be in dispute, however, was the nonsense of Noel Dempsey's answer to Phil Hogan's question. Neither the Department of Education nor the Church could possibly have gone into the Secret Deal without recognising the gravity of what they contemplated in respect of the indemnity offered by the State to the Church. It was in the Church's interest to make sure every Folder had every relevant document in it. And it was in the Department's interest to revise and research the full remit of cases, complaints, reports, documents, memoranda and recorded phone calls bearing upon all abuse cases that were to be embraced in the Secret Deal.

So comprehensive was the State's offer of indemnity to the Church that, beyond the Folders, it comprehended litigation threats in the future. It comprehended future requests for information or records, future detail before Lafoy, and anything 'which a Contributing Congregation has inadvertently omitted to submit for inclusion in any one of Folders One to Four'.

I wrote at the time:

> Have we ever had the like of this in the history of the State? Have we ever had a parallel for the insolence of the Minister, telling a deputy in the Dáil that it would be 'neither effective nor appropriate' for the Minister to do what secretly he had already done? Or for the Minister to suggest that the deputy should do what the law precludes him from doing? Or for the Minister to defer from a 'thorough examination of a very significant number of documents' which must have been examined anyway in pursuit of the terms of the Secret Agreement?

At the time, the Redress Board was advertising for claimants. Those responding needed to be warned of the perilous difference between the State's public attitude of collective concern, and the private inconsistencies about critical information. In due course the Minister for Education, Noel Dempsey, replied to the series of articles by myself published in the *Irish Independent* in January 2003. It was published in the newspaper on 30 January.

The article was not written by Noel Dempsey. It came to the newspaper as a Word document from the desk of Tom Boland, Head of Policy in the Department of Education, a post to which he was promoted before Christmas 2002. There was a reshuffle of senior Department of Education personnel later, in 2003, and on 23 September Tom Boland left the Department of Education to become chief executive of the Higher Education Authority. He had overseen legal strategy during the whole period in which the policy on the victims of abuse in the industrial schools had been constructed. The Word document was initially entitled by Boland 'Providing redress to people who as children suffered abuse while in residential care must be primarily concerned with the need'. These words express the line taken by Noel Dempsey when he appeared on *Prime Time* on RTÉ.

The article was completed a week before it was sent in, at the time when Minister Dempsey originally asked for right of reply. It went through three departmental revisions. The full, final text appears as Appendix 3.

The article's defence of the Minister seemed comprehensive enough, but Noel Dempsey's arguments were countered in a letter to the *Irish Independent* from Dagenham, in Essex, written by Ron McCartan.[3] Moreover, since the Redress Board now had Senior Counsel looking into its own legality, there was obviously a question over that. The legal position was further undermined: the Minister did not conform to the Statutory Instruments Act of 1947 when he signed the crucial ministerial orders immediately before Christmas, sending the signed instrument—the Establishment Day Order—to the Redress Board by fax!

What was significant about Tom Boland's authorship of the Minister's reply was the fact that Boland, only recently made Head of Policy in the Department, was the key figure with Michael Woods in the processing of redress and Lafoy legislation and administration. Perhaps most important of all, he was the key figure behind the Secret Deal.

Boland was brought into the public eye during the course of the two parliamentary committee investigations. Public interest concentrated on how a deal with the Church could have been made with so many advantages to the Church and so few to the State. The issue of taxpayers' money was quite properly central.

Also necessary and important was the investigation by the Dáil of how the supposedly compassionate arrangements for those who had been sexually abused in institutions were constructed. Under normal Statute of Limitation constraints, both in civil and criminal action, there were time limits. These, generally speaking, had precluded the victims of widespread deprivation in the reformatories and industrial schools from their legal rights. This was done because the State, for reasons that could be seen as compassionate, but could also be seen as devious, limiting and self-serving, singled out sexual abuse for Statute delimitation in respect of the wrong done. This allowed appeal, or court action, depending on the chosen route taken by the abused.

What was puzzling was the deliberate choice of sexual, as opposed to other, abuse. Sexual abuse is the most contentious of the various forms of abuse. It is obviously one of the most damaging, and the kind of abuse most likely to be vigorously fought or concealed. It is also the form of abuse that was most private in the institutions referred to, and therefore the form of abuse least applicable to the charge that the State was negligent in its duty to protect the children through a regime of inspection and control. This meant a compelling focus on the Church and the religious organisations that ran the institutions, and away from the State. The State in fact was hugely vulnerable to a whole range of fundamental abuse of the rights of the children it committed—'condemned and imprisoned' might be

---

3   In 2007 McCartan successfully sued the State, winning a substantial award. He had never subscribed to the redress system.

a better phrase—to these places.

The rights to sentence review, not to be committed at all and to have other options investigated were all ignored. In many cases warrants and court orders were invalid. Charges were wrong. But this was not part of the enlarged Statute of Limitation remit.

The Taoiseach, Bertie Ahern, entered the fray at the beginning of February 2003. He spoke in the Dáil on the position of the CORI side of the Secret Deal between Church and State. He reminded us that Church coffers were not bottomless. He also warned of the dangers of a witch hunt directed against religious organisations that were responsible, for well over a century, for the young girls and boys committed to them.

The grave difficulties that were being faced by everyone involved in the issue of child abuse in reformatories and industrial schools were huge in number and the efforts being made to resolve them were complex. Central to these difficulties was the Secret Deal of 5 June 2002. The Taoiseach was questioned on this in the Dáil, particularly in respect of the indemnity. He made the case that the religious organisations might be 'destabilised' if too much cash were demanded of them.

For his answer to have had any validity, however, it would have been necessary to demonstrate that the CORI side of the deal presented the State with a full record of its properties and other financial holdings and that these were assessed by the State in the context of the deal that was then struck. Without such actuarial assessment, the appeal implicit in the Taoiseach's reply, on behalf of the Church organisations involved, was merely an emotional one unsupported by the kind of evidence that was crucial in the circumstances. Factually he was wrong to claim that the Church organisations did what they did 'on behalf of the State'. They were paid to do it, and they did it with enthusiasm for three reasons: firstly, it was profitable, in giving them labour to help in the often extensive output of the institutions—they were, after all, 'industrial' schools; secondly, there were the per capita payments, which not only kept pace with inflation but were also parallel with the average agricultural wages, more than sufficient for the care that was needed; finally, it brought 'souls' within the Church's remit.

These were simply not organisations or institutions that had been imposed on by the State and it was disingenuous of Ahern to say they were. But it was consistent with the general slant of his attitude on the industrial schools. These were not religious bodies that had generously undertaken to help out Ireland in redressing the hurt and damage done to generations of Irish children unable to fend for themselves or rely on their parents.

In the arrangements that led to the remarkably short-sighted agreement, potentially of great embarrassment to the Government, and expensive for the taxpayer, the only justifications for fixing on a figure which accommodated the resources of the religious organisations had to depend on proper audit. In the circumstances, where there was so much disparity between Church and State, the Government was entitled to know what the religious owned. The Government was also entitled to a moratorium on the disposal of assets. Finally, the Government was entitled to clear covenants from the religious in respect of their total worth. There is no evidence that any of this was covered.

Even the fulfilment of these conditions, had it taken place, hardly justified a deal that involved the State in granting blanket indemnity to the religious in terms of legal action, and exempted them from all but a limited and increasingly small percentage of the likely total cost of the redress to victims of abuse.

Public outrage was tempered by a sensible and indeed compassionate judgment of the work done for good by the organisations involved in the Secret Deal. Little was known, either of good or evil, about these groups. But the present circumstances were concerned with another dimension, that of extensive abuse for which the State has promised redress.

The progress of that redress at this stage, in the early part of 2003, was in a state of uncertainty, confusion and, in certain circumstances, chaos. The Lafoy Commission was effectively stalled. The State-funded centre for the organisations of abused people, NOVA, was losing the confidence of its members. The organisations working for the abused were uncertain about the State's commitment, uncertain about each other, and uncertain about the lawyers working on behalf of individual claimants under the scheme.

The Redress Board was uncertain about its legal position. Despite the assertions by the Minister for Education, Noel Dempsey, writing in reply to articles in the *Irish Independent*, that nothing illegal had happened in the setting up of the Redress Board, the Board asked for Senior Counsel's legal opinion on its status, and this was awaited.

The Department of Education became involved in work on behalf of the organisations for the abused. It offered funding and educational help to SOCA UK, Right of Place, the Aislinn Centre for Healing, One in Four, and to other organisations. It helped to fund venues used for meetings of the abused. It did so without revealing the Secret Deal with CORI and the deal's mutual arrangement over the defence of legal and other challenges. Once this became known, it inevitably represented a conflict of interest. Though details became clearer, they did not become transparent.

The CORI parties to the Secret Deal, according to the list of financial, property and service provisions outlined in the document, were directly involved in counselling the victims of abuse who were abused in the institutions they operated. This also represented a considerable conflict of interest issue. In many cases the origins and religious associations of those engaged in such work were concealed.

Though much of the Secret Deal was suspect, a good part of it was also potentially beneficial. The deal included provisions, in Section 16, for disputes and their resolution. The State and the Contributing Congregations can 'meet and endeavour to resolve . . . dispute in good faith and in an expeditious manner'. There was a 30-day time limit. If this failed, there was still provision for resolving difference by calling in an independent expert who, if agreement on the person were not forthcoming, should be the President of the Law Society of Ireland. His or her decision, according to the Deal, would be final. It was clear how serious and comprehensive this document was. It derived exclusively from the two defendant organisations. This was without the knowledge of, or consultation with, those whose rights had been affected. From the beginning, with the Taoiseach's Apology, to this point, there had been secrecy, covert observation of the representative organisations, distribution of taxpayers' money without supervision by the Dáil or the Department of Finance, and misrepresentation of the degree of progress made.

The rights of children changed with the 1937 Constitution. They were changed in respect of institutionalised children, but then the legal system employed to commit such children was used with unintended severity, quite out of line with developments in child care reform elsewhere in Europe and notably within the United Kingdom. The State was required, both in law and under the 1937 Constitution, once it came in, to ensure a proper and 'equal' education for these children. Time and again, evident in a huge body of documentation, there were cases of fundamental abuse of this right. In summary, the children were used as slave labour—as adults were sentenced to what had once been 'hard labour'—for much of the time they should have been at their desks. Unfortunately, for many of them, when they *were* at their desks, petrifying fear undermined their capacity to learn.

The State was responsible for feeding these children. It provided the money for this, and for medical care, for clothing and warmth. The perpetual cry of Artane boys, and of those from Upton, Letterfrack, Daingean and almost everywhere else, was about their gnawing hunger. Scraps thrown from the staff tables to feed the pigs were fought over by the children. At Artane they fought for chocolate waste from the Rowntree factory dumped on the school's land.

By concentrating on sexual abuse, this whole raft of fundamental abuse was set aside. No Statute of Limitation reform came to the aid of the thousands who suffered permanent and crippling loss, and lifelong emotional and intellectual deprivation.

A long-suffering view, reinforced by sensational revelations, led people to concede that the State could not deal with all these rights and was probably correct to follow the sexual abuse trail if their following of it had been an honest and caring one. But the evidence that has emerged from the workings of the Lafoy Commission, from the Redress Board, from the Secret Deal, from the conflict between the private and public positions of the Minister principally responsible, Michael Woods, was that there was no caring and reliable examination of this. It was the easiest accusation to defend against; this was the course taken. It was the Church that was protected, and, in company with the State, is committed to a protection of the State as well. Meanwhile, the abused will remain abused.

In summary, it needs to be underlined that the State made no provision for controlling Church assets and freezing them in respect of legal obligations over crimes of the most serious kind. It did the least it possibly could do in preventing the destruction of documents, or the transfer of money, belonging to the religious orders, out of Ireland. There are no penalties against individuals or organisations cited in the Redress Act for possible abuse. All they get are indemnities. The religious are indemnified for their very existence, for all but a small proportion of their expenses, and against any calumny whatever. The abused remain on the legal fringes of our society, their legal status often in limbo, still looking, still waiting for the modest recompense that most of them would settle for if it were to be given in the right spirit.

Baltimore Fisheries School, the only industrial school where the investigation was completed before Ms Justice Mary Lafoy resigned. The findings were deeply shocking. (*Courtesy of the National Library of Ireland*)

Daingean reformatory, run by the Oblates of Mary Immaculate, was a former military detention centre completely surrounded by high walls. Daingean and Letterfrack were widely regarded as the worst of the institutions. (*RTÉ Stills Library*)

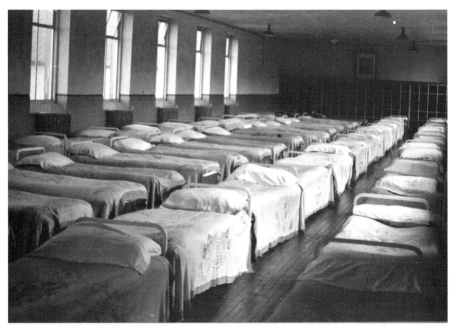

A dormitory in Daingean reformatory; severe corporal punishment was carried out at night in the stairwell, audible to all the inmates in the dormitories above. (*RTÉ Stills Library*)

Artane Industrial School, with more than 800 certified inmates was, at its peak, the largest industrial school in Ireland, of which the Christian Brothers were most proud. Subsequent revelations have deeply tarnished their image. (*Courtesy of the National Library of Ireland*)

Letterfrack Industrial School, also a Christian Brother industrial school and reformatory, with a dark and terrible reputation brought vividly to life by Peter Tyrrell's book, *Founded on Fear*. (*Courtesy of the National Library of Ireland*)

Letterfrack Industrial School, showing the remote Connemara wilderness in which it was set. From it many boys vainly tried to run away and were savagely punished when captured. (*Courtesy of the National Library of Ireland*)

Tomás Derrig, Minister for Education during successive administrations in the 1930s and 1940s. He repeatedly blocked investigation of cruelty and neglect in various industrial schools. (*Topfoto*)

Eamon de Valera briefly took over the Department of Education from Derrig for the passing of the 1941 Children Act. This legislative weapon was in part used to block relations between men serving in the British Army and their children in industrial schools. (*Getty*)

John Charles McQuaid rapidly became the dominant voice of Roman Catholic Ireland after his 1940 consecration. Eamon de Valera undoubtedly deferred to him, in public, forming a bond between conservative Fianna Fáil politics and an authoritarian Church. This did little for the victims of child abuse in the industrial schools. (*Courtesy of Dublin Diocesan Archives*)

Ms Justice Mary Lafoy, first chairperson of the Commission to Inquire into Child Abuse. She resigned when impeded in her work by the Department of Education, expressing the view that there was conflict of interest in the Department being in charge of the investigation into itself. (*The Irish Times*)

Mr Justice Seán Ryan, who succeeded Mary Lafoy as chairperson of the Commission. He had advised the Government on changes to the legislation scaling down its original obligations to see all who wanted to appear before the Commission. (*Collins Photos*)

Father Seán Fortune was a serious and serial abuser of young boys who helped to serve Mass at his church in the Ferns diocese. He was exposed in a BBC documentary. The scandal led to the resignation of Bishop Brendan Comiskey and a wider recognition of clerical sex abuse. (*The Irish Times*)

District Justice Eileen Kennedy, the first woman to be appointed to the Bench in Ireland, chaired the Kennedy Commission into Industrial Schools and Reformatories, set up in January 1967. Its 1970 report set in train the dismantling of the Gulag. (*The Irish Times*)

Bertie Ahern announced the Government's response to child abuse in institutions, including the industrial schools, in his famous Speech of Apology in May 1999. In the background on the right is John Kelly of Irish SOCA.(*Photocall*)

Micheál Martin was Minister for Education 1997–2000, during the preparatory period when Government policy on abuse was being put in place. He was the main spokesperson, with the Taoiseach, Bertie Ahern. (*Collins Photos*)

Michael Woods was Minister for the Marine when the plans were made for helping those abused in the institutions but was on the Cabinet subcommittee. As Minister for Education (2000–2002), he steered through all the early legislation. (*RTÉ Stills Library*)

Noel Dempsey succeeded Michael Woods as Minister for Education in 2002 and remained in that position during the controversial resignation of Mary Lafoy. (*Photocall*)

Mary Hanafin was appointed Minister for Education and Science in September 2004. She brought a new Bill before the Dáil, amending the Commission to Inquire into Child Abuse Act. This gave effect to Mr Justice Seán Ryan's recommendations, made before his appointment. (*Collins Photos*)

Batt O'Keeffe, Minister for Education under Brian Cowen's leadership, will be the recipient of the final, five-volume report of the Commission to Inquire into Child Abuse, published in 2009. (*The Irish Times*)

Mary Raftery, author of the book *Suffer the Little Children* and of three ground-breaking *States of Fear* television programmes on child abuse in State institutions. These were first shown, to great acclaim, in spring 1999. (*RTÉ Stills Library*)

Tom Sweeney, seen here on hunger strike outside the Dáil, challenged the restrictive terms and the secrecy of the legislation and won a new deal on his own claim for compensation. (*Photocall*)

Father Michael Mernagh walked from Cobh to Dublin as an act of contrition on behalf of the Church. He was praised for this by Archbishop Diarmuid Martin, whose desire to bring conclusion to the issue had a positive impact on the Hierarchy and the public. (*Collins Photos*)

Father Henry Moore, the author of the controversial Artane Report commissioned by Archbishop John Charles McQuaid. It was submitted in 1962 and laid bare the true conditions within the institution. It was suppressed by the State until 2006. (*Father Henry Moore*)

Chapter 13 ✍

THE CASE TAKEN BY THE
CHRISTIAN BROTHERS

The case taken in the High Court by the Christian Brothers was to challenge the powers of the Lafoy Commission. Legal argument revolved around key legal principles of natural justice and the constitutionality of what the Lafoy Commission was attempting. Among other things, the Christian Brothers properly challenged the idea implicit in the State's position: that no man can be a judge in his own cause. There is also the principle that, in any legal action, the other side must be heard.

Many of the cases concerning institutional abuse involved defendants who were dead or too old to plead. The Christian Brothers argued this, claiming that what had become known as the Lafoy Commission was a kind of court. In all this the State was the defendant. Yet the State had set up and was paying for the compensatory bodies and the people involved. It was argued that the State had acted as judge and jury in its own case.

The procedures followed had taken the process away from the natural place for it, the courts, and put it into a controlled set of organisations established by the Government. The injustice of this was part of the argument brought before the High Court. It was entirely legitimate to pursue this and no organisation was better suited to the legal action than the Christian Brothers, with their worldwide involvement in education. They had a reputation worth protecting.

All this, as it emerged in court, was increasingly embarrassing to the Government. The key Government document was the inter-departmental report on child sexual abuse. This report went through various drafts. The subcommittee, according to Micheál Martin, was set up in December 1998. Its remit was to draw up a range of initiatives, developing a proposal to establish a commission into abuse. Martin was chairperson. An inter-departmental committee, not a Cabinet grouping, had done the earlier work on the terms of reference. The committee included the Tánaiste, Mary Harney, and four ministers. The Minister for Marine and Natural Resources, Michael Woods, was one of them. The Attorney General and a junior minister were also on the committee. In a Dáil speech made on 13 May 1999, Martin said, 'we were not driven by a concern to find legal ways out of taking action', the meaning of which is obscure, to say the least, but 'our very purpose was to find a means of moving away from the conservative approach which had informed previous responses to revelations'. The only 'conservative approach' in use and pending was the law of the land. The report was submitted in its final form in April 1999. It had been this that had set out the strategy for what followed. Unwittingly, the approach adopted through that report had invited the action in the High Court. Significant parts of the document were still being withheld under legal privilege. Nevertheless, from what was obtained under Freedom of Information legislation, a clear picture emerged of Government policy and intent.

The direct involvement of the Church had to be assumed then and is still, to this day, not proven. The possible linkages are far from clear. However, what had happened in respect of the Christian Brothers was that there had been a complete reversal in their attitude, between their initial apology, about abuse, and their High Court confrontation with the Commission. They were central to the issue, since they ran a number of the industrial schools and reformatories in which there were many recorded cases of abuse. The Christian Brothers were also in the forefront of the reconciliatory approach that was fostered both by Church and State in the 1990s.

It was Brother Edmund Garvey, Head of the Christian Brothers in Ireland at the time, who took public responsibility for what was a landmark apology. This was made by the Order on 16 April 1997. It was made in respect of the abuse of boys within the institutions run by the Christian Brothers, among which, of course, were Artane, with up to 800 boys, and Letterfrack. In different ways these were among the most notorious.

As part of his apology, Brother Garvey said:

All I can do is ask forgiveness. People have had negative experiences with the Christian Brothers and schools. I cannot deny that. Nor do I want to. I don't want any ambiguity in the minds of people who have been hurt or damaged by anything that has been done. Obviously, I cannot accept every allegation but I do believe that every allegation has to be fully investigated. I am sorry to say that at times, with some of our men, we reflected some of that harshness and cruelty only too adequately.

Further and more briefly worded apologies followed. These were in the form of advertisements in newspapers during March 1998. This 1997 apology preceded by more than two years the Taoiseach's Apology, which began the Government's planned programme of investigation and redress.

The Christian Brothers' apologies were prompted, in part, by a wave of Garda Síochána investigations and prosecutions at that time. They came well before the showing of Mary Raftery's *States of Fear* programmes on RTÉ, which were even more of a landmark in their information and their impact.

The place of the apologies in the abuse chronology, however, is significant for other reasons. Two sentences in the statement are of importance in the light of subsequent events. The first is 'All I can do is ask forgiveness.' This is by nature of being a passive acceptance of what was to come in the way of investigation of the growing numbers of allegations. The second sentence is more positive in tone: 'I do believe that every allegation has to be fully investigated.'

The plea for forgiveness is only a starting point. To show their commitment, the Christian Brothers should have made available their records. They have never done this. Without this, the statement about the investigation of 'every allegation' carries no serious conviction. Whatever lay ahead, in the period beyond 1997, and more particularly after 1998, when serious discussion began between CORI and the State over what to do about the abused in institutions, the honouring of Brother Garvey's commitment to have things 'fully investigated' depended on the records.

Brother Garvey's sensitivity over this is expressed in his letter to the *Irish Independent* (published on 29 October), where he says: 'the Christian Brothers have not destroyed, either deliberately or accidentally, any evidence concerning residential institutions'.

In August 1998 a former inmate of Artane, visiting the school in pursuit of information for a book he was writing, witnessed a bonfire of documents which could not have taken place without the authorisation of the Christian Brothers. The man rescued some documents and photographs from the fire. He described the fire as 'huge—10 feet across'. This was not an unusual event. Many documents from the industrial schools were destroyed when they were closed, and this process was widespread. Documents within the Department of Education have been destroyed or lost as a result of accident. Serious loss occurred in Talbot House. The Cussen Report documents have been mislaid or lost, as have the very important documents connected with the Kennedy Report.

In the case of the Christian Brothers, as reported in a lengthy article in *Community Care*, the British professional publication for care workers, their files are held in Rome. Specific documents connected with abuse in Irish industrial schools have been moved there, and have not been made available. Certainly, the idea of State investigation, then and later, was, by implication, impeded by the fact of the records not being readily available in Ireland, whatever may be the stated aim of co-operation and involvement.

The availability of documentation is a key aspect, but only one of many. The greater compliance and openness by present and former members of the religious orders was equally important.

Events at that time, when trust in the institutions being investigated and in the investigators was increasingly in question, included much testimony expressive of doubt. There was an added and growing complication coming from within the ranks of the abused. One example was offered by Tom Hayes of the Alliance Victim Support Group, and published in the *Irish Catholic* on 29 May 2003. This suggested possible misrepresentation of their experiences by the abused. The evidence he supplied was that 'dozens of calls' had come in from people wanting details about names, dress and routine in industrial schools. This introduced a new twist to the abuse story. It envisages fraud on a growing scale by people intent on pretending that they were abused in places to which they had never been sent. However, it is imprecise and is obviously a matter for the Guards, rather than for media speculation. It has created a new and quite different abuse equation: between those who had good experiences as against those who had bad ones and those who had none at all.

Interesting though this new equation might well become, it was at that time a small part of what confronted the public over the processes being pursued by the Commission and the Redress Board and the unsatisfactory rate of progress. Nevertheless, their work concerned the abused and those who abused them. Both the Commission, still under Ms Justice Mary Lafoy, and the Redress Board were showing considerable determination and energy in challenging people who might be guilty of misrepresentation of their cases. They were also trying, against legal obstruction, to persuade the alleged culprits to co-operate more and not to fall back on a blanket challenge to the authority or the remit of the structure set up to bring justice to a dark series of events in the country's life. This made the action by the Christian Brothers particularly difficult for everyone.

If what Brother Garvey had said in his apology, more than six years before, had any meaning at all, it was certainly not expressed in a statement in November 2003. This offered a 'now established perception' of widespread abuse which he described as 'systematic', and this he rightly denied. But of course it wasn't systematic. Nor was it 'methodical, according to a plan' as the dictionary defines the word 'systematic'. Bells did not ring to announce abuse time. There was no rota.

The unresolved issue remained. There was abuse. The State was committed to rectifying its damage and recompensing its victims. Yet the State's actions, its institutions—both permanent, like the Department of Education, and temporary, like the Commission and the Redress Board—were not operating smoothly or with clear intent. One of them had ground to a halt, leading to the resignation of a capable and balanced High Court judge; the other was facing doubts and questions about the relationship of its awards to the real life of abuse in the courts.

There is a substantial literature in defence of those who ran the institutions that were part of the industrial school system, and the general tenor of the argument is that the abuse, particularly the sexual abuse, was limited and isolated. By contrast, the schools were generally well run and the work of the religious in them was one of lifelong dedication.

This view was expressed by the Christian Brothers themselves to reinforce their new pleading at the time of the High Court action and following the announcement of Ms Justice Mary Lafoy's resignation. Without giving number, dates, names or evidence, the Order initiated a whitewash of itself. It used the phrase 'the now established perception' to justify something on which it denies investigation and refuses evidence. Things, it said, were not as bad as had been stated. The public had no clear measure of what had been stated, for or against, so that the Christian Brothers' statement was largely meaningless. But it clearly evoked sympathy.

Of all the religious orders, the Christian Brothers, with their worldwide system of education, had the most to lose by high profile exposure over Artane.

With more than 800 inmates possible under its management agreement, Artane Industrial School did not have a library. It had other odd facilities not usual for a school, such as an on-site mortuary and an on-site cemetery. The remains of upwards of 248 child inmates lie in a mass grave on the Artane lands. This was Ireland's strange flagship industrial school, once a jewel in the crown of the British Empire, visited by William Gladstone, Edward VII and Queen Victoria, who took tea there on Saturday, 21 April 1900.

The State knew, through the Department of Education, that Artane did not provide secondary education. Even so, the Department claimed the opposite in its Annual Reports. 'The policy of extending vocational and secondary education to the children fitted to benefit there from was continued during the year under review.' (Annual Report 1959/60) 'The practice of sending children, who were likely to benefit thereby, to secondary and vocational schools was continued.' (Annual Report 1960/61) 'The physical and educational needs of the children were adequately catered for in the past twelve months and those of them who were fitted for post-primary education were enrolled in secondary or vocational classes on completion of their primary school programme.' (Annual Report 1961/2) 'Where it was considered that pupils who had completed the primary school programme would benefit from secondary or vocational classes they were enrolled in such classes.' (Annual Report 1962/3) 'Pupils who were considered suitable for secondary and vocational courses were advanced to such courses.' (Annual Report 1963/4)

Sympathy for Brother Garvey was shown in late November 2003 and came in the form of support from a new organisation led by Florence Horsman-Hogan. It was called Let Our Voices Emerge, or LOVE, for short. Florence Horsman-Hogan's objective was to discover 'good news' stories and publicise them. Obviously, if it was to gain any credibility at all, it needed to provide numbers, dates and occasions. Its membership and what they had to say would, in the circumstances of what we had already heard from victims, have needed to be comprehensive and convincing. It never achieved this comprehensiveness and five years later it was dissolved.

In her Saturday column in the *Irish Times* on 6 September 2003, Breda O'Brien wrote in the same terms as the Christian Brothers, claiming it was 'not all bad', and 'not as bad as had been stated'. It is not possible to explain what these phrases mean. She gave nine lines in her article to the testimony of a former inmate of

Artane, and even this individual told her 'it was not so bad'. Nineteen lines were given to the 'idealistic young men' (the Christian Brothers running the place) whose lives were 'nearly broken' by the experience of working there and doing their best for the children. Well over half of her article was in defence of the system, while at the same time calling for us to look 'honestly and completely' at what happened. The problem is, the evidence of abuse, a great deal of it unbearably painful to hear and to read, is overwhelming. Alternative evidence, from people who sailed through these schools as happy, well-fed and well-cared for inmates, is at best thin and unconvincing. Moreover, the institutions, very notably Artane among them, had either deliberately destroyed evidence of the life in the schools, or had been the victims of an alarming number of fires which always seemed to take place where the records were kept.

Furthermore, those who should have been able to tell us, from memory, of the circumstances, and answer questions about charges laid against them, either individually or collectively, had by then erected impregnable defences.

Teams of lawyers and publicity spokespersons, on behalf of CORI and the individual orders, again notably the Christian Brothers, had made nonsense of the stated objectives of the ongoing process of reconciliation and truth. As in Northern Ireland, openness and transparency were required. What was actually happening was the further criminalising of the victims and the attempted exoneration of the orders and their members, save where actual crimes had been identified with charges and in many cases sentences following after.

The defence of the Church, by CORI, and by well-meaning individuals or organisations set up to defend those who have been accused of abuse in a wide range of situations, was premature. But its pursuit was gaining ground. We needed the process. We needed the evidence. We needed the orders to give us facts and documents about what they did and how they did it. We needed an audit of the money involved. We needed to know what had happened to the State's per capita grant to the institutions. Where did the profits go? What had happened to the victims' own personal documents? What were the punishments? What had happened to the 'punishment books'?

There was a further truly disgraceful aspect that was becoming obvious. It bore directly on the issue of supporters of the system seeking a blanket pardon without anyone being brought to account. This was the manifest evil of the total membership of all the orders that were engaged in the so-called care of the children. They had become comprehensively incapable of remembering a single occasion of wrongdoing, of brutality in punishment, of particular wrongs done by brothers or nuns whose names were frequently mentioned by different victims. They expressed no recall whatever. There had been no record of confessional reaction. There was no humility about what was done, no evidence available on the incontrovertible cases where the damage to men and women within the system had been sworn to and had been lifelong.

How was it possible that no one in the orders—and they cared for between

70,000 and 80,000 young people if we go back to the foundation of the State—could remember or tell us of a single episode of brutality, deprivation of rights, starvation, poor or neglectful educational opportunity, or sexual abuse? Was there not one person, male or female, on the Church's side, who witnessed what happened in the Magdalen laundries, in Daingean, in Letterfrack, in Clonakilty, in Clifden, and was able to remember anything at all? This stifling code of silence—and guilty silence at that, unless tens of thousands of people are simply inventing the hell that was their childhood—had now become a defence that called for our pity.

There was yet another alarming development at this time. The Church, through certain bishops and other spokespersons, began putting out the idea that the motivation of commentators was either anti-religion, or anti-Catholic. There is no evidence being offered for this. It was laid in the autumn of 2003 by a United Kingdom Roman Catholic bishop against the BBC. Here it was being voiced very generally against the media. Unfortunately, it was taken up and responded to by the media, giving it further currency without the questions being asked: Where is the evidence? What is it?

PART FOUR

Testimony

Chapter 14 ∿

TESTIMONY OF THE ABUSED I

I
t is worth recording here the testimony that was still coming out from individuals. The first two accounts that follow are by female victims, one of whom we shall call Annie, the other Brigid. This is followed by the testimony of a former Daingean inmate and in the next chapter that of one who was in Artane. Mary Norris's story and James Martin's testimony are given later. Then comes a personal recollection of Letterfrack and an encounter there with a former inmate. There is the Commission's record of the fate of a sad group of individuals who were in the Baltimore Fisheries School. Their suffering was fully investigated, and published in 2003, by Ms Justice Mary Lafoy. They all serve as reminders of what this process was meant to resolve and highlight the question of what went wrong.

Annie's earliest memories are of being in the workhouse in Clonakilty. She had a twin sister, Mary. Both were under three when left there by their unmarried mother. Annie has no early memories. She remembers being looked after by 'a tiny little lady' in the workhouse. This angel of her early years she described as 'a kind of mother who made pretty little dresses' for both sisters to wear. These first recollections, despite being of life in a workhouse, were happy ones, perhaps her only happy childhood memories. She had the comfort of her twin sister and the luck that the two of them remained together.

They were put into the Clonakilty Industrial School, St Aloysius, on 12 April 1939, charged with being 'destitute'. Annie's personal records show that her mother came from Dunmanway. The sentence handed down by District Justice J.F. Crotty was for a period of 13 years.

She remembers the beatings, she remembers the bed-wetting and having to stand up in front of everyone with wet bedclothes. 'They beat me awful,' she told me, 'with rulers, sticks, anything they could lay their hands on.' Her sister was treated more cruelly. She was left-handed and was punished for this. It was 'the divil in her'. She was beaten and made to kneel in front of the class and pray out loud 'for the devil to go out of her'.

Clonakilty Industrial School was a prison. The gates were guarded and there were high walls. Annie said she suffered six breakdowns. She couldn't eat or sleep. She walked in her sleep and was strapped into her bed at night. Those who gave the children the worst time of all were the lay workers, sometimes drawn from other institutions, rather than the nuns, but the cruellest beatings came from the sisters in charge of them. They all seemed 'unhappy in their own lives', Annie said. The brutality was a kind of disease within the convent, spreading from the nuns to the others, learnt by new nuns from the older ones.

'The beatings of the little children were terrible to witness,' Annie said to me. 'They were helpless and would huddle together and be lashed with big lashes.' Then the lay sisters, or at times the nuns, would leave, slamming the door. 'We would pick up the little children, and comfort them. What were they punished for? They were punished for nothing.'

Of her education she said: 'The classroom was a place of punishment. It was where we watched people being sadistically beaten. If we were ambitious to study, they did not like that.' There were exceptions. Sister Peter was one. When Annie was sent out from class as a punishment and told to wash the floor, Sister Peter remonstrated with the teacher. 'This girl, who wants to learn, should be at her lessons. Send out the ones who don't want to learn.'

Annie kept coming back to her memory of scabies. Everyone in the school had it. They also had chilblains. The nuns had a way of treating both ailments. They took stiff-bristled floor scrubbing brushes and scrubbed the children's hands until they screamed. Their flesh was often red and bleeding.

Scabies was eliminated in due course because people no longer slept on straw. The mites causing the disease bred in straw and multiplied in dirty straw, which was what the girls slept on at the Clonakilty Industrial School. Annie told me that when a Department of Education inspection was imminent—and the nuns mysteriously knew when this was to happen—the girls removed all the old and dirty palliasses and brought down clean, freshly packed ones from the attics. They were given clean clothes. Soap was put out. They had nice food. The new palliasses were never used. They were returned to their storage places immediately after the visit of the inspectors and the dirty ones came back. It was the height of ignorance to do this, encouraging the development of the disease.

It was doubly ignorant of the nuns to treat scabies in the way they did. Apart from being intensely cruel, the hard scrubbing spread the disease, distributing the infected pus to other abrasions, including those caused by the deliberate damage to the skin affected by chilblains.

After the inspector's visit, the good clothes and soap were put away. Bad food returned. On one occasion there was a slip-up. A female inspector arrived unannounced. 'It was a shock to the system,' Annie remembered. They all queued up to be inspected. Annie had been badly beaten, her body had many marks. She was told by the sister in charge to say that an older girl had done it. The sister then hid in the kitchens. Annie did as she was told, but the inspector knew and, when the sister came back, she challenged her.

They were a bit more careful after that. 'You would have to cup the tips of your fingers together and they would beat you on the tips of your fingers with a ruler or a stick and this would leave scabs which would turn green.'

Health and hygiene were perfunctory. The children shared cold and dirty bath water, three or four girls in turn despite the infectious scabies. They never saw toothbrush, toothpaste, or soap. Annie suffered from abscesses and other complaints. She learnt later that she had TB. Her sight was damaged by the scabies. She later lost it completely in her right eye. She now wears dark glasses and walks with a white stick.

After her release she went to England. Medical problems continued. The hospitals in England needed medical records. When she tried to get these, she was told by the nuns, 'Clonakilty does not keep records.' This reply was given to nurses from Queen Charlotte's Hospital in London when they sought help with Annie's treatment. Annie's story is one of thousands from those who went through the reformatory and industrial school system in Ireland. Many moved to England; according to my researches, many had worse stories than Annie's. Some have suppressed or buried the memories; a few only have got over the early experiences and have since lived out reasonable lives.

Annie, with a host of other people who had read my stories in the *Irish Independent* was losing faith in the process. Is it any wonder?

Brigid's is a painful case. In May 1935 she was committed to the Goldenbridge Industrial School under the 1908 Children Act amended by the Children Act of 1929. The detention order, made with the consent of her unmarried mother, was for 14 years. She would be released on 29 May 1949. When she entered Goldenbridge, the report said that she was 'well nourished and clean'. She was then aged one year and eleven months. She was two foot six high and weighed one stone eight pounds. She had a fair complexion, light red hair and blue eyes. She had a small nose. She was put down on the admission form thus: 'To go to factory work'.

She fared well for her first 10 months, but by April 1937 the record showed 'dirty habits' and in September 1939 she was described as having 'dirty habits' again, and being 'troublesome'. Anyone of sound mind would recognise the symptoms of love withdrawn, punishment, cruelty or neglect in these few facts about her early life in Goldenbridge up to the age of five.

During those early years of her incarceration, the 1937 Constitution was drafted, debated and passed by the people. It made certain of the laws governing Brigid's position unconstitutional as well as bestowing on her a number of rights to a proper education, food and clothing, under the State's care. Perhaps most importantly of all, it should have guarded her against being brutalised, mentally or physically, by those who had charge of her.

These rights were abused and her changed status ignored. Most of the abuse she suffered was outside the terms of reference covered by the abuse legislation. This was designed to compensate the inmates of reformatories, industrial schools, homes and other institutions which were under the control of the State but which were administered by the Church. The religious bodies responsible for these homes were guilty of a terrible misuse of power.

Brigid is still alive and is in touch with me. She will not qualify for redress though she was the victim of a gross and terrible sequence of damaging and depriving acts carried out against her mind and body. She has lived with them all her life. To a large extent they have ruined that life. She particularly resents the fact that she was 'a defendant' when committed. That is hard to bear. She is just one of scores of men and women who have sent me their files. And she represents one complicated saga of hardship, years and years of damage inflicted by the Irish State.

What did Bertie Ahern really set in motion, when he made his May 1999 Speech of Apology? This was meant to have been a process of healing. What had happened in practice was a disaster. The State was faced with a duty of recompense, but also with the needs of the abused to come to terms with their wrecked lives. For this purpose the Lafoy Commission was promised as a forum at the same time as the Taoiseach's speech. For reasons already examined in earlier chapters, it failed during Ms Justice Lafoy's tenure to fulfil its remit. By the time she resigned, effectively in December 2003, only a small number of abuse victims had given testimony.

At the same time, the process of preparing legislation for redress in the form of compensation was set in train. The Taoiseach moved Micheál Martin out of the Department of Education and put in Michael Woods.

The Lafoy Commission had a persuasive exterior, and many abused men and women wrote to it or applied to be involved and make their statements. Indeed, there were many people who wanted to confront their abusers in circumstances of what appeared to be State sympathy for what they had suffered. Where this happened, the experience tended to be far more traumatic than expected.

A report on redress was prepared, setting out terms of compensation. It was sound if conservative and led to the Redress Bill which was then hurried through the Dáil in difficult circumstances during the final months before the general election of 2002. Debating time was truncated, the guillotine was used at the important Committee Stage, the Minister denied amendments from the Opposition on the grounds of expediency and then introduced many that were not debated. The legislation is unfairly tilted in favour of the Church, for whom protective clauses abound, and against the abused, who are the only people involved in the legal procedure for whom serious penalties are enshrined in what became an Act in April 2002.

The Minister for Justice, Brian Lenihan, presented an illogical answer on the issue of the Freedom of Information Act and how it had to be used with the Department of Education. He suggested that 'the FOI Act does not provide a mechanism' for addressing 'often sensitive issues'. This was not the point; it was the State's duty to do that. But the State did nothing. The State, through the

Department, could have relaxed the legal privilege and changed the service all on its own. It could have covered any legislative requirements in the substantial acts that went through, allegedly to help the abused. It did none of this. This fact is of course part of the shortcomings of the State in dealing with the problem. Though not yet established on any legal footing, a database of documents for those who had been incarcerated was then in the process of being transferred to the children's charity Barnardos. It was later decided that the Department would be keeping the Freedom of Information approach, but in tandem with Barnardos' supposedly 'more caring approach'. It raised questions as to why. Why pretend to be 'more comprehensive, compassionate and supportive' when every act of the past three years had been in the opposite direction?

Brian Lenihan claimed that 'prior to the transfer of the records to Barnardos, the Department consulted with the Office of the Data Protection Commissioner and took data protection requirements into account in framing proposals for the new service'. There were, however, no 'proposals'. 'Taking into account' is not a parliamentary guarantee; there was no legislative backing. Part of the trouble was that Barnardos had not resolved the ways in which its services in the United Kingdom might work for the Irish abused. Methods of handling this were still, at that stage, 'being explored'. No legally binding State agreement, involving the Freedom of Information Act, which is a major part of the regulating legislation, could be signed if part of its remit, within the United Kingdom, could not also be embraced.

Though Brian Lenihan said that the Department had consulted widely, he provided no evidence of this. The Department did not consult with all the representative groups, and two have come out strongly against the scheme. The response was not, as he said, 'generally positive'. It was generally bewildered and, when informed, negative. How could it have been otherwise?

During his response on that night to Joan Burton, who questioned the move of archive records from the Department to Barnardos, the Minister admitted that the Ombudsman Act would not relate to the new arrangement, but only to the situation where the Department of Education is used under Freedom of Information. The onus of choice is on the abused, many of whom were very damaged people. They were unable to choose what to do. Having delayed the process of help for more than three years, Minister Lenihan told us 'a separate statutory agency would delay the assistance which the individuals concerned require'.

There seemed to be a misguided Government determination to continue to shoulder the major part of accountability for this abuse, and it is coupled with an apparent desire to allow the Church to hide its own responsibilities behind this cloak of protection. On Tuesday, following her private member's debate, the Minister for Finance, Charlie McCreevy, told Joan Burton that the religious congregations had a choice to become involved in the Government's scheme of redress and that, because their approach on this was voluntary, any audit of their assets was 'not relevant'. It was an extraordinary confession of feebleness, uncharacteristic of this particular Minister, well known for his outspokenness and candour. It was also seriously at odds with his frequently declared approach on public finances, which is that both the taxpayer and the Exchequer should be the primary interests that he would protect.

Here McCreevy expressed the opposite. What his words meant were that, because of Church 'reluctance' to become involved with the State in bringing 'some healing and closure to the victims of child abuse', the State would have had to take on the entire burden. And it would have done so without the increasingly disparaged Secret Deal, seen by the Minister as some kind of help.

Later in the week, the Minister for Education, Noel Dempsey, made a rather different defence in answer to Jan O'Sullivan of the Labour Party, when he ruled out any review of the deal. What he said was this: 'There is no provision for re-negotiation in the indemnity agreement and there are therefore no plans to review it.' He was both right and wrong in this statement. He was right in saying there were no provisions for re-negotiation. He was wrong in saying that this precluded reviewing it. It could be reviewed, and it could be altered. It will be recalled that the terms of the deal do specifically allow for disputes to arise and for these to be the subject, either of voluntary resolution, or of a system whereby dispute between the parties can be referred for adjudication to 'An Expert'. This can arise in respect of a number of issues contained in the Agreement. These are not evident at present, but are likely to arise in the future, when victims of abuse, losing patience entirely with the crumbling monument the State has built to achieve 'healing' and 'closure', go back to the courts, and carry their anger eventually to Europe.

The CORI spokespersons—notably Sister Elizabeth Maxwell and Sister Helena O'Donoghue, the latter one of the signatories of the Secret Deal—had been absolutely clear in stating that the organisations they represented would not give way to the requirement that runs right through the series of abuse measures. This was for a confessional approach. Quite the reverse was the stance adopted, and it was expressed by Sister Helena when she said on RTÉ: 'We cannot as congregations be indicted as abusers.' This attitude, essentially adversarial, is one of denial of the whole framework of abuse and of everything done so far to mitigate it. It makes nonsense of what is now almost four years of supposed redress, reconciliation, healing and the assuaging of pain.

CORI's position should be read, of course, in the context of the key paragraph in the Secret Deal. This paragraph was not presented to the public by Michael Woods when he gave the 'good news' about the CORI–Government deal in the summer of 2002. This was the legally binding commitment required of CORI, and signed by representatives of the religious organisations, to assist the State in defence of claims, and not in the acceptance of them.

Despite the good efforts of several opposition deputies, and the leaders of the Labour Party and Fine Gael, the Dáil was being denied its right of review. It should have been allowed this, since the country was now facing a set of circumstances that would gravely impinge on taxpayers, on the right to a fair hearing by the abused, and of the resolution of a huge and terrible series of crimes committed jointly by the State and the Church.

Interest in the abuse saga continued in the Dáil. The debates and the questioning of members of the Government had generally yielded little but had aired many of the doubts and puzzles that were felt about the official handling of what was clearly a national scandal. Then, on 12 February 2003, in answer to questions from Pat Rabbitte about the scale of abuse cases likely to be settled at the taxpayers' expense, Bertie Ahern, referring back to the 1999 Speech of Apology, said: 'Following intensive negotiations, a date in May was agreed, and I apologised on behalf of the government to those people affected over the years.'

This was the first time that such negotiations had been referred to. The admission threw an entirely new light on a process that had been generally presented as the work of Minister Michael Woods operating with CORI. Both he and other ministers engaged in that process, including the Attorney General at the time, Michael McDowell, had already presented a picture of two teams wrestling to produce mutual involvement and agreement. However, this was all presented as coming after the Government decision to make good the damaged lives. In other words, it was claimed that it *followed* the Taoiseach's speech.

If the process took place before the speech, and if there were 'intensive negotiations', it suggested a quite different approach which was begun before the matter became a CORI operation. It raised a number of questions. Was the Taoiseach himself primarily involved? If so, with whom did he negotiate? Was it with the Church, and at 'the highest level'? Were the measures contained in the Government package, and was this hammered out with the then Archbishop of Dublin, now Cardinal Connell? Was Connell able to speak for the Vatican, to which the religious organisations were generally answerable? And why did the Taoiseach not tell us then what he let slip in his answer to Pat Rabbitte in the Dáil?

One thing was inescapably sure: he did not negotiate with the abused. The Speech of Apology contained no reference whatsoever to 'intensive negotiations'. It did not once mention the Church nor were there any references to the religious orders. He referred in the speech only to a political process that involved work but was not contentious. He apologised on behalf of the State, promised 'proper structures', went back over Government discussions and departmental views, and came up with the comprehensive package. There was not a word then, not even a single line, to reveal to us that this had been intensively negotiated, nor with whom.

It is necessary to recall the context. Mary Raftery's excellent *States of Fear* ran in the weeks before the speech, giving a huge public platform to the Taoiseach and the obvious creation of an opportunity almost heaven-sent—to enter the arena with a 'solution'. The third and final part went out on the day of his speech,

11 May. It is obvious within this context that a lot of work had already been done, including the recruitment of Ms Justice Lafoy and her team. And the speech was then applauded by the Christian Brothers and by the Bishops' Committee on Child Abuse, knowingly, one must assume, since they would hardly have approved a set of objectives, aimed at bringing them to account, which had not been carefully considered and negotiated.

Against this disintegrating situation, it is worth adding to the story of Annie another insight into the experiences and the present attitudes of the abused. The forum for this was an Irish Survivors of Child Abuse (SOCA) public meeting in March 2003.

In recent times the conscience of Ireland was stirred by the wrong done to these abused children from the 1930s on. It was like distant trumpets of hope, a faint and uncertain intrusion, not altogether welcome because it brought back unhappy memories. Books like *Children of the Poor Clares*, a growing tide of newspaper articles, radio and television documentaries like *States of Fear*, and *Dear Daughter*, told all of us, as it told those who had been victims, that a terrible and sustained wrong had been done. The wrong was part of the system. It was carried out under State control using State laws, implemented by the courts, executed by the Garda Síochána, and then run by the Church. There weren't any loopholes. No communities were spared. It had the comprehensive surveillance of Nazism or Russian Communism. Yet it was carried out in the broad and ostensibly benign pursuit of Roman Catholic conformity. It was apparently legal and constitutional. In those days, the concepts of human rights, family rights and review of children in care were controlled and stifled by a rigid, bigoted interpretation, or misinterpretation, of the law. The plethora of controls was as high, thick and impenetrable as the walls of Daingean reformatory.

Daingean is often talked of as the very worst of all the places in which boys were incarcerated. They were young enough when they went there but stayed longer, many of them past the industrial school age limit of 16, remaining until they were 18. One of these, a man who, at the time of writing in 2003, was aged 75, I first encountered at the Irish SOCA meeting in Liberty Hall in March that year. Tommy O'Reilly was sitting in front of me and it was shortly before I spoke. He turned and handed me a document. It was a poem, 'Daingean Reformatory Recalled'. It began:

Boys were incarcerated in Daingean
For small crimes and sometimes none.
The prison walls were high in Daingean
They blotted out the sun.

He was attending what he viewed as a protest meeting. It was not about past treatment of the abused. That matter lay in the past. It was a protest about the present, about the manifold failures of the previous five years to honour the Government's declaration of recompense; it was about the charade of promise and apology; it was about the lies.

The abused had started out with a brief but encouraging period when they thought they were going to be rescued. Like Annie, most of them recorded in their minds lifelong anguish. Their youthful experiences had condemned them to that. What the Government and State had now done was to turn their past into a living nightmare.

That meeting in Liberty Hall was a passionate, emotional event, attended by about 200 angry people. They passed a No Confidence motion in the Lafoy Commission. They also passed a motion proposing that Bertie Ahern's Speech of Apology made in 1999 should be returned to him. The speech had become widely regarded by soca supporters as dishonest. What angered them greatly was that Bertie Ahern had said, without having any facts to justify it, that the numbers of abused were not as many as people were claiming; they were certainly not in thousands. He had belittled them.

Yet the Redress Board had invited the whole age range, and specifically invited application from those acting on behalf of those who were then under 18 years old, meaning that we were looking at abuse of the present generation of young people. The Board had recently advertised in Ireland, but had then stopped the programme. A similar programme for the United Kingdom had at that stage been put off.

Though in his speech of May 1999 the Taoiseach had promised a Commission to Inquire into Child Abuse, this was now mired in legal wrangling and argument. Irish soca has long regarded the Commission as a convenient tool of the Department of Education. Though this was not the case, as the events of September and December 2003 would prove, at that stage, in the spring of 2003, no explanation of the delays had emerged and the meeting of Irish soca, with its rejection of the Commission, was in the light of this.

Bertie Ahern promised redress. The necessary redress legislation was passed, but it was guillotined in the Dáil and contained very serious shortcomings. Most serious was the fact that the legislation favoured the religious, who did the abusing, and contains serious penalties for the abused victims of religious communities should they reveal or expose what they faced before the Redress Board.

The Taoiseach's speech was no more than a gush of words and he had made the position far worse with the Freedom of Information Amendment Bill. He claimed, falsely, that the amended legislation would not affect individuals getting details relevant to their lives. And this, almost by definition, meant abused people. But the Freedom of Information Commissioner had contradicted the truth of this.

It seemed, on that March day, that almost everything concerned with the abuse saga had turned sour. In a single sentence of a parliamentary reply in the

Dáil in mid-February, the Taoiseach seemed to have suggested that there had been 'intensive negotiations' bfore his Speech of Apology. If so, it casts fundamental doubt on the genuineness of what was done, and the integrity of his and the Government's actions. Far from it being a recompense, it now seems certain that it was a structure of legislation and promises designed to protect both Church and State from the enormities of their past guilt. It was hardly surprising that Bertie Ahern's speech was at this stage roundly rejected. Why would Irish SOCA not return it to him? The men and women that day, who had once thought Ahern genuine, were now disillusioned and angry.

On the private side, organisations representing the abused sprang up, as did an army of eager solicitors, ready to represent the abused when they went for compensation to the Residential Institutions Redress Board or when appearing before the Commission.

The evidence of a stacked deck against the abused was further confirmed by the direct involvement of the Department of Education in running, funding and creating the code of conduct for organisations that were meant to be independent, and were meant to be serving the needs of the abused.

The Department became selective in the organisations it would deal with, and those it refused to meet. Irish SOCA, which rightly refused State funding, for a time was refused contact or debate about the problems of the abused. This was later modified and one executive in the organisation, Patrick Walsh, did become involved and served on a board concerned with education.

Then there were the punitive clauses in the Redress Act itself. These applied to applicants for financial recompense as a protection for the defendants—those religious and State authorities against whom the abused men and women are bringing their cases.

When the resolution sending back the Taoiseach's letter was put to the crowded hall on that Saturday afternoon, Tommy O'Reilly from Daingean raised his hand firmly to its full height. There was a kind of fervour, the fervour of desperation, in the decisive gesture. I bent my head and re-read two more stanzas from his poem:

No humanity was shown there
Only the five foot leather strap.
Floggings were received there
For even the slightest mishap.

A regime of terror reigned there
No kindness ever shown.
You could not report the brutality
Because behind the walls of Daingean,
You were on your own.

He gave me an account, in February of the following year, after we had exchanged letters and discussed what had happened to him. He began with Father Fitzsimons who managed Daingean reformatory:

He was the first person I met in his office after I entered the gates of the very high prison walls, and after the shock of the high walls, his whole treatment of you, left you in no doubt that you were incarcerated in a very oppressive place of internment and it certainly turned out to be so. He would know how badly we were fed and clothed. He would know that myself and others were getting no schooling or training of any kind, in fact many times he saw me pushing a very heavy wheelbarrow full of wet sand, this was heavy labouring work which should have been carried out by a fully grown strong man and not a light, five foot, fifteen year old (that was their description of me in their records). I did this kind of labouring work for twenty one months of the twenty two months I was imprisoned there.

He would have known that the shop in Daingean sold five cigarettes to those boys that had the money. This was on a daily basis but the place was closed when any boy escaped. Father Fitzsimons knew that closing the shop, because of the boy escaping, would enrage the rest of the boys. This meant that they would take it out on the runaway when he was caught. I saw this happening a few times.

When a runaway boy was brought back to Daingean, they cut off all his hair and put him on dry bread and water which he ate on his knees in the Refectory. They gave him an unmerciful flogging, so much that he could be heard screaming all over the place, and if that was not enough, they then let him down in the 'play' yard and turned their backs, so that the enraged boys who had been stopped their cigarettes would give him another beating. Father Fitzsimons knew this because it was him that closed the shop for that very purpose.

As manager he would know that we got no dental or medical examinations. I had scabies like many of the other boys from being so badly fed. I also had welts and chilblains from the hard work I was doing in all weathers out of doors. I also had trouble straightening my shoulders, due to the heavy wheelbarrow work I was doing at such a young age. The army man, who came out to drill and march us, often shouted at me to straighten up.

Father Fitzsimons would know that the only place we could sit down in the 'play' area, was on thick planks. These held the dampness after the rain for a long time. The result was I got haemorrhoids. We were never supplied with underwear.

He would know about the flogging carried out by Brother Dunne. The four to five foot thick strap he used for these floggings was made in the shoe repair shop. He was in charge of a regime that left the likes of me leaving Daingean without the ability to love, or have compassion or understanding. I was only left with the animal instinct to defend and protect.

I have had some counselling last year. It has helped me to talk and write about things which I have kept silent about for fifty-five years. The time I needed the counselling was when I was released.

The biggest breach of my constitutional rights was the conspiracy between Father Fitzsimons and the Minister of Defence to conscript me into the Defence Forces, at the age of sixteen. The Second World War was on. The Country was in a state of alert. There was no conscription in the rest of the Country, but we were not treated like ordinary human beings in that hell hole called Daingean.

This is how it happened to me. One Sunday morning I woke up to find a uniform, boots and leggings on the bed. The Brother in charge told me to put them on, I was in the army. So I had to do what I was told. I remember how rough the trousers were on the skin. As you know, we were not supplied with underwear. An army man came in and taught us how to march and drill, we were supplied with a rifle. Though we were not given bullets we were shown how to open and load the rifles. An army officer came in (I remember he was a small man) he instructed us in the use of hand grenades. I ask myself what was the purpose of all this training? Was it the intention to use us in the event of an invasion? It was certainly not for fun, there must have been purpose in it.

Father Fitzsimons knew about the boy terribly beaten by the Brother in charge of the staff kitchen. This boy was so badly beaten that he was taken away and we never saw him again. I am sure this boy's name was Roche. Father Fitzsimons would know what happened to him.

Then there was Brother Conroy. This Brother was in charge of the wood work shop, where I spent the first three to four weeks I was in Daingean. I thought I was going to like the hours in the day that I would spend working there, but it did not work out like that. Brother Conroy started to touch and rub against me, he kept doing this every day and I would move and push him away. After three or four weeks he moved me from the wood work shop and put me to work as a builder's labourer with a man called Ned who was employed by the management of Daingean and carried out building and other work for them. I did labouring work with this man. He was old and had a terrible ill temper. I was young and too light to carry this heavy labouring work. Not having any knowledge of building work I often made mistakes. I often let the heavy wheelbarrow turn over and this man thought nothing of giving you a belt of a lump of wood or a shovel and on one occasion he flung a plaster board full of plaster and dust down on my head, while he was on a ladder, because the plaster went hard, my head bled a lot and my eyes were sore for many a day from the plaster dust. It was hard labouring working with Ned, in fact it was hard in every way that is painful, fearful and very unpleasant.

Brother Dunne, whom I have already mentioned, carried out all the flogging while I was incarcerated in Daingean. I don't know what else he did, but he was very busy giving floggings, as they were given for even the smallest mistakes. He carried out these floggings in a room with a cold floor beside the upstairs toilets. The strap he used was about a half inch thick, four to five feet long, and was made of leather in the shoe repair shop.

I was flogged four times while I was there. I know that, as well as taking some kind of enjoyment in inflicting terrible pain, he was also taking sexual pleasure of having me on my knees and exposing my bare buttocks. If my shirt fell down he would also make sure to touch me while he was pulling it up. He also had a look of someone very pleased when he was finished flogging you, he had a look of enjoyment or something on his face.

Brother Aherne was the man in charge of the washing room, where you went to wash in a basin of cold and sometimes iced-over water, first thing every morning. I don't ever remember having the use of hot water in the twenty two months I was there. Even so cold water was the least of your worries when Brother Aherne was around.

I first saw him in action the first morning I was in that wash room. He boxed and kicked a few boys every morning. This is how your day started in Daingean, with fear and terror from Brother Aherne, all the time I was there. I often hoped I would not wake up at all. I got a few boxes and kicks from him a few times, when he caught me asking another boy for a bit of toothpaste or something. He was a coward who took enjoyment in inflicting pain on small boys who could not defend themselves.

I left Daingean with no schooling, no training, with a record that would stop me getting certain jobs, and a hatred in my heart because of the way I was treated there. I was never shown kindness, understanding or compassion, and that rubbed off to such an extent I would never have a real, loving relationship.

Reading Tommy's story, I wondered, would anything good happen for him? Would his cry, from the imaginary prison to which his youthful experiences have condemned him, lifelong, remain unanswered until his death? The process should have been concluded by the end of 2003; it went on until the end of 2008, with the final Commission report due in May 2009. By then Tommy O'Reilly was dead.

Chapter 15 ∾

TESTIMONY OF THE ABUSED II

Jim Beresford was born in Trim and was raised on a farm with his four sisters and younger brother. He was committed to Artane where he was interned from 1961 to 1963. He was sent there when he was 13, with his younger brother Thomas, who was 10. It is Beresford's view that the Irish State decided his English parents were unfit to look after him. He describes his experiences as 'two years of hell … Every child was exploited for their labour. It was child abuse on a grand scale—organised slavery that was State sponsored.' He claims he was sent to the industrial school after his mother was reported to the authorities by the Catholic lay group the Legion of Mary, because 'she was having marital difficulties'. Beresford also claimed that the fact that he had English parents marked him out at Artane, where he described the brothers as 'fanatical republicans who hated any association with England'. He said the priests targeted him for more abuse than most and claims the evenings were the worst when there was an 'orgy of beating' in the dormitory. 'They did not need a real reason for it. I got the feeling that they did it for sadistic reasons. The priests feasted like kings while they starved the children and fed them slops.' In an article entitled 'I was abuse victim of Irish Catholic priests', Jim Beresford told Jane Yelland of the *Huddersfield Daily Examiner* that he was sexually abused by two of the brothers and raped by one.

> They were men sworn to a celibate life and they used the boys as sexual objects. Of course the thing about it was that they got away with it. They were free to do whatever they liked. What eventually stopped them abusing me was the fact that I had parents, and that I was articulate. Most of the other children were inarticulate and illiterate because they had spent their whole life in the institution. Others were orphans and some were mentally handicapped.[1]

Jim Beresford and his brother left Artane when their mother successfully pleaded with the authorities to release her sons to visit their father, who was dying in a London hospital. He and his brother then refused to go back.

[1] The article by Jane Yelland appeared in the *Huddersfield Daily Examiner*, on 19 December 2002.

As with so many others, his time at Artane left an indelible mark on him.

He suffers from acute anxiety, his only marriage failed and he did not have children. He is one of the great sceptics about what has been done and a trenchant member, along with Patrick Walsh and John Kelly, of Irish Survivors of Child Abuse (Irish SOCA). 'We want a proper inquiry, run by people from outside Ireland, where we can tell the truth about what happened to us and not give the Irish Government's version,' he said in the *Huddersfield Daily Examiner* interview.

The direct reference by a victim of abuse to Legion of Mary involvement in committal procedures is the only case known to me of this aspect of the court appearances, which preceded incarceration. However, there is another source in the testimony given to the Commission. This includes the evidence given by both Eoin O'Sullivan and James Martin, two important witnesses. O'Sullivan makes a point that is quite different from the testimony of Jim Beresford, given in the newspaper interview, in respect of the Legion of Mary, and this point refers to the Legion's founder, Frank Duff. O'Sullivan describes him as 'one of the more interesting commentators on the industrial school system', who was particularly critical of them because he felt they broke up families and this went against his fundamental Catholic beliefs on the sanctity of the family. According to O'Sullivan, Frank Duff wrote a series of memos to the Department of Health about the breaking up of families and the placing of children in industrial schools.

This designation of Frank Duff's position is accurate. He shared with the Archbishop of Dublin, John Charles McQuaid—with whom he was friendly—an abhorrence of the industrial school 'solution' to child poverty and the instability in many poor and disrupted or broken families. He referred disdainfully on one occasion to the children being 'shovelled into' the institutions. Frank Duff's view is confirmed by Eoin O'Sullivan who saw the organisation as critical of the industrial school system:

> Again, I think there is consistent evidence from the Legion of Mary about the deleterious effects of institutionalization of children. Again, I suppose the key point is that the sanctity of the family, anything that breaks up the family unit should be severely checked, so that this is inconsistent in the Legion of Mary's view with Christian social principles, and Catholic social principles more particularly.

However, this interpretation of the wider position of the Legion of Mary and of other Roman Catholic organisations engaged in proselytising sits uneasily with the account given by Jim Beresford, about his own committal. There is an alternative and disturbing view given by James Martin, assistant secretary in the Department of Justice, Equality and Law Reform, to the Commission. On Monday, 19 June 2006 Martin told the Commission to Inquire into Child Abuse that there were no professionally qualified probation officers before the 1960s.

There were six full-time, paid probation officers at that time, but not professionally qualified, and they were all based in Dublin. Instead, use was made for court probationary purposes, of men and women from the voluntary societies of St Vincent de Paul and the Legion of Mary. Those who worked in this probationary field, according to Martin, were expected to have experience of or interest in social work. Yet twice in his testimony this witness asserted that the religion of the probation officer was significant. He himself asked the question:

> Can I just note one thing, am I right and I may be wrong, in thinking that there would be an ambivalence perhaps in having people from either the Vincent de Paul or the Legion of Mary functioning professionally at that level? For instance, people might consider there was some slur on the family or that there was some moral judgment being made on them?

This was a very muted judgment on the intensity of religious fervour inspiring both organisations in the 1950s and on the invasive zeal with which they sought to help people and families, not to be better, more prudent people and more cohesive, loving families, but to be better Catholics.

The membership of the Legion of Mary in Ireland in the 1980s well exceeded 10,000. A similar number operated within the St Vincent de Paul Society. As late as 1983 the lay members of the Vincent de Paul organisation, which laid stress on person-to-person contact, visited 10,000 families a week, 7,000 elderly people and virtually every hospital and long-stay institution in the country. The Legion of Mary, like the Knights of Columbanus or Opus Dei, is more secretive, and its statistics are not available in the same way. Its meetings were in private, its minutes not publicly available, its members instructed to maintain secrecy on all matters discussed at meetings.[2] Nevertheless, the *Official Handbook of the Legion of Mary*, in its new and revised edition, published in 1953, gives a detailed insight into the intense, apostolate nature of the organisation. The 340-page handbook, with the imprimatur of Archbishop John Charles McQuaid, has been republished regularly and is a monument to the huge impact the Legion's founder, Frank Duff, had on the life of the country.

From its foundation in 1923 it had flourished, as Pope Pius XII told Frank Duff, in a letter on 22 July 1953, 'on the fertile soul of Catholic Ireland'. The book gives a very detailed explanation of how 'home visiting' should be conducted. It was comprehensive, not selective; it was intrusive and fact-finding. The facts were reported back to the *praesidia*, which operated and held weekly meetings in the villages and towns of Ireland, reporting upwards, through the Legion's governing structures, through the *Curia, Comitium, Senatus* and *Concilium Legionis*. It was an organisation that did immense beneficial work for good Catholics. However, its zeal to purify was a pernicious force among liberals, freethinkers, unmarried

---

2 See Tom Inglis, *Moral Monopoly*, University College Dublin Press, 1987, pp 53–7.

mothers, mixed-marriage couples, those generally who did not conform or respond to the 'beautiful and holy work' identified by Pope Pius xi, in a letter sent on 16 September 1933, 20 years earlier than the one from his successor mentioned above.

In the Gulag parallel, which is a parallel between two great faiths in the twentieth century—Communism and Roman Catholicism—the Legion of Mary, according to Jim Beresford, who is uniquely bitter about the role of that organisation, is matched by the NKVD. He recalled for me the actual kind visits carried out, and feared for himself and his family, since his parents were of different religions, or of none, and had no emblems or outward signs of holiness and Christian identity in their house; he said that Stalin would have given his eye teeth to have the equivalent of the Legion of Mary in the Soviet Union.

It was put to James Martin that 'the probation officers, in theory, if the system was functioning, could firstly make some class of a report to a judge on a juvenile offender prior to sentence; isn't that right?' It was further put to him: 'So, there seems to have been no disquiet at the idea that either the Legion of Mary or the Vincent de Paul, both of a reasonably strong religious impulse, were going to be involved in non-residential minding of people who have gotten into trouble?'

James Martin did not know how to answer the questions. At second hand he had learnt from people involved in voluntary work about the participation of the religious orders and he added, 'obviously some of the more significant bodies would have been of a religious nature'. The only thing he could say was that the 1908 Act referred to the duty of a probation officer to befriend the offender. 'The legislation did not envisage them as necessarily professional people, it was more a kind of guardian or a role model.' While current practice, he said, was for the probation officer to do an assessment for the judge, he had seen 'no evidence in any of the files that they came up with a kind of a structured assessment of children or what should be done'.

It was not needed. Sadly, it seems, the nod and the wink sufficed. There is no record in any of the many District Court 'Orders of Detention in a Certified Industrial School' that I have seen, of the reporting, in open court, by the so-called probation officer surrogates, of the reasoning behind the presentation of a child or children by a member of the Garda Síochána and a representative of the NSPCC. These legally approved officers were not required to present a case but the District Justice was required, by the Children Act of 1908, to hear one. It never did. Jim Beresford has given me details of a case well-known through the first episode of Mary Raftery's programme *States of Fear*.

Mary Norris was one of the women who took part in the series. She was in St Joseph's Industrial School in Killarney, run by the Sisters of Mercy. Her father died and her mother took a lover, a local man who visited the house, was kind to the children, sometimes stayed the night 'and we saw our mother a bit happy'. Mary Norris and her siblings were arrested and brought to court in Sneem, County Kerry. She and all her siblings were marched through the town, watched by neighbours. The male companion was in the house. Mary tried to comfort the others, who were all crying. They were committed to industrial schools, put in the car and she was sent to the 'orphanage' in Killarney. (It was common for the industrial schools to be so called, though they did not contain orphans.) There was no charge, no indictment; no crime had been committed. Their mother was not destitute. Seeing the man and sleeping with him were not offences, even under Irish law. Most significant of all, the Children Act 1908, under Section 58.1 requires, under the committal procedure, that there should be a court inquiry. Clearly this could not take place in the presence of, or using, the NSPCC inspector or the Guard, for testimony or witness, unless parallel witness and support were available to the mother. It did not happen and this was an illegal process. All over Ireland similar committals took place without the 'inquiry' demanded by the law. No victim of abuse known to me recalls any inquiry. Their committal proceedings were perfunctory, tearful, unexplained and swiftly completed. It is this aspect that has been consistently ruled out of consideration by Ministers for Education and by the Commission and Redress Board. It is a black hole, unexamined in any of the abuse cases.

In *Suffer the Little Children*, Mary Raftery and Eoin O'Sullivan summarise the committal procedures:

> Approximately eighty per cent of all children committed, and over ninety per cent of the girls, came under the category 'lack of proper guardianship'. In practice, this was a catch-all heading which included children of unmarried mothers not eligible for adoption, children who had lost one or both parents, those whose parents were incapacitated through illness, or whose families were unable to look after them due to poverty. Homeless children came within this category, as did those whose families had been broken up because of desertion or the imprisonment of one parent. However, in all these cases, the language and procedure of the courts was to place the onus of guilt on the child. And the State, rather than attempting to address the poverty that existed in these families, chose instead to fund religious orders to effectively incarcerate these children.
>
> About ten per cent of the total were committed for non-attendance at school. However, it is important to remember that these children had committed no offence. Rather it was the parents of the child who were guilty of a breach of the law. But in all cases, it was their children who paid the price, ending up detained in industrial schools for periods as long as eight years.[3]

Mary Lafoy, in her Third Interim Report, published in December 2003, gives a detailed summary of what legislation was in force—the Children Act of 1908, the employment of Children Act, the Children Amendment Act of 1949 and the

---

3   Raftery and O'Sullivan, *Suffer the Little Children*, p. 22.

School Attendance Acts 1926–68—and in some cases how these Acts were used. When they were used, they resulted in the committal of children to industrial schools or to reformatories, in one case specifically providing for transfer of children to St Anne's reformatory in Kilmacud. Comprehensively, the legislation had the ultimate effect, contained in *Suffer the Little Children*'s summary, that all the children who were committed ended up in the Gulag.[4]

A great deal of secrecy surrounds the role played by the Legion of Mary—and, incidentally, the role of the Society of St Vincent de Paul—as surrogate probation officers in the service of the courts concerned with the committal of children. It is probable that this secrecy meant that Frank Duff, who would have disapproved, did not know of what I can only construe to have been a reporting function by the Legion, unsupported by the open presentation of any kind of evidence before the District Court.

Martin was asked by the Commission lawyer:

Just to expand on that, probation officers, in theory, if the system was functioning, could firstly make some class of a report to a judge on a juvenile offender prior to sentence; isn't that right?

Martin said that in trying to look at the type of information that was available to judges in the 1940s and 1950s in relation to juveniles, there seemed no indication as to what class of information a probation officer could bring other than a bit of family background. It was said that there was no evidence in any of the files that such probation officers came up with any kind of a structured assessment of children or what should be done with them. It seems that, in the highly unlikely circumstances of a child not being sent to an institution, there would be probationary supervision.

James Martin said such children would be put on probation. 'It didn't necessarily mean supervision by a probation officer, it could be supervision by any individual, it could be by St Vincent de Paul, the Legion of Mary, there was a kind of informal arrangement. But it could be a probation officer, but it wasn't necessarily a probation officer.'

James Martin was asked if there would be any ambivalence in having people from either the Society of St Vincent de Paul or the Legion of Mary functioning professionally at that level. For instance, people might consider there was some slur on the family or that there was a moral judgment being made on them.

James Martin answered:

Possibly. The only thing I would say is that in the 1908 Probation Act it refers to the duty of a probation officer to befriend the offender. So it wasn't the legislation for probation that didn't envisage them as necessarily professional people, it was more a kind of guardian or a role model.

4   Commission to Inquire into Child Abuse, Third Interim Report, December 2003, Table F6, pp 53–5.

The point was not lost on his Commission interrogator, that a situation existed where the surrogate probation officers, who were members of religious societies or organisations, would in certain circumstances have been aiding the process of turning children over to institutions also run by religious orders or directly run by the Church, as was the case with the Baltimore Fisheries School. Given that parish priests were also involved in many of the committal procedures and that NSPCC officers were carrying out inspections of families on grounds of neglect or cruelty, it did at times seem that the country was really in the grip of a powerful crusade made up of more than just social concern; religious and moral issues were also being dealt with. This in turn was further fuelled by the urgency with which the managers of the industrial schools pressed the State to send more and more children, thus providing grant-aid for the sustenance of the child prisons.

Jim Beresford and his brother were the victims of a curious case where intense religious prejudice and bigotry resulted in them being imprisoned illegally. Jim's parents' marriage became unstable as a result of ISPCC intervention, and it eventually broke up. A case was brought against his father, again with ISPCC involvement. No summons was served and the prosecution went ahead in the father's absence. He was characterised as a freethinker, and someone who did not believe in God.

Before Jim's father's prosecution, which he did not attend, an officer of the ISPCC came to the house where the children were with the mother, and brought them all to the court. He gave assurances that this was just a formality. In his absence, the father was found guilty of child neglect. During this part of the procedure the two brothers were kept outside the court.

When they appeared before the judge, with their mother, it was to face an extraordinary diatribe. He told them all that if parents wanted children, they had a duty to bring them up in the love and fear of God. If they failed to do this, then the State would take over. On the spot, the District Justice committed the children to Artane. There was no assessment or examination of their needs or their family circumstances.

A promise was given in the court. When the mother, who was going to England, had a house, the children would be released. At Artane this was repeated, and it coloured Beresford's attitude, which was to assume early release on foot of the promise. He was confident he would get out and it made him defiant towards the brothers. It did not happen. The mother found a house, but the children stayed in Artane. And because of his Protestant background, and his rebellious attitude, Jim suffered terrible abuse and punishment. 'Christ!' he said to me at the London meeting, where I interviewed him, 'It was Hell on Earth!'

It was a legally untenable decision, later recognised as such by the Attorney General and by the Chief State Solicitor, who ensured that the resultant decision to retain the children and not release them to the mother had the personal imprimatur of the Minister for Education. Principally for this reason, it seems, the Department later claimed legal privilege whenever Beresford tried to get his documents. In anticipation of the visit to London by Noel Dempsey for a 'Survivors' Conference', Jim Beresford wrote an angry letter to him reminding him that the meeting was to be an 'Open Information Day of direct relevance to survivors of institutional abuse'. He succeeded in obtaining most of the documents, but certain key and deeply incriminating papers were refused. He has been angry ever since.

He told the Minister that his department held secret child abuse documents on him that had been shown to third parties, according to the answer to a Dáil question on 13 February 2003. He concluded his letter to Noel Dempsey: 'It would be particularly apt for you to hand the secret child abuse file over to me publicly at your "Open Information Day". I will be there to accept it from you, so pack it with your luggage before you set off to London. Don't come without it. Perhaps you could pack the 43,000 other files in case anyone else wants theirs. We could then have a real "Open Information Day".'

Noel Dempsey, a good political barnstormer, did better. Three days after receiving Jim Beresford's request, and in a letter that was personally signed, the Minister surrendered the complete file, including the legally sensitive papers. 'My Department has agreed to waive its right to legal privilege and grant full access to these records.'

It was clear from the documentation that the Attorney General and the Chief State Solicitor were acutely aware, in the light of the Doyle case, that if the matter came to court it would be virtually impossible to defend the *ne temere* grounds for committal by the judge. There was also obvious serious concern about the extraordinary reversal of the court promise. Since this had led to gross and punitive abuse of the two brothers, the Department's position, up to that time, was understandable, though still quite unforgivable. It also strongly reinforced the illegal nature of so much that was done at that time in respect of children.

A third serious issue also emerged. The Department of Education had decided to set up a NOVA committee to administer €12.7 million of the Secret Deal money to provide education grants. This appeared to be an illegal use of CORI funding. The argument was that the funding was part of the Secret Deal. There is no statutory provision for its use unless the deal, which is essentially an indemnity agreement, is made part of the Redress Act. This has not been done, and is unlikely to be done. Once funds are paid into the special account, they can be used only for purposes outlined in Section 23 of the Act.

I visited Letterfrack during the June Bank Holiday weekend 2003. In misting rain I spent time on the Sunday evening in the graveyard of St Joseph's Industrial School. It has been smartened up and changed. It has a dreadful new memorial at one end with plaster figures of child angels and naked female children, the one a piece of nonsense, the other inappropriate. At the other end stands the old memorial, erected in the late 1950s, with the names of the 78 boys who died between 1893 and 1956. We know now that the total is higher, and that boys are suspected of having been buried in the woods as well. The full story of misery, deprivation, fear, hunger and punishment, not to mention sexual abuse, will never be told.

A party of four people had come up to the graveyard, one of them a woman whose friend, Martin, in Cork, had asked her to visit for him. I stood and talked with these four; the conversations were strange, interrupted by stabs of grief and their telling expression in tears. A fifth person stood apart. He was clearly looking for a particular name. The original names have been copied onto heart-shaped stones decorated with coloured flowers and arranged in rows across the green, cropped grass. He eventually found what he was looking for: the grave of George Glynn, who had died towards the end of March 1953.

I asked him about George Glynn but he was too upset to reply. We later walked around the former industrial school and he told me of his experiences. He was one of the luckier ones, there with his brother because his mother had TB and could not look after them, but released and returned home after less than two years. Both the brothers and their sister, who was in St Joseph's Industrial School in Clifden, had a bad time, and he told me about that as well.

He showed me round the buildings. It was his first visit in 50 years. He had been eight and his brother seven. He was recovering the past, and he had a sympathetic audience of one. I tried to assess what had been irrecoverably lost in his life. What stood out particularly was education.

St Joseph's at Letterfrack ran a self-contained farm on some 400 acres. The boys did a great deal of the work. This meant they were not in class, they were not properly taught, their prospects intellectually had a very low threshold. The best most of them could expect was labouring.

Two episodes stuck in his mind. The first was a terrible beating with a broom handle because he changed the slices of bread on his and his neighbour's plates at suppertime. There was an understandable craving for bread with thick husks on it, because of the acute hunger. The second was working in the hay field, the long line of boys bent double, with their fingers splayed like a rake, gathering up the cut. If they stood up to ease their aching backs, the farmer hit them with a stick. This was a part of their education.

Ms Justice Mary Lafoy found that the same kind of floggings as occurred in other institutions such as Letterfrack, and have been reported in earlier pages, were widespread at the Baltimore Fisheries School. Her final report, published in December 2003 and representing her signing-off as chairperson, contained the only report on an individual industrial school completed during the whole 10-year period of investigation that had been initiated by Bertie Ahern's Apology, back in 1999. Her Baltimore Report, chapter 8 of the Third Interim Report of the Commission to Inquire into Child Abuse (pp 105–44) is a searing indictment of the whole system and caused a great deal of public disquiet. On the specific issue of punishment Ms Justice Lafoy claims that 'a common theme of the evidence was that the most serious form of punishment was severe beating on the bare buttocks with a strap, stick or cane' (p. 114) and goes on to call these grave assaults by flogging 'child abuse'. Of course they were, by current and modern standards. Yet they were fully permitted by the Rules and Regulations. They carried the authorisation, as was the case in every industrial school, of the Minister for Education, who was responsible for the punishment code that was universally followed. Mary Lafoy may have had the view that 'the type of punishment described by the witnesses (former Baltimore inmates who appeared before her Investigative Committee) was qualitatively and quantitatively different from the type of personal chastisement envisaged in the 1933 Rules'. Yet this is not and cannot be the case, since no such 'envisaging' took place. No inspectorate records, legal investigations, court cases or other checks by the State, by parents or by managers in the institutions created any framework for the 'envisaging' of how the rules were implemented and to what tolerance. There is no measure of the tolerance of those receiving the floggings and nothing whatever in the Derrig rules of 1933 of any quality or quantity in the degree or severity of those floggings. Rule 13 'Punishment' contains no restriction. Mary Lafoy's frame of reference, in judging the undoubted wrongdoing of the floggings as humane or inhumane behaviour, by those running the Baltimore Fisheries School, was drawn from the Commission to Inquire into Child Abuse Act of 2000. Of course under that Act it was child abuse, but in the sense of this becoming the basis of judgment, it constituted a deception and levelled the crime against those who had charge of the boys, removing it as a guilt at the time deriving directly from the ministerial authorisation of extreme forms of punishment. Throughout all consideration of the cruelty and brutality that prevailed within the child prison system, this transfer of guilt is an underlying theme: the State is more or less exonerated from direct guilt. It failed to inspect and regulate, but it is never seen as the initiator of the system, thus carrying the primary burden of guilt.

Mary Lafoy additionally found, at Baltimore, wretched conditions that justify the severest condemnation of the Department of Education and the Irish State. The children were starved. They were not properly clothed; their garments were so ragged and inadequate as to be embarrassing. The children scavenged for food scraps in the dustbins of Baltimore and begged for help and sustenance from the local people. These were hard times; nevertheless, the expenditure of the actual grant for each boy at Baltimore would have clothed, warmed and fed them adequately. Instead, that money was used elsewhere and the boys were sustained at a level that compares with the worst conditions in Gulag camps in Russia or indeed concentration camps in Nazi Germany. That is the true extrapolation of the evidence heard by the Investigation Committee of the Commission.

Originally 26 former pupils offered evidence. Two died before the hearings commenced, two withdrew. All those involved in the school's administration were dead, or believed dead, at the time of the hearings. The Bishop of Ross, Patrick Casey, was, as chairman of the governors of the school, ultimately responsible from 1935 to 1940, and his successor, Denis Moynihan, from 1941 until 1953, three years after the school itself closed. The Baltimore parish priest from 1936 until 1951, Father Thomas Hill, was also ex-officio governor.

Those men who gave evidence were born between 1926 and 1935. Their ages emphasise the urgency about completing the Commission's investigations, stressed repeatedly by Ms Justice Mary Lafoy in her correspondence with the State and in her letter of resignation. More than half the boys giving evidence were 'non-marital children' with no home or family contact and came from other institutions. One was from a Dublin children's home and was committed on the application of an NSPCC inspector, the court order for his incarceration citing him having 'been found ... receiving alms'. Two witnesses came from foster care. Others were committed under the 1908 Children Act; they were destitute orphans, either both parents being dead or the mother being dead. Two were committed under the School Attendance Act of 1926 for 'truancy'. An 11-year-old was committed for house-breaking.

Mary Lafoy records the most startling failure as being related to food and diet. The children were not merely hungry, they were starving. 'They were compelled to supplement their diet by eating raw vegetables and vegetation—potatoes, turnips, mangolds, carrots and sorrel, by eating barnacles at the sea shore and by scavenging, begging and stealing in the village of Baltimore.' Witnesses attributed their small stature to poor diet. 'The Committee noted that the lack of physical stature was still observable.' Living conditions were appalling, dormitories dirty, beds flea-invested and urine-saturated. Boys drank from cracked mugs or jam jars, used outdoor, dry closets, only had hot water 'if a cartload of dry turf was to hand' and bathed six in succession in the same water. They had no toothbrushes or toothpaste, combs, brushes or personal towels. There were outbreaks of scabies; their bedding was verminous. 'For one witness his worst experience of life in Baltimore School was living through that winter [1947] dressed only in light clothes in a building with no heating, feeling, as he put it, "perished".' Christmas was a non-event; there were no letters or visitors and no holidays.

Severe physical punishment was systemic and humiliating. Beatings were recalled that were administered indiscriminately to any part of the body and at times included the use of other pupils to restrain offenders. There is sufficient evidence cited in the Commission report of one adult who engaged in frequent, gross sexual abuse, including anal and oral intercourse with boys. Clearly here was a sexual predator, 'probably a homosexual paedophile', systematically preying on vulnerable children 'in a pervasive and indiscriminate manner, regularly and over a period of time'. Former pupils were employed in or near to the school and were perpetrators of abuse.

The school and the teachers were inspected by the Department of Education, including those teachers who were the subject of complaint by survivors in their evidence to the Commission. The reports survive and indicate no awareness of any of the above defects in the management of Baltimore.

The Lafoy evidence on Baltimore is of great significance in that it confirms what has otherwise, during the eight-year period of the industrial school abuse process, derived from survivors. Mary Lafoy's approach is balanced and fair, cautious and restrained. In spite of this, the picture that emerges is one of appalling treatment and deprivation. This extended to the stigma felt at having been in an industrial school, the embarrassment of having no family, no parents, the impact of these factors on children's subsequent lives right up to the present, even the practical difficulties of obtaining a birth certificate or a passport. The Commission found that all the Baltimore witnesses suffered psychiatric illness, in some cases severe. Without any vestige of nurturing as children, in adult life they had psychological and psycho-sexual problems. These are directly related to 'severe discipline, bullying, fear and sexual abuse'.

Dr Anna McCabe's reports on Baltimore have survived and show general confusion, in that she finds improvement on an annual basis from 1939 and yet in 1946, four years before the institution's closure, she says: 'I am not satisfied with this school and never have been. It is easily the worst of all the schools and stands alone for inefficiency, slackness and neglect.' Though the chairman of the governors, the Bishop of Ross, professed 'interest in the school', her view was that 'he had [not] the slightest interest in the place'. Departmental records show that Bishop Casey persistently sought from the Department an increase in the numbers of boys sent to Baltimore in order to get a corresponding increase in the capitation grants. Because there was a policy of keeping institutionalised children near to their parents or families, Bishop Casey sought to have the most vulnerable sent to Baltimore, those without any families. In time this led to Baltimore becoming overcrowded and having numbers that exceeded the legal limit of 170 boys. What should have been a 'Fisheries School' was run commercially, tendering for business, and this precluded nautical education of any kind. Boys provided unskilled labour for the money-making pursuits of that part of the Baltimore enterprise.

No report has been published by the Commission between the Third Interim Report in December 2003, when Ms Justice Lafoy's resignation became effective, and the early summer of 2009 when, in five further volumes, all other institutions and issues were the subject of Mr Justice Ryan's final report. One hopes that this will be modelled closely on the Baltimore Fisheries School investigation which took place during the summer of 2002.

There is no 'appropriate' place in this book for consideration of the issue of committals by the courts. Nevertheless, in the context of the mixed testimony in this chapter, which may be seen by many as the heart of the suffering of a small cross-section of victims of abuse in the Irish child prisons that were euphemistically called 'schools', it might be appropriate to end with an examination of this, the worst event in the whole cycle of their lives, whichever way it is considered. After they entered the industrial school to which they were sent, bewildered by the reasoning behind the committals, Hell's Gates opened for many of them. They closed again, the clang echoing for lengthy periods of their youthful years. But the overwhelmingly terrible decision that began this awful trajectory in their lives was unarguably a legal one, carrying with it the stigma of a court procedure and a court committal ending in detention by the State.

There is no 'appropriate' place in this book because the subject of committal was ruled out by the State in the drafting of the legislation covering the supposed redress and compensation. It had no place. The raising of it was not permitted, except in the most general way, and consideration of it as 'an abuse' was not permitted under the legislation. A fuller examination of how this came about, by the State's deliberate suppression of it, including coverage of its debate in the Dáil, will be found in Chapter 9. However, in her introductory remarks at the beginning of Chapter 5 of her Third Interim Report, Ms Justice Mary Lafoy touches on the issue when she deals with the personal terms of reference of the witnesses who had appeared, or were to appear, before the Confidential Committee. She deals with the period from the establishment of the Commission, 23 May 2000, to 31 October 2003. At that stage she had announced her own resignation and was completing the Third Interim Report. The Confidential Committee had already completed a 'final' two-part report, covering 340 witnesses, all of whom had left institutional care by 1960; 272 of them were in industrial schools or reformatories.

The completed report contains detailed information on the circumstances of the witnesses before their admission to the care of the institutions, their experiences in the institutions and their life after they left the institutions. The Commission has decided, based on legal advice, not to publish that completed report at this time.

The reasoning for this may be inferred from the defined functions of this Confidential Committee, which was to hear the evidence of people 'who had suffered abuse in institutions during their childhood' and who relied on being free to do this 'on an entirely confidential basis'. The Commission received evidence, and was free to make a general report, but the Act gave no opportunity for those involved in running the institutions to challenge the veracity of statements.

Because of what this report dealt with, it inevitably gave details of the reasons for admission, at least in respect of those completing their incarceration before 1960 who had come before the Confidential Committee. Of the 616 witnesses from industrial schools and reformatories, 498 were committed by the courts, 458 of these under the 1908 Children Act and 40 under the various School Attendance Acts 1926–68. Almost certainly this meant prison terms for truancy or non-attendance at school, or for a variety of human shortcomings or moral errors, such as illegitimacy, mixed-marriage parentage, liberal wilfulness and loose living. The committals were generally without proper investigation of the family circumstances as provided for in the Act. A further 118 witnesses not committed by the courts had no knowledge of the formal arrangements made for their imprisonment. All but one of the truancy offenders were boys. The same was the case with the 40 found guilty of criminal offences, which in most cases were thefts of food, fuel, clothing, money and bicycles. There were only a small number guilty of breaking and entering or attacks on the person. There were 470 witnesses from two-parent families; 191 of the children were born to single mothers, though it is not specified whether or not they were illegitimate; 55 witnesses had no knowledge of their parents' marital status; and 55 witnesses were 'admitted to care', meaning they were imprisoned 'in the context of family disruption caused by parental separation or as a result of extra-marital relationships'. The deaths or serious illnesses of parents, particularly the deaths of mothers, were significant; the main causes of death were TB, childbirth, cancer and heart disease. NSPCC inspectors were certainly involved, according to public record, in 281 committals, not clearly involved or not involved in a further 155 cases, and definitely not involved in 229 admissions.

These are sad statistics and do give some support to the view that committal was better than the possible choices facing many of these children. It is a view profoundly qualified by what actually happened to so many of the abused who, when they arrived in the places designated for their care as children, they began a lengthy period of suffering and of cruelty often far worse than the set of conditions from which the NSPCC had supposedly 'rescued' them. However, the findings of the Society were also at times horrific.

The work of the NSPCC is the material for a book on its own, but some mention of its attitudes as well as selected examples of cases will help in giving a perspective to the difficult choices that were made in respect of the families the Society inspected. Before turning to these cases it is worth indicating that the Society was the object of concern on the part of the Archbishop, John Charles McQuaid, and the founder of the Legion of Mary, Frank Duff.

The officers of the NSPCC were not exclusively of one Church or denomination, and there were some who caused disquiet. One of these was a Mrs Clarke, about whom Frank Duff raised concerns. He reported her as being responsible for an over-zealous instinct to have children committed to industrial schools. Duff's attention was drawn to the work of the NSPCC by Archbishop McQuaid, who wrote to him on 4 June 1941, sending him a copy of the 1939/40 Dublin Branch Annual Report, inviting him to look through the specimen cases, which give fairly harrowing accounts of exceptional levels of poverty and neglect.

Duff's response was one of serious disquiet. He was of a view that children were being committed to the industrial schools 'far too easily'. He went on in his letter:

I profoundly distrust every word and action of one of the Society's Inspectors, Mrs Clarke. I go further and I say that I regard her as a danger. She is quite capable (by which I mean she has already done it) of distorting facts to suit any point of view she is trying to make. She exercised an ascendancy over ex-

Justice Little, and between them they simply shovelled children into Industrial Schools.

It seems that Mrs Clarke's view may have been an exceptional one. In the Annual Report of the NSPCC for 1948/9 it states that a large number of children were placed in industrial schools 'chiefly because their parents were unable to maintain them, but in some cases because their home conditions were so undesirable as to make it necessary to remove them'.

The Society's view, stated in that report, was that it would be much better if they could avoid sending children to these institutions since it deprived them of home influences. It was regarded as preferable to send the children to foster homes. However, such homes were not easily found. Nor were they favoured by the Roman Catholic Church, either as a substitute for the family or as a solution generally for child care.

The report of 1948/9 states that only a small percentage of children in the schools were there because of juvenile delinquency. In the public eye, however, 'all children in the schools were tarred with the same brush'. The NSPCC held emphatically to the view that this stigma 'was not the fault of the schools concerned'. It favoured the idea of classifying the schools in such a way that 'delinquents' would be segregated from the other children.

On a quite different issue, which ties in with the findings of the OECD Report 20 years later, the NSPCC Report also lamented the lack of employment for 16-year-olds after finishing in the industrial schools. On this, if not on other accounts, 'it is not surprising that many of our more experienced officers try to avoid the easy course of committal, even where the task of bringing about suitable home conditions seems almost insuperable'.[5] It is surprising, however, with this weight of opposition to the use of the industrial schools as a broad child care answer, and with the powerful involvement of the Archbishop of Dublin, who had the Taoiseach's ear, that the religious orders continued to receive a steady flow of new inmates.

Among the cases taken selectively from the NSPCC Annual Reports 1934–66, the following offer insights into the circumstances behind industrial school committals.

The father in this case was earning money but an alcoholic, while the mother was uninterested. The six children ranged in age from 3 to 14 ½ years old and were found malnourished and infested with vermin. Some of the children had sores, while others suffered from adenoidal problems. The oldest, a 14 ½ year old girl, had enlarged tonsils, was almost deaf and had problems speaking. The parents had apparently made no attempt to get the children treated by a doctor.

The inspector called in the local doctor and the children were taken to Union Hospital for treatment. Both the parents were prosecuted. The father was

5   NSPCC Annual Report, 1948/9, National Library of Ireland, pp 5–6.

originally given two months in prison doing hard labour and the mother six weeks hard labour. Both the cases were adjourned and were fined instead £1.

Eventually five of the children were committed to Industrial Schools, and the father was ordered to pay 1s. 6d. per week for each child towards the cost of their maintenance. The oldest girl was treated for her medical problems and went to live with her grandmother.
(Specimen case, 'Gross Neglect of Six Children', in Annual Report, 1935/6, pp 9–10)

This case originally came to the attention of the NSPCC two years prior when the stepfather (of all but one child out of eight children under sixteen years old) attempted to murder the mother. His sentence was suspended and the couple were re-united. The family lived off benefits and the father drank. He was warned several times but nothing changed, so he was prosecuted for neglect and was sentenced to six weeks' imprisonment. Meanwhile, seven of the eight children under 16 were committed to industrial schools, the mother being left with the baby.

Through proceedings it was found that the father was in debt and had sold all the house's furniture, as well as the children's underclothes. Charities cleared the debt and the family were moved to a smaller house. 'The new home, although not quite so large as the old, has three large rooms, to which the children, if it is found desirable, can be, in due course, brought back from the Industrial School.'
(Specimen case, 'Reconstruction of a Home', in Annual Report, 1947/8, p. 10)

This case concerned a family of six, living in crowded conditions. The father was living in London and sending money home regularly, while the mother was reportedly 'apathetic' towards the children. Due to the crowded conditions the Inspector said that the mother must apply for a house.

The eldest boy, aged 11, was in 'bad company' and would not attend school. The family were promised a house, but, meanwhile, first the boy was sent to an industrial school for non-attendance at school. When this happened the mother sold up and went to London, but the family were made to return home by the parish priest. A house in Dublin was provided and was furnished from charitable donations. The father returned four weeks later and claimed he would stay if a job could be found for him. 'The Inspector found him a job, and the family are now reunited in a good home and may hope to get the boy back in due course from the Industrial School'.
(Specimen case, 'Remaking a Home', in Annual Report, 1953/4, pp 13–15)

Both parents were in and out of mental hospitals on several occasions, while at least five of the children were thought to be 'mentally retarded'. The family were viewed as a problem family by Dublin social welfare departments.

Some of the children were admitted to industrial schools and convalescent

homes at different times to allow the parents to recuperate after coming out of hospital. 'Mentally retarded children cannot be "committed" to a school, so parents take them out at will whenever they are sent for a period to any institution, usually after they have been fully clothed!' The inspector visited this family once a week for close supervision.
(Specimen case, 'The Society in Action' Case No. 4. 'Mr and Mrs "D" and Nine Children, 14 years to one year')

It is perhaps appropriate to conclude with a singular case study of an inspector for the NSPCC, Joseph Browne, the father of the Left-wing politician and Dáil deputy, Noel Browne. Joseph Browne was from a small farming family in Galway. He was unskilled and unemployed at the time of Noel Browne's birth, in 1915, in Waterford, and took the job of inspector in Athlone. With it went a large house.

Noel Browne's mother, a devout Catholic, wore herself out with childbearing, while his father destroyed himself cycling the roads of midland Ireland in the early 1920s, 'out virtually all day and home later, dead tired with little to say to us'. His work, as Browne describes it, was 'the protection of children from deliberate cruelty', yet the 'usual causes' were 'widespread poverty and the fact that most families were too large to manage'.[6] Joseph Browne was assaulted and shot at in a job which his son described from first-hand experience as 'distasteful' because it involved taking children from their homes on court orders in cases where, in Joseph Browne's view, they were enduring needless suffering. It is implausible to assert that he could possibly have investigated this on his own. Yet no account is given by his son of the complex background required for each and every committal. The hostility to such an inspector could be frightening:

> The most awesome demonstration of hostility happened one afternoon in mid-summer. We children were playing with our tops outside our house when we heard the sound of wailing women, crying and shouting. They came from the direction of Lower Irishtown and were heading our way. Amongst the crowd there was a distinctive lady, the centre of the cursing, jeering and shouting crowd, which continued to gather outside our house. She was a distinctly frightening, powerfully-built, very old woman. We children scattered up the lane and into the house by the back door to watch her and the crowd from a safe distance, behind the curtains of the parlour windows. This old lady had long, tangled, rusty-grey, curly hair, which reached down to her shoulders and around her neck. Her loose wrinkled skin had the awful yellow dirty colour, which is sometimes seen on the aged who have lived their lives indoors, in semi-darkness. Her clothes were simply an old skirt, green with age, and her once black shawl. Her eyes were of a watery blue, washed with tears of anger or distress. Her mouth had long since lost all its teeth. Like a great Diva playing a sequence in Grand Opera, she sank slowly to her knees.

6   Noel Browne, *Against the Tide*, Gill & Macmillan, Dublin, 1986/2007, pp 2–15.

She then opened her powerful lungs and in a mighty voice, and with great feeling, called on God, his angels, and his saints, to curse and damn for ever my father, with all 'his breed and seed'. She then turned to each of us children, and wished us unending disaster and unhappiness to all our children, and to their children throughout their lives, with a death in the end for all of us of great agony and pain, to be followed by never-ending torment by the devils in deepest hell. Her curses on our house and home completed, exhausted but happy, she slowly rose and, with imposing dignity, moved away, the crowd following her. Whatever my father's real or imagined crime had been against her family, horror and damnation were facing us in reprisal. Looking at the life of each one of us since, much of it tragic, the peasant in me sometimes wonders about the power of an old lady's maledictions.

Chapter 16 ∾

DAINGEAN REFORMATORY AND THE OBLATE FATHERS

For its first hundred years Daingean was an Army garrison and a prison. For the next hundred years it was a reformatory for boys. The dates are almost exact. The garrison was established in 1776, the reformatory in 1870 and the closure—recommended by the Kennedy Report of 1970—took place in 1973. Since then, Daingean has been largely forgotten. It is now a decayed place of sad and fearful memories for those who were inmates and of shameful ones for those responsible for its operation.

On Saturday, 29 April 2006 there was an Open Day organised by Tom Parlon, the Progressive Democrat deputy who was then in charge of the Board of Works. He asked me to give an address as part of the programme, which I did. I had already visited the grim interior. On that first occasion, organised two years earlier through the Office of Public Works, I arranged to bring with me two former inmates who had become friends, John Kelly and Tommy O'Reilly; it was Tommy O'Reilly who wrote to me after the event:

> I wish to thank you for getting me the opportunity to visit Daingean Reformatory. I can only say that from the time I went through that gate with yourself and John Kelly until we came out two hours later, I was in some kind of time lock or dream, which I have been trying to untangle. I will have to visit the place again in order to see it more clearly, however, it was fortunate for me there were four other people around [we had a guide with us from the Office of Public Works] as I revisited some of the different places inside the high stone wall. On my way back to Enniscorthy the whole thing got to me and I got very emotional and had to stop outside Carlow for over half an hour to compose myself before I could continue my journey. Parts of Daingean were in fact worse in appearance than I remembered back in 43–45 especially the long dark corridor to the Refectory, but it is still the same fearsome place (as you saw for yourself) and when you add to that the regime of fear, oppression and neglect that the Order of o.m.i. [Oblates of Mary Immaculate] added to

the place you get some idea of the hell hole that it was. Just imagine spending hour after hour in the Prison Yard surrounded by the high stone walls. On Saturday and Sunday you could be there for eight hours each day with absolutely nothing to do, it was soul destroying, no wonder some lads went mad. As John Kelly has said, that every one who spent time incarcerated in Daingean was abused under at least two headings of neglect and emotional abuse, many of the boys also suffered either physical or sexual abuse or both.

There was no empathy or affinity between the boys and the Oblate Order who managed the place, and their excuse now is they were not trained for the job. As Priests or Brothers, were they not even trained to behave like human beings? Because all that was required was that we be treated humanely. They failed to do that.

Tommy O'Reilly was born in Dublin on 9 March 1928. At the age of 16 he was brought before the District Court.

I was sentenced by the court to two years in St Conleth's Industrial School (Daingean Reformatory) for what could only be described as very minor offences. I feel I was not treated properly in the way the Gardaí handled my case. There was never any adult present and I was detained in a house in Summerhill for several days. When the judge sentenced me using the words 'two years to Daingean Reformatory' there was very loud gasp from the people in the Court. I was soon to find out why they made that loud gasp.

The account Tommy gives of Daingean, in which the charges echo and resonate with all inmates of all reformatory and industrial school institutions in Ireland over a period of more than 50 years, were recalled with calm objectivity reinforced by a use of language that appealed to me from my very first encounter, when he had given me the poem which is quoted elsewhere. But abuse needs names and Tommy O'Reilly gives them in a clear and objective part of the statement he gave to me which is printed above.

On the Open Day many former inmates and members of their families visited as well. I wrote about the experience, trying to make sense of the complex feelings of my companions, Tommy O'Reilly and John Kelly. They traced among the derelict buildings and the overgrown paths and yards their own youthful experiences which were far from happy. They recounted them, and I was shocked. At the same time I remember the matter-of-fact approach they both adopted. One of them was angry and became heated with his rage, the other resigned and philosophic about what he had endured.

They were both survivors. They would never come to terms with what they had suffered, but they had both spread a lifetime between then and now and were living within the flawed comfort of what life had to offer. If there is guilt, shame, culpability for what they endured half a century ago, it rests on the shoulders of others. And whatever may be done about Daingean, that is an unchanging fact about the place.

The Grand Canal, which was built in 1797, passes beside Daingean and provided during the nineteenth century a ready access for canal trade, a significant and cheap means of shipping provisions, horses, weaponry and building materials. As already indicated, a gaol was constructed beside the barracks and this became a convict prison in mid-century where prisoners, sentenced to deportation, were held before shipment, mainly to Australia. For the hundred-year period from Daingean's foundation until it was passed to the Oblates of Mary Immaculate, its history was an unexceptional one of service to the British Army in all its many and diverse roles.

The Oblates of Mary Immaculate was a French order founded in 1816. It ran two reformatories in Ireland, both of them famous. St Kevin's in Glencree was visited by John M. Synge who had a cottage nearby and wrote amusingly of one particular and rather daring inmate who escaped and masqueraded successfully as a woman collecting for charity. The Order operated in Daingean from 1870, in St Kevin's from an earlier date. In both institutions the Order was subject to the British legal system which included regular supervisory inspections. Some of the sentences passed on boys prior to independence were very harsh: five years for stealing two suits of clothes, almost as long for stealing apples and pears. The reformist principles followed were religious and moral, supposedly aimed at creating in the boys a 'normal' outlook. There is now little argument that fairly fundamental changes took place after 1922 and included an alliance between the revolutionary politicians who had brought the State into being and the Roman Catholic Church. Inevitably there were power struggles, but these were won convincingly by the Church, and undoubtedly, where reformatories were concerned, this had a retrograde effect.

A small insight has been provided for me. In 1924 Liam Ó Daimhain, a local politician, asked a question in the Dáil of the Minister for Local Government, J.A. Burke (Minister, but not a member of the Cabinet). He asked if the Minister would state the number of children at present detained at Daingean (Phillipstown) Reformatory School. He asked also for the cost to State funds. The deputy pointed out that several business firms were anxious to secure the premises for starting industries. This, he said, would give much-needed employment in the district.

The deputy thought those detained in Daingean might be moved to another reformatory. Then the business firm might move in and secure the premises for the trade.

The Minister rejected this proposal. He said that there were 34 boys at present in the school. The cost of their maintenance ordinarily was £706 yearly, but a special grant of £800 was made the year before (1923) to meet a portion of a deficit that had arisen from a fall in the admissions owing to the abnormal conditions.

As to the idea of business stepping in, the Minister said: 'I am not prepared to take the steps suggested in the question. The premises are the property of the religious community which conducts the reformatory.' Respect for the rights of the Church decided the question. So the cruel life at Daingean went on.

The legal safety mechanisms designed to protect institutionalised children were surrendered in those baleful years. The reformatory schools, which were for children convicted of criminal offences, were different from the much larger number of industrial schools. The offences were often very minor but the punitive regimes were notorious and the sentences imposed by the courts were quite out of proportion to the crimes with which the children were charged.

In 1940 St Kevin's Reformatory in Glencree was closed and the boys transferred to Daingean. This was then the only reformatory for boys in the State. It had lasted for just over 100 years. Latterly it became infamous and was singled out for immediate closure by the Kennedy Report of 1970, but it should be made clear that the context for this was not so much the regime within the institution as deep dissatisfaction with the reformatory system. Inmates of Letterfrack, for example, who had also been in Daingean, said it was far worse in the Connemara industrial school. Nevertheless, Daingean was rightly feared as an institution and its shadow falls over many lives.

Between the entrance gate and the first building, the original barracks, there is a garden. Two huge copper-beech trees stand on a mown lawn, and between them is the figure of St Conleth. The atmosphere is benign, almost inviting. The priests and brothers of the Oblates of Mary Immaculate had rooms in the barrack buildings, which also housed the kitchen and refectory. On arrival, one passes through an entrance and then two doors into a long, dark corridor stretching to left and right.

Whatever an inmate's sentence, during its term he never again saw that garden or the outside world beyond it. The walls, 20 feet high, in places several feet thick, run round this world of punishment. They close it in completely. The laundry, the prison yard, the chapel, the bakery, the huge dormitories, various workshops, all of them scenes of oppression, created a world of fear with nowhere to go. Daingean stands today as a bleak reminder of those times.

Tommy O'Reilly has described for me the physical punishment which was always carried out by the same brother. Punishment took place in the same room, near the toilets and on the same floor as the dormitory. It had a cold tiled floor and young offenders were taken there from the dormitory at night, or brought from the prison yard during the daytime.

The Brother then told you to take off your trousers and also your shirt if it had a long tail. You were then naked. You were not supplied with underwear. You were then made to kneel down and forward onto your hands so that your buttocks and sometimes your back could be flogged with a leather that was made in the shoe repair shop.

This particular leather strap Tommy O'Reilly remembered as much larger than the ones carried by the brothers to punish inmates on the hands. 'It was about four feet six inches long, one and a half inches wide, and about 3/8 of an inch thick. It left black and blue raised marks on your buttocks for weeks and sometimes they would bleed.'

In the 1940s the boys were compliant and did what they were told, including submitting themselves to what were excessive punishments. In later years things were different. According to much other testimony, all of it now widely known, the brother giving the punishment in the 1960s needed help from other brothers to hold down the victim for flogging. The punishment by then was carried out at night in the main stairwell leading up to the dormitories. It was intended that the cries of pain would heard by everyone in the dormitories above.

My correspondent, who visited Daingean with me, was flogged four times during his two years there. We spent a long time together in the different gloomy and derelict parts of the former institution. It was being used at the time to store artefacts from the National Museum. Even the carts and carriages, the plaster casts and pieces of furniture, make it more homely than it was. He brooded to himself about his time there and confessed afterwards that he had been overwhelmed.

When he was at Daingean there were as many as 200 boys detained. The ratio of staff to inmates was roughly 1 to 12 and the boys were aged from 12 to 18.

It has been admitted, on behalf of the Order, that reliance on physical punishment was heavy. There was a climate of fear; members of the Order imposed it, but they also felt it in respect of the older boys, many of whom had reached the age of manhood. The punitive regime is confirmed; one inmate reckons there were around two severe floggings a week. It may have been more. Some of the victims thought there was a sexual aspect to the punishment, always carried out by the same 'prefect' of the Order, always in degrading circumstances and always excessively harsh.

There were other beatings on the hands and arms. Seán Burke who sprang George Blake from Wormwood Scrubs in 1966, and was himself an inmate of Daingean, gives a frightening description of a boy being beaten in this way. The assault left him with swollen and bleeding hands, the fingers of which he was unable to use.

Nothing of this cruelty, excessive brutality or possible sexual sadism has come out in the testimony presented to the Commission on Child Abuse during its public hearings under Mr Justice Seán Ryan's chairmanship. Neither the Department of Education nor of Health have added to our knowledge of this. Quite the reverse is the case. Departmental knowledge, as expressed by the Department of Education's Secretary General, John Dennehy, was seriously limited. And when a spokesperson for the Oblates of Mary Immaculate gave testimony, it provided so different a report on the punishment at Daingean as to represent a quite separate and wholly imaginary institution.

Father Tom Murphy, who represented the Order before the Commission of Inquiry on 23 July 2005, claimed that there were only six instances of complaint about excessive physical punishment from 1963 until Daingean closed 10 years later. He also said that earlier records were either not available or had been lost, and that no records were ever taken of the interviews that followed such complaints. How he knew this, since the records were not made available of the earlier period, is a puzzle.

Father Murphy made the point that before the Taoiseach's Apology the complaints were very few in number, a total of six, but they increased rapidly afterwards, rising to 322 by 2002. 'There was,' he said, 'deep shock, deep disbelief' at the idea that there was ever any excessive physical or sexual abuse. The former staff were shocked at the growing numbers of people coming forward claiming sexual or physical abuse. All former surviving staff members would insist, Father Murphy said, 'that they had no knowledge of abuse on that scale at all, at all, or on any scale actually.' The implication, not expressed, seems to be that the complaints were a product of the political acknowledgment of a need for the State to apologise.

Again, contrary to first-hand information, Father Murphy claimed that the 'punishment on the buttocks' was reserved to the prefect. The one surviving member of staff who was appointed to that position had claimed that the beatings were always delivered 'in his office' and during the day.

Punishment of the kind inmates described to me went unrecorded. Members of the Order do not remember. Those who were there deny knowledge. When all else fails, the possibility of abusive cruelty is mitigated by reference to 'the times' in which it all happened.

The record of the Order over the years has not been impressive. Though incidents where the State intervened in the running of reformatories or industrial schools are rare, the Oblates at Daingean came in for criticism from the Secretary of the Department of Education following a visit he made in 1955. He found that the cattle on the well-run and profitable reformatory farm were better fed and better cared for than the boys. For many years previously there had been pressure on the Order to improve, both in material terms and over their education. The Department of Education inspector had repeatedly been told that there were inadequate funds.

Daingean was a special case, being the only reformatory in its last years. It deserved the opprobrium heaped on it. Inmates during the later years refer to the climate of fear with special regard to the fact that the upper age of the boys was 18, whereas the inmates of industrial schools left when they reached their sixteenth birthday. This meant that the Oblates at Daingean were dealing, in many cases, with starved, angry, hostile young men. They, too, were frightened, and fear made them vicious. But it is their ignorance and inhumanity that astonishes every time there is a recollection of what it meant to be sent there.

A future for Daingean was in the minds of the officials from the Board of Works as well as the Minister responsible, in whose constituency Daingean stood, when the Open Day was arranged. And the ideas they had did not include using the former reformatory as a memorial to the past. Yet that was precisely what the former inmates wanted and the idea of erasing the physical substance of their unhappy early years was intolerable.

Daingean's past is a sorry tale of systems that were hopelessly ill-considered and unsuitable. The State's control was inadequate. The introduction of modern practices in the care for young offenders and their rehabilitation hardly progressed in the period up to Daingean's closure in 1973. The looming opportunity for Ireland, of EEC membership, led to revised thinking about the whole structure of detention centres for the young. This examination was given reinforced urgency by the OECD Report in 1965. The report included embarrassing observations about Ireland's neglect of this section of its young population.

With the closure of Daingean, the entire complex became for many years a 'Lost Domain'. It was deserted and closed up, its rooms filled with museum artefacts that were being stored there. The courtyards and pathways became overgrown with weeds. Many of the buildings, of poor quality in some cases, fell into disuse and decay. They were cleaned up and tidied for the Open Day. But it did not inspire thoughts of what it might become which was Tom Parlon's wish. Daingean should not be allowed to vanish, the fate of other institutions. Like Auschwitz or Dachau, Daingean should be a memorial to the inmates of all the industrial schools and reformatories and to the many people who went through them. It should be national and it should focus on children. There are many survivors and they are a credit to the recovery powers of the human spirit under adversities that were nearly always not of their making. They should not be forgotten or overlooked.

Chapter 17

THE LONDON MEETING

I sat in the great hall of Imperial College in South Kensington and listened as a man called Patrick told his story. It was very simple. His mother had been raped at the age of 10 and a half. He was the result of this, and had been born when she was 11 years and three months old. The family had not been indigent or inadequate. There had been money, and until he was four and a half years old he had lived at home. Then, he had been put into the orphanage in Kilkenny. He said a little about this but his testimony—and his question—was really of secondary importance to the unloading of a heavy heart. Later he told me a poignant story of how, before her teens even, his mother had been given a red coat. It was paid for at the rate of 2s 6d a week.

When, eventually, he met her again, at the age of 50, he said to her: 'What happened the red coat?' She paled and looked shocked and crossed herself. 'You remember the red coat?' 'Indeed I do,' he said, unlocking a heavy but silver-lined door into his own and her past.

He sat in the audience, sweet-faced, in a pure white shirt, and recovered snatches of his distant life as a child in an orphanage run by the Sisters of Charity to which he was committed through the intervention of an officer of the NSPCC in Tipperary.

This London event was a 'Survivors' Conference 2003' and was well attended. Coaches travelled to London from Birmingham, Manchester, Coventry, Sheffield and other cities in which there were Irish abuse support organisations with significant memberships. The meeting was organised by SOCA UK.

Noel Dempsey, the Minister for Education, gave an undertaking that he would go to London and be at that meeting on 30 March. He was as good as his word and addressed the men and women who had been abused in Irish reformatories and industrial schools.

Delegates from the Redress Board and the Lafoy Commission were also there. Part of the confusion with which abused people had to contend was the presence of women such as Sister Teresa Gallagher. She was director of Immigrant Counselling and Psychotherapy (ICAP) and a member of the Loreto Order which in turn is part of CORI. She attempted to give an account of ICAP's work. Sister Gallagher had clearly not been in front of an audience of this kind and she came in for serious, sustained and angry objection to the fact that she was a member of a religious community. She tried to speak above the interruptions but was so heckled and shouted at that eventually she gave up.

Noel Dempsey's speech was full of pain and hurt but short on specifics. He referred to a meeting in December 2002 at which it was indicated that the survivors of abuse in institutions in the United Kingdom were being left out of account. He claimed he wanted to rectify this. The Taoiseach's Apology, he said, was not given to victims in the United Kingdom. Jim Beresford of Irish SOCA, whose story was told in Chapter 15, sitting near the front, raised a banner: 'Stuff Your Apology'.

It was clear that Dempsey had misjudged his audience. He talked of people being 'gravely wronged'. As I recorded it, he said the unthinkable: 'I detect your pain'! He could have been a bishop! I noted down: 'Not pain—crime.' He went on to say the purpose of Government thinking was that this would not happen again, and that a range of measures had been put in place to this end. He outlined them in rather limited, stolid terms: the Lafoy Commission, the Confidential Committee, the Investigation Committee, the Redress Board, further refinements to these bodies. He gave heavy emphasis to why the abuse and hardship had happened, how it had happened and he hoped that it would not happen again. But he admitted nothing beyond the broad guilt and the wish to end the pain. He did not go far enough. His apology was minimal and ungenerous. Worst of all, it was unspecific.

We had questions at 12.30 p.m. Albert King, who was there on behalf of his wife, Mary, asked the following:

How can the Minister justify the Michael Woods–CORI Agreement of June 5 2002 which includes the indemnity agreement when it is clear the intensive negotiations are without the majority of Survivors of Child Abuse? Can the Minister accept the paltry and pathetic figure of €128 million being paid to the State in bits and pieces of cash and property from the Church when it is quite clear it is far less than they would have to pay through the courts and far less than the gold mine of land assets the Church in Ireland is sitting on according to property experts? Why has the Minister not made the terms of the indemnity agreement very clear because the terms do allow for disputes between the parties to be referred for adjudication to an expert and can be reviewed and altered? Does the Minister understand that his failure to respond to our letters is a failure in his duty? Is this failure due to the fact the Minister, including the former minister Michael Woods TD with the Church and State, had already done intensive negotiations related to the Michael Woods–CORI Agreement? Finally, did the Minister Noel Dempsey TD have a role in the amendments to the Freedom of Information Act to deny certain records of information to Survivors incarcerated in State institutions?

This was clearly a well-rehearsed assault, worked out in detail and related deliberately to issues in which Dempsey himself had been involved. It seemed to throw Dempsey, this concerted and critical questioning. He put up poor arguments, denying capacity to answer or denying knowledge. He had no proper defence on CORI and the State and was clearly surprised by the virulence of Albert King's opening salvo. Later, when the nature of a woman's committal proceedings were recounted, he said: 'If anyone has a written record, a criminal record, let me have that and I'll come back.' He seemed unaware that almost all the men and women who had gone through the industrial school system had, at least in theory, court records of the process by which they had been committed, records that were in the possession of the Department over which Dempsey presided; moreover, they were records that had been extracted from the Department with the greatest difficulty. They were the heart of the problem. They were the pernicious evidence of the distorted use of the Irish court system to arrest and confine boys and girls for years in industrial schools all over Ireland.

Tom Cronin wanted to know whether the Minister had the funds for the compensation. Were they in place? Had they been put through the Book of Estimates? He also asked about the trust fund for education. How would it be implemented and made accessible?

The answers to these questions, as was the case in all Dempsey's answers throughout the day, were ambiguous or negative. The money was not in any firm form at all. It would, said the Minister, 'be available as and when required'. There had been no special vote, there were no paragraphs in the estimates. The accounting was worse than it had been for industrial schools in the 1960s.

Another speaker raised a critical issue: that of the receipt of compensation among English-resident abuse victims and the effect of this compensation on their social welfare benefits. Dempsey was more specific on this, but gave a very limited prospect of a good answer. There is in fact no agreement and no preparedness on the British side to accommodate the victims if they received redress. There had been talks—he mentioned a meeting with Charles Clark, a member of Tony Blair's Cabinet—but they had got nowhere. It was a matter for United Kingdom law; change in this was not foreseeable. Dempsey had an answer, but it represented minimal information. He should have had a briefing document on this to guide him, with details of what was planned for the future, or how the Department of Education actually saw the solution. What were its targets? The absence of such an approach was increasingly suspicious. Perhaps nothing would be done?

Patrick then told his story, about the red coat. His difficulty, and his mother's, was that she had later married and had a family. Who was he to intrude? How was he to represent himself? He passed himself off as a friend of their father, probably the last person he could have been a friend of. It was a heart-stopping pivotal point in the proceedings.

Daisy Day spoke next. She wanted to know why there was so much delay.

Eleven victims of abuse known to her had died since the beginning of the year. On the issue of compensation, Dempsey made a mistake at this point in answering the question about delay. 'I know in general,' he said, 'there will be money to pay compensation as quickly as ever I could. *I will cut through the procedures.*' I made a note at this point: The Minister is saying that everything is being done. But he is not saying that bad things are being done. I thought particularly of the records. On these he was challenged. He said that 4,000 applications were in the pipeline. There was a six-month delay. They were being treated in 'chronological order'. This seemed a daft word to use. Did it mean by date of incarceration, date of receipt, date of departure?

The issue of education for people in the United Kingdom came up. Dempsey talked about the €12.7 million 'entrusted' for education. Patrick Walsh of SOCA corrected this. He raised the issue of the indemnity agreement. If it were to be made part of the Redress Act, this would be acceptable. But unless this were done, what the Minister was proposing to do with the money was illegal.

The issue of therapy was raised. This was in response to the rather poor performance of Sister Gallagher. On the question of ICAP, the representative of the Department of Health said that people could have therapists independent of ICAP and these would be paid for. Apparently, many are already in this position. I was astonished.

Mary Tyndall spoke. She was in Summerhill, in Athlone, and her family, she said, did not know. She got no education, could not read or write. She was followed by others. The session became ragged and quite angry before the break for lunch.

In the afternoon Kevin Brady, who ran NOVA, spoke about the education programme. He seemed to me a boy sent on a man's errand. He did not know the British educational system. He was in the process of finding out.

Michael O'Beirne of the Redress Board was the best speaker of the day. He spoke from notes, but it seemed like a script. He subsequently answered questions clearly and well. He explained what the Redress Board had been doing, before establishment day and after. The early work included meeting with NOVA and other outreach groups. The Redress Board was engaged in issuing forms and accepting applications. At that stage there had been 861 applications, that is, 12 per day since establishment day. Of these, 35 per cent—340—were complete, the rest incomplete, some needing further information, some—34 or 4 per cent—rejected as coming from the wrong source, i.e. victims of supposed abuse in national schools. These are not covered by the legislation. To date there have been 11 interim payments.

Mary Ellen Ring, a Senior Counsel attached to the Lafoy Commission, spoke about her work as an advisor to the Confidential Committee. She drew attention to the fact that the Commission faced a legal wrangle with the Christian Brothers, and she gave important statistics. She said there had been 1,152 applications; 660 were met in Dublin, the United Kingdom, the United States and France. On 452 applications progress lay in the future. There was a case in the courts on 13 May which would impede the situation. She did not spell it out. It later emerged that this was the challenge by the Christian Brothers against Ms Justice Mary Lafoy. She said that the mandate for the Commission had already been extended to 2005 and would probably be extended further.

We moved on to questions at this stage and Ron McCartan questioned Dempsey. On Freedom of Information, Dempsey simply denied any legal impediment in the amended legislation. This somehow rang false; one could tell from his expression that he doubted what he was saying. Ron also asked him about the funding of selected survivor groups. The response to this was that the Department 'facilitated groups and survivors as much as possible'. Dempsey said he thought the method currently followed was the best. There was some discussion of NOVA. The consensus of the meeting was clearly of dissatisfaction with it.

Eddie Birmingham spoke. He had been in Letterfrack from 1959 to 1963. He said quite simply that it had ruined his life—his wife, his children, drink, violence. He was not entirely coherent, but later, in personal testimony to me, I could see that his experiences had been excruciating. They were clearly expressed in his meagre physique, his lined and punished face, his language.

Dempsey said that it would have been 'a lot cheaper for the State for people to go to court'. It was an extraordinary remark, received with audible disbelief. It rendered cold and political the whole structure of aid and recompense. But, more deeply, it indicated part of the day's strategy, which was to emphasise the value to victims of going down the route of redress and not returning to the courts. This was, of course, suitable to the Government, frightened of the court road, as well they might be. Dempsey reiterated the argument: it would be cheaper for the Government if people went to the courts. He wanted to recommend redress. Redress was a more simple option. Victims would not be challenged legally at the Redress Board.

John McDonagh, a Senior Counsel, spoke for the Redress Board. He had no answers that satisfied the audience. A woman called Yvonne talked about her life. 'It's my life I want back and I cannot get it back. The Minister has made me cry for it again.' Ron McCartan came in again and raised the argument that the date for redress should begin with the first award.

The meeting overran its time. It did not end until five o'clock in the evening. I chatted with friends and with the Irish Ambassador, exchanging addresses and phone numbers. I told Michael O'Beirne, who had appeared on behalf of the Redress Board that he had been the best platform performer. He was non-committal.

It was a lovely afternoon. The sun blazed down and there were crowds everywhere. I gazed in a kind of numbed disbelief over the meaning of happiness and at the sight of lovers lying together in the warm sunlight on the dry spring grass. There had been no rain for many days. Children were playing and the

Round Pond in Kensington Gardens, besides which I had enjoyed so many happy days in childhood watching the boats and flying my kite, was full of birds. There were wild geese and swans. They made me think of Chekhov.

The London meeting was unique. Nothing as elaborate had been achieved by the abused. They had discomforted an Irish Minister, dismissed many of the alleged helpers and advisers provided by the Irish State, asked questions and received dusty answers, demonstrated their power and their disenchantment. They had established that there was a lot wrong with what was being done, and very little that really met their demands.

By any judgment, Noel Dempsey was in some trouble with the issues raised, to which he had given very limited answers. His need had been that of attempting to justify the State's deal with the Church. It had satisfied no one. He had tried to respond to the growing tide of criticism levelled against himself and his department over the workings of the various bodies established by legislation. This had not gone well either. He had reiterated some of the main points from the Taoiseach's Speech of Apology of May 1999 but they had made little sense in the intolerant atmosphere at the meeting. The May 1999 speech had in any case been unanimously rejected by Irish SOCA, one of the organisations working on behalf of the abused.

Dempsey's real problem, however, lay with the organisations representing abused people and their growing despondency about their dependency on departmental influence, personnel and funding. This despondency and the reasons behind it were expressed in London throughout the day of the meeting. Strongly declared was a perception among the former victims of abuse that many of the structures set up by the Department of Education were primarily concerned with controlling the victims rather than helping them. NOVA is the umbrella organisation for several abuse organisations, all but one of which are part-funded by the Department of Education. Though described by the Lafoy Commission as a place where 'fair and impartial advice' can be obtained, NOVA was seen by the abused as predominantly a Department of Education organisation. Its funding, members of its staff, and its programme all bore the heavy stamp of departmental influence. There is a conflict of interest in this. As ministers, including the Minister for Justice, had made clear at this time, it was the State that wronged the boys and girls in sending them to the institutions and then not protecting them, and central to this wrongdoing was the Department of Education. It ran the inspection service that so dismally failed those who were abused. Both the failure and the abuse continued until at least 1995.

Many former victims of abuse in London said that the State–CORI Secret Deal was overly favourable to the Church. The Department held the power. As they saw it, members of CORI who were directly involved were given a blanket indemnity. In addition to the Department of Education funding and staffing NOVA, its officials were also responsible for the organisation's code of conduct. The details were written by an officer from the Department of Education.

Departmental officials were seen as close to Michael Woods in the negotiation with CORI of the Secret Deal. Altogether, six civil servants, three from the Department of Finance, two from Education and one from the Attorney General's office, in February 2001 and earlier, prepared the guidelines for the final stages of negotiation with CORI.

A draft memorandum of that February meeting obtained at the time by the *Irish Independent* indicated an expectation of a 50 per cent deal between Church and State. The possibility of the figure being 'capped' was mentioned, but if so it would be at 'a significant sum'. The officials who attended meetings on the Government side in respect of this negotiation had since then become closely involved in monitoring the development of the organisations acting for the abused. There is no suggestion that Department officials acted improperly, but a conflict of interest is obvious.

The extent of the Department of Education's involvement in abuse organisations can be gauged from its financial support. In a letter sent to Tom Cronin, a former member of Right of Place, in Cork, in September 2001, the Department of Education wrote of being 'committed to support the activities of NOVA groups that will assist past victims of institutional abuse in accessing information'. The letter, a copy of which was held then by the *Irish Independent*, also endorsed departmental financial support to the groups, giving them what are described as 'dedicated budgets'. Its author outlines the figures.

ICAP, the Immigrant Counselling and Psychotherapy service, was given a rough time at the London meeting. This organisation was run by Teresa Gallagher a nun in the Loreto Order, one of the CORI institutions. ICAP is under contract to the Department of Health to supply counselling. It is recommended to abused people in the United Kingdom by the Lafoy Commission and by health board counselling service personnel. This is done without informing the abused that the director is a nun of the Loreto Order. To many of the abuse survivors, the involvement of a member of a religious order attached to CORI is a significant issue. This is a clear conflict of interest.

One of the trustees of ICAP at the time was Father Jerry Kivlehan, a priest of the Oblates of Mary Immaculate, another CORI institution. This order ran St Conleth's reformatory, Daingean, the most notorious of the reformatories and far more brutal than the industrial schools. Its immediate closure, on account of its harsh and brutal regime, was recommended by the Kennedy Report in 1970. The Oblate Order refused to co-operate fully with the Lafoy Commission. This involvement represented another conflict of interest.

In all this there is evidence of substantial, over-zealous and in many respects ill-judged involvement by the Department of Education and, to a lesser extent, by the Department of Health, in the running of the abuse organisations. This is coupled with examples of co-operation with the religious organisations and their activity among the abused people, particularly in Britain, but also in Cork.

The London meeting was a very public display of a number of issues that had undermined the confidence of the abused in the processes set up by the Irish Government in 1999. Very little was resolved as a result of it. Despite his strong showing, the man at the heart of the rumbling storm that went on all that day, Noel Dempsey, failed in assuaging fears or settling doubts. Other people had been exposed as being too involved on either side of the wall dividing those who represented the Church or the State and those who had been abused. These people, like the Minister, left the event unsure of what would happen next. They were relying on an unstable set of provisions and on people who at some level or other were engaged in a cover-up. The London meeting was a watershed in the chronology of distrust, not one of progress.

Chapter 18 ❧

⏐ THE ISSUE OF REDRESS

The need for a compensation scheme for survivors was raised before the Commission to Inquire into Child Abuse by a firm of solicitors representing a number of solicitors throughout the country who were acting on behalf of many, but not all the survivors of institutional child abuse. As early as 20 July 2000, at the Commission's second public sitting, the matter was referred to as having a significant impact on the Investigation Committee's remit. The solicitors asserted collaterally, in their submission, that on the question of compensation—as was the case in many other matters, and was referred to in these terms many times over by Ms Justice Mary Lafoy—there was a basic conflict of interest within the Department of Education. This was because the Department had consistently denied liability in civil proceedings, a number of which had already been brought against it by survivors alleging abuse. It was a stock defence to be found in all defence correspondence against such legal claims. The Commission quite properly saw it side by side with demands for a scheme for the payment of lawyers involved in representing the survivors who were claiming they had been abused.

The two issues were seen as significant stumbling blocks. It need hardly be added that both issues were so central to the achievement of the Commission's objectives that it is little short of astonishing that they had not been attended to in the primary legislation, rather than left to applications coming from the survivors; this is particularly so in the case of the compensation or redress scheme.

Nothing was done. When the Commission held its next public sitting, at the end of December, there had been no progress on either issue. This chapter deals with the compensation scheme, not with legal fees, but the Department's failure to devise a scheme on fees meant that a significant number of solicitors would not make submissions on behalf of abused people.

While the Commission recognised that compensation was a policy issue for Government, it did so within the clearly expressed view that it was an issue on which it was empowered to make recommendations and that, in the context of the Taoiseach's Apology and the announcement of measures designed 'to redress the wrongs done to victims of abuse', the Government should commit in principle to compensation. All the Department of Education would say was that 'it was intended by the end of October 2000 that a report would be submitted by the Department to the Cabinet Sub-committee on Child Abuse'. Compensation was agreed 'in principle' on 3 October and announced by the Minister for Education, Noel Dempsey, without consulting the Commission, as Mary Lafoy had suggested. Instead, the Minister made a second announcement, on 27 February 2001, that the Government 'had agreed to my proposals for a compensation scheme'. The exclusion of the Commission from contributing to the modalities of a compensation scheme was 'regretted', not without good reason since, apart from the many stories coming from abused people, the only statutory examination of such allegations was contained in the work carried out by the Commission and would have been of considerable value. Instead, the scheme was worked out essentially by the Department of Education!

The Commission regretted the delays, the prevarication and the exclusion of its staff from involvement in the construction of the scheme, in part because it had led to public confusion and had divided the solicitors acting on behalf of abuse victims into those who would not submit without there being a legal payments scheme, those who wanted both a legal payments scheme and a compensation scheme to be in place, and those who were prepared to submit without either being finalised. The Commission argued that the compensation scheme—whatever form it eventually took—and the Commission's own work were inextricably interlocked. 'All persons entitled to pursue a claim for compensation under the scheme envisaged in the Government decisions will also come within the remit of the Commission's inquiry.'

The public confusion, referred to by the Commission, was widely in evidence in the views taken by the abused. As a result, quite undeserved, negative reflections were made about Ms Justice Lafoy, who was blamed for inordinate delays in the procedures of the Commission. This situation was aggravated by the fact that the Minister for Education had implied in his statement of 27 February 2001 that the Government had accepted 'his' proposal, which was strictly true, although the reality was that the need for such a scheme came directly from the Lafoy Commission. Nor would it have been anything other than a reluctant course to take by the Government on its own. What confronted Bertie Ahern and his Minister for Education was the real risk of work within the Commission, which had already ground to a stop, being terminated because the abused were faced with two blockages: fees for their lawyers, and compensation payments for themselves.

The Government continued to drag its feet, having agreed 'in principle'. It had accepted, from the start, the fact of large numbers of people wishing to confront their tormentors or to get off their chests their recollections of what they had suffered during their childhood incarcerations. The additional dimension of them being recompensed, in financial terms that would have to measure up, in part, to the kind of awards that were being given in the courts, represented a formidable administrative and financial problem.

There were close to 30,000 people, born since 1930, who had been committed by the courts to industrial and reformatory schools. Further significant numbers which the Department of Education could not accurately quantify, were committed by parents. The fact that records on these committals proved inadequate was then, as it had been in previous years, a bone of contention. What had the Department done with its prison records?

What Noel Dempsey had outlined in relation to redress was couched in terms of the undesirability of court cases being taken side by side with the work undertaken by the Commission. It was inconsistent with the Taoiseach's Apology. Dempsey was of the opinion that 'there was a compelling case for setting up procedures outside the court system for dealing with claims from victims of abuse, in order to avoid significant delays and costs in litigation'. This view had to be taken with a pinch of salt in the light of the protracted delays, both before Dempsey's recommendation to the Government—prompted by Ms Justice Lafoy—and after it. In reality it was a form of self-protection against a substantial number of prospective claims that had started off the whole process.

The Minister was right to point out that victims would face difficulties and that it was appropriate to offer a quicker and less demanding process for the award of monetary compensation. But it was offered in a hollow chamber of increasing negligence over the operation of the process initiated by the Taoiseach's Apology. Not entirely to anyone's surprise, CORI, also 'in principle', indicated its willingness to become involved.

In February 2001, the Government approved the drafting of the Victims of Child Abuse Compensation Tribunal Bill, which would 'validate claims in a non-adversarial way'. It did not indicate that it would be something of a Star Chamber, private, secret and with huge penalties of up to €25,000 fines and six-month terms in prison for those abused who accepted money and made the details public.

The Redress Bill was enacted into law, on 10 April 2002, as the Residential Institutions Redress Act 2002 and under it the Residential Institutions Redress Board was established. Men and women who, as children, were resident in certain institutions and suffered injuries that were consistent with abuse received there would qualify for compensation. A total of 123 institutions in the child prison system, or working closely with its inmates in other categories, were listed—87 of these were the responsibility of the Department of Education or were supervised by the Department; 82 of them were managed by religious congregations represented by CORI. The apparent distinction between State and Church is misleading: the Church, or 'Religious' as they were termed, worked for and were financed by the State in their role as 'guardians' of the incarcerated.

There followed what I term the Secret Deal (dealt with in Chapter 11), indemnifying the 'Religious' in return for financial involvement in the redress scheme. In January 2002 the Minister announced that agreement, in principle, had been reached with the congregations about the level of their contribution.

Further negotiations took place, culminating in the approval by the Government, in June 2002, of an agreement under which the congregations would make a contribution of €128 million inclusive of some past contributions. I argued, after the scheme had been in operation for a limited period, that the cost of it to the State would be in the region of £1,000 million—a figure that is now accepted as modest—and that the contribution by the religious was derisory. Moreover, it included gifts in kind, in the form of properties, some of which had dubious value or questionable title.

In return for this limited Church commitment, the State agreed to indemnify the congregations in respect of all cases where a person would have been eligible to make a claim under the Act, with the indemnity to apply to those cases where litigation was commenced within the following six years. Though the deal was signed on 5 June 2002, with 18 religious congregations as signatories, the public was given only part of the detail.

The redress scheme raised a number of questions, not least the fact that the Board was established to determine awards, while an independent Residential Institutions Review Committee was established to review them, which it appears to have done in miserly terms. The penal secrecy has prevented any analysis or comparison between civil awards and redress awards but such information as has become available indicates a substantial disparity.

The Board had two main functions: firstly the making of awards and secondly a search 'to ensure that those who were resident in the institutions listed in the Act are made aware of the Board's existence so that they may apply for redress'. Applicants for redress had to establish identity, incarceration in one of the institutions designated by the Act, the nature of the abuse and injury and to do so 'within three years of the establishment of the Board on 16 December 2002'. Provision was made, in the event of the death of a claimant, for a spouse or children to apply.

Medical and psychological tests preceded the placing of an applicant within the bands that had been set up by the Board and the Review Committee. 'If the applicant accepted the award, then he or she had to agree in writing to waive any right of action against a public body or a person who had made a contribution under the Act.'

There was uncertainty from the beginning, with doubts about the State's liability, about a number of other contingencies and possible future events. After less than a year of the Board being in operation, questions were raised about the number of claimants, the extent of the awards set against the nature of the abuse suffered. This is slightly but significantly at odds with the Board's interpretation of its function, after advertising its purpose, based on Section 5 of the Act:

> It is then the Board's function in relation to each case in which an application is made to determine whether the applicant is entitled to an award, and, if so, to make an award in accordance with the Act which is fair and reasonable

having regard to the unique circumstances of the applicant.

In its first Annual Report, published in 2003, the Redress Board gave an account of its operation. In order to fulfil the first part of its remit, an advertising campaign was conducted in Ireland in January and February 2003. In December 2003, 15,000 documents, including posters, short guides to the redress scheme and single-page leaflets, were sent to Irish Centres in the United Kingdom. In the 54 weeks to 31 December 2003, the Board has received a total of 2,573 applications, averaging 48 applications per week. The statutory steps and times allowed for each step laid down in the Act and Regulations occupied, in that first period, a minimum of 14 weeks.

At that stage the Board anticipated receiving between 6,500 and 7,000 applications in the time allowed by the Redress Act 2002. This was a tentative estimate.

As already pointed out, a Compensation Advisory Committee was established by the Minister in 2001—before the Act was passed—which brought together expertise from a range of disciplines, including law, medicine, psychiatry and psychology. The Committee considered the experience in other countries. It published a report, *Towards Redress and Recovery*, known as the Ryan Report. This was presented to the Minister in January 2002 and included, *inter alia*, recommendations for the assessment of redress. The Committee recommended that redress should be assessed under four headings dealing with severity, medical, physical and psychiatric verification, possible illness and loss of life opportunity.

There were five 'weightings'; 70 was the most severe, earning €200,000 to €300,000; 55 to 69 earned €150,000 to €200,000; 40–54, €100,000 to €150,000; 25–39, €50,000 to €100,000; and less than 25 up to €50,000. This schema was incorporated into the redress scheme. The Board had leeway to make further payments of up to '20% of the assessed award in exceptional circumstances'. The Board then commenced making awards in May 2003 and by 31 December 2003 had completed the process in 587 cases. The average value of awards to 31 December 2003 was approximately €80,000, the largest award being €270,000; in one case no award was made.

By way of comparison, this trend is borne out by the level of average awards from three of the compensation schemes which operated in Canada, where awards made were, broadly speaking, based on matrices similar to those recommended by the Ryan Report and adopted in the Irish Regulations.

PART FIVE

Ms Justice Mary Lafoy Replaced by Mr
Justice Seán Ryan

Chapter 19 ∾

A SECOND LOOK AT MS JUSTICE MARY LAFOY'S RESIGNATION LETTER

Those members of the Government with a reasonably well-informed idea of how they were viewed by abuse victims and the survivor groups included only the Ministers for Education and for Health and the Taoiseach. These three were informed because they had received many letters of complaint and criticism. I received copies of these letters, accompanied by letters from former inmates, and was astonished at the anger, dismay and disdain they contained. Other Government members were largely in the dark because the ministers concerned, with the Taoiseach, handled knowledge of these letters badly, keeping them away from collective Cabinet consideration. There was no requirement to do otherwise, but it has left those politically responsible in a difficult position when it comes to explaining why the soft-soap approach—dismally offered on radio by Dermot Ahern on the day Ms Justice Mary Lafoy's resignation letter was published—aggravated a situation in which confidence in the Government had been lost. All members of the Government, other than those who have played a direct part in abuse action—whether the wide-ranging acts by the Taoiseach, or the specific ones of the two ministers closest to the problem—would need answers. Or so it seemed to me. At that stage, with Government and Cabinet changes, we were beginning to get a cast of characters who had occupied the hot seat in the Department of Education, with other new faces in Health and Justice, all having a part of the responsibility. In fact it did not really matter. There would be a replacement for Mary Lafoy, answers to her criticisms and the show would go on.

The truth was that the abused had by now, in mid-2003, lost all trust in the Government. The carefully orchestrated process, begun in May 1999, had fallen apart. The Redress Board's actions were not trusted. The average payment, somewhere near 10 per cent of what the courts might give for the serious abuses that were done to these people when they were imprisoned children, was seen as derisory. The Lafoy Commission, from the point of view of the abused, was not trusted either.

It was clear that there would be no rescue for those facing the crisis into which the State had been plunged by Mary Lafoy unless the answers were comprehensive, serious and far-reaching. The likelihood of this, so long as Noel Dempsey remained Minister for Education, and so long as the issue remained the responsibility of the Department of Education, was slim indeed. And even if answers were to be found—very difficult to see happening—different incumbents would be required to implement it.

The political side was only part of the problem. This was not a situation where a promise to do better would make any difference. Mary Lafoy had exposed a political nightmare contained within the legislation. It was defective from the outset, and this was proved by the three-year turmoil through which she tried to work her way. The fact that it was a cover-up, and not a genuine attempt to settle retrospectively the circumstances of widespread abuse, caused the nightmare. Untangling it was too huge a problem.

The proposed changes, under the Government's first review of the Commission's workings, were not designed to put right these faults in the legislation. They were designed to change the legislation for entirely short-term and dishonest cost-saving and time-saving purposes. The process needed to be speeded up in order to get it and the whole abuse controversy out of the way. Morally reprehensible, this approach was also legally difficult if not impossible, as Mary Lafoy had outlined in her letter. There were too many people involved—legal representatives, servants of the Commission and advisers—to make it tenable for the procedures to be put right.

There was no way back to the original legislation because it had been found deeply damaging to the process and also ineffective. No judge of merit would be willing to undertake that road forward. The legislation could not be effectively revised, because the framework for so doing had been irreversibly prejudiced by the Minister's actions in trying to formulate change as part of a time and motion study. It was difficult to see how the legislature could possibly go forward on any legislative proposal put before it by Noel Dempsey, and backed by this Government, after Ms Justice Lafoy's position became clear.

Nor could we look into the future, and accept any remedy consistent with the Taoiseach's speech, since few people believed that speech any longer. It had been so profoundly traduced by the events of the four years since he had made it. The abused had been marginalised and were now the major stumbling block to progress. They had been seen at the outset as flawed and damaged individuals, looking for answers. This interpretation, given what they had gone through, was quite wrong. It failed to recognise that many of the leading figures were also highly intelligent—though denied the proper education which was their birthright—and extremely angry.

There were brilliant minds at work among the survivor groups. They understood the law, they asked difficult questions, they embarrassed ministers and the Taoiseach, and in a piecemeal way, despite obstruction, they were slowly getting the right answers. But they were not sufficiently well supported legally to undertake the challenge that seemed to be invited by the change of direction that had led to Mary Lafoy's resignation.

There were good reasons for the majority of the abused no longer wanting the Lafoy Commission, with Ms Justice Mary Lafoy or without her. But their reasoning, which embraced the idea that the Commission had ceased to serve them, and was serving instead the interest of CORI and the lawyers, was unfair. Not until Mary Lafoy's letter of resignation, with its detailing of Department of Education obstruction of her work, did the abused begin to revise their judgments about her.

From then on, the abused saw the future as a political vista of further Government prevarication and deviousness. This was undoubtedly what followed and it was a confirmation for the abused that their worst fears had been realised. It had been predicted, not least in numerous articles published earlier that year in the *Irish Independent*. There was no pleasure in referring to this during the crisis provoked by Ms Justice Mary Lafoy. Most people in the country wanted the abused to get a fair deal. They deserved to be rescued from the legal limbo into which they felt they had been placed when committed to the industrial schools for what turned out to be around 10 per cent of their natural lives. This latter aspect would never be resolved since the Government had ruled it out of account. But sorting out the other difficulties should have been possible with the proper will. Yet that will was simply not there. The Department of Education and its Ministers, both Noel Dempsey and his predecessors, Michael Woods and Micheál Martin, were guilty of a shameful dereliction of duty, embracing prevarications, exclusions, the imposition of penalty clauses in legislation, all designed to hedge in the prospects of the abused and put them under threat. It is notable that, throughout her Third Interim Report, Mary Lafoy repeatedly brings to the forefront of her thinking her concern for the aging victims of the industrial school system.

Neither trust nor confidence could be easily recovered in the embarrassing circumstances that emerged in September and were emphatically confirmed with the publication in December of the Commission's Third Interim Report. This seemed to have more in it about delays and obstructions, as well as legal difficulties and anomalies, than it did about direct inquiry into abuse. Only one inquiry had been completed. This was into the Baltimore Fisheries School, closed more than half a century before. Another, Our Lady of Succour Industrial School, Newtownforbes, County Longford, was dealt with in a chapter about the module for investigation, though no evidence had been heard and the only material available was in the form of allegations. That was how the first four years had been spent, and the achievement was very small indeed. This situation would now be further complicated by proposed amendments to legislation. The change of direction had now become a critical factor in the crisis. It was virtually impossible, any more, to define the Government's purpose; and even if this were so, no one believed any longer that it was to benefit the abused.

It is at this point appropriate to consider in greater detail the content of Mary Lafoy's letter of resignation. Broadly speaking, the letter divides into two unequal parts. The first and lesser of these is concerned with how the Department of Education and the Government, for a variety of reasons, obstructed and brought to a standstill Ms Justice Lafoy's attempts to fulfil her mandate. She stresses that this mandate was given her by the Oireachtas, then changed and, by default, taken away, by the Government and by the Minister for Education, acting on behalf of the Government. Whatever about these decisions, which she recognises were matters of policy, she maintains that

> … my role was to preserve intact the process put in place by the Oireachtas in the Act of 2002. However, I believe that the cumulative effect of those factors, each of which has been characterized by long periods of uncertainty for the Commission, has effectively negatived the guarantee of independence in the performance of its functions conferred on the Commission by section 3(3) of the Act of 2000 and has militated against the Commission being able to perform its statutory functions as envisaged by the Oireachtas with reasonable expedition.

These changes were, perforce, endorsed by the Houses of the Oireachtas. As in the passage of the first Commission to Inquire into Child Abuse Act of 2000, the amending Act of 2005 was presented and passed in contentious circumstances— as has been so much legislation in respect of this institutional child abuse issue— and had still not produced, as Mary Lafoy pointed out in her letter, anything beyond an unqualified mandate for its operation. This is not unusual in Irish law-making. Various barrow-loads of documentation have been trundled in and out of court-rooms in respect of tribunals, in efforts to tidy up the search for criminal corruption in planning, bribery and other acts of chicanery. In this case the circumstances were different. Mary Lafoy took seriously the position of chairperson of the Commission which she had accepted in advance of the first Act, took on trust the legislation itself, believing that it would be funded correctly and pursued without hindrance.

She must have ground her teeth a little at the end of 2002, when the Department of Education asked her to justify the request for sufficient resources for the Investigation Committee to separate into four divisions and complete Phase One of its work by the end of July 2005. Nevertheless, she responded by telling her sponsoring Department that there were both legal and moral consequences in further delays. Her concerns were:

> The need to bring closure for the Complainants and for other victims of abuse in childhood, many of whom are old and in bad health. The avoidance of unfairness to individuals against whom allegations have been made, which

may not stand up following investigation. Many of the individual respondents are very old. Some are in bad health. It may be that in certain cases, the end of their lives are being unfairly blighted by the stress of a prolonged investigation. Issues of fairness also arise in relation to individuals against whom allegations have been made, who are still of working age, whose capacity to work in institutions may be affected.

The Government's response was bizarre. Instead of meeting Ms Justice Lafoy's request, it immediately made the decision to review the mandate. Nine months then elapsed during which time she repeatedly reminded the Department of her concern for the persons concerned by the process.

> I believe that the further indefinite protraction of the uncertainty as to the task which the Commission will ultimately be mandated to carry out announced in the Press Release is detrimental to the interests of the persons for whose benefit the Commission was established—the men and women, many of whom are now elderly, who allege that they suffered abuse in institutions in the State during childhood, who, at not inconsiderable cost, have indicated a willingness to assist the inquiry. They deserve to see the inquiry, which they were promised over four years ago, concluded within a reasonable timeframe. More-over, I believe that the inevitable future delay has the potential to give rise to unfairness and injustice to individuals against whom allegations have been made and persons with management or regulatory responsibility for institutions in which abuse is alleged to have occurred. They are entitled to expect that such allegations will be dealt with within a reasonable timeframe.

This paragraph in Ms Justice Lafoy's letter represented her view of the human iniquity being done by the State after a period of four troubled years in which the abused had been left outside the door of State deliberations, as indeed had she. But the legal view she had come to was even more serious. The alteration of the mandate put the Commission in the position of working in the future 'to a mandate potentially radically different from that currently in force', and rendered its investigations 'redundant or incorrectly focused'. The current mandate, still on the statute book, was 'inoperable'. No one knew what the new mandate would be. Apart from the practical and financial implications, there were legal ones and on these Mary Lafoy took legal advice, and decided, in spite of its independent statutory status, that the Commission could not continue, and that, furthermore, it had to make public that it was stymied.

In summary, what had happened was as follows: in November 2002 Mary Lafoy, in response to the request to 'justify' the need for funding, on grounds of satisfying the interests of the parties involved in the process, who had been unfairly delayed, had to abandon her already overdue interim report. She and the

Commission additionally concluded that the Investigation Committee would not be in a position to complete its statutory mandate; in December 2002 the Government decided to review the mandate. She expected this to be done expeditiously; her view was by Easter 2003. Instead, it dragged on for nine months, with her office repeatedly stressing the concern felt for the people involved. This concern, which lay at the heart of everything that she had done—though it was clearly not at the heart of Government thinking—was backed by another consideration.

> A subsidiary consideration which has weighed with me in reaching the decision is that there appears to be some risk that a Commission which works first to one mandate, and then to a substantially different mandate, would leave itself open to legal challenge on the ground that, in the course of exercising its first mandate, it obtained information or formed impressions which would affect its capacity to exercise the second mandate with a fully open mind. While, on the basis of independent legal advice which I have obtained, I believe that this risk is a slight one, nonetheless, even a slight risk may be unacceptable in a matter of this importance.

How slight has never been tested in the courts or challenged in the Dáil. Mary Lafoy ended her letter by assuring the Government that she would 'take all necessary steps to ensure that the public interest is protected'. Her letter was clear in that regard. The full content of it is as severe an indictment of judicial process marred by political uncertainty and prevarication as we have seen in recent years, affecting many lives and possibly undermining the rest of the abuse process.

Mary Lafoy's letter, together with the sequence of events that led to her resignation, would have put off the stoutest heart from taking on the challenges she left behind her amidst the debris of her departure. In the event, there was a ready-made replacement in the person of Seán Ryan, who was elevated to the Bench and made a High Court judge by President Mary McAleese on 10 December 2003. He was 55 years old, Senior Counsel since 1983 and, since 2001, if not earlier, had been involved within the Department of Education in giving legal advice. He had been appointed on 30 August 2001 to chair the Compensation Advisory Committee. This made a report, *Towards Redress and Recovery*, in January 2002. This Committee was appointed under section 14 of the Residential Institutions Redress Bill 2001. Others on the committee were Dr Helen Cummiskey, Dr Marion Gibson, Professor Desmond Greer and Professor Martin McHugh.

The announcement of Ryan's appointment said that he was to be made a judge of the High Court. This was as a preamble to putting him in charge of the Commission to Inquire into Child Abuse. Strangely, Noel Dempsey made the announcement at a marine event in Cork. He gave even stranger undertakings about the appointment and the immediate duties facing Ms Justice Mary Lafoy's replacement.

The judicial appointment was not a legal requirement. The Act does not stipulate a High Court judge. However, for a Senior Counsel to take on the job would inevitably have a bearing on his career if, in the future, he had to return to the Bar. Being on the Bench at the outset was probably a wise move for him and may have been a necessity for those appointing him. It was possible that accepting the position was conditional on the judicial appointment. Certainly, Seán Ryan was accepting a poisoned chalice, though poisoned quite by whom is a profound and complicated question.

At the beginning of October the Dáil returned to business. The Taoiseach and the Minister for Education were faced with embarrassing questions, to which they had added what seemed to be both an extraordinary error of judgement, and an even greater one on timing, when it made the Seán Ryan announcement.

Seán Ryan had been involved in abuse issues for some time and had worked with the Department of Education. He had been attached to the Ferns Inquiry as a lawyer advising the members of that body and, as chairperson of the Compensation Advisory Committee, had been engaged in hearing testimony from abuse organisations and individuals two years earlier. When his appointment was announced, doubts were expressed as to whether or not this work rendered him unsuitable, since those he had questioned were among those seeking hearings for themselves before the Commission he was now to chair. However, Ryan is experienced in what is a highly complex field of legal work.

Seán Ryan had also been responsible for the review that was undertaken by the Government while Ms Justice Lafoy was still struggling to get answers from the Department of Education.

The Government did not publish the review. It treated both reviews as 'a matter of priority' and Noel Dempsey brought them to Government on 4 March 2003. Late in March the Commission tried to find out what was happening. After a three-week delay, the Minister said the review would accompany publication of the Bill. In due course the review was released without the Bill.

Still thinking of the future, and now in the light of a substantial indictment of the Department of Education, it is appropriate to consider how Mr Justice Seán Ryan dealt with the problem. As he says himself, he was 'asked to conduct a review of the working of the Commission having regard to the interests of victims of abuse'. He says he was given 'every assistance' by Ms Justice Lafoy and her associates in the Commission and all the 'facilities' were made available.

It is inconceivable that Mr Justice Ryan was left unaware of the review involving the Attorney General. Nor is it conceivable that he was left ignorant about the reservations of Ms Justice Lafoy on the Department of Education's conflict of interest. The conflict of interest arises on the two issues—of servicing and of being a respondent—and of having negotiated a 'mutual protection' arrangement with the religious orders which was then kept secret, either on the orders of the Government, or by the Department on its own initiative.

In his own report Seán Ryan avoided the question altogether. There are five paragraphs in his report that deal with the Department, one of them on money. The second is significant, since it highlights the fact that the Department is a respondent in every one of the 314 Artane cases before the Commission. Seán Ryan proposed to 'sub-divide' them. The only other respondent, again in every case, is the Christian Brothers Order. This also would seem to be evidence of conflict of interest. Here is a Department of State and a religious order, both joined in mutual protection by a secret legal agreement, both answerable to the Commission; yet at the same time one of the two, the Department, is responsible for the Commission's resources, including funding, and is blocking an increase in these. This matter was later passed over wordlessly by the new chairperson of the Commission. He expressed a new objective; he was in favour of the decision to make the hearings briefer and presumably more palatable.

Mr Justice Ryan's final reference to the Department of Education was also significant, not for its funding relevance, in trying to get the resources to multiply the Committee divisions, but because he says: 'Then began the exchanges that led to the Attorney General's review of the Committee. The events that followed, culminating in the announcement of her resignation by Ms Lafoy, are not a matter for this review.'

If the Government asked him to review the workings of the Commission, then central to that were the issues of non-performance or poor performance by the Department, and the question raised by Ms Justice Lafoy about it being the 'statutory sponsor'. Astonishingly, these matters were not just part of the review, but an absolutely central part of it, and had affected the Commission's workings from the beginning. This important piece of evidence was not then dealt with by Seán Ryan and there is no explanation for this omission.

At the time, I raised some concerns about the method of Seán Ryan's appointment, which was made outside the conditions that were established in 1996 for judicial appointments. These required advertisement of the job, application for it and interview by a selection committee, including the Chief Justice. Apart from an aborted attempt to bypass this committee in 1998— aborted because the committee threatened to resign—all appointments since then had followed the procedure. On this occasion it seemed quite likely that the judiciary found itself nonplussed by the fact that no judge had wanted to take over from Ms Justice Mary Lafoy, though that is no more than informed speculation.

A further problem was that the High Court Bench was full. To appoint a High Court judge in such circumstances would require new legislation. In addition, and as a result of Ms Justice Lafoy's strictures in her long resignation letter, further legislation was required to amend the terms under which the Commission would now operate under its new chairperson.

Anomalous in a different way was a further question: how could Seán Ryan know what it was he had agreed to chair? Moreover, how could he agree in advance to an appointment to the High Court, which was being specifically made by the Government, according to Noel Dempsey's announcement of his appointment, 'to guarantee that the integrity and independence of the chairman [of the Commission] will be maintained'?

We had here a disturbing political situation. The sovereign law-making body in the State had neither seen nor debated the terms of either piece of legislation, but were being offered the person whose two appointments—to the Bench and to the Commission—had already been announced. One of these appointments was not in accordance with the terms for judicial appointments, nor was there space on the Bench for it. The other was to take up a role whose terms had been changed but were not yet specified. Nor had the relevant amending legislation been brought before the Houses of the Oireachtas. Seán Ryan could not know that his first appointment would be approved, and he could not know what the details of the job, which apparently he had accepted, would be, after the due legislative processes had taken place and, assuming that they were successful, including acceptance by the judiciary.

What we faced in the appointment of a High Court judge in this particular way, chosen by the Government, was the intrusion of a political mandate in shaping the judiciary. The appointment to the High Court appeared to pre-empt the constitutionality of what was being done. This represented a more serious problem than the others. The nature of the mandate announced by the Minister for Education, in advance of the appointment, though not at all clear, was unarguably for an express purpose that had been provoked by a confrontation between a respected member of the judiciary and the State, and, in so far as it could be understood—since it had not been worked out, nor the legislation drafted—it was very narrow in its design. The nature of the mandate, as announced by Noel Dempsey—and he said it quite clearly—is to protect the integrity and independence, not of the position of the new High Court judge under the Constitution, but of that judge's position as chairperson of the Commission to Inquire into Child Abuse. Yet that independence had just been obliterated, in part on grounds of the impugned integrity of Mr Justice Ryan's predecessor if she had chosen to stay in office. How could either the integrity or the independence be protected without first having been restored? And what hope was there of this being done in the circumstances of the Lafoy letter? Was the Commission itself hopelessly damaged by what had happened? And had not the new appointment been contrary to the constitutional protections for the judiciary on which depend their integrity and independence? The only independence and integrity applicable to any member of the judiciary is as defined under the Constitution. Neither the Government nor the Oireachtas can in law, or should in judgment, appoint judges in the way that was announced by Noel Dempsey in September 2003.

This piece of constitutional juggling was nonsensical and was creating a nightmare. It was deliberately and knowingly bypassing the State's due process for appointments to the judiciary. A new judge was being given a special duty to an existing Commission instead of what he would normally face if he were to be put on the Bench like other judges. And was not the Commission itself in need of redefinition in terms of its mandate, its future role, in funding and in the very law itself on which it would depend to complete the job that had been so negligently delayed by Government inaction and prevarication?

A judicial appointment superfluous to the legally approved number of High Court judges had happened once before. In 1982, after he had lost the second of the two general elections of that year, Charles Haughey tried to appoint Judge Laffan, to occupy a specific planning appointment, one that required a High Court judge. When the impropriety of the appointment was published in the *Irish Independent*, Haughey had to undo what he had done before going out of office and he made a public announcement to that effect. The Ryan case was slightly different, but it still carried a special set of circumstances that were embarrassing. It did not conform to established procedure, nor, it seemed, with legal and constitutional requirements.

This was a curious sequence, of government before the fact. In this case, we had a decision and a public announcement before the Oireachtas had seen the necessary legislation. We lacked a law under which to be governed on this issue. Yet we had the strange case of the Minister presenting a candidate for a crucially important task—that of chairperson of the Commission in respect of the lives and suffering of innocent people—before we knew that the Dáil and Senate had agreed to procedures under which this would be done.

As to the final question: why create a High Court judgeship for Seán Ryan in advance? And why announce this before the Houses of the Oireachtas have met? Might it have been part of another Secret Deal? Furthermore, according to the Minister, Seán Ryan was given a role of research and investigation, aimed at expediency and economy in the future operation of the Commission to Inquire into Child Abuse, of which he was intended to be the next chairperson. This was done in advance of the appointment, which could take place only on the publication of Ms Justice Lafoy's Third Interim Report. So Seán Ryan would be working for three months before becoming Commission chairperson and while Ms Justice Mary Lafoy remained in her position, completing her report. The relevant legislation was, of course, the Commission to Inquire into Child Abuse Act. (It had not at that stage been amended.) This Act does not allow for the Minister for Education, or indeed for the Government, to instruct the next chairperson, whose appointment must wait until new legislation has been passed, to carry out this research and investigation. This work, under Section 24 of the Act, can be ordered only by the Commission. Its chairperson, Ms Justice Lafoy, did not appear to have been consulted by the Minister for the purpose of then ordering her successor to investigate what she had been doing, and how it could be changed.

As matters stood, the Commission was in existence. Its work had been partially suspended by Ms Justice Lafoy. She had given the reasons to the Government in her letter three weeks previously. Part only of the Commission's work was ongoing. In such circumstances another section of the Act is relevant. Section 29 states: 'A person who by act or omission obstructs or hinders the Commission or a Committee or a person carrying out an examination pursuant to Section 14(5) [which concerns the central working of the Investigation Committee of the Commission] shall be guilty of an offence.'

We knew, at this stage and all too well, that this Investigation Committee was suspended. But in order to carry out the task given to him by the Minister, Seán Ryan would have had to invade the remit of that Committee or his task made no sense. He had to know how and why there were delays. To find this out, he needed to interrogate those responsible. Under the terms of the Act he was already in conflict with its powers under Section 24. He would now undoubtedly be treading on thin ice with the actual chairperson of the Commission, Ms Justice Lafoy, if he attempted to fulfil the proper inquiry that Noel Dempsey had asked for.

Ms Justice Mary Lafoy announced her decision to resign in September, but this was only to take effect after she had completed and published her Third Interim Report. One suspects that she did it this way in order to maintain the statutory powers under which she was operating until she had safely seen the document through into print. It is difficult, reading some of the passages, to imagine that it would have been secure if passed to the Department of Education without it being supported by the inescapable powers she had as Commission chairperson. Going back over the performance of the Department of Education, in respect of published reports and closely held personal documents of abused persons, the trustworthiness of the public servants serving the Commission chairperson had to be regarded with suspicion. It was even more the case with both the Department of Education and of the Taoiseach during the previous four years. Indeed, it is consistent with the Department's performance on everything connected with the industrial schools.

Mary Lafoy welcomed Mr Justice Seán Ryan's appointment. She said she would give him every co-operation and that the other members were looking forward to working with him. The Government request, that Ryan would undertake his own independent review of the Commission, was also mentioned. He was to have regard to 'the interests of the abused'. He was also to complete the Commission's work 'within a reasonable period and not incur exorbitant costs'.

There was a sting in the tail. Having 'lauded' (a rare word meaning 'praise' and used almost exclusively in Protestant hymns) the Government's emphasis on a speedy conclusion, these last words still seemed to be pregnant with nothing short of foreboding.

We faced a situation, at the beginning of 2004, in which the Commission, now operating under Mr Justice Seán Ryan, awaited changes to its legislation, therefore due to come before the Houses of the Oireachtas. The process of amendment would be open to debate and possible reform. Whether or not it was really in need of reform was at the time unclear, and really remained so, certainly in Ms Justice Mary Lafoy's judgment, though clearly not in the view of Seán Ryan. Though it had not worked effectively, this was hardly a fault of the legislation. It was the poor servicing of the Commission, by the Department of Education, which had driven its former chairperson, Mary Lafoy, to resign.

Chapter 20

THE COMING OF A NEW ARCHBISHOP

The Coadjutor Archbishop of Dublin, Dr Diarmuid Martin, who was later to succeed Cardinal Desmond Connell, said, in respect of abuse, that it was important to learn 'very deep lessons' about the past. He had been eloquent about his experiences, 40 years before, when he had first visited Artane. It seemed, from what he said, that he had seen and knew what was happening there when it was effectively concealed from everyone else. And he talked about Archbishop John Charles McQuaid, who knew very fully what was going on in Artane, having 'extreme concern' about the situation. Archbishop Martin remembered a nun being appointed to help out. This was in the last days of Artane, not too long before it closed its doors.

Archbishop Martin, having spent much of the previous 25 years working at the Vatican, returned to Dublin in August 2003. Shortly after this arrival in Dublin, he told the Association of European Journalists, at a luncheon, that for this reason he could not discuss the current abuse controversy. The view was expressed that he would need to learn fast. Diarmuid Martin is a sharp man, one of the Vatican's brightest and best. He was made aware of the problems in Ireland well before he came. He had been able to read up on the controversy, receive briefings from Sister Elizabeth Maxwell, former Secretary General of CORI, and its spokesperson, Sister Helena O'Donoghue, and perhaps he should have been able to give a better first presentation of himself than he did. However, there was time for improvement. His perplexity was genuine. With the best of advice, he was still dealing with a very complicated set of issues and with many different kinds of advice coming to him from within the Dublin Diocese.

What was clear was that he had no intention of following what appeared to be the new Church policy of drawing a line between what had gone before, on which the Church had been generally speaking, defensively shrewd, and what was to happen from then on.

Ireland was still in some degree of shock over the Secret Deal. Father Seán Healy, for example, who was CORI's spokesperson on justice, presented himself on RTÉ's *Questions and Answers* that autumn, as he had done the previous Friday, at a CORI conference, as not having read the Secret Deal and not wanting to read it. He declared himself as not being in a position to comment on it. He said it was not his job anyway to take any responsibility for the agreement struck between the Government, through Michael Woods, and the 18 religious orders who had signed the deal. He studiously avoided any reference to the fact that CORI—acting on behalf of the religious orders—had actually negotiated the deal. As its spokesperson on justice, Father Healy's first priority might have been expected to be the study of this legal instrument crucial to his appointment and his main work.

He was having things otherwise, however. He drew a clear and distinct line between CORI and the 18 religious orders, cutting them adrift from his care and concern, which was cruel, and cutting them off from his professional responsibility, which left commentators with a serious problem. Not too much importance was attached to Father Healy's view that the 18 religious orders should, might, or would work out a methodology for some kind of public audit of their assets. So what? This would then conform, in anticipation, to the long overdue charitable status legislation. It was a long way from surrendering those assets.

The 18 religious orders would not have minded all this, however. Being cut adrift, after the deal was done and they had their indemnity and their money still, was a profitable position to be in. But the abused, for whom Father Healy expressed words of compassion, were not satisfied. To their likely dismay, he had no specific remedies, when he appeared on that *Questions and Answers* programme. He seemed oblivious to the fact that specific remedies were what they wanted.

Sister Maxwell was central to the CORI negotiations on behalf of the congregations. Until June 2003 she, with her associate, Sister O'Donoghue, answered for and defended these congregations involved in the residential institutions. Sister O'Donoghue was from one of those orders, the Sisters of Mercy. Sister Maxwell's hand in the negotiations and in the Secret Deal was deliberate and sustained. As Secretary General of CORI, for example, she welcomed the announcement of a redress scheme in 2000 and knew that early in 1998 the Christian Brothers had approached the Government about setting up just such a compensation body but, extraordinarily, in the light of what followed, had been turned down.

In 1998? Had we missed something here? The Taoiseach's Speech of Apology was in May 1999. What had been going on in 1998 between the Government and the religious? They were obviously talking, at least a year *before* the Apology, possibly longer. The talks were serious enough if they covered the idea of a scheme for victim redress. Once again we were brought back to the key document—there since before the Apology—the *Report on Measures to Assist Victims of Childhood Sexual Abuse*. This report, the second of two prepared during the time Michael Woods was in Education, established the overall strategy for what followed, including Bertie Ahern's Apology and the setting up of the

Lafoy Commission. In due course, out of the Lafoy Commission came the Redress Board. Consistently protected, within this report, was a 30-page submission by Senior Counsel, Gerry Durcan, and the Attorney General. Legal privilege was invoked to protect both these documents. Content may be inferred from the fact that, in December 1998, the Cabinet subcommittee had a meeting which sought to identify 'the projected scale of cases against the State' and what impact a Commission might have on State liability in litigation. However, there was another draft document that made reference to protected information, revealing that by April 2001 a total of 900 claims 'had already been made against the State'. As to the religious congregations, the Department of Education had been given a figure 'of a possible 2,000 claims', that is, more than twice the number faced by the State.

Well before this time, in fact in March 1999, the Department of Education had carried out a check of its database on the abused men and women who were committed by the courts and had then passed through the system. Separating those born before 1940 from those born since January of that year, it had come up with 23,520 children born since 1940 who had gone through the industrial schools. Clearly, a potential explosion in numbers threatened, as the rights of these men and women, under the scheme for recompense, became more widely known. Something had to be done to head off this threat. This need, rather than any compassion, inspired the Taoiseach's apology speech.

The numbers were clearly incomplete. They still are to this day. It was widely and correctly assumed, in considering the legal measures taken against the abused, that the majority of them were imprisoned by the State through the courts. And this process frequently involved the Church, through parish priests, and was aided and officially monitored by inspectors who were from the NSPCC or the ISPCC, working with the State in the largely illegal, but lively and sustained, imprisonment of children whom they judged to be in need of moral protection. At times this committal extended to adults and was used to perpetuate incarceration of young people beyond the legal industrial school age for committal of sixteen years. In an unknown number of cases this process by-passed the courts. The law was frequently taken into the hands of the religious, particularly in cases were women were placed in the Magdalene laundries without any State authorisation, against the will of the women themselves; in a covert and maternalistic way, the physical slavery of these women extended, sometimes indefinitely.

The evidence suggests that the State, well aware that the legal threats against the Church involved more than twice the numbers facing them, nevertheless negotiated the Secret Deal. In this the State took all the blame, indemnified the Church for cases it might face, and did so for the mess of potage amounting at face value to €128 million, but in fact totalling much less. John Purcell, the Comptroller and Auditor General, has been conservative so far in his estimates of the numbers of the abused and the cost to the State and restrained in criticising the politicians who had got us into this dreadful mess.

The Archbishop's return to Ireland, which in due course would have a considerable impact on both Church and State, came not many months before the publication of Ms Justice Mary Lafoy's Third Interim Report—which included the first and second reports as well—and this gave him as full an update as he needed to come to grips with the situation surrounding the institutional abuse story, the solution and conclusion of which, so many people believed, lay in his appointment.

Among other things there were the lamentable and criticised circumstances—detailed in chapter 10 of the report, which must have been on his desk from the outset of his Dublin ministry—of the Department of Education both as the Commission's statutory sponsor and as respondent in its capacity of statutory guardian of the men and women who, as children, were abused. Diarmuid Martin must have wondered at the Ireland to which he had returned. It is extraordinary that the Commission, through its Investigation Committee, had to 'schedule procedural hearings to procure the co-operation of the Department and secure compliance with statutory requests and directions'. On two occasions it was necessary 'to require the attendance of the Secretary General of the Department on foot of a direction to attend under the Act'.

The principal worry was undoubtedly in respect of the discovery of documents. On this score there were delays and difficulties, some of which could be traced to staff shortages, meaning shortages of funds. The fact of this is inconsistent with the declared determination, by the Taoiseach, and by his two successive Ministers of Education, Michael Woods and Noel Dempsey, an inconsistency that runs through the whole supposed operation of the abuse investigation.

But perhaps more importantly, the report specifically identifies the Director of Strategic Policy and Legal Services in the Department as swearing an affidavit listing documents described as primary sources, and an apparent claim of privilege over such documents. This impasse was resolved when lawyers for both sides sat down together and perused the documents. It turned out that many documents were irrelevant and that the Department had 'no record of contemporaneous knowledge of sexual abuse by a person in authority'. The discovery direction was disputed by the Department, but its objections were withdrawn at a public hearing.

The purpose of this detail is merely to give a flavour of the level of argument and obstruction that arose at times between the Department and the Commission, and was now public knowledge, as well as being part of the complex issue controversy with which Archbishop Martin had to deal.

This in turn had to be taken in the context of Ms Justice Lafoy's submission to the Attorney General's review. The publication of her final statement reminded people also that she had questioned the appropriateness of the Commission being dependent on the Department, when 'The Department's conduct is being investigated by the Commission' and where the Department 'has a contractual arrangement with the religious orders which managed residential institutions in the past'. She had invited the Government to consider reposing the Commission's functions in another department. She quite properly excluded Health and Justice, since they also had roles in referring children to institutions. But in any case nothing was done on this score.

The Archbishop had to deal with, and respond to, much more pressing events. The tide of media interest was reinforced during 2003 by the public role played by the One in Four organisation, led by Colm O'Gorman. Colm O'Gorman had shown courage and clarity at the time of his award of €300,000 in April of that year. It was accompanied by the all-important admission of negligence by the Catholic Church. The documentary he made for the BBC, *Suing the Pope*, and the fallout from it rightly led to the resignation of the Bishop of Ferns, Brendan Comiskey, and should have changed the circumstances surrounding the plight of the abused in Ireland.

O'Gorman had already been running One in Four for a year at that stage and within 18 months he received €633,000 from the Department of Education to help fund counselling. He had also received funding through Faoiseagh, a counselling service organised and funded by the Catholic Church. The financial basis for his main service to the abused victims who came to the One in Four organisation was therefore a combination of Church and State aid. While this did not preclude him from expressing criticisms of the State and of the Church, on behalf of the abused, it did represent a conflict of interest. In a highly emotional press conference in October 2003, Colm O'Gorman alleged Government disquiet at his public criticisms, and suggested that these had possibly influenced the decision to call a halt to funding.

This was strenuously denied by the Minister for Education, Micheál Martin, in a later interview. Martin categorically ruled out the possibility of any State spokesperson suggesting that funding might be withdrawn because of the criticisms. But he was in difficulty over the issue of whether or not to enter further talks to rectify the position of One in Four for the future. The problem was that the Minister should never have allowed himself to get into the position he was in. He already had a countrywide professional National Counselling Service based in the 10 Health Boards. This was set up following the Taoiseach's apology speech, and up to that time €17 million had been expended. The huge investment here, originally made for an initial three-year period, was now in doubt for the future. It was designed to deal objectively, without direct Church involvement, with abused people.

It had run into trouble as a result of the State trying to reduce expenditure. A much larger team of psychotherapists than those involved with One in Four had seen their contracts come to an end without renewal proposals that were satisfactory.

In effect, the State was as much in chaos as Colm O'Gorman claims his own organisation faced in the light of the need for further funding. O'Gorman's press statement raised major questions about the whole funding of services for the abused. And the apparently *ad hoc* offer, aired in an RTÉ interview by Minister Martin, to reopen negotiations with One in Four was a further example of confusion in the face of challenges from that organisation.

Two Departments of State, Health and Education, were both involved in the provision of counselling, funding, buildings for abused people to use, and in some cases to live in, and organisations to represent the abused. There was an Education Fund. This was under some kind of State management, using money given by the signatories to the Secret Deal.

The hand-to-mouth provisions evident from the Minister's confused response to Colm O'Gorman's shock announcement of possible closure demanded a proper parliamentary audit of what was being done and how it was being monitored or controlled. Nothing was to be served, except the interests of those who wanted further confusion, by any short-term rescue operation for One in Four. The Dáil needed to call a halt to a chaotic framework that had been erected around the tragedy of institutional and clerical abuse in the State.

The One in Four group became quite outspoken on behalf of the abused generally at this time and countered what it called an attempt to rewrite the history of sexual abuse. This was a welcome declaration on behalf of victims. Other support groups reinforced the message. But it was a sad development to see this inadequate and under-researched defence before the criticisms had been heard. Moreover, the hearing of evidence was being blocked. The Christian Brothers, and other member groups of CORI, were increasingly active in what had all the appearance of deliberate obstruction.

It seemed appropriate, during that gloomy period from the autumn of 2003 into the operations of the Commission under Mr Justice Seán Ryan, still in an atmosphere of uncertainty and distrust, to ask again some of the basic questions that were being provoked by the faltering and apparently wayward actions of the Government, four years after putting in place a process of recompense. The following are the questions.

We have in this State a comprehensive system of redress that applies to people who believe they have been wronged. It is called the law. It operates essentially through the courts of the land and is governed by legislation. There is additional redress through the Constitution. This document is the bedrock of rights and duties in the State. It has been widely and effectively used by many people since its promulgation in 1938. They include me. And there is a real purpose: to achieve the righting of wrongs. Beyond this there is an international dimension, through the European Convention on Human Rights.

None of the courses of action covered by these protections and redress mechanisms is easy, but they are the best way by which a democratic state regulates wrongdoing. When such a State sets this structure aside and introduces a quite different one, it is exercising a dangerous mandate, one that contains many pitfalls and is open to treacherous and manipulative actions that may in the end have to be righted by the law and the Constitution that have been, in a sense, usurped in their purpose.

In 1999, the Taoiseach, Bertie Ahern, took the option of an alternative route. In October 2003, as a result of criticism of what had happened in the Commission, he disparaged and dismissed previous governments, including the Rainbow Coalition, which had immediately preceded his first administration, for having done nothing for the abused men and women who were in the industrial school system.

Previous governments, long before that particular administration, knew of the abuses done to those people and left the matter to the law and the courts. Though many members of the Government led by Ahern had pleaded lack of knowledge of what was going on, Charlie McCreevy, ever an outspoken person and at that time Minister for Finance, had said, only days before Ahern's disparagement of those who had 'done nothing', that we all knew about this abuse in industrial schools 30 years ago. What he was saying was that he, who had been much of that time a legislator and a member of the Oireachtas, knew of gross and terrible crimes done within a system under State control. Like his colleagues, he had done nothing, leaving the matter, as they did, to the courts.

Rape, starvation, deprivation, physical and mental cruelty and lifelong damage to people in the care of the State went on and was remarked on but not rectified nor recompensed. It was left to the law. It is not unreasonable to ask why legislators remained so passive. There was enough negative evidence of failure to question or confront, within the legislature, the catalogue of abuse that stretched back to the Second World War and beyond and is outlined in an earlier part of this book. But it did not happen, except in isolated cases.

It is not sufficient to rest any elected representative's case on the presence of laws and the Constitution. There was an additional 'fear of the collar'. It was widespread. It affected, at least potentially, the individual deputy's electoral prospects. And the cases are rare indeed—Noel Browne being one, Owen Sheehy Skeffington another—where elected members of the Houses of the Oireachtas took personal action in defence of the abused and in criticism of the Church for its desire to cover up.

The alternative adopted by the Taoiseach in 1999 seemed at the time to have been provoked or initiated by television documentaries. The perception in 2003 was quite different. The growing conviction was that it was for different reasons altogether. The first and most obvious was the prospect of more court cases against the State by lawyers representing abused men and women. But this does not fully account for Ahern's approach, which also seemed to have been based on prior negotiation with the Church. Was this in preparation for what eventually emerged: a joint Church–State protection agreement? Whatever about that probability, it can certainly be said that it was not debated with the abused.

Ahern was faced with an option of investigation, redress and, much later and under pressure, compensation. He presented this in a particular light. His actual words were: 'What the Government has decided on today is not a break with the past, it is a facing up to the past and all that this involves.' For many people these were mere words; for the abused they had a very real intensity. The abused had spent their lives trying to escape the past, forget the past, set it aside and rescue their lives. It had been, as is always the case with abuse, a desolate and largely impossible quest. The past is not recoverable. Damage to the heart and mind, imposed with arbitrary cruelty, leaves permanent stains. Even physical deprivation—which at the time caused tooth decay, loss of clear eyesight, rickets, skin disease, ear infections and other illnesses deriving from poor diet and lack of medical care—usually leaves a permanent mark. The remedies for these stains on life are never complete in their achievement of recovery. Drink, mental breakdown, the inability to have normal loving relationships and the impossibility of acts of affection haunted the abused, in many cases wrecked them, so that even the act of survival was itself a huge triumph.

The idea of the Government 'facing up to the past', confronting it, putting things right, meant a huge amount, and it created a mood of euphoria. There was, for a time, a remarkable degree of trust in what the Taoiseach laid out as the solution. The idea, in the closing months of 2003, that this was a betrayal,was indeed hard to bear.

The simple truth is, however, that the Government did not face up to the past. Instead, it sided with the past. It constructed a protection mechanism for itself, for all the wrongdoers, including the Church, and against the interests of the very people to whom the Taoiseach had apologised—the victims.

When the *Irish Independent* published the full details of the indemnity agreement, in January 2003, no one had any clear conception of the strength and intensity of ministerial, civil servant and political self-defence that would result. This was a deal that was deliberately kept secret. The Minister, Noel Dempsey, pretended it had been published. That was his first defence. He went on to present other arguments. What he did not do, and what the Taoiseach failed to do, was to admit the catalogue of wrongdoing by the State that followed the Apology. The State made it more rather than less difficult for the abused to obtain documents. It blocked requests and prevaricated over detail. Instead of increasing staff to cope with an inevitable increase in requests, it seems it did the opposite, leading to six- and eight-month delays in releasing material.

The State made no attempt to place constraints on the members of CORI in respect of their documentation. It made no attempt to assess the numbers of abused and the potential applications under the schemes for investigation that followed the Taoiseach's Apology.

It was truly hard to listen to the evidence given by the Secretary General of the Department of Education, John Dennehy, to the Public Accounts Committee. His department had floundered over numbers for five years, hiding its inadequacies behind Freedom of Information protection. He took John Purcell to task over his analysis of potential survivors. Yet the Comptroller was the only public official who had attempted any kind of predictive analysis of the number of abused and the potential financial burden of their claims to the State.

The Taoiseach adopted a critical and confrontational attitude to this same constitutional officer. If companies or private individuals have such attitudes to their accountants, they sack them. If not, they accept their accounting processes. The State has an accountant, under the Constitution, whose job is 'to control on behalf of the State all disbursements and to audit all accounts of moneys administered by or under the authority of the Oireachtas'. He is removed from office for misbehaviour or incapacity, and this is done only by the Oireachtas. These two attacks on Purcell were a disgrace. They indicated an unwarranted and improper defence of their own un-researched and inadequate factual presentation.

As we know from the Lafoy fiasco, the Department of Education, with the knowledge of the Government, frustrated and handicapped the work of the Commission to an inexcusable degree. It then came up with an alternative approach that changed fundamentally the purpose of the Commission's work, departing, yet again, from the needs of the survivors. This was further evidence of the hollowness of the original 1999 Apology, which placed a premium value on the Commission and gave it by far the most important position in that speech.

The case was made by the Minister for Education, Noel Dempsey, by the Taoiseach and by other members or former members of the Government, that the Redress Board was working well. In the course of my own discussions with men and women who have been before the Redress Board, this was already, in 2003, seriously open to question. The methods of interrogation and the manner of dealing with individuals and their documents were at least questionable. The levels of awards and the degrees of abuse for which disgracefully small amounts were being offered were also open to question. There was an inexcusably slow pace of processing plaintiffs which, together with the secrecy of the Board's work, gave growing grounds for concern, if not alarm.

Those appearing before the Redress Board reportedly found a mood of disparagement and scepticism, together with less than comprehensive management of evidence. This also gave grounds for alarm. If true, then proper investigation was being hampered by the legal penalties in the Act on those who disclosed information. Strenuous argument against the secrecy of this process was widespread; unfortunately, the legislation had been drafted to protect the process of recompense from analysis. This was wrong in principle. It was the equivalent of a Star Chamber approach. It was particularly wrong in the circumstances where judgment of evidence and the handling of testimony had been so fraught with psychological disorder, instability and timidity among plaintiffs. Some victims were prepared to brave this, but it was disingenuous of members of the Government to pretend that Ms Justice Mary Lafoy was an exception to the smooth running of the whole system set up following the

Taoiseach's speech.

Where had we gone wrong? Instead of facing up to the past, we were indeed recreating its worst aspects, of secrecy, evasion and a one-sided approach towards power—in this case the power of the Church. The State had maintained a process of manipulation of data, prevarication and delays in the release of documents. The infiltration of abused people's organisations by the Department of Education and the Church, and the widespread misrepresentation of the facts by officials, have been offered as the fulfilment of a solemn and long-overdue promise.

There was a postscript to this, and to the dismal record on the treatment of abused people. It came towards the end of that year, with the publication of *Time to Listen: Confronting Child Sexual Abuse by Catholic Clergy in Ireland*.[1] This provided another overdue piece of the jigsaw puzzle that was being slowly and painfully put together in response to the Church's grim catalogue of concealment and prevarication over decades. It was welcomed for its scholarly treatment of the subject. Carried out by the Health Services Research Centre in the Department of Psychology at the Royal College of Surgeons in Ireland, its authors would have been the first to admit its limitations. But it was a solid study of one part of a huge problem that was facing us all.

The Church seized on it. It provided the Primate, Archbishop Seán Brady, with an occasion for another apology. And this, in turn, was greeted as evidence of a 'watershed' in Church thinking and in the Church's attitude. Archbishop Brady said, in an article published in the *Irish Independent* on 5 December: 'For several years nothing has received higher priority from the Bishops than the effort to address the problem of child sexual abuse within the Church.'

This was not in fact the case. At that time the Church had collectively been more concerned about its own main issue, that of scandal in the Church. There could be no doubt at the end of 2003 that both Church and State had consistently failed to resolve the wider problems of abuse. These included conformity with the law, the prosecution of offenders, the investigation of charges by men and women who were abused, particularly in the industrial schools and reformatories, the protection and availability of documentation, and the answerability of those directly responsible.

Both Church and State, particularly the Department of Education, had shown themselves almost relentlessly obstructive, casual, inept, even at times dishonest, about one particular problem, that of documentary evidence. While Archbishop Brady spoke persuasively about the documentary support for this report, he knew better than most clerics how great the gulf was for many who were seeking to gain access to critical files on all aspects of abuse.

Specific religious bodies directly involved in industrial school and reformatory management, from well before the foundation of the State and including, notably, the Christian Brothers, were still maintaining the fiction of

---

[1] Helen Goode, Hannah McGee and Ciaran O'Boyle, *Time to Listen: Confronting Child Sexual Abuse by Catholic Clergy in Ireland*, the Liffey Press, Dublin, 2003.

collective ignorance about what had happened in their many institutions and were still not surrendering documentation.

There was a parallel at the time: the series of tribunals on corruption. After years of investigation, many millions of euro spent on lawyers' and defendants' fees, the huge work of the Criminal Assets Bureau and the collective condemnation by politicians of dishonesty in public life, no fundamental change had been made to the law on corruption. What had been there for decades was patently inadequate and there was little to bring to an end the practices about which so much public concern had been expressed. One elderly public official had gone to prison, guilty of some misdemeanours but in the end found not guilty of corruption, and two members of the Oireachtas had been found guilty of corruption.

The same situation prevailed with the Church. A very modest, legally watertight payment of compensation had been stitched up between Church and State on the issue of abuse. Very few offenders had been voluntarily handed over to the State or had been the subject of co-operative criminal investigation in the spirit or in the letter of the apologies that were regularly issued. These still concern themselves with 'pain' and 'hurt'. They do not concern themselves with broken lives and the criminal acts that did the breaking.

The report, *Time to Listen*, is exclusively about sexual abuse. The weight of evidence in it concerns abuse outside the institutions. The number of abused interviewed is very small indeed, a total of 21, 14 of whom were interviewed over the telephone. Moreover, those who were interviewed face-to-face were obtained through diocesan delegates, therefore within the Church. There was no testimony obtained independently.

Predominantly, the survey was about attitudes to the Church and to sexual abuse within it. The general public featured with a disproportionately huge 1,000 respondents compared with a total of 48 specialist interviewees, among whom abuse victims were a minority. The response rate, from abuser or victim, was low.

An effective public launch transformed an interesting but quite limited scholarly investigation into what appeared to be a triumph for the bishops. What was alarming in Archbishop (now Cardinal) Brady's statement was the distortion in favour of the present and the future, and its virtual disregard of the past. No bishops today can plead ignorance of the law. Thirty years ago, even 10 years ago, they could, and they did, and they got away with it. Archbishop Brady said at the launch of the report: 'Wrongs from the past cannot always be fully righted.' He went on to express the hope that 'the Church, the media, and wider society, can all work constructively together to bring healing to those who have suffered in the past'. This was code for offering the ubiquitous 'healing' in place of investigative action.

The Church was giving a dismal message to the sufferers of the past. Life is long for those who were in Artane, or Daingean, or Letterfrack in the 1950s, and they are still struggling with what happened to them. The damage to their lives does not go away. It is there until they die. And that damage is an immense and ignored blight on the Church. It would have been more balanced to have heard more from the Church on that score.

Brother Tobin operated in 'the past', from 1959 to 1974, brutally abusing innumerable victims. More than a quarter of a century later he went to prison with a 12-year sentence.

We do not know how many others like him operated within that system, quite apart from those who abused in parishes and communities. But their victims were many. I suspect that, from among the 40,000 who went into institutions and were abused in every other way possible as well as sexually, the majority would repudiate the supposed healing balm of yet another apology.

The state of the Church, in terms of continuing faith and trust, was still, at that time, a matter for confidence and reassurance. Currently, the scale of abuse, under the informed and more watchful eyes of parents, children themselves and the Church, is likely to remain small. Nevertheless, a problem remained. Pastoral care would never be entirely free from embarrassment and potential shame until the legal redress of abuse, present, past and future, is confronted by action rather than apology. An apology has little merit in the eyes of an abused person whose injury and damage remains, and who has not had the benefit of a proper hearing and such action as the offence requires. This, in spite of the fact that the report had been commissioned by the Bishops' Conference, did not seem to be part of the Church's thinking. It was not part of *Time to Listen*, and that was overdue in its need to be remedied.

Senior officers of the Redress Board went to London on the last weekend of March 2004. They held meetings with victims of abuse in Irish industrial schools and reformatories. Further meetings were held in other cities in the United Kingdom during the following days. The Board's secretary, Michael O'Beirne, led the team from the Redress Board. He had been at the day-long London meeting, where he had spoken well. Other officers attending were Deirdre Lawlor, the administrator, and Patricia Kavanagh, the office manager. The agenda for the meetings consisted of descriptions by the three individuals of their work, followed by questions.

Those attending the meetings were angry that no legal representative from the Redress Board was present. No legal questions of any kind were allowed, though the majority of problems expressed by abused men and women concerned their legal rights and the sections of the Redress Act that impose legal restrictions on them.

Men and women who reported on the meetings said that they knew enough already about what the Redress Board said it was doing, and how it did it. They do not wish to hear any more about office management or the membership of the Board. All they wanted, they said, were answers to their individual and collective problems. Questions on psychiatric help for the abused, and on counselling, had also not been answered, and could not be answered, since those attending were involved exclusively in administrative work. Those attending were simply there to give information about what the Redress Board did.

One former inmate of an industrial school told me: 'They could not answer my questions, nor those of other people attending. There was no information new to us. We know how the Board works. We want to know why it is not working for us, and why our questions about compensation are not being answered at all.' According to a woman attending a meeting in London, the meetings had not been advertised in the London Irish newspapers, the *Irish Post* and the *Irish World*, but in the Irish national papers. These are not widely read by the Irish community in Britain. It is astonishing, after five years, that a comprehensive ledger containing all personal contact details of abused men and women had not been put together in order to achieve the contacts which were still being attempted through Irish national newspaper advertisements!

Conflicting views were being given about Redress Board compensation payments. Outreach organisations in London, according to one victim of abuse, were advising that appeals led to reduced compensation. The Redress Board staff countered this with a different view, but were not able to give legal answers because no lawyer from the Board was present.

More women than men attended the meetings. They continued during the week in provincial cities, including Coventry and Leeds. According to Irish soca in the United Kingdom, no reasons could be given for the non-attendance of legal officers. Michael O'Beirne reportedly said it was 'strictly confidential', as was the reason for using the Department of Education's outreach services in London to promote the meetings and choose invitees. Irish soca claimed that these outreach services denied it access. They claimed that 'the real purpose is a publicity drive' and that it would allow the Minister for Education to claim that 'wide consultation in the United Kingdom' had taken place about redress and about the reconstituted Lafoy Commission. No one reporting on the meetings agreed that any consultation at all had taken place.

No public statements were made about the London visit by the Redress Board, whether the atmosphere had been emollient or sulphurous, or whether or not any valuable information had been divulged by the abused that might help the Redress Board. It moved about its business—when it did move—as silently as it operated in Ireland.

However, this equanimity was seriously disturbed, less than four weeks later. This was as a result of Tom Sweeney's hunger strike outside Leinster House. The location was directly outside the Kildare Street entrance to the Houses of the Oireachtas and Tom Sweeney was accompanied by his son, Mark, also on hunger strike and supported by other members of the family, from the Tallaght suburb. Tom Sweeney, who was then aged 57, was in dispute with the findings of the Redress Board in respect of his experiences in Artane. He was physically abused there and also in St Joseph's, Salthill, Galway, where he was physically and sexually abused over a period of three years.

His first award, under the settlement stage in the redress scheme, was for €113,333. He took this to the second stage hearing, where the amount was reduced by €50,000. In every category of the points scheme used by the Redress Board, he was downgraded. In the third review stage the overall figure was increased by a small amount, but still stood at just over half the original award. Tom Sweeney declined to accept this and went on hunger strike.

He described what he had been through with the Redress Board as the worst experience of his life. His wife and six children, aware already of the time he had spent in Artane and in St Joseph's, had to go through the full details of the experiences in both places as these were assessed and reassessed by the Board.

Tom Sweeney was among an increasing number of men and women who had gone before the Redress Board and had met with a range of reactions and contradictions which left them bewildered, angry and dissatisfied. He was the first such applicant to carry his distress to the extreme position of a hunger strike outside the Dáil. During the first week in August he was visited by Archbishop Martin, who spent up to an hour talking with him. The Archbishop, soon to replace Cardinal Connell, was known to be worried and concerned at the way in which abuse had been handled by both Church and State and said at the time that he was anxious to remedy a situation that had begun to look unending.

The Archbishop already had a huge portfolio of material to absorb. He now had a more immediate, practical problem to tackle in this potentially intractable hunger strike. It was to last 22 days. Sweeney eventually received awards totalling €150,000—€113,000 from the State, €37,000 from the Christian Brothers—together with an apology from the Christian Brothers. Costs and interest were paid as well. Sweeney did not receive the money until the autumn and it was not until the third week in November 2004 that he got the full text of the apology from the Christian Brothers. Only part of this had been read to him previously. This apologised for the hurt he had experienced whilst at Artane Industrial School and at St Joseph's Industrial School in Salthill. Subsequently six Christian Brothers who had worked at Salthill were charged with abuse offences. Tom Sweeney had asked several times for the release of the text of the apology. When he eventually received it, he claimed that it contained details of a confidentiality agreement. The terms of this, he said, were not pointed out to him at the time. The document went on to say that, in the event of publication of the details of the apology and payments, the Christian Brothers reserved the right to comment on the settlement.

The involvement of the Archbishop changed the balance of influence within the Tom Sweeney case. The Taoiseach's office also became involved in negotiations. Noel Dempsey agreed to 'reactivate' the original High Court action and allow a financial settlement to be made. This persuaded Tom Sweeney to give up the demonstration outside the gates of Leinster House.

Tom Sweeney broke new ground on behalf of those men and women who were abused within the industrial school system. The Government gave in to the hunger strike, and in an unprecedented move, allowed Sweeney to go back to the High Court for a hearing and a settlement that had been agreed in advance.

In his statement on 6 May, the Minister for Education, on behalf of the Government, accepted that the case would proceed, but 'solely on the basis of assessment of damages'. Yet the Redress Act has a penal clause in it to prevent such cases succeeding or, to make it more difficult, by the lodgement of money in the High Court to the value of any rejected award. According to the Minister, this clause would remain in force for other cases, but was not invoked in the Sweeney case. Other cases would be 'examined on their own merits'.

The key problem facing the Government and the victims at the time was that the Board, brought into operation following Government legislation passed in 2002, was simply not giving the results that the State had promised. This had been shown to be true with both pieces of legislation, the first being the Commission to Inquire into Child Abuse Act, passed in 2000 and enacted on 26 April of that year, and the second the Residential Institutions Redress Act, passed two years later and enacted on 10 April 2002. On two critical occasions during the framing and passage of the first piece of legislation concerned with the abused, which set up the Commission to Inquire into Child Abuse, over which Ms Justice Lafoy presided until her resignation in 2003, and the Redress Board under Mr Justice Seán O'Leary, Michael Woods, who was responsible for both, claimed that the awards made for abuse would parallel the substantial awards made in the High Court.

The State's investigation of what should be paid, and how it should be done, had concluded in January 2002 with a particular view. This was that 'the "injuries" received by a number of victims of abuse are among the most serious kinds of personal injury known to the law; many survivors not only "lost" their childhood, but much of their adulthood as well'. The best guidance for the Government came from within the State and should be 'by reference to the level of awards made by the Irish courts for pain and suffering and loss of amenities arising from serious personal injury'. Such an award would also be 'the award likely to be made if … an applicant elects to pursue a claim for damages in the High Court'.

This had simply not happened. Like so much else, the undertakings vanished within the text of the legislation. By comparison with court awards for sexual abuse, or the agreed settlements that have been made on foot of threatened court proceedings, the offers and the handouts from the Redress Board have been much less, often to a point that was derisory.

One example may be relevant. In August 2003 the High Court made an award of €75,000 to a man who had been sexually abused in Kilkenny in the mid-1970s. It was a single abusive action, and was rated as being at 'the lowest end of the scale of sexual abuse'. By comparison, the sustained sufferings of institutionalised men and sometimes women merited substantial awards. Many of those presenting themselves before the Redress Board had been the victims of gross, usually brutal, and often sustained acts of sexual and physical abuse. For them, the State created a legal process based on secret hearings where neither the public nor the media could discover—as they generally can in the case of court procedures—what was being done in what in effect were legal cases, heard ultimately before a High Court judge. This was an abuse of the European Convention on Human Rights. Openness in public hearings was vital for all parties. Archbishop Martin was himself clearly aware of this, and was concerned at the continuing damage to the Church of a system that was meant to resolve the distress of past victims and bring to an end the controversy.

Tom Sweeney's hunger strike was effective. He achieved a major breakthrough for victims of industrial school abuse in their fight for a far better deal than the one given them on foot of Bertie Ahern's Apology five years before. He forced upon the Government a changed attitude towards the Redress Board and a potential change in the Redress Act. He gained access to the High Court in circumstances that were materially different from those provided for in the Redress Act. If his achievement were to be equated with the circumstances of other victims of institutional abuse, this then represented a considerable advance.

He had raised the profile of suffering of those men and women who originally believed their troubles were being addressed, through the Lafoy Commission, the Redress Board and the apparent co-operation between the Church and State over compensation but now had growing doubts. Whether or not the Sisters of Mercy chose to issue their generous and very welcome apology at the time of Tom Sweeney's hunger strike deliberately to ease fears about the Church's lack of compassion, it definitely had the effect of very positive reaction from those who suffered. In the light of this they saw the Order as breaking ranks with other orders involved in running the schools. They anticipated further such apologies, and looked with particularly keen interest on the other orders.

The hands-on involvement of the new Archbishop of Dublin, in the increasingly tense period of the 22-day hunger strike outside the Dáil, was particularly welcome. Archbishop Martin faced a huge task in achieving the necessary change, but he seemed during the difficult period in no way daunted by the challenge. He adopted throughout an approach that would be of considerable importance in the immediate future.

The events that brought an end to Tom Sweeney's hunger strike had shaken the stability of the Redress Act and the operation of the Redress Board. It had also thrown into question the relevance of the Secret Deal between Church and State. The Sisters of Mercy alone, by their apology, had raised fundamental questions as to how the State and the Church could sustain the mutual protection pact they had signed committing both to defend each other against the victims. Despite the fact that they had said that the deal would stand, in the shaking of the veil that was taking place, who knew what would crumble?

When the Minister for Education, Noel Dempsey, noted, in his press statement of 6 May, that 'the integrity of the Redress process has been maintained', he was fundamentally wrong. It was not maintained in the case of

Tom Sweeney. Who else might shake it was yet to be seen. The 'Redress process', as he called it, was made up of the Redress Act, the Redress Board and the victims. All have been changed by the events of those few days outside Dáil Éireann. The so-called integrity of the process—which is not worth all that much—was damaged.

Towards the end of the hunger strike, in an attempt at compromise, the Taoiseach issued a conditional promise to Tom Sweeney. This was on 30 April. He stated then, 'I believe that the Redress Board would be willing to offer the last amount (circa €68,000) if they know that Mr Sweeney would accept it as being a final settlement.'

In so doing he was proposing the breaching of the Board's terms of reference and this implied an amendment to the Act. The amount quoted turned out to be wrong, and the proposal made no progress. But the terms contained in it represented evidence of serious concern that the system imposed by the State was not working, and could—indeed, perhaps, should—be changed. The Taoiseach, under advice from others not in the Department of Education, was acting with the best intentions and was all too well aware that there had to be change. He also offered the High Court provision, though without the limitation to assessment of damage only.

The change came from Noel Dempsey. He introduced a variation in the referral to the High Court which was not part of the Redress Act. That Act, which contains in Section 25 provision for appeal to the High Court, was constructed as a disincentive to abused people, making it risky to make an appeal since the Minister could lodge funds against such an appeal, putting plaintiffs at risk, and the State would be fighting the case in terms of material evidence.

By making the new provision, 'that the case should proceed solely on the basis of assessment of damages', the Minister appeared to have taken away from such legal action the risk factor for the abused. If he had not done so, and now proceeded to lodge the amount of the rejected offer to Tom Sweeney—which he had not made clear—then it would be a travesty of the supposed justice with which this sorry affair was concluded.

If he made this new approach free of such lodgment, then he unilaterally altered the powers of the Act in respect of Tom Sweeney. If for Tom Sweeney, then why not for all victims who were unhappy about the miserable awards that were being handed down by the Redress Board? And if this were not the case, then did we face a succession of hunger strikes along the same lines, and for the same reasons?

The ambivalent situation was inherently untrustworthy. It was difficult to take, in the light of the past performance of the Government, the Minister for Education, his department, the Redress Board and everyone else on the State's side. It seemed preferable, therefore, that it should be writ in law and not in printed promises.

The Sisters of Mercy made a full and generous apology. It made nonsense of the puerile attempts at that time by some organisations to muddy the waters in terms of the supposed wrongful blaming of people. But at that time they had been slow to produce any evidence. In contrast, the Sisters of Mercy had dealt in what was real and actual, and were to be commended for this.

They had challenged the core thinking that lay within the indemnity deal. The terms of this still stood; but the defensive principles were a dead letter. The programme of protective action by Church and State working together was no longer acceptable. This fact raised substantial problems for the future.

Archbishop Martin had impressed people on all sides of the crisis, stepping into the difficult hunger strike situation and adopting a supportive approach within only a day of his appointment being ratified by the Pope. His Holiness had accepted the resignation of Cardinal Connell, ending a grey era for the Church in Ireland. The Archbishop had shown himself to be an activist, and one deeply concerned at wrong turnings taken in the past. He and the Sisters of Mercy had acted on the side of the abused. It was in marked contrast to the fact that, during the previous five years, the State and the Church had not been more firmly on the side of right but on the side of self-protection; this meant continued oppression of those who had suffered the loss of their childhood.

There was a further symbolic act that struck a fresh chord with the public. This was when Father Michael Mernagh, an Augustinian priest who was 70, made a 300 km 'walk of atonement' from Cobh to Dublin. It was an apology for the sex abuse at the hands of the clergy. He was greeted on the steps of the Pro-Cathedral by Archbishop Martin. The main Roman Catholic Cathedral in the city is, ironically, opposite the Department of Education. The Archbishop described the priest as a man of principle and said that the day he ended the walk was 'a credit to him'. Father Mernagh had been calling for the resignation of the Bishop of Cloyne, Dr John Magee, whose handling of allegations of sex abuse in his own diocese had led to a public outcry; this resulted in due course in the Bishop's replacement. Father Mernagh said that though his walk was ending, 'our journey to give justice and to make atonement is only beginning'.

PART SIX

Political Testimony

Chapter 21 ⚬

MR JUSTICE SEÁN RYAN HEARS BERTIE AHERN'S TESTIMONY

The Taoiseach appeared before the Commission to Inquire into Child Abuse on the morning of Monday, 5 July 2004. His Apology to victims of abuse, given in the Dáil on 11 May 1999, was pivotal to the whole process, which, in the hands of a good tribunal interrogator, would be crucial. The Apology had led to the establishment of the Commission. More tentatively and with some reluctance, it had also led to the Redress Act and the Redress Board responsible for recompense. These have been examined extensively in the foregoing pages, in as forensic a way as possible. No apology is given for this, but much of the criticism was made against virtually all the provisions made for the abused and some of it was directed at Seán Ryan himself. Good reasons had been frequently put forward for a detailed interrogation of the Taoiseach. Would it happen? Would all the key issues be examined fully?

Bertie Ahern's testimony altered the approach of abused people and their legal representatives to the Irish State and also to the religious communities. With much more careful planning than was evident in the emotional frame of references offered at the time of the Apology, Ahern had set in train the negotiations that led to the indemnity deal between the Government and members of CORI. These members are listed in the Redress Act as responsible for the industrial school system, and hence for the decades of abuse affecting the lives of tens of thousands of men and women. On their behalf Ahern had encouraged a very large number of men and women to put their trust in the process that had been constructed for them. They were now, in varying degrees, unhappy and distrustful. Tom Sweeney was one very public example; there were myriad others more private, more frightened, more insecure. What of them?

Five years after that Speech of Apology, the initial trust of the abused, which was immense and was accompanied by relief at not having to go through the courts, was shattered. The willingness and the competence of the Redress Board to deliver adequate compensation were seen as a sham. The collapse of the

Commission under Ms Justice Mary Lafoy and her replacement by the present chairperson, Mr Justice Ryan, was regarded as wasteful and its deliberations as repetitive.

Five years of bad decisions, obstructive legal arguments and actions in the courts, punctuated by the deaths of some of the abused, many of whose complaints date back into the 1930s, have made a mockery of the Taoiseach's fine words. The exposure, 18 months earlier, of the full details of the Indemnity Agreement between Church and State further damaged the credibility of the process. This had been presented as one of healing when, increasingly, it seemed to be one of self-protection by those responsible for the safety of the children committed to the State's care in huge numbers over decades.

Despite criticism, despite growing anger and dismay among the abused, and within the various representative organisations, this had still not been put right.

A new approach had been signalled in Mr Justice Ryan's various statements since his appointment to take over from Ms Justice Lafoy. They indicated a number of differences in process and in law. He spoke in ways that suggested a new mood of *peristroika* or 'openness'. For various reasons, not necessarily of her making, this approach had not been available to Ms Justice Lafoy. Given the magnitude of her task, and the difficulties put in her way, there was much involvement by the abused in her work. The new mood was accompanied by selectivity. Originally, all who wanted to appear before the Commission were free to do so. Now, it was on a selective basis.

The new approach was also characterised by Mr Justice Ryan's apparently vast resources of energy. He was clearly tackling a huge task and indicating that he would do it comprehensively. In many key respects he was starting over again. It looked impressive to have a rerun of how the abuse had started, when people became aware of it, and what they planned to do. But the justification for this, the factual testimony indicating a need for it, was not very convincing. Was he right in a comprehensive approach to whether or not abuse had taken place, while at the same time the representation of abused people before his Commission was being curtailed?

There was undoubtedly a new dimension present, one that was represented by a mood of broad confession of wrongdoing, though exemplified only in rare examples, one of them being from the Sisters of Mercy in their statement of 5 May 2004. This was brave and new. So far, ministerial and public servant testimony has echoed this only 'in principle' and in a muted way.

Those who had been following the abuse story looked on these modest changes coldly. For example, there has been conflict over who became aware of what, and when. The picture presented by Micheál Martin, who was Minister for Education at the time of the Apology, Michael Woods, who succeeded him and was responsible for the redress legislation and for the indemnity deal, and their civil servants, does not hold together. They have given in various statements huge and justified credit to the *States of Fear* programmes and the *Dear Daughter* documentary, as well as to the abused who came to them with complaints of how they had been treated. They have given much less detail about Government sub-committee discussions of the threat of legal action. Yet it was this that mobilised State strategies. These, covertly aimed at diverting the cases threatened by the abused, wanted to direct them away from the courts and into the flawed set-up we have now.

The Commission had to be in possession of the Cabinet documentation as well as the inter-departmental subcommittee's reports that preceded the Apology. (After all, even I had them.) It could not have done its work up to that point without them. It certainly could not pursue Seán Ryan's enlarged programme without them.

Yet in the questioning of ministers and civil servants up to the point when Bertie Ahern took the stand, there had been little or no reference to the matter there contained. There had been no raising of the question of legal cases threatening the Government, how many there were and the seriousness of the potential charges. This was absolutely crucial if we were to get at the truth. We had to presume, though we had not been told so, that the testimony of the lawyer who had advised the Government on this matter, together with his report, would be made public.

There is conflict over whether the Government asked the religious institutions to support the indemnity funding or if the institutions offered to do so. The State claimed on 24 June, through ministerial and public servant testimony, that the religious orders came forward and offered to be involved, but that the scheme would be State-funded anyway. The religious orders, through Sister Breege O'Neill of the Sisters of Mercy, claim that the scheme was announced and they were then asked to contribute. If this was true, then the negotiating position of the State was sold out before any discussion had taken place. Having stated vehemently in the Dáil and in all subsequent exchanges that court committals of those who were then abused would not be examined, responsible politicians at the time were now faced with the fact that Mr Justice Ryan was planning to go to Government to have this changed.

We had, in the early months of 2004, what appeared to be a new strategy. Up to that point, however, it looked very like the old plan dressed up.

The Taoiseach needed to change this perception and explain what the State would do in legal terms to meet the implied promises and undertakings that were now being made. His credibility, on the matter of abuse within the industrial school system, was pretty threadbare on the eve of his Commission appearance. He made much of the Apology. He needed now to make people believe all over again, and much more strongly, that he was still on the side of the victims of abuse.

Bertie Ahern failed to do so. True, his performance on 5 July 2004, before the Commission was certainly clear and unequivocal. He appeared before Mr Justice Ryan with a message. He delivered it with a concern and passion that impressed the audience, including many of the victims of abuse and their spokespersons. The message was that the Apology of May 1999 came as a result of the impact made on him and his ministers by the representative groups of the abused and by the individual members. His interrogator throughout was Noel McMahon sc. After quoting back to the Taoiseach the words of the public Apology, he said: 'Perhaps you might speak to the Committee about the political thinking behind the making of that apology?' Virtually the whole of the Taoiseach's evidence thereafter was concerned with his explanation of Government thinking at the time.

Bertie Ahern said:

> ... the political thinking ... was coming from victims and representative groups of victims that were either calling individually or in groups or collectively on politicians, me included, indicating what was happening or what did happen, and asking us to deal with the issue.

He referred also to the inter-departmental working party and its 1999 report, saying specifically that 'the issue of the apology was not in the report'. He repeated that the Apology 'came from meetings that I had with Minister Martin and meetings that I had with representatives of the various groups and individuals on their own'.

> In fairness to the Working Group, I don't think they ever discussed the issue of the apology ... I fairly well remember the day I made the decision, it was after I met a large group of the individuals ... I remember one such meeting where I attended the Sycamore meeting in Government Buildings and there was a large attendance of representative groups ... So that is when we made the decision that we would try to deal with this in as upfront and honest a way as we could, and that is where the history of the apology came.

The giving of his testimony was an impressive performance by Bertie Ahern. However, there was a problem with what he said. It was in complete conflict with the evidence given by the Minister for Education, Micheál Martin, by the former Minister, Michael Woods, and by Tom Boland, who was the key figure in the whole creation of the strategy for dealing with the victims of abuse. It was also in direct conflict with the facts surrounding the representative groups that the Taoiseach claims he met in advance of making the Apology.

Let us deal with the groups first. The Alliance Victim Support Group was formed in May 1999 after the Apology and as a direct result of that Apology. Christine Buckley was originally part of this group, but later separated and formed the Aislinn Centre for Healing, but *after* the Apology.

The Survivors of Child Abuse, known as soca, was formed in June 1999, following the Apology, and led by Mick Waters. There was a split in February of the following year, 2000, and two SOCA organisations subsequently existed, one in the United Kingdom, the other in Ireland. Right of Place/Second Chance, which then represented the Upton School inmates and was based in Cork, was formed in June 1999, also *after* the Apology. Right of Place was founded by Noel Barry.

With Government support an umbrella organisation, the National Office for Victims of Abuse (NOVA), was established in November 2000, well after the Apology. It was part of a process by which Government money was put into the abuse victims' representative groups. There was yet another group, Right to Peace, formed in Clonmel even later; finally, and much later still, there came Colm O'Gorman's One in Four, formed in 2003 and not specifically aimed at the abused from the industrial schools and reformatories.

While the Taoiseach may possibly have met abuse victims, either singly or together, *before* the Apology—though there is no record of this—he could never have met a representative group before the Apology since there were none. It is difficult to see how individuals could have swayed him into making so momentous an Apology. More seriously, the evidence given to the Commission in the previous two weeks by senior figures in Government is also completely at odds with the Taoiseach's testimony.

On 23 June, for example, Micheál Martin, Minister for Education at the time, gave testimony. Frank Clarke SC put it to him that the 'Cabinet subcommittee recommended a number of measures to Government at that time, of which the Apology was one, and indeed the establishment of the Commission was another; is that correct?' And Minister Martin replied: 'That's correct, yes.'

Confirmation of this was also given the next day by Michael Woods, a fellow-member of the Government and Martin's successor in Education who put through the subsequent legislation. Noel McMahon SC, asked: 'Is it the case that the Government's desire, and indeed your desire was to bring about a situation where there was closure to the whole issue of past institutional abuse?' Michael Woods replied: 'Yes. That was very consistent with the Taoiseach's Apology. The Taoiseach was apologising on behalf of the Government, and of course on behalf of the Nation. That was a policy objective from the Government's point of view from a very early stage.'

Noel McMahon later that day questioned Tom Boland, the central figure in planning Government strategy, and the author of the report to Government. Boland told him: 'A very important recommendation was that the State was to apologise to victims of childhood abuse.' Noel McMahon put a question to Tom Boland: 'Is it fair to say that it is because of the work that had been done over the previous year leading up to that time that the Government was in a position and the Taoiseach was in a position to make the apology and the subsequent announcements?' He answered: 'Absolutely.'

The recommendation in favour of an apology was contained on page five of the *Report on Measures to Assist Victims of Childhood Sexual Abuse* and went to the Government in April 1999. The Apology was made a month later.

At the time it was seen perhaps as a matter of modest significance. The Taoiseach's recollection was faulty. We were, of course, to learn later, in other forums, that this faulty recollection, on a serial scale, was part of Ahern's political make-up. But at this stage it needed careful, forensic address.

What he was claiming had happened was in direct conflict with the evidence of those closest to him, on the issue, at that time. Moreover, it was plainly wrong. It was, in the descriptive phrase used by Hillary Clinton during her unsuccessful struggle for the Democratic Party nomination, an example of 'misspeak'. Two years later, when Bertie Ahern began to find himself in trouble over a sustained involvement in misspeak about his personal finances, during the Mahon Tribunal hearings, it made better sense. In the latter case he was correctly and relentlessly pursued by the Mahon Tribunal lawyers and in due course the exposure of what turned out to be a tissue of lies led to his disgrace and his resignation from office. In contrast, the Commission hearings in 2004 did not pursue him at all. When it was pointed out, as a result of research by Irish soca, and published in the *Irish Independent*, with the suggestion that the Taoiseach should be asked back to clarify the matter, nothing was done.

The response, in fact, was entirely different, and it came in the form of a failure by the Commission chairperson, Mr Justice Seán Ryan, not just in leaving the misleading evidence on the record, but in actually failing to follow up on his own advice to himself.

Well before the June 2004 hearings cited above, he issued a statement on 7 May 2004 saying the following: 'The Taoiseach's apology of the 11th May 1999 marked a transformation in attitudes. How did this change take place and why? It seems to us that this is a legitimate area of inquiry and we want to ask those who apologised to victims of abuse and who contributed to the redress fund—we want to ask them: "How did you come to apologise?"'

Given the fact that Minister Martin, former Minister Michael Woods and the central figure, Tom Boland, had all said that the idea and recommendation for the Apology had come from within Government, while Bertie Ahern had said something quite different and circumstantially wrong, why did the chairperson not return to the question he had previously said was important, and ask the Taoiseach to reconsider his entirely different interpretation of events? After all, the testimony given to the Commission was all made under oath. Why was Noel McMahon not given the opportunity to quote back to the Taoiseach what his own Government members and civil servant had said about the Apology and to rectify his conflicting views?

From all this, the conclusion seems to be that the current strategy of the Government is to claim that it had no strategy at all and that the chairperson of the Commission abandoned the very terms of reference he had given himself at the outset of his occupation of the position.

The Taoiseach said he was moved to apologise by members of groups that did not exist at the time of the Apology. Indeed, according to his ministers, this

Apology was recommended a year before as part of a strategy that is now being made to vanish. We now have more questions to be answered than ever we had before.

Chapter 22 ～

THE RYAN COMMISSION'S SHORTCOMINGS

Before investigating abuse in the lengthy and much publicised accounts to the Commission, which were to continue for the next four years, Mr Justice Seán Ryan gave a lengthy address in the Shelbourne Hotel about what he was going to do. In it he said:

> The function of the inquiry at its most basic is, as we see it, to find out whether child abuse took place; if so what was the nature of the abuse; where did it happen; why did it happen; why was it not discovered and stopped; how widespread was it in any institution and how many institutions were contaminated by child abuse. We plan to begin our inquiry work proper with a hearing into the emergence of child abuse as an issue in Ireland.

It was difficult, at the time, not to form the opinion, from testimony, that the outcome up to that point had been a travesty. From the choice of witnesses and the exclusion of witnesses, from the conflict of evidence between those who were at the heart of the process from 1999 to 2004, from the questions asked, as well as those that were seemingly and deliberately not asked, it seemed that it was all aimed at the opposite of the objective stated by Mr Justice Ryan. We were being asked to believe that no one knew, no one took action, no guidelines were issued. We have been guided towards the idea that the Taoiseach's Apology was prompted by the survivor groups, whereas none of them existed at the time. Mr Justice Ryan could hardly be proud of his first six months in office.

It seemed, on the face of it, that Mr Justice Ryan was now offering a programme that had at its heart a central conflict. On the one hand he was saying that he would

> … examine all available documentation either from the institution or from other sources which throws light on the issues [as to] whether abuse happened in the institution and if so how widespread and of what nature.

And to this he added:

> We are considering hearing as many witnesses as to individual experience of
> abuse as is necessary to reach a conclusion whether abuse happened, if so of
> what nature was it and how widespread.

Then, on the other hand, he was saying:

> The real job that the Investigation Committee has to carry out is not to act like
> a court hearing dispute between rival parties, it follows that any inquiring
> body must have the power itself to decide where the inquiry should go, what
> areas to explore and specifically what witnesses can assist in the inquiry
> process. The Investigation Committee accordingly cannot be deprived of the
> power to decide which witnesses it is going to call.

This was not what had been laid down in the original Act. It should not have been
a matter for Mr Justice Ryan's discretion. When Ms Justice Mary Lafoy
announced her resignation, he had already accepted a task from the Government,
to look into the Commission's statutory remit, report his findings and make
recommendations. To this was subsequently added the supreme job of chairing
the Commission. To begin with, Seán Ryan was chairperson-designate of the
body he was investigating at the Government's instigation. The law did not allow
either the Government or its designated chairperson to do this. Only the
Commission, under the Child Abuse Act, can research its own functions and Mr
Justice Ryan was neither a judge, nor chairperson, nor a member of the
Commission, when he carried out this function. Out of that questionable
investigation emerged new and different rules.

It should be remembered that Ms Justice Lafoy, faced with the derelict and
deficient behaviour of the Department of Education in withholding information
she regarded as essential to her work, and withholding funding, wrote in strong
terms to the Minister for Education, Noel Dempsey, in August 2003. She told him
that legal advice sought by the Commission was that consultation with a view to
reviewing the Commission's remit was not appropriate. The Government, as we
know, took the opposite view. Mr Justice Ryan went ahead with his research. He
ignored his predecessor's view, which was taken with legal advice, that this review
should not have been attempted. There was always the possibility of this being
tested, either in the Dáil or in the courts, but this did not happen.

The judge was in a difficult position, having succeeded Mr Justice Mary Lafoy
in highly controversial circumstances. Her resignation from the chairmanship of
the Commission had been provoked by non-co-operation by the Department of
Education and her explanation, in a published letter, had been highly
embarrassing to the Taoiseach, the Government and in particular the Minister for
Education, Noel Dempsey. Mr Justice Ryan therefore had to take up a poisoned

chalice, and restoring confidence in the process was his key priority. Furthermore, he had to satisfy those coming before the Commission, as well as the wider public, of his own credentials. He had been appointed to the High Court and had taken up the post of chairperson on that basis. This itself was irregular and departed from the normal practice of judicial appointments.

Of far greater concern, however—and this is particularly the case for the survivors in their assessment of something being done for them—the judge had been deeply involved already in the Commission's work. He it was who carried out for the Government the review made necessary by the delays and blockages faced by Ms Justice Lafoy.

He had certainly quickened the pace. He had taken over as chairperson of the Commission at the end of four years' delay through the obstructions of the Department of Education. That Department, working to satisfy the Government's concern, then reviewed its own bad behaviour. It carried out two reviews, one of them through the person of Seán Ryan. He therefore adjudicated on the way forward. He was then appointed a judge specifically to implement the changes proposed when the previous system, largely through the Department of Education's fault, ran into the sand.

There were undoubtedly shortcomings in his review. At the heart of these was the apparent failure of Mr Justice Ryan to deal fairly and judicially with the central issue. He declared himself acting in 'the interests of victims of abuse'. He was aware of Ms Justice Lafoy's charge of conflict of interest within the Department of Education, since she had published this in full, in her Third Interim Report. He was also aware—as everyone was, from its frequent media examination—of the 'mutual protection' arrangement between the Government and religious orders exemplified in the Secret Deal.

None of this was dealt with in his review. He declared himself committed to helping the abused and speeding up the process. Yet he passed over wordlessly the issue of serious and prolonged conflict of interest that had undermined the relationship between the Government and the Department of Education on the one hand and the Commission under Ms Justice Lafoy on the other. He set aside the exchanges between Ms Justice Lafoy and the Government that had put him in his job. They were not, he said, 'a matter for this review'. To some, at least, including the more outspoken of the representative organisations for the abused, it seemed that he was looking the other way on a crucial matter. I shared this view and said so at the time. I still believe it was an extraordinary omission on the new chairperson's part not to have dealt in some detail with the broader issues raised by Ms Justice Lafoy. I still believe it to be the case in view of the loss of confidence occasioned not so much by her resignation, which itself was a bombshell, but by the greater part of her letter in which she raises questions that are rather larger than the outcome of Department of Education delays and prevarications. Rather more generously than the circumstances required, she referred to these specifics as 'matters of policy for the Government', but then said their cumulative effect had 'negatived the guarantee of independence in the performance of its functions conferred on the Commission by section 3(3) of the Act of 2000 and has militated against the Commission being able to perform its statutory functions as envisaged by the Oireachtas with reasonable expedition'. One would have thought some reassuring deliberation on this aspect alone was an essential part of the change of leadership. Ms Justice Lafoy said that Mr Justice Ryan's review 'and the publication of information in relation to that decision in the Press Release' had compounded 'the sense of powerlessness', making it impossible to deduce the nature of the functions likely to be conferred on the Commission 'post review, save that they will be substantially different from its current functions'. All this will no doubt be covered in the five-volume final report of the Commission.

The Government terminated the Commission's statutory mandate under Mary Lafoy. It decided against her suggestion to enable the Investigation Committee to suspend the operation of its current procedure pending completion of the review and the enactment of necessary legislation giving effect to the outcome of the review, leaving the Commission with an unqualified mandate from the Oireachtas.

In her carefully considered view, contained in her resignation letter, Ms Justice Lafoy said that the same Commission personnel over whom she had resided knew that they would in due course

> ... end up working and reporting to a mandate potentially radically differently from that currently in force. It follows that the procedures under which the Commission has operated and the investigations which it has conducted up to now may transpire to be redundant or incorrectly focused in the light of some future, but as yet unknown, mandate.

There is an almost Churchillian picture here, of a body 'buggering on' with a complex process affecting the lives of former inmates of the Gulag, having failed in any comprehensive redirection of forces, either at Government, Department or chairperson level. For further details on the lengthy summary by Ms Justice Lafoy of her misgivings, readers are referred to the full text of her letter in Appendix 7. But we shall have to reconsider all this in the light of the preamble to the forthcoming further report of the Commission, where the transfer of personnel and the writing of new legislation will no doubt be explained and analysed.

Among other things, people will wonder at the further delays mentioned in Ms Justice Lafoy's later point:

> I had hoped that the outcome of the review and any legislation necessary to give effect to it would have been published around Easter last [that is, Easter of 2003]. Instead, the process had already dragged on for seven months by the time the Commission was notified of the most recent Government decision. I have come to the conclusion to abide, without protest, the outcome of the

future radical review now proposed, whenever it may be concluded, would be a complete abrogation or the independence which the Oireachtas intended the Commission to enjoy and would seriously undermine my credibility as Chairperson of the Commission.

It seems that Mr Justice Seán Ryan took a different view. We will know more of this in due course.

Mr Justice Ryan paused in the hearing before him, as chairperson of the Commission to Inquire into Child Abuse, in early August 2004, having finished an intensive series of hearings before the Investigation Committee. This conformed to his statutory duties requiring hearings in public for one of the two committees, the other being confidential. They had included testimony from the Taoiseach, from present and former Ministers for Health and Education, from abuse survivors, representatives of orders and others.

At the end of two months of public hearings, during June and July 2004, a number of serious shortcomings had emerged from those hearings. They raised, again, the credibility of the Commission and its chairperson in handling conflicts of evidence and in getting full and truthful testimony from those appearing before the Commission. The first of these concerned the Taoiseach and has already been dealt with. What the judge had not dealt with, nor questioned, was the issue of rectifying the false record. He never did this. It remains the published version.

He had, however, made no bones about this being central to his inquiry. He had declared his desire for the truth on the reasons behind the Apology, how it came about, whether it was planned. Yet he was happy to leave Bertie Ahern, the architect of the whole scheme of recovery, 'healing' and compensation, on the record as saying the Apology was unplanned, when in fact this was not the case. His ministers and a key official had said it was carefully planned and was central to Government strategy. Faced with two contradictory versions, Mr Justice Ryan did nothing to pursue the matter. Nor has he addressed it since then.

Other issues had been dealt with, also in a way that is seriously open to question. One of them—absolutely central to the anxiety and remembered fear of most abuse victims—concerned corporal punishment. When the Secretary General of the Department of Education appeared before the Commission, he was asked:

Is there a general view within the Department as to the extent to which the circulars and guidelines were in fact adhered to? I suppose I am thinking in particular in relation to the corporal punishment guidelines, but also the other ones?

John Dennehy replied: 'I am afraid I just couldn't be helpful to you there, because again it would be speculation.' He was beginning another sentence with the words

'I do know that certainly—'when the chairperson intervened and said: 'I am glad you can't be helpful to us. I don't know how you could answer it to be honest.'

All 'general views' are speculation, and that was what was being requested. The reason why John Dennehy could be expected to answer this question much more fully than he did, a reason well known to Mr Justice Ryan, was that Mr Dennehy had been a central figure in all the Government discussions about physical and sexual abuse since 1998, before the Apology. This fact is referred to. Yet in his testimony John Dennehy deals with only one 1987 document and otherwise with the 1990s as far as sexual abuse and non-accidental injury are concerned. (Non-accidental injury mainly refers to physical injuries sustained through floggings or physical assaults on children in institutions.)

The Secretary General was specifically asked:

Is it the case, Mr Dennehy, that other than the guidelines and regulations to which you have referred there are no other guidelines, whether statutory, non-statutory or otherwise, circulars that you are in a position to indicate the existence of to the Committee?

And he answered: 'Certainly, I am not aware of any others that were available.' Yet it was known—in the sense that knowing is a public service responsibility when referring to circulars and directives—that the amending non-statutory directive on punishment of 1948 was one such set of guidelines. This document was advisory and indeed ameliorated the statutory set of 'Rules and Regulations for the Certified Industrial Schools in Saorstát Éireann' where these applied to punishment. But they did not alter the legal position and, like all such directives, were comprehensively ignored throughout the industrial school system. In the light of the evidence already given, on the whole issue of punishment regulations, going back to the time of Tomás Derrig and before, it was extraordinary that this was the totality of evidence on the rules for beatings.

More generally, John Dennehy was able to deliver to the Commission an array of relevant documents quite extensive in their range and date. Noel McMahon, counsel for the Commission, at one point said to him:

Going through the list of documents which you were kind enough to furnish with your statement, there appears to be a document from 1938, one from 1941, one from 1943, one from 1950, one from 1951, 1952, 1964, dealing with formal complaints in national schools, 1956 and then 1970.

So the Secretary General had therefore come before the Commission well-equipped with a variety of documents, but was vague about such documentation within the industrial school system.

John Dennehy had been a school inspector as far back as 1978, the year in which the Department of Health issued guidelines on sexual abuse and had them circulated to other departments. However, he told the Commission that he knew nothing of these guidelines. Yet their existence was clearly confirmed in a letter written by Barry Desmond, Minister for Health, on 24 May 1983, where he referred to:

> ... the Department of Health ... set of guidelines on procedures for the identification, investigation and management of non-accidental injury—including sexual abuse—to children in 1978.

By 1983 the protocols were widely in place, with responsibility in the hands of directors of community care in each Health Board round the country. Because the nature of the problem arose from physical injury, it came through the Department of Health. But details and the regulations were circulated to other departments. Moreover, given his own very considerable involvement in issues related to this problem of 'non-acccidental injury including sexual abuse', there is a major question to be asked: why did Mr Justice Ryan not pursue John Dennehy in his examination of this issue?

This whole episode before the Commission was simply not in conformity with both public and departmental knowledge. It was inconceivable in a decade that included the Kincora[1] reports in 1980, in Northern Ireland, the convictions that followed in 1981, Sir George Terry's[2] report of October 1983, together with parallel events in the Republic, including guidelines being circulated between Government departments, that a quite different presentation of the truth was not available, if not suppressed. Surely, even a little speculation might have gone a long way towards delivering a quite different verdict on events and on knowledge?

It is a further side issue, but this particular problem did come up in another form. The problem that John Dennehy found so overwhelming, and for which he could not find an answer, was relatively simple. It did not need the chairperson to intervene and absolve him from giving an answer. It simply needed the Commission to accept testimony offered by one of the representatives of the victims of Donal Dunne, who was sent to prison for sexual abuse. This witness had extensive material knowledge of a specific case and the measures taken about it but the Commission refused to hear their testimony. In contrast, Colm

---

1   Kincora was a home for working-class boys in Belfast known to the police but not investigated because of MI5 links with the manager, William McGrath, leader of an obscure loyalist paramilitary group called Tara. Allegations of the widespread prostitution of the boys were made but not substantiated. The tabloid press linked the home with a whole series of establishment figures without any evidence being provided.

2   George Terry was Chief Constable of Sussex. In 1981, after the prosecution of five people held responsible for child abuse in the homes and hostels in Northern Ireland involved in the Kincora affair, James Prior, Secretary of State for Northern Ireland, appointed Terry to investigate other allegations about the involvement of police officers and other high-ranking people in homosexual offences against the boys. No prosecutions followed.

O'Gorman, who was a fluent contributor to the general abuse debate, and was called before the Commission, was not in a position to offer any first-hand information on abuse within institutions. His experience is of a quite different, diocesan area of abuse. Any wider first-hand knowledge he might have had was mainly governed by therapy confidentiality. This was reflected in the generalised nature of his contribution on 21 July.

The Donal Dunne case is crucial to any examination of how abuse became an issue, and this was the heart of the hearings during June and July. Donal Dunne was a teacher from the early 1940s and an abuser over many years. Those who sought to help his victims knew the circumstances in which abuse was handled through half a century. They were looking for an inquiry well before the Taoiseach's Apology. Yet they were not called before the Commission; their offer to appear was declined.

PART SEVEN
Stories

Chapter 23 ᴄᴠ

MARY HANAFIN TAKES
OVER

In September 2004 there was a Cabinet reshuffle and Mary Hanafin was appointed Minister for Education. She was faced with bringing a new Bill before the Dáil, to amend the Commission to Inquire into Child Abuse Act. She said it was intended to have it enacted before the following summer. She announced in her press statement at the time:

> The main purpose of this Bill is to give effect to Mr Justice Seán Ryan's Report and recommendations on the workings of the Commission following his consultation at that time with all the parties concerned. The amendments proposed in the Bill will enable the Commission to carry out its inquiry into child abuse within a more reasonable timeframe and cost than earlier envisaged. The Bill will also establish a statutory framework for the operation of a €12.7 million Education Fund for former residents of institutions and their families provided under the Indemnity Agreement with the religious congregations. It also includes a number of technical amendments to the Residential Institutions Redress Act 2002.

The shortcut in the legislation was simple enough. It removed the obligation on the Commission's Investigation Committee to hold a full hearing into each and every allegation of abuse referred to it. The Committee considered this unnecessary for the purposes of its inquiry. It 'would result in long drawn out proceedings over many years at considerable cost in legal fees'. For the abused, this was an inexcusable curtailment of their rights. They had already lived through three and a half years under the chairmanship of Ms Justice Mary Lafoy, during which time the penny-pinching and prevarications of the Department of Education, seriously curtailing her work, had resulted in a very small number of them being able to appear before the Investigation Committee. Now, with the new amending Act, this delay was made statutory.

The legislative changes meant that all complainants wishing to pursue their cases with the Committee would be interviewed—approximately 1,300—but that, following this, the Committee would call as many witnesses to a formal hearing 'as are required for the purposes of the inquiry'.

Mary Hanafin claimed considerable progress by the Commission in its inquiry to date and she expressed her confidence that, with the help of this amending legislation and the ongoing support of her department, it would be well placed to complete its work and report on its findings within the next few years.

The amending of the terms under which the Education Fund was administered, making them statutory too, was a disgracefully belated intervention by the State in a process that had been the subject of much disquiet over how the money had been used.

The legislation reached the Senate for its Second Stage debate there late the following June. Mary Hanafin went over the ground again, telling senators that Seán Ryan, when he was made chairperson-designate of the commission, in September on the announcement by Mary Lafoy of her intended resignation,

> the Government requested Mr Justice Ryan to undertake immediately his own independent review of the working of the commission. Mr Justice Ryan's report was published on 15 January 2004, together with the review completed by the Office of the Attorney General. The Government accepted the recommendations contained in Mr Justice Ryan's report. Following the publication of this report, the investigation committee held consultation meetings with all interested parties and representative groups to facilitate them in expressing their views regarding the content of both reports and to enable them to make suggestions in respect of the future operation of the investigation committee. A formal hearing of the investigation committee took place on 24 May 2004 to receive submissions on identifying institutions and persons under the Act. Representative groups were also given an opportunity to express their views on the matter. On 16 June 2004, Mr Justice Ryan publicly stated that the commission had decided to proceed in accordance with the position paper published on 7 May 2004.

Giving opportunities, particularly to the abused, to 'express their views' concealed much disquiet and growing uncertainty.

Mary Hanafin also claimed that 'the confidential committee of the commission continues to operate as normal'. It was not possible to define what 'normal' meant at this stage. By 17 June 2005 the Confidential Committee had heard evidence from 1,082 witnesses. It would continue to hear evidence from remaining witnesses and after that would prepare its report and present it to the Commission.

Minister Mary Hanafin took on the legislation, largely drafted by Mr Justice Seán Ryan and designed to speed up the work and the working circumstances that defeated Ms Justice Lafoy. Even writing this at the time, there was the feeling of how soon dreadful events become history. There must have been people who were saying, 'And who is Ms Justice Lafoy?'

Mary Hanafin saw through the Second Stage and the Committee Stage of the Bill, and faced the polishing off of the Report Stage. It had been slightly delayed, not least by the abused she consulted who subjected her to stern questioning. This took place on 17 May. One of the main complaints made at that meeting was the lack of clarity and openness in the legislation about the role of the courts.

At least Mary Hanafin saw them. She was reportedly unhappy in her departmental role where it applied to the abuse of children committed to State care by the courts from the 1930s to the 1960s. Constantly supported by officials, her responses were neither confident nor well-supported by the facts. She preferred purer educational work, responsibility for the young, for their parents, for schools and their teachers and managers. This fitted her political background as a representative in a generally well-to-do South County Dublin constituency for which she was a popular and successful representative.

One of the abused who took part in a session on 17 May spoke of the encounter, saying that Maria Grogan, a key figure in the unit dealing with abuse issues, 'sat next to the Minister and gave her any assistance on the various legislative measures taken over the past five years. Though he is the Head of the Unit, John Fanning sat quietly and said nothing throughout the meeting.' This witness is from a group not affiliated with NOVA.

Mary Hanafin can be forgiven for not being on top of this vast, unwieldy and pernicious acreage of legislation and documentation, behind which are the silent wails of innumerable victims. It is poisoned ground. Nothing grows on it any more.

One of the many issues that the abused are angry or bewildered about is the role of the courts. The entirely unjustified criminal records of abused people is another. The Minister, guided by Maria Grogan, claimed that the matter of criminality had been resolved in both the 2001 Childrens Act and the Redress Act. This was decidedly not the view put to her at the meeting. Nor is it true. One representative of an abused organisation pointed out that, as in post-Nazi Germany, there was a need among the abused to be absolved from the same criminal status that victims of Nazism suffered. The parallel was an unwelcome one. An even more unwelcome analogy was the one with the Soviet Gulag system. Tens of thousands of children had been committed by a child prison system that deprived them of fundamental rights, including education, food, clothing and good health, while subjecting them to the brutalities of harsh punishment and sexual abuse. The reasoning behind this supposed care had been a kind of moral clean-up operation, putting into compulsory detention the children who came from a variety of backgrounds but were collectively seen as 'out of line' in the strict Catholic environment that prevailed from the 1920s up to and including the 1970s. How could Mary Hanafin, a practising Catholic herself, cope with this extraordinary confrontation? As Minister, she undertook to look into this and other matters, in putting through the legislation; the hope was expressed in an

Irish Independent article that the Opposition would watch carefully over the detail at Report Stage, but it was a forlorn aspiration.

Mary Hanafin was under fire on a number of fronts. She confirmed, in a new law, the despicable legal structure that allowed representatives of the orders, in public sessions of the Commission to Inquire into Child Abuse, to make veiled rather than formal acknowledgments of the abuse, while at the same time defending their record. By contrast, the abused are heard in private. Their testimony has no public stage to counteract the carefully contrived work of the State, since Bertie Ahern's Apology, to protect the Church and eventually settle all claims.

The Minister faced continuing embarrassment, not of her own making, in other areas, including the funding of education for the abused and their families. Would making this 'statutory' actually work? For over two years the money had been distributed with clear evidence of a conflict of interest among those administering it. Her willingness to face the reality of a botched and dishonest treatment of the abused, in this as in other matters, was still to be proved.

Whether or not Mary Hanafin was right in claiming wide-ranging contacts with abused people and organisations, the net effect of her first period in office was to identify her as not on top of this particular brief, and heavily dependent on her advisers.

No aspect of the problem was going to be simple, least of all the confusion of concern, with muddled legislation and selective choice of future witnesses. At the same time the numbers of those coming forward were increasing and the potential cost to the State was rising. As reported in the *Irish Times* on 1 August 2005, the number of people applying to the State's compensation scheme for institutional child abuse and neglect, established late in 2002, was estimated to be heading towards 9,000. There had been a doubling in the rate, in previous months, at which people were applying. The Residential Institutions Redress Board claimed that it had received 7,046 applications, a rate of 400 a month.

In a controversial deal approved by the Government, the religious orders made a contribution of €128 million at the time, based on an estimate by the Department of Education that the cost of the scheme would be between €250 million and €500 million. This was the estimate by the Comptroller and Auditor General two years earlier. The amount was questioned at the time by the Department of Education. According to the latest figures (2005), the Residential Institutions Redress Board's settlements of the 3,665 awards dealt with to date, averaging €77,100 each, came to €282 million. If the current compensation rates continued, the potential cost was likely to be in the region of €800 million.

In November 2005 Bertie Ahern made a speech in which he claimed that he had given the child sex abuse issue the highest priority during his two terms as Taoiseach, and there was undoubted truth in the statement. This is what he said:

I have put child protection in the context of sex abuse within religious institutions and by clergy at the forefront of the work of my term as Taoiseach. My record in relation to the investigation and exposing of child sex abuse is second to none. As Taoiseach I oversaw the establishment of the Commission of Inquiry into Child Abuse and the Ferns Inquiry. And it is through this process of inquiry and disclosure that we as a society are enabled to ensure that the abuse and dereliction of duty in the past does not recur.

As has been clearly demonstrated, the Taoiseach's concern reflected the State's reaction to the rapidly growing threat of court action in respect of sexual abuse in Church-run institutions over decades. The programme of action initiated under Bertie Ahern's first term as Taoiseach was intended to deal with this problem.

Documentation shows that the Department of Education, in the mid-1990s, conscious of this, and also advised in part by legal opinion about the level of cases that might come to court, brought to the Government proposals for obviating this threat.

Bertie Ahern did indeed take action, but principally for three reasons. The first was to protect the State by creating an alternative process, through the Commission to Inquire into Child Abuse. The second was to protect the Roman Catholic Church from the same threat of widespread legal action for abuse and deprivation. The third reason was fear of the revelations, which were emerging through television and articles, and which were likely to snowball in number and expand the shaming range of perverse and abusive behaviour.

The legislation then introduced by the Government was couched in terms that were protective of the Church and of the State. Bertie Ahern opposed the idea of redress, which was brought to Government only as a necessary additional measure. Without it the legal challenges were likely to have been mounted anyway. It was done at the express demand of Ms Justice Lafoy.

This process was accompanied by the Secret Deal with the Church, which put the financial burden of redress on the State, and therefore the taxpayer, and absolved the Church with payment of less than 10 per cent of the likely eventual charge on the State for what had been done in more than a hundred institutions around Ireland.

Bertie Ahern's declaration about the Church's place in Irish society was ill-judged. We were still in the position, as a modern State, of having yet to get to grips with the full problem of abuse. It did not lie in the past. It had substantially become a heavy and frightening present anxiety for thousands of victims and was an embarrassment to the Irish people.

This is the text of the Irish SOCA statement in response to Bertie Ahern:

There are no heavenly or earthly scales that will ever allow the weighing of the abuse of young people against the provision of any physical services whatever and in suggesting there is Mr Ahern displays a lamentable shortfall in clear thinking from both a legal and moral perspective.

We fully support and congratulate the recent call by Ms Liz O'Donnell TD and others for the ending of the cosy relationship (power sharing) that still exists between government and the Catholic Church in Ireland.

[That] the Indemnity Agreement of 5th June 2002 whereby Catholic Church liability for widespread abuse of the young in enclosed institutions is fixed at €128m whilst the public liability remains open-ended is one of the most grotesque manifestations of the 'cosy relationship' in recent years conducted under the premiership of Mr Ahern.

Contrary to Mr Ahern's utterances this morning the legal system has not properly dealt with abusive priests and religious personnel over the past five years—that is a complete myth.

This was signed for Irish SOCA by its co-ordinator, John Kelly. He referred also to the inter-departmental working party and its report, saying specifically that 'the issue of the apology was not in the report'. He repeated that the Apology 'came from meetings that I had with Minister Martin and meetings that I had with representatives of the various groups and individuals on their own'.

Bertie Ahern presided over three successive Governments—and the Department of Education under four ministers, Michael Woods, Micheál Martin, Noel Dempsey and Mary Hanafin (who was retained after the 2007 general election but moved to Social and Family Affairs in May 2008)—consistently claiming the same record on behalf of the abused. The ministers all followed the same policy.

The purpose of the Commission, for example, had always been to satisfy the needs of the men and women who claimed they had been abused. There were not really other purposes to consider. The outcome of this thinking will be fully revealed only with publication of the Commission's final report.

The earlier process had arguably been purer in its concept and purpose. This was certainly how Ms Justice Lafoy saw it and so argued in her letter of resignation. By doing so, she blew the whistle on what was happening. She took on the Government for its hypocrisy in not funding or supporting the very inquiry that Bertie Ahern claimed was his great gift to solving the institutional abuse issue.

She blew the whistle in another and much more fundamental way by publishing the only full account of gross ill-treatment by the Church of young people in the Baltimore Fisheries School. This, the only institution that had been the subject of a completed report when Ms Justice Lafoy left office in December 2003, described the near-starvation of the inmates who lived in squalor and in rags, without proper medical or educational care.

Mary Lafoy was a watershed figure. After her, the State changed the law. Since then there have been lengthy inquiries into different institutions. The stated purpose of these inquiry sessions has been to assess whether or not what is alleged to have happened actually did happen. These inquiries, where the institution is being questioned, have been in public. The individual inquiries where abused people were interviewed were held in private. The public statements and answers, usually given by religious orders who were not in the institutions and did not know what happened, have, in my opinion, mainly been whitewash operations.

It is not damages or civil actions that are relevant, it is prosecution for crimes of violence against innocent and powerless victims, and against senior members of the Church who have consistently, over long periods of time, protected the abusers and the regimes under which the abuse became chronic and insidious.

The practical proposals that repeatedly came from Government concerned investigation. They dealt in hopes about improvement. There was no real underpinning of legal intent. The process was actually going on almost exactly as before, only it had become much slacker and more gregarious.

The Church continued to wrestle with its conscience and with its own response to abuse, past and present. This response, contained in *Our Children, Our Church*, the child protection guidelines published by the Church before Christmas 2005, was in trouble over the document's lack of precision and over legal issues that had not been resolved or legislated for by the State. The law was in an unsatisfactory state in respect of the reporting of suspected child abuse. Because such reporting was not mandatory, the Church could argue quite strongly on behalf of its own guidelines. These are essentially self-protective, continuing to give discretion to bishops over the reporting of sexual abuse allegations, instead of making such reporting automatic in every case.

The debate about this had gone very much against the Church. This had been anticipated, since the Church, in *Our Children, Our Church*, has gone back on one of the fundamentals of the guideline document of 10 years previously, that all allegations of sexual abuse by clergy or religious should be reported to the civil authorities. That vital word, 'all', had been compromised and set aside, and the criticism has been justifiably severe.

The Church had encouraged and supported a very one-sided legislative programme. This strengthened its position and weakened that of its victims. The weight of evidence suggests that Michael Woods, Bertie Ahern and other members of the first partnership Government (1997–2002), succumbed to Church influence on the legislative process and this apparent submission became a significant factor in the drafting of legislation. It is also likely that Church interest played a part in the clear distinction there was between the shaping of the Offences Against the State (Amendment) Act of 1997, which brought in mandatory reporting for terrorist offences, and the specific exclusion of mandatory reporting for sexual offences. This was at the height of revelations of clerical sexual abuse and at a time when terrorist offences were declining, soon to be marginalised as the Good Friday Agreement took hold.

Somehow, the Church managed to evade the imposition of mandatory reporting. It was therefore better placed to combat the looming conflict. The likelihood was that the Church would plead the following: it has put in place guidelines that have Vatican approval; therefore it should be given a chance, since its guidelines broadly conform to 'best practice'.

The opportunities for presenting this case by the Church have been numerous. Yet somehow the pinning down of the Church has never actually been achieved. If the Church is able to walk away from the many public encounters with its guidelines intact and having achieved a breathing space, preventing or putting off any legislative action for the time being, it will have won its battle. The likelihood of the politicians preventing this is thin indeed. They are not united. They are nervous about public opinion. They are perpetually facing an election of one kind or another, and offending the Church, or being seen to be aggressively in conflict with it, will not help. Robust truthfulness and courage will be at odds with the temptation to compromise. And among our elected representatives compromise has been the pathetic and endemic record of the majority. They have generally failed to examine crucial issues of the Church's behaviour over abuse, both currently and historically.

The public investigations by the Commission to Inquire into Child Abuse went on. In January 2006 it held public sessions of its Investigation Committee. Three institutions were involved, all of them called after St Joseph. The Sisters of Mercy ran the schools in Dundalk and Clifden, the latter notorious for the harshness of its regime. The Christian Brothers ran the industrial school in Tralee. The hearings were widely reported in the media. Particular attention was given to the extreme brutality of one Christian Brother whose teaching was reinforced by violent beatings, one of which resulted in a child's jaw being broken.

The Sisters of Mercy representative appeared, apologised, expressed regret, and made the disingenuous claim that the first the Order knew of the cruelties and the suffering was in October 1999. Since one of the sisters was provincial leader of the Order, this was hard to accept. But in common with almost all the testimony that has come before the Commission in its public sessions, the norm has been for the spokesperson to be at arm's length from the events, and therefore from responsibility for charges made to the Commission and its chairperson, Mr Justice Seán Ryan.

It is a different matter when the Investigation Committee meets in a private session. Then, there is indeed direct conflict of evidence, with victims giving details and naming their tormentors, and with those charged with abuse defending themselves, or being defended by lawyers.

In respect of St Joseph's Industrial School in Tralee, run by the Christian Brothers, the case for the defence was presented by Brother Seamus Nolan, a member of the provincial leadership of the Christian Brothers, but one who never worked within the industrial school system. In respect of his general testimony, which included a statement made before the hearing, no defence was offered for the brutality of the unnamed teaching brother, his acknowledged violence and the extremity of this behaviour, nor was there any apology for the failure by the Christian Brothers to put a stop to his severe punishment regime. Instead, like sexual abusers among clerics within dioceses, the relocation of this offender, and presumably others, was the automatic and only response. This spread the violence from school to school, and implicit in this and in other evidence—including that of a boy who died, possibly as a result of a brutal beating—was a very dismal indication of what went on.

Brother Nolan was a relaxed and plausible witness. He used the word 'unfortunate' many times. Records were kept only minimally, statements of complaint—were any victims brave enough to make them?—were not taken, and all this was 'unfortunate'. So, too, was the fact that the legal requirement, of keeping a punishment record, or 'punishment book', was widely abandoned, as early as the 1920s. This was universal within the Order. Brother Nolan said that the programme for discipline was the same in all Christian Brother institutions, that is, there was no record and therefore there could be no recollection of sadism, brutality or excessive physical assault.

Brother Nolan told the hearing that the Christian Brothers participated in the annual meetings of all the congregations that ran this Gulag of child prisons spread across Ireland, and additionally used to hold Christian Brother meetings either the day before the general meeting or the day after. One wonders what they discussed. Did it include the whereabouts of punishment records, teaching records, health records? Did they tell the other congregations they had abandoned keeping 'all that stuff'? Did they discuss the slack and 'unfortunate' lack of law-abiding management and co-operation with Department of Education regulations?

Brother Nolan acknowledged that washing facilities had been 'inadequate'. It is a constant theme throughout the industrial schools. The washing arrangements in Daingean, seen by me, and in Letterfrack before it was cleaned up, were appalling. Throughout the records there is constant reference to the fact that the children did not have toothbrushes. Dental havoc has been one of many lifelong miseries for many of the victims of abuse. It was indeed a form of abuse, as was neglect of the care of the eyesight of the children. This was all 'unfortunate'. Brother Nolan told this public session that 'improvements were discussed but not progressed'. The toilets were in the yard. They never 'managed' to modernise them. 'Unfortunate.'

The lawyer took a compliant Brother Nolan gently through all this, relying on a script—the statement previously furnished. The lawyer for the Commission did not deal with the controversial issues in a way that managed to cut to the heart of them at all. He did not cover the question of funding, allowing the unsustainable fiction about limited Government funds, with much more money available within the United Kingdom. This simply was not the case.

Mr Justice Seán Ryan intervened rarely, and without much additional bite or penetration. The room was packed. The elderly victims, in comparative silence, heard a sanitised version of what might have happened, and all of it was described by Brother Nolan as 'unfortunate'.

Reports from the confidential sessions present a different version of what was 'unfortunate'. There, the abused confront their abusers and real argument is in the air. In one such session, lawyers for the Christian Brothers attempted to cross-examine an abused plaintiff on his membership of Irish soca. Despite the intimidating environment, the man challenged their right to adopt such an approach. They were, he said, obliged to deal with his case, not his affiliations with an organisation that has done more than any other to bring out the truth. After some argument Mr Justice Ryan sustained this view.

Another session in 2006 involved two alleged victims who were present for the cross-examination of a brother. One victim's brutal punishment was acknowledged by the brother who had charge of him at Artane. But the same brother fiercely denied a charge of extreme sexual abuse made against him and other brothers accused of regular sexual assault in a dormitory at Artane. It turned out that the allegation could not be sustained or supported by the Commission because the brother in question was on sabbatical throughout the period identified in the false accusation. Truth was upheld on the one hand; falsehood detected on the other. Will we ever arrive at the truth of what happened, unwrapping the innumerable layers of deception that still surround the Commission in its work?

Chapter 24 ∾

THE CHRISTIAN BROTHERS AND THE MOORE REPORT

Apivotal and controversial document, throughout the whole period covered by this book, was the 1962 *Private Report on Artane Industrial School* written by the school chaplain, Father Henry Moore, at the request of the then Archbishop of Dublin, John Charles McQuaid. It was designated 'Private and Confidential' and was sent to Archbishop McQuaid on 7 July 1962 from Father Moore's home in Harmonstown Avenue, Artane. The Archbishop had requested it on 18 May. In his covering letter Father Moore refers to the scope being limited by the wide terms of reference. It was completed in seven weeks.

My Lord Archbishop,
      In a letter of 18th May Your Grace requested me to submit a report on Artane Industrial School. I have pleasure in presenting herewith the findings of my enquiry.
      Due to the confidential nature of my task and the wide terms of reference I was obliged to restrict my observations to personal experience. The details are none the less factual and complete.

Here follows my summary of the report, originally published in the *Irish Independent* in August 2007. The full text of the report is given as Appendix 6.

Father Moore's report, without doubt, shines a clear light of judgment upon the iniquities of Artane and upon the wider iniquities of the industrial school system for letting what happened at Artane and elsewhere continue unchecked for decades. The Annual Reports year after year, told the same lies on industrial schools, that 'the physical and educational needs of the children were adequately catered for', that those 'fitted for post-primary education were enrolled in secondary or vocational classes', and that 'where it was considered that pupils ... would benefit from secondary or vocational classes they were enrolled in such classes'. These regular mantras were simply not true.

Moore's report was the result of a confidential charge given him by Archbishop McQuaid. It was factual and complete. It was also, it must be said, written intelligently and with style. It followed a careful reading of the Cussen Report of 1936, itself a damning indictment of Artane, and Father Moore found—26 years later—that nothing had changed.

Moore endorses the Cussen finding, 'that in Artane industrial school only the minimum standard of literary education required by the regulations is provided' and, furthermore, that the trades taught—many obsolescent—were 'useful to the schools rather than to providing a groundwork for future employment ... the boys apparently being regarded as a rule merely as juvenile labourers'.

Moore said Artane 'is in need of drastic revision'. The management methods employed 'are obsolete, proper training is neglected, and there is no attempt at adequate rehabilitation'. Artane is 'in dilapidated condition, colourless and uninspiring, and reflects the interior spirit'.

The boys were admitted 'indiscriminately' without 'regard to their background, medical history, antecedents or suitability for the training which they are to receive'. Medical history would not have mattered anyway because, in Moore's judgment, the Department of Education inspectors were entirely indifferent to 'the seriously inadequate medical facilities in the school'—no matron or nurse, but run by an unqualified brother 'transferred from the care of the poultry farm'.

Food was sufficient, but plain and unappetising. Methods of serving were crude and unhealthy. Clothing was inadequate, uncomfortable, unhygienic and dirty, as were the boys. The winter during which Moore surveyed conditions was cold, and the one that followed his report was one of the coldest of the last century. 'It is pathetic,' Moore wrote, 'to observe hundreds of boys walking the roads of the district on Sunday mornings even in deep winter without overcoats.' All the clothing was indiscriminately shared. 'Handkerchiefs are not used.' A trifle, in the broader spectrum of a place run like a prison, but Moore comments: 'This fundamental disregard for personal attention inevitably generates insecurity, instability and an amoral concern for the private property of others. This I consider to be a causative factor in the habits of stealing frequently encountered among ex-pupils.'

Discipline he found outrageously severe—'regimentation', 'no proportion', 'a boy was severely beaten on the face for an insignificant misdemeanour' are phrases used. The result was 'undue fear and anxiety', loss of self-esteem and an inability to establish relationships.

He condemned the chapel as dirty and damaged, with mouse droppings in the Chasuble and Corporal.

His most severe judgments were against the levels of education, with widespread illiteracy in boys up to the age of 14. Technical training was completely out of date, vocational guidance non-existent, choice of trade training bore no relation to the wishes or capacities of the boys. All of this, and much more, was done contrary to the Children Act *of 1908*!

The report remained private and confidential from 1962 until well after 2000, when the work of the Commission to Inquire into Child Abuse had started and the abused had begun to look for documents that related to their experiences.

At that time—the year 2000—Irish SOCA had been founded. One of its members was Jim Beresford. Father Moore was appointed chaplain to Artane in 1961, the same year that Beresford was sent there. He got to know the young priest quite well because he worked in the monastery (called 'The Brothers' House').

Living in the monastery for most of my waking hours I had constant contact with all of the monks and with their activities. I was forced to wait on them hand and foot and serve them their meals. That was my 'trade'; I was a 'houseboy' and there were five of us in the monastery. Father Moore was a visiting chaplain only; his main work was in a nearby parish. He travelled into Artane by car and saw to his duties—celebrating Mass, hearing Confession, supervising choir sessions. As I recall, many of the inmates found him cold and aloof—as indeed I did at first. I think he cultivated an air of mystique. Father Moore took his meals, usually alone, within the monastery—in a fine parlour … Whenever I served him, Father Moore invariably sought to engage me in conversation with what seemed to me rather intrusive questions. Of course I didn't know at the time that he was compiling a report for McQuaid nor did he give me any hint of that. As time went by he gradually gained my confidence and I realised that he was quite unlike the Christian Brothers. He was highly strung and superficially snobbish. But I discovered that he was a civil and civilized man who, unlike the philistine monks, could hold a conversation on almost any subject from Aristotle to zoology—and that impressed me greatly. I was desperate for something beyond violence and mind-numbing drudgery, any kind of human contact felt like a deliverance. Moore sometimes gave me a silver sixpence as a sort of waiter's tip—that too impressed me!

Beresford also knew about the report, his memory having been refreshed by *States of Fear*. In the first episode the panning shot of a page from what seemed to be the Moore Report is sufficient evidence of both its existence and its importance. The page could not be read on the screen, but Jim Beresford took a succession of images, freeze-framing them on his computer. By carefully manipulating the images, he obtained a fairly readable image of the page. Father Moore confirmed that he had given a verbal account of his report to the joint Education and Justice Committee. The image was a page from Moore's verbatim aide-mémoire.

On 25 March 2000 Jim Beresford wrote to the Archbishop of Dublin, Desmond Connell, asking for a copy of the report. He got an acknowledgment. Beresford had explained to the Archbishop that he had a personal relationship with Moore during his time in Artane, which was true, and he felt it was just possible that something he had told the chaplain might be in the report or even that he might be mentioned by name in it.

Beresford had no response from the Archbishop. He asked the Diocesan Archivist, David Sheehy, and was advised to try again. He did so, by letter, on 16 June 2000. (He had been told by Sheehy that a committee would have to sit to decide on the request and that the committee had not convened.)

Jim Beresford made a five-page submission to the Lafoy Commission, requesting, among other documents, a copy of the Moore Report. After much delay, on 5 February 2001, he was refused. He was told that any document produced or discovered to the Commission could not be disclosed to a third party and that such documents held by the Commission could not be obtained under Freedom of Information legislation. He asked if he would be shown the Moore Report if he decided to give testimony to the Commission and wanted 'a yes or no answer', but was told only that he 'would be shown anything that the Commission considered relevant to the investigation of his case'.

He corresponded with Archbishop Connell during 2001 and with Bishop Eamonn Walsh, then Dublin Auxiliary Bishop. This simply led to more stonewalling. In 2002 Archbishop Connell, who by then was Cardinal Connell, planned to attend the Irish Christian Brothers' bicentennial celebrations at the Royal Dublin Society in Ballsbridge. Beresford cautioned him not to go, but without success. The Cardinal said at the celebrations:

> To appreciate what the Christian Brothers have accomplished we must go back to the point where it started. The service Edmund Rice hoped to offer was a liberation, in the broadest sense, a great liberation of the Christian Faith, a liberation from slavery and oppression. For 200 years the Brothers have been faithful to that vision.

Not long after, on 6 October 2002, Cardinal Connell delivered a sermon in which he mentioned child abuse and begged forgiveness for his Church and its errant clergy. He failed to respond to Beresford's request for the report but, in a letter to Beresford of 25 October 2002, he said:

> It is my intention that any documents in our possession which relate to the industrial school at Artane and which are considered by the Commission to Inquire into Child Abuse to be of relevance to its investigation will be made available to that Commission.

It is reasonable to surmise that this was the point at which the Moore Report was sent by the Archdiocese to the Commission. It seems extraordinary that such records had not been handed over well before October 2002 (if indeed they were handed over at that point). It seems a clear possibility that they were sent much later. If, as is possible, the Commission had not obtained the Diocesan records by 2004, then what had been going on in the four-year period of the Commission's work, central to which were records covering Artane?

The process was simple enough in theory. The Commission would request voluntary discovery (say from the Archdiocese of Dublin). Only if that failed would a compulsory discovery order be issued. It would be very surprising if the Moore Report was ever specifically the subject of a discovery order, but it may have been. What is clear, from Ms Justice Mary Lafoy's Third Interim Report of December 2003, is the fact that comprehensive discovery directions were made by her during 'the evidence gathering phase of the Committee's inquiry', and that this comprehended 'Congregations which managed institutions in which abuse is alleged to have taken place'. This clearly included the Christian Brothers not just in respect of Artane, but of Letterfrack and other places. It included also 'Departments of State with regulatory responsibility for institutions in which abuse is alleged to have taken place … Bishops and Diocesan Archives'. Under this direction the Moore Report and its summary version would have been filed several times over; this would have been done well before the appointment of Mr Justice Seán Ryan. Ms Justice Lafoy refers to a certain leniency over some documentation, partly because of the long period—'up to sixty years'—that had elapsed. But this could not have applied to so central and significant an item as the Moore Report.

Parallel with his letters to the Commission and to the Archbishop, Jim Beresford also engaged in lengthy correspondence with the Departments of Education and Justice. He wanted to extract from them a copy of the Moore Report, as well as other documents. His requests were consistently refused. The Department of Education consistently denied that the notes on Moore's testimony existed in its archives and also said that it had never had the report. When eventually Jim Beresford sent them the page from *States of Fear*, they acknowledged having the document but refused him access to it. Cardinal Connell's office considered the matter for over six months before refusing him access.

In 2003, Jim Beresford made his first contact with Archbishop Diarmuid Martin. He had made the understandable mistake of thinking that the sending of the report to the Commission had placed it 'in the public domain' and he said this. It may be an over-generous interpretation of the facts, but it seems that Archbishop Martin had not at that stage read the small print of the Act setting up the Commission. This was carefully worded to prevent any documentation being passed on to third parties. The Archbishop did ask Beresford to put his request in writing. This was in 2004. Again, nothing happened for two years.

In 2006 Patrick Walsh of soca, who had been in Artane, also raised the issue of the Moore Report with Archbishop Martin who told him in June that he could not release the report because lawyers for the Ryan Commission had told him not to do so. Up to then he had been willing to release it, he said. It is not clear when the exchange between the Archbishop and the Commission took place or when the report was handed over.

Both Church and State wanted to keep the Moore Report secret. This alone intensified interest in it regardless of its content. The attitude represented an index of official anxiety. As will be seen, its content is evidence of woeful conditions in Artane, most of them long since revealed from other sources. But it had been ordered by the Archbishop, delivered by a trusted priest, read and absorbed. And then very little was done about it, though the Archbishop attempted to bring in reforms.

In reading a suppressed document we are also reading the minds of those who wanted to keep it secret. Thus, although the report reveals little not already known widely, by way of the media, its content becomes explosive in relation to the fact that Church and State wanted to conceal it. It was also of interest for another reason: when read in conjunction with the reports of the inspectors it raises major questions of the integrity of those reports and the departmental officials who wrote them.

Father Moore's report is a severe indictment of the Christian Brothers and their regime at Artane. Father Moore's findings confirmed the worst fears engendered by the testimony of inmates but not acknowledged by those responsible for their care. A different version of the management of Artane has been consistently delivered by the Christian Brothers to the Commission to Inquire into Child Abuse. The view taken by the Christian Brothers has been broad in its application, covering the whole period under examination in this book. It is a view that has also been endorsed by the Department of Education and broadly accepted, when put before hearings, by the chairperson of the Commission, Mr Justice Seán Ryan.

Moore's painfully honest account, stylish and economical, found Artane to be in need of drastic and comprehensive reform. This included every aspect of education, health, general care, including food and clothing, and after-care for inmates when they left. He condemned in the report the savage and unfair punishment regime, beatings that were completely out of balance with the offences. One 'small boy' was punished with a hurley stick for a negligible offence. He recounts one occasion when

> … a boy was punished so excessively and for so long a period that he broke away from the Brother and came to my house a mile away for assistance. The time was 10.45 p.m., almost two hours after the boys retired to bed. For coming to me in those circumstances he was again punished with equal severity.

The lives of the children, aged from 8 to 14, were blighted by this treatment. Bed-wetting—a product of emotional fear, uncertainty and other psychological problems—was widespread, even among older boys. Father Moore found a particularly strict regime as far as sexual misbehaviour was concerned. It was euphemistically referred to as 'badness'. If boys were caught or reported on, they were called out and beaten outside the classrooms during school hours. Boys generally were asked to report on such activity. The boys were terrified of this practice of beating in the classrooms and terrified too of the revelation of suspicion of 'badness'.

Moore wrote his report on Artane in 1962. He submitted it to Archbishop McQuaid and in late December repeated its contents in verbal testimony to the Interdepartmental Committee on Crime Prevention and Treatment of Offenders, chaired by the Justice Department Secretary, Peter Berry. The Education Department Secretary, Dr T.R. Ó Raifeartaigh, also sat on the Committee. He constantly interrupted Moore's interview to angrily reject his criticisms of Artane. Berry insisted on Moore being heard. Ó Raifeartaigh gave Moore a very rough ride and Moore left the committee room shaking. The Education Department received a written complaint about this from Archbishop McQuaid. The Committee persuaded the reluctant Ó Raifeartaigh to send his inspectors to Artane and they arrived there on 20 December 1962 to begin their Special Inspection in order to discredit Moore's complaints. The Christian Brothers were tipped off (probably by Ó Raifeartaigh) about the imminent inspection, which gave them time for a bit of window-dressing. The three inspectors' reports (delivered in January 1963) misrepresented conditions within the institution, a fact confirmed when the Department of Justice, following Moore's findings, ordered the issue of better clothing. The Department of Education reports were an attempt to discredit Moore—just as the Government had tried to discredit Father Flanagan, the Boystown Schools founder, by presenting false facts about the industrial schools in 1946. But in their attempts to discredit Father Moore, the inspectors went too far, describing how no fault could be found with the school. This was so obviously not the case and everyone knew it at the time.

Beresford decided to seek out Father Moore and the two men met in Dublin.

> We reminisced on events in the prison and discussed his 1962 report in detail.
> We also discussed his own background, the events that led to his appointment,
> his dealings with the Artane jailors and with Dr McQuaid and his treatment
> by the Church and State when and after he spilled the beans on Artane. He
> told me, among other things, that McQuaid had appointed him to inspect
> Artane and report back. His memory of the events surrounding the Special
> Inspection was extremely sharp—as sharp as mine.

Moore was himself denied access to his own report by Church and State, until many years later when he was sent a copy of it ahead of his appearance before the

Commission. His documentation and films on Artane were taken into police control.[1] The report bears out Beresford's own observations on the school at the time.

Moore was told by the Christian Brothers that their education had benefited the boys and that they had introduced psychological reporting on the boys during Moore's time at Artane. Moore saw little evidence, either of beneficial education or of help from psychological reporting. He had some understanding of this from his acquaintanceship with the Archbishop's nephew, Dr Paul McQuaid, who was the chief psychologist at the Mater Hospital and who worked in Artane in the late 1960s.

During his seven years at Artane there were some improvements. Overall numbers dropped. Better clothing was provided. At the same time nothing substantial was done and there continued to be no preparation of the boys for the outside world. They left inadequately prepared. There was no personal training before their departure, the date for which was fixed under law as their sixteenth birthday. A very elderly brother was responsible for what he called 'after care'. The result was that the majority ended up in dead-end jobs.

It has often been asserted that the Boys' Band was the only worthwhile feature at Artane because training in music was given. Nevertheless, it was a rigid and inflexible training. Boys were simply told what instruments they would play. Moreover, some of the pupils regarded the director, Brother O'Connor, as a brutal and abusive man. He was certainly a perfectionist, obsessed with achievement. He had been in charge of the poultry at Artane and had produced prize-winning hens. He had been in charge of Gaelic games and winning was a central point with him, not the enjoyment and understanding of the sport. Many Artane boys were successful, the musical ones ending up in the Army Number One Band and in the RTÉ Symphony Orchestra. Those who were successful generally did not want it known that they had been at Artane.

Archbishop McQuaid became actively involved in the welfare of the Artane boys. He set up a hostel for them in Eccles Street. Moore became involved in the work there. The brothers' involvement in job-finding for the boys was at a very primitive level—they found them positions as 'kitchen porters' and other unskilled work. The Countess of Wicklow helped, employing them as houseboys herself and trying to place boys elsewhere. She trained them well before they moved on. She persuaded the wife of the chairperson of the British Overseas Airways Corporation to take an Artane boy and she got one of her houseboys employed in an airline job. He went on to be successful. The regime changed during the last years at Artane; sisters came on to the staff in 1966 and the number of boys declined steeply, so that in the end there were about 30 and they resided in the infirmary.

The Archbishop arranged for nuns from the Daughters of Charity to help in the Eccles Street hostel. He also arranged for the Holy Family Sisters, an English

[1]   They have since been returned.

Order of nuns, to become involved in Artane itself where they helped in the infirmary.

Behind the scenes the Archbishop sought to have Artane closed. He claimed, 'Artane is the "Plague Spot" of my diocese.' On another occasion he reportedly said, 'I would burn Artane to the ground.' But the Archbishop recognised that he was dealing with a powerful organisation; moreover, it did not come directly under diocesan control. The Christian Brothers were powerful and independent and they had a network of educational establishments around the country that were held in high public regard. Their success in the field of education was absolutely critical and it had predisposed them never to admit wrongdoing; yet in Artane, Letterfrack and the many other industrial schools and institutions they ran it was palpably the fact that they had failed lamentably to deliver even rudimentary education. They were also incapable of dealing with damaged children, and even more, dealing with penal cases who were under the kind of restraint maintained in both Letterfrack and Artane. The Christian Brothers had an ingrained inability to admit their own failures. Their view of the institutions they ran was to maintain 'an autonomous, independent attitude: We run this show'. They countered criticism by referring to shortage of money: it was a mantra. Singling out for investigation places like Artane and Letterfrack would have been a kick in the teeth to educational success stories by the Christian Brothers elsewhere. The Christian Brothers at Artane resented Moore. They did not know about the request from the Archbishop that Moore should write a report on Artane.

It is ironic that Father Moore himself came from a very deprived background. His parents had been married for just two years when his father died following an operation for appendicitis. Moore was born six months later. His mother was destitute. Her father had been a publican and was an alcoholic. They were a Milltown family with land, but that had all gone. As a child, even with the decline in her father's fortunes, her grandmother had sent her to Muckross Park in Dublin where she studied, among other things, the piano and became quite good.

Henry Moore was fostered out but his mother joined him in the foster home, which included four others, making it a foster family of five with Moore's mother as a helper in the household. As was the practice at the time, four of the children went to industrial schools, two to Artane, one to Baltimore and the only girl to Cavan. This was Maureen Connolly.[2] She went to St Joseph's in Cavan in about 1939. She survived the Cavan fire by jumping clear of the conflagration. She was terribly wounded, with bones broken, and the young Moore went to see her in hospital, all tied up with slings for her broken limbs. She recovered and went to England where she met a hairdresser and married him. She had two children, a boy and a girl, and the boy died in his teens. She went to Australia. She is still alive and lives in Melbourne.

The foster home was a small cottage and the life in it was impoverished. The

---

2   See Arnold and Laskey, *Children of the Poor Clares*, pp 15–23.

woman was called Mrs Ivors, seen by the children as an 'endearing woman'. It was normal form for this fosterage of poor children in early childhood to be followed by industrial school. Mrs Moore left the foster home to become a clerk in the Hospital Trust.

Moore did not go to an industrial school but to an orphanage, St Vincent's in Glasnevin, and was there for 10 years. This was also under the Christian Brothers. The regime was very severe. He suffered from neglect and physical abuse. Like Goldenbridge, there was an automatic feeling of inferiority and the children were not allowed to mix with non-orphanage schoolchildren at the same orphanage. A few boys at the orphanage went on to Artane. Of the two boys who were in the foster family with Moore, one joined the Army. The other, James Jordan, left Artane and was very delicate. He was in a dead-end job, got TB and died at Peamount at the age of 23. Later, as chaplain at Artane, Moore saw his records, which recorded: 'he tended to be lazy'. The boy who went to Baltimore was Noel Corbally. He went into the RAF as a mechanic and died in ther latter half of the 1980s.

Moore's view was that the education at Artane was so inadequate as to be pathetic. Moreover, there was no attention whatever to human development, to the formation of character, or any attempt to provide basic psychological care and monitoring. Moore felt he could never interfere himself in discipline because of his spiritual role as a priest and chaplain to the boys. The Catholic Church thinking at the time was pre-Vatican II, a time when discipline and obedience were paramount in the Roman Catholic Church. Moore felt strongly enough about the situation to meet with the Christian Brother Provincial Superior, J.C. Mulholland, to complain about what was going on at Artane. Mulholland's reaction was simple enough: 'If I were to do what you ask me to do in Artane, I would have to send angels there.' Moore then went to the Superior General, Edward Clancy, in Marino, the head of the Christian Brothers worldwide. Moore's views on the industrial school were listened to, but the reaction was not encouraging. The Superior General, like those at the head of the Church generally, was simply at pains to avoid publicity at all costs.

Father Moore retained one image of two small boys who came to Artane from Rathdrum on a summer's day, dressed in light tops and shorts, each of them bringing a jam jar with goldfish inside. He later saw them in woollen clothes with hobnailed boots, the fish gone. 'They were little goldfish themselves!'

Chapter 25 ❧

THE KEY TO IT ALL:
EDUCATION

What must have caused acute upset to the Department of Education, in Father Henry Moore's report, were the criticisms of widespread illiteracy, criticisms that could be extrapolated throughout the Irish Gulag. Boys up to 14 years old at Artane either could not write, or found difficulty and needed help. The system of technical education, which should have given boys a chance of employment, was completely inadequate; wrong and obsolete technical training was given, its sole purpose to service Artane's needs, not to educate the boys. In the year of the report, of 18 who sat the Vocational School Examinations—the least onerous intellectually at the time—only five passed. How could the Department of Education, responsible for the running of Artane and its regular inspections on an annual basis, have flintily denied, year on year in successive Annual Reports, this blatant abuse, in the form of deprivation of every Irish child's constitutional right, a proper education?

The Department of Education had good reason to fear publicity about Artane in respect of the failure to educate the boys there and the fear was to be augmented very shortly, with the decision of the Government to apply for EEC membership. This brought the OECD into the picture and presented the Department and the Government with a serious headache, not just in respect of the educational failure at Artane, but almost universally throughout the industrial school set-up, nationwide. It is this that explains the extraordinary overreaction on the part of the Department of Education and the Christian Brothers. It had been known for decades that Artane provided only a bare literacy standard of education at best. That fact had been noted by the Cussen Report in 1936. Father Moore had read the report and he mentioned the fact before the Commission to Inquire into Child Abuse.

The significance of this is that Cussen had the following to say:

> We note with regret that in Artane industrial school, with over 700 pupils, only the minimum standard of literary education required by the regulations is provided, and pupils, however promising, cannot, as a rule, proceed beyond

the sixth standard.[1]

As for what passed as 'industrial training' in the industrial schools, Cussen is scathing:

> It appears to us that in the majority of the [industrial reformatory] schools the trades taught—many of which are obsolescent—have in view the needs of the institutions rather than the future of the boys … [the training] is generally of a kind adapted to making [the boys] useful to the schools rather than to providing a groundwork for future employment…the boys apparently being regarded as a rule merely as juvenile labourers.[2]

Father Moore used the term 'juvenile labourer'. As far as 'aftercare' was concerned, Moore said that it had not improved in the 26 years since Cussen. Neither had the educational provision. One person at Artane during the period covered by the Moore Report had already begun secondary education in September 1961 when he was imprisoned. He received no secondary education whatever in the two years he spent in Artane. He was used instead as a juvenile labourer.

This looked as if the Department and a major Irish religious teaching order were deliberately and wilfully robbing children of their right to education in an institution that they called a school. Moreover, the Department and the Christian Brothers had been found out lying repeatedly about the provision of education in both this and other institutions. There are many examples of this.

When Moore mentioned the deprivation in education at Artane, it was clear that he had to be silenced and, in due course, discredited. His charge of educational deprivation levelled against Artane has consistently been denied by the Department and by the Brotherhood. That was the main reason his report was kept secret. The Artane inspection reports (General, Medical, Educational) and Artane exam results are still not being released to former inmates.

Father Moore told the Interdepartmental Committee that Artane was turning out 'social misfits'. This was no surprise to anyone at the time or later. He noted that most of the Artane inmates were functionally illiterate even at the age of 14 and older.

In his letter to the Secretary of the Department of Education, Dr T.R. Ó Raifeartaigh, Peter Berry, then the Secretary of the Department of Justice, said: 'I am being given information which goes to show that there is something very, very wrong with the way the industrial school system is functioning.' He went on:

> I feel it necessary to say that having heard Fr X [Moore] twice, having carefully

---

[1] *Commission of Inquiry Report into the Reformatory and Industrial School System, 1934–1936*, p. 26. This report is better known as the Cussen Report, after the Commission's chairman, George Cussen, KC, one-time Senior Justice in the Metropolitan Children's Court, Dublin.

[2] Cussen Report, pp 30–33.

re-read your letter of 3rd December [1962] (with some of the conclusions of which I do not agree) and having listened to your cross-examination [of Moore] on 13th December [1962], I am entirely satisfied in my own mind that conditions in Artane Industrial School are not what they should be and that the Chaplain's basic complaints of under-financing and bad management, producing social misfits in afterlife are well-founded. On the subject of bad management, you will recollect that I told you in our talk the(?) morning of(?) Wednesday, 5th December that your Inspector of Reformatory and Industrial Schools [Turlough McDevitt] had weeks earlier described the manager of Artane school [Brother Slattery] to me as being entirely inadequate.[3]

Even Moore's complaint about mouse droppings in the Communion chalice would not explain the need for a cover-up. That finding may have enraged Archbishop John Charles McQuaid but it was marginal in terms of the State's reaction. Moore had some misconceptions about Artane. He had been in the institution a relatively short time and the Christian Brothers would barely speak to him, regarding him as a spy in the camp. He thought the Artane Boys' Band was a financial burden on the school. In fact it was a source of income. He thought that many of the inmates were orphans. In fact there were few, if any, orphans in Artane. He suggested that some of the inmates were 'mentally handicapped' and that they needed the services of a psychiatrist. This was probably a misreading of some measure of psychological damage after periods of between 10 and 14 years spent in a brutal and unregulated prison for children.

Moore's report gave the three departmental inspectors a list of items to check when they carried out their Special Inspection. One of those things was clothing, and in particular Moore's charge that the boys lacked overcoats. Of all Moore's complaints, this appears to be among the least significant. However, the facts that the clothing was not only inadequate but was also degrading and a source of embarrassment were very significant to the inmates, as widely reported in evidence to me. The fact that overcoats were not supplied was something that the inspectors could readily confirm or deny and clearly they lied. Moore charged that 'Overcoats are not supplied except where a boy can pay £3 to £4 in advance, which must come from his own pocket. It is pathetic to observe hundreds of boys walking the roads of the district on Sunday mornings even in deep winter without overcoats.' The Department of Justice later obliquely refused the Department of Education when it arranged for overcoats to be issued.

One needs also to remember that the winter of 1962–3 was the coldest for 200 years. In eastern Ireland and western Britain a freeze began in December 1962 and the temperature didn't rise above zero until the following March. Air temperatures as low as −8 °C were common by day. Icicles hung from every roof and packed snow lay deep on the ground. One inmate has given testimony of how

---

3   Commission to Inquire into Child Abuse, Brother Martin Reynolds' testimony on 15 September 2005, pp 88–9.

he spent the whole of that winter dressed in skimpy shorts and an ill-fitting jacket, which would not button up. He had no overcoat.

> I can show you a photo taken in that winter of myself and my brother together with my mother and three sisters when they visited Artane. All in the picture are clad in hefty overcoats except myself and my brother. My parents had offered to provide clothing for myself and my brother (including overcoats) but the Brothers wouldn't allow that.

The freeze had begun when the three inspectors arrived in Artane on 20 December 1962. They sat in the warmth of the reception office and observed through the window hundreds of inmates milling about in the prison yard—without overcoats. They spent two days in the school—long enough to settle the question of whether or not the children possessed overcoats. It is interesting to see how they dealt with the clothing question. Dr Anna McCabe claimed that the boys had warm comfortable clothing. She lied. McDaid, another member of the inspection team, answered the question more fully. After the two-day visit he wrote in his report on clothing in Artane:

> Before turning to other premises visited, I think it appropriate to comment at this stage on the clothing of the boys, the outward show by which the uninformed public must perforce judge the work of the school. Tenets of criticism inevitably change once the criticism is a ward of the State and/or in the control of the Religious. The cherry-nosed, ruddy-faced boy playing coatless in the muddy street on a winter's day will at once be the happy despair of his mother for his appearance and his father's pride for his rude health. Place the same child within the gates of an institutional school and he immediately earns a label 'neglected and exploited'. All the boys on review were warmly clad and, though possessing overcoats of some sort (either raincoats or topcoats), few wore them though the weather was sharp.
>
> There were only two in the sick-bay out of a complement of 413 which testified to the care of the children. And the difficulty of getting boys to wear overcoats when going out to play is not new. But to be frank, the clothing in most cases was of the rough-type tweed and the familiar poor-house colours of light red brick rust and drab grey, automatically identifying the wearer. Sunday clothes were in some cases of a finer material but equally drab in colour and unimaginative in pattern. What a difference a fleck of bright thread in the weave would make in this material and since the cloth is woven and the suit is tailored in the school workshop, a woman with ideas could do really good work in that direction in this department.
>
> Socks, pullovers and jerseys are also made in the knitting workshop for which the wool is dyed on the premises. Neither the dye selected for the wools nor the patterns chosen for the pullovers or jerseys were to the credit of the

workshop. While not to the same extent as girls, clothes for boys need to be chosen with some regard to the harmony of the garment and the clothes. Several youngsters wore black boots with maroon coloured stockings bearing a single white burn near the top, tweed suits, some unmatched of the colours as described and—to cap it all—sported light blue jersey pullovers with single creamy stripes across the chest. Add to this shirts buttoned or unbuttoned at the neck and no ties, and even the most presentable boys are handicapped in appearance. I do not wish to convey the opinion that all the boys were so ill-assortedly garbed but rather to stress the poor use made of such fine raw materials with such harmful advertisement.

There is nothing wrong with the clothing of the children that a woman would not at once put right given the necessary authority and she would probably insist on shoes instead of boots in most cases, especially for Sunday wear. The following is a list of clothing which the Bursar claimed was supplied to each boy during 1962. Replacements were to be made as required by 1963.

Item: On paper this looks a generous issue but is not supported by the appearance of the boys. This once again emphasises the need for selection, variation etc.—a natural instinct which most women in the field possess but not possessed by men to the same degree.[4]

What is most shameful of all is the treatment given, 45 years later, to the report and to Moore's reputation by the Commission. Father Moore was at Artane from 1960 until 1967, with additional pastoral duties in the Coolock parish. He began to take alcohol for the first time many years after leaving Artane. In his late forties he became an alcoholic and it was during this period that a single, isolated sexual abuse episode took place. Moore's non-custodial conviction was some 20 years later. In a move that was disappointing and distasteful, this completely irrelevant court appearance by Moore, 30 years after the date of his report, was brought up before the Commission by the Christian Brothers in circumstances that can only be seen as aimed at discrediting him.

As to the charges on education, clothing, care, food, recreation and all the other matters dealt with by Moore, the Commission did not discuss, debate or raise them in a direct and open way, putting each of Moore's criticisms into the public arena for debate and cross-examination. It did not even discuss the circumstances of the commissioning and writing of the report.

There was a cover-up about Artane and the other industrial schools. The Moore Report was an attempt to breach that cover-up at the instigation of Archbishop McQuaid. It failed and the cover-up went on. It continued through and after 1962. It was still in operation during the various media investigations, article, magazines and television documentaries. It has continued to this day. The purpose was to conceal State crimes against children.

4   McDaid's report on the Special Inspection of Artane conducted on 20 and 21 December 1962.

The process was one of faking Irish history. It is very dangerous to indulge in it. On Ireland's habit of inventing history, the historian and author T.W. Moody had this to say in a 1977 essay entitled 'Irish History and Mythology':

> If 'history' is used in its proper sense of a continuing, probing critical search for truth about the past, my argument would be that it is not Irish history but Irish mythology that has been ruinous to us and may prove even more lethal. History is a matter of facing the facts of the Irish past, however painful some of them may be; mythology is a way of refusing to face the historical facts.

The controversial Moore Report, held under wraps by the Department of Education for 45 years, was made public on 18 August 2007. The release of a copy held by Dr Diarmuid Martin, Archbishop of Dublin, made this possible. Repeated requests for it eventually persuaded the Archbishop to honour a pledge he had made, when he first arrived back in Ireland, that the only possible resolution of the child sexual abuse scandal would be when everything came out. The report was not published with State backing or acknowledgment. It appeared on websites aimed at those who were abused within the industrial school system, among them the widely followed Paddy Doyle website, www.paddydoyle.com. It also went to the press.

The report was blocked by the Department of Education, despite numerous attempts by interested parties, including victims and their lawyers, to gain access. It was also blocked by the Commission to Inquire into Child Abuse set up in 2001. Mr Justice Seán Ryan, who took over from Ms Justice Mary Lafoy at the end of 2003, when she resigned in protest at the way the Department of Education was responding to her, tried to prevent the Archbishop releasing the document when the Dublin Diocese sent it to the Commission.

Moreover, for the Commission to have allowed this report to be largely bypassed or deliberately discredited and marginalised is a terrible indictment of the programme of redress that had gone on since 1999. The Archbishop's release of the document was a welcome challenge to the State on its attempt to whitewash the whole abuse story.

Archbishop Martin's release of the *Private Report on Artane Industrial School*, which was furnished to his predecessor, Archbishop McQuaid on 7 July 1962, raised him in the eyes of the victims and gave them some hope of future support.

Archbishop Martin also said: '… there are no short cuts. Over the past five years there has been change in the Church's handling of the issue with a policy of openness and of rapidly addressing problems.' This was immediately disputed, since there was considerable disparity between what happened in other countries and what had happened in Ireland. But the Archbishop appeared to emerge at the time as a new broom and showed his sympathy, over the Father Moore affair, by respecting Jim Beresford's request for the document.

By doing so, Archbishop Martin put himself at odds with the Government. He also offended the more reactionary elements in the Church, in respect of the abuse issue. This was where the release of the Moore Report represented an important change of direction. In practical terms it came too late. By the time he released the document, the Commission had concluded its public hearings. The chairperson, Mr Justice Seán Ryan, was apparently going to prepare his report. That report inevitably would be a flawed document. Evidence of this is clear from what has already been said of the flawed testimony of the Taoiseach, over the background to the Apology, and over the treatment of Father Moore's report. Many other examples of Commission shortcomings have already been touched on.

What seemed to be a growing possibility, on the basis of the long drawn-out operation of the Commission, was that its conclusions would be a whitewash of Church and State, with at least some possibility of the charge against the abused that many of them presented 'corrupted' testimony.

Whatever the degree of fault on either side, it was the growing conviction of a large number of people concerned directly in the process, that what should have been a scrupulous investigation was turning out to be a flawed one. The action of the Archbishop, in releasing the Moore Report, unwittingly gave huge public attention to the possibilities, not of corrupt testimony by the abused, but of corrupt handling of that testimony by those entrusted with its honest and careful assessment. Archbishop Martin had drawn public attention, perhaps unintentionally, to the dishonest and biased handling of the Moore Report and its content in the hearings before the Commission.

What happened was a truly reprehensible handling by the Commission, under Mr Justice Seán Ryan, and by the Christian Brothers, of the Moore Report in direct conjunction with Father Moore's later life and his reputation. This included, among other things, the completely unsubstantiated claim that Father Moore was 'actuated by malice'. To this was then added the idea, again unspecified and unrelated to any factual data, that 'there was an agenda at work'.

Neither for the first nor last time, Brother Martin Reynolds, who appeared for the Christian Brothers at the Commission talking about Father Moore, found himself 'in difficulties'. These 'difficulties' were the case against Father Moore for sexual abuse brought in 1994, 30 years after his report. The following is how Brother Reynolds started his testimony:

I am so sorry, I need some direction as to whether—or unfortunately I meant to do this before a name was mentioned and I am now—it has caught up with me. I am not too sure—I am not too sure how to put this without saying what I want to say. I am not too sure how I am going to deal with this—let's put it this way, Mr Chairman, you know what I am referring to.

Instead of stopping him there and then, Seán Ryan said:

I think the problem that arises is in the public domain … We would want to retain the capacity to make a decision as to how much of the surrounding factual area in regard to this matter is relevant and is necessary for us to explore. In one sense, the matter can be regarded as being in the public domain, but unrelated entirely to any activities of ours. In another area evidence was explored in private hearings so it goes beyond simply what the report says … it should be possible to explore the area without trespassing into an area that we want to retain the right to make a decision about.

It is astonishing that Mr Justice Ryan then allowed the discussion to continue for several minutes. He allowed explicit references to the conviction of Father Moore for sexual abuse to be aired before the Commission's public hearing into the Moore Report. Undoubtedly, the fact that this conviction was raised in the course of the hearing before the Commission could only lessen the integrity of Moore's work for Archbishop McQuaid, 45 years earlier, and thus cast doubt on the report. And the judge let this happen. It was a truly disreputable episode in the Commission's long series of public interrogations and was inexcusable.

For those people, many of whom now live in England, from where they watch, not without residual twinges of fear and loathing for the system that damaged their lives, this was the worst event in the hypocritical and twisted process of the previous eight years—ostensibly designed to bring them justice—but now concluding on an inevitably sour, hypocritical and profoundly unhelpful note.

In a press statement released on Monday 20 August 2007, Brother Edmund Garvey, head of the Christian Brothers in Ireland, claimed that the Department of Education inspection of Artane, following Father Moore's report, and made by two senior inspectors together with Dr Anna McCabe, the medical inspector, was *not* notified in advance. He said: 'The Brothers in Artane at the time did not have prior notice of the inspection, contrary to reports in recent media commentary.' It was, however, quite regular practice, in all industrial schools, whether for boys or girls, for prior notification to be given to the institution of coming inspections. As a result, and in preparation for them, special food was served, clean clothing issued and a general smartening up went on. Countless inmates have testified to this fact.

On its own it is not sufficient to challenge what Brother Garvey has said about the inaccuracy on this point in *Irish Independent* coverage. There is more evidence, however. Jim Beresford who served meals to Father Moore and worked in the Brothers' House knew of the inspection in advance and knew also that Father Moore expected it and, as soon as the inspectors arrived, drove out of Artane and back to his house. There was no doubt, in Father Moore's and the boys' minds, as well as in gossip among the brothers overheard by the boy, that there was prior knowledge of the visit.

But the conflict of evidence goes much deeper. Reading the sustained and unrelentingly negative judgments of the whole of Father Moore's report, it is inconceivable that a two-day visit by inspectors could in any way whatever refute the testimony. And it is a disgrace that the two approaches were treated in a way designed to let them cancel out each other.

The initial report was concerned with every aspect of Artane witnessed over almost two years (Father Moore remained at Artane as chaplain for seven years).

The other, done more or less on the orders of the chairperson of the inter-departmental committee, Peter Berry, was motivated by departmental alarm—expressed very strongly at meetings of the committee—and a desire to rebuff everything the priest had said. To do so would have needed a stay at Artane of months, rather than a two-day visit. It was done as a 'response' to Father Moore, according to Bridget McManus, present Secretary General of the Department of Education, in her testimony to the Commission on 12 June 2006. She made the astonishing claim that, in two days, the inspectors, whose brief was 'to state the facts reasonably and with discretion, good and bad to be included', managed to look 'at virtually every aspect of life in Artane … including food that the children were eating and the clothes that they were wearing … the relationship between the boys and the teachers … virtually every heading … [and] the Department's report was very satisfied that there was *no substance* to the allegations of Fr Moore'.

According to Bridget McManus, 'there was some criticism I think subsequently in the Interdepartmental Committee minutes and discussions that perhaps they hadn't dealt with all headings'. Hardly surprising if their assessment was confined to two days, as indeed it was.

Subsequently, the medical inspector, Dr McCabe—known to generations of inmates, male and female, and not with too much sympathy—agreed with part of Father Moore's report but in general rejected its findings over food. This was later to have a comic postscript.

When Dr McCabe retired in 1965 she visited Artane for some kind of farewell lunch, a macabre concept. She was a formidable lady and was dressed for the occasion in a tweed suit. She also wore a smart tweed hat with a feather in it, a slightly Tyrolean presentation. Ruling Christian Brothers accompanied her at the time. Informed in advance, as was the general practice, the boys, given the usual 'special day' food of boiled pork chops, decided to prepare their own reception. Dr McCabe came into the dining hall, beaming on all around her. The boys, who were intrigued by this novel food, were picking up the chops and inspecting them. Deciding that their food came by grace of Dr McCabe, and on the basis of her generally distorted reports on conditions in the industrial schools as she found them, those near the entrance threw their chops at her, covering her in gravy and meat fragments. Both she and the senior brothers beat a hasty retreat. Within minutes a large detachment of brothers entered the dining hall. Anyone without a chop on his plate was flogged on the spot. The event became known as giving Dr McCabe 'the chop'.

Father Moore's report from 1962 highlights the widespread illiteracy amongst the children at Artane and this was in a place run by Ireland's premier teaching order. Artane was 'a school' in existence for 99 years without a library—yet we know that the children in the band were used to raise money for their and other Christian Brother schools around Ireland, such as Sullivan's Christian Brothers School in Cork, in need of new libraries or science labs—Artane had neither of these things and it must be inferred that it was because the brothers didn't want such things for the Artane children.

Father Moore also lamented the violent methods used to 'teach religion'. This was obviously a matter for the then Archbishop of Dublin who had employed Moore and commissioned the report from him. Education was his territory; he must have been rightly appalled that the children were coming to associate religion with classroom violence of an extreme kind and wholesale oppression.

This is the proof, if proof were needed, that as guardians of the faith and true followers of their founder, Edmund Rice, the Christian Brothers were not fit for purpose. It must have appeared to Archbishop McQuaid, as he read Moore's report, that the anti-Christ was about his evil work in the Archdiocese. It is obvious that you cannot bring the young (or anyone) 'to the love of God' through violence but violence was their creed and God's love was jettisoned in its mad and wicked pursuit. The written testimony of Father Moore could in no way be refuted by the whitewash undertaken by the inspection team from the Department of Education on those two ice-cold days in December 1962.

Not only was the Commission open to the most serious criticism for its handling of the Moore Report, it is also suspect in that there is no record of it seeking the important Archbishop McQuaid correspondence relating to Artane. This included correspondence with the Government and with Father Moore. In a letter to Moore dated 18 December 1962, the Archbishop wrote: 'If by an act of God Artane could disappear today, I would be a much less anxious Archbishop.' Clearly he was not happy with the 'goings on' in Artane. Why else would he have requested Moore to prepare a report in the first place?

Father Moore maintained that there was a flurry of correspondence between Archbishop McQuaid and the Government following the rough handling he received when summoned to appear before the committee representative of the Departments of Education, Health and Justice. The Archbishop had written a letter of complaint to the Government. Though this was requested from Archbishop Martin in 2004 and from others who might have had copies, it has not yet become part of the public domain.

John Cooney, in his biography of Archbishop McQuaid, says that he was a meticulous record keeper. He claims that the Archbishop's system of archives was the envy of J. Edgar Hoover, the FBI chief! More recently, the Dublin Diocesan Archives Archivist, David Sheehy, said that the DDA has an extensive file on Artane.

Chapter 26 ∾

| THE RYAN REPORT

T he account of abuse of children in Irish industrial schools is living history, involving many men and women still alive who suffered within the system. They are the main protagonists, the chief people in an unhappy and tragic saga involving, above all else, a betrayal of them by the Irish State. The living history falls into two quite distinct parts. One of these parts predates, at its outset, the lives that are being considered and are still central because so many of the men and women who were incarcerated within the Irish Gulag are still with us. It is a necessary part because it contains details of the legislative and administrative framework within which those lives were distorted, damaged and wrecked by the State.

The Roman Catholic Church has carried an unfair share of the burden of blame. This is a fact and not a mitigation of the ignorance, perversity, cruelty and neglect that characterised the lives of those placed within the industrial schools and reformatories. These were run by religious orders, notably the Sisters of Mercy, the Christian Brothers, the Oblate Fathers. They seem to have known so little of the need for love and compassion towards their charges. Their regimes were dominated by cruelty and punishment and this was aggravated by neglect in all departments of the lives of the inmates: their health, welfare, education and training. To this was added two further terrible dimensions: there was brutal and illegal punishment and there was sexual abuse.

Yet in order for this widespread regime to exist at all there had to be distortion of the laws, going back to the Children Act of 1908, and indeed to earlier legislation, and distortion as well of the Rules and Regulations fashioned for the whole system. These were the State's responsibility and the State not only failed to regulate but actually covered up, in official and statutory investigations, what was going on and what constraints were being universally overturned.

In addition, as is argued from the early pages of this book, the system of committal was widely misused to the disadvantage of the children brought before the courts. No one spoke or acted for them. Their incarceration was widely predetermined. It was imposed on the basis that the State, not the Church, was acting, in the first instance, *in loco parentis*, handing over this responsibility—

which is a responsibility for individual lives—to untrained and unsympathetic organisations predisposed to care for what they termed the souls of the inmates while persecuting and invading their minds and bodies in a perverse, cruel and extortionate exaction of mindless submission to their authority.

This phase in the living history then went through a change of focus and direction. What had been seen in a generally benign light was fundamentally challenged by journalists, writers, campaigners for the truth and by the abused people themselves. It was also challenged in the courts. There had been a massive and sustained cover-up, by the State, by the Church, by many devout, conservative Christian men and women who, out of duty to the Church and their own faith, could not accept that a terrible wrong had been perpetuated in Irish society and had gone on in many institutions spread around the country.

This discovery, at first half comprehended and questioned by doubt and disbelief, led to the second phase, the real living history of a new saga unfolded principally by Bertie Ahern under the pretence that he was responding to what journalists were discovering, in particular in relation to the *States of Fear* programmes on RTÉ. As I have tried to show in previous chapters, his was a hypocritical Apology concealing a carefully organised and orchestrated response by the State to a growing threat of litigation which could well have snowballed out of control and overwhelmed his administration. Ahern's Apology offered a mitigating and supposedly compassionate alternative to the legal route, the main ingredient of which was the setting up of a Commission to Inquire into Child Abuse. (The added commitment to recompense, through the Redress Board, came later.)

Ahern deliberately misled the public by adding his own entirely fictitious motivation for the Apology, claiming that this had been inspired by members of the various groups representing the abused. The truth was that these representative bodies did not exist in May 1999.

From that Apology there began the reconstruction of the past through the Commission, first under Ms Justice Mary Lafoy and, since her resignation of December 2003, under Mr Justice Seán Ryan. The account of this fills the greater part of this book. The sequence of events faced a major crisis when Mary Lafoy resigned. She threw the process into confusion by confronting the Department of Education with a detailed account of its foot-dragging and obstruction. She had earlier expressed her grave doubts about the evident conflict of interest in the Department of Education—primarily responsible for the control and management of the industrial school and reformatory system—being her authority under the legislation. Now she presented a formidable indictment of the travesty in the events through which she had struggled. She warned that the process, which aimed to alleviate distress among the abused, expose the irregularities within the system and come to some kind of final judgment, had been prejudiced, possibly irrevocably.

At this stage there was widespread lack of confidence among the abused people directly affected. By December 2003 I had already written numerous articles with the underlying doubt and suspicion that this was a flawed process, not to be trusted. Mary Lafoy's successor—well-flagged in advance of her resignation as Seán Ryan, a Senior Counsel who was appointed a High Court judge before taking over—was taking up a bittersweet promotion.

Whether or not this is true will take time to judge from the huge body of material contained in the five-volume Final Report of the Commission to Inquire into Child Abuse. The purpose of this book and its final chapter is to set the scene for that judgment but not, for the present, to make it. That will be carried out in a revised edition.

Here it is sufficient to indicate some of the historical points that have not been explained, or not covered adequately or in detail up to the present time. For Seán Ryan to make sense of what he accepted in 2003 and what he told us he would try to achieve in statements he made in 2004, he has to do the following.

Firstly, he has to present a satisfactory explanation of the true motive for Bertie Ahern making the Apology and setting up the Commission. The evidence given to the sitting which dealt with this was flawed. Ahern told a lie. He was not recalled to rectify this and it remains a serious issue for the abused. Was the process based on recompense, or was it based on a quite different Government concern? Was the State attempting to protect its integrity and taxpayers' money— as it was duty-bound to do—rather than indicting the Church and the religious orders for what they had done during the entire existence of the State? In order to answer these questions, we need discovery of departmental and Cabinet documents and minutes from the period during which the State's response— made public in Ahern's Apology—was worked out.

Seán Ryan, in his own forecasting of what he would seek to achieve, does not refer to this matter. He was consulted by the Government on how the investigative process could be speeded up and his report on this was seminal in the changes that followed Ms Justice Mary Lafoy's resignation. In the event, the amending legislation was not presented in draft form until March 2005 and passed later that year.

It was in mid-June 2004 that Mr Justice Seán Ryan presented in detail points from his own policy which he would be following. Unsurprisingly, this did not allude to the basic issue of why we had gone through five years of delayed action on behalf of the abused. He emphasised that there would be no naming of individual perpetrators of abuse unless they had been found guilty in the courts. Irish tribunals generally, of which there have been many others, have not been so shy of naming those guilty of criminal acts.

Seán Ryan put his own approach down to the fact that the inquiry's remit extended from the late 1930s for some 60 years and he made the point that there was conflict in the interests and wishes of victims of abuse. He made clear that this approach was supported by the Commission to Inquire into Child Abuse Act of 2000 which forbade findings in relation to particular instances of the alleged abuse of children.

> We tried to look at the point and purpose and value of the inquiry mandated by the Act of 2000, and whether they were going to be achieved by examining many hundreds of individual cases in a long sequence of trials.

Mr Justice Ryan's position paper, which preceded his statement, contained a full review of the Act and the issues in relation to naming individuals who have not been convicted of abuse. He went on to say that he was looking for a process

> ... that met the legal requirements laid down by the courts, promised a proper investigation into what happened and why it happened, would not be prolonged to a degree that is unfair and unreasonable and disappointing to everyone involved as well as the public, and was practical and focused and sensitive to participants.

He claimed that a round of consultations followed, leading to submissions on which the groups acting for the abused were invited 'to comment'. We shall have to see what the final judgment of these groups is.

Mr Justice Ryan said he would proceed in a spirit of inclusiveness but would also conduct the inquiry in what he saw as the most effective and valuable way. He did not expect everyone to agree.

> We have a job to do and we cannot avoid the responsibility of deciding difficult questions. But we do want people to understand what we are doing and why and our approach is to be as open and considerate as possible. We are not passing the buck and abrogating our duty to choose between different options. We hope that all the participants in the inquiry will understand what we are trying to do, even if some of them don't always agree with us.

At the time I was not impressed by what I considered was an ill-judged attempt at ameliorative language, at the expense of clear judicial presentation, well before the terms of the amending legislation became clear. The comparison may seem unfair, but looking at the impeccable, forensic explanation by Ms Justice Mary Lafoy in the early parts of her Third Report and in the extensive appendices on her dealings with the Department of Education, which take up close to half the 434 pages, I find distressing the uncertainty and woolliness of Mr Justice Ryan's presentation in advance of the case that has now led us to the Final Report. We shall see whether or not the requirements of the public and the abused people are satisfied.

Mr Justice Sean Ryan had made the point that it was time for the investigation to get under way and that there had been 'enough or even too many reviews and reports and discussions about ways and means' which provoked the thought that this was primarily a product of the apparently deliberate frustrations from the Department of Education that had brought into existence his own role and his own writing of the reports and reviews that were now seen as an impediment.

Without saying what 'the major issue' was, he said debating it further was not helpful.

He has two essential purposes: 'Not to name individual perpetrators of abuse unless they were convicted in the courts, and to call witnesses to give evidence of abuse suffered by them to the extent necessary for the inquiry'. That extent was not spelled out. Its acceptability and fulfilment, to the satisfaction, first, of the abused people, and then of the general public, is central to the forthcoming Final Report. He said there had been some disagreement and some agreement and then later added, in what seems like an afterthought:

> Nobody put forward a rival scheme that could meet the requirements we set out in our documents and which I very briefly summarised at the beginning. The challenge was to see whether some other modus operandi could be devised that would better meet the needs of the situation as agreed all round. None was proposed. In the result, our decision was inevitable.

Given Seán Ryan's position, this was strange language indeed.

Though amending legislation was required, Mr Justice Seán Ryan was determined

> ... to get on with our work and to inquire into child abuse in institutions as we are required to do under the legislation. We must of course bear in mind, before we get the amendments that we are looking for, that we have to comply with the existing legislation. We will do that by proceeding as we are announcing here but we do not think that it will be possible to produce an interim report before we get the legislation changed.

Mr Justice Ryan indicated the prospect of an interim report, or interim reports, based on the investigations, but only after the legislation had been amended. It was so amended, as announced by Mary Hanafin, but no interim reports appeared. It might have been better if they had, spreading the load that now at the end comes to us in several volumes.

One of the most significant points he made, in respect of investigating past failures within the industrial school system, was that it was important 'not to ignore the methods by which children came to be placed in institutions'. This issue of committal was never meant to be part of the process. It came far too close to the derelictions of the State—its betrayal of the innocent children—than was comfortable. It had been precluded by Michael Woods when he steered through the original legislation setting up the Commission to Inquire into Child Abuse.

Ms Justice Mary Lafoy covered it, but only in a detailed listing of the various legislative provisions by which children were committed and how they operated. Since this was already in the public domain, what Seán Ryan said was seen at the time, and now appears, in the words 'not to ignore the methods', to be an extension of what she had done. An extension was and is certainly necessary. As this book stoutly asserts, there was almost complete lack of balance in the views taken by the courts and these views represented a grievous abuse of human rights.

The children were not represented. Their circumstances were not properly investigated. They were, as the founder of the Legion of Mary, Frank Duff, asserted in a letter to Archbishop John Charles McQuaid, 'shovelled' into the industrial schools. What Seán Ryan has to say about this, if he fulfils his quite burdensome undertaking properly, will be keenly looked at by the abused. Committal was probably the worst shock they experienced. What he said, in spelling out his intentions, is interesting:

> I mentioned the role of the Courts and the relevance of that question to the matters that we have to investigate. The Committee had previously rejected such an approach because it felt that this matter was not within the terms of reference of the Commission. Our continuing investigations have alerted the Investigation Committee to the materiality of this topic. The importance of the issue to some victims is hard to exaggerate. People were heartened by the reference in my speech to this question and were enthusiastic at the prospect that this area would be followed up by the inquiry. It seems to us that it would be unsatisfactory to ignore this part of the history that we have to explore. In the circumstances, we propose to seek an appropriate amendment to remove any doubt about the relevance of this area to the inquiry into child abuse.

Mr Justice Seán Ryan undertook to investigate the training of teachers, staff, managers and supervisors, the recruitment of religious and the engagement of staff, and their educational level. Following this the education of the children would also be inquired into. He was advised by Patrick Walsh of Irish soca, when Walsh made an appearance at a hearing of the whole oecd investigation of institutionalised children and their educational attainment and he undertook consideration of this.

Ryan did not seem to see this information, of itself, as abuse. He said of it:

> When we have ascertained a lot of the background information about the institution and we know what attitude is being taken to the suggestion of abuse and what extra information is available about abuse, we will be in a position to decide how many of the complainants we need to call in order to fill out the picture.

He expected institution representatives, where it was backed by evidence, to acknowledge the essential truth of the complaints and believed this would make it easier to find out the scale of the abuse. When it came to the hearings, my own limited experience was of denial by the spokespersons representing the institutions. And it therefore seemed simple-minded to anticipate a high level of co-operation that would then make it unnecessary to call 'a large number of witnesses'. How many were heard would depend on what remained in dispute in regard to the abuse and the needs of the inquiry to get background information as to the detail of the abuse after acknowledgments were taken into account.

This giving of a variety of theoretical examples of what might happen seemed a strange approach by a judge who had been aware of several years of investigation by his predecessor, including the model hearing of the Baltimore Fisheries School testimony.

> We cannot lay down a specific procedure. We have to say to people that the way we approach the institution depends on the issues appropriate to that situation. We intend to call as witnesses a sufficient number of complainants to deal with the issues relevant to the particular institution. Once we have satisfied ourselves by considering the necessary quantum of evidence there will, I expect, remain a body of complainants (and indeed individual respondents) who have not been called to give evidence.

Mr Justice Seán Ryan said he would be happy to discuss with complainants and respondents how best to conduct the inquiry into the particular institution. 'The decision ultimately must be one for the Investigation Committee as to how to carry out the inquiry, but in broad terms, that is what we intend.'

One issue on which Mr Justice Seán Ryan gave no assurances was the troubled question of documents. This has bedevilled the process and worried the abused men and women throughout the past 10 years. There were Government documents covering the setting up of the Commission and including Department of Education memoranda, inter-departmental papers and Cabinet subcommittee papers. These should be a part of any final audit of the Commission's work. The long-standing failure of the Department of Education, in facilitating abused people in respect of personal documents, is another area of failure and frustration on which the public should be informed and about which the chairperson should be making some kind of judgment. He should be doing the same in respect of the Church and the religious orders. They had at first-hand responsibility for countless lives and the documentation of this should have been preserved carefully as a legal requirement in respect of the care process in which they were engaged. Such evidence as we have suggests that this was treated with casual indifference. But we need to have the chairperson's views on this. In all these categories the loss and deliberate destruction of important papers, of records of punishment, of health and identity records on inmates and of other material of seminal—and now historic—importance, is an essential part of the final report to Government.

The softness of the intended approach was evident in the following appeal:

We hope that respondent congregations and institutions will feel able to co-operate as fully as possible with the work of the Investigation Committee. In fairness, it has to be acknowledged that a number of religious congregations have taken a position of spectacular Christian concern for the victims of abuse and for finding out the truth.

Our inquiry is not a process to see whether the Committee can come up with evidence which establishes that abuse took place in a particular institution, in the teeth of opposition from that institution which denies everything and which says that every single allegation made by the complainants is wrong. We want to up-end that process and I hope that congregations will accept that they have responsibilities to the victims of abuse and those who complain, even if some of them are thought to be in the wrong, and to the community as a whole and also to the congregations and their own members. No devout religious can feel comfortable putting victims of abuse through further trauma and distress if that can be avoided.

There is a fear among some of those who are co-operating fully with the inquiry in ascertaining the extent of abuse in their institutions that other congregations who resist what we are trying to do will fare better in the final result of the inquiry process. In other words, there will be condemnation of the co-operating congregations while those who oppose and resist the inquiry will escape any sanction or even a finding that abuse took place in their institutions. I wish that we could dismiss such a fear as being unfounded.

But the real fear, overriding every other fear, was the fear among the abused that their betrayal was nearing an unresolved conclusion from which they were being excluded. We shall see if this is true or not.

Chapter 27 ❧

RYAN REPORT BETRAYS VICTIMS OF INDUSTRIAL SCHOOL SYSTEM

The five-volume Report of the Commission to Inquire into Child Abuse is a vast document. It attempts to cover six of the 10 years since Bertie Ahern made his public apology to those who had suffered abuse in the industrial schools and, together with Ms Justice Mary Lafoy's Third Interim Report, published in December 2003, it completes the record of the Commission's work.

Its main achievement is the painstaking and imperfect knitting together of various strands of testimony about a selection of industrial schools where abuse was central. Their names are well-known to us. Much of the testimony coming from their former inmates contained in this report is also well-known. It was exposed, debated and argued over at public hearings of the Investigation Committee of the Commission. These began under Ms Justice Mary Lafoy and went on under Mr Justice Seán Ryan after he took over the chairmanship.

This testimony is now presented in extensive and sickening detail about Artane, Letterfrack, Tralee, Carriglea, Glin, Salthill, Cabra, Daingean, Marlborough House, Upton, Ferryhouse, Greenmount, Lota, Goldenbridge, Cappoquin, Clifden, Newtownforbes, Dundalk, Kilkenny and Beechpark. From the earlier Third Interim Report there is the further testimony of what happened in another bleak, grim place: Baltimore Fisheries School.

The two volumes covering these institutions run to 1,400 pages and they deal with only a selection of testimony by inmates of the 60 industrial schools and reformatories listed and mapped at the beginning of *The Irish Gulag* and spread across the whole country. There is a disproportionate emphasis on the institutions for boys, where much of the abuse was pervasively gross; but violence in the girls' industrial schools was also terrible and merited far greater attention than it has been given. Confronted by the massive amount of material, it is easy to overlook the central contribution brought to the Commission's work by Mr Justice Seán Ryan, and this was to short-circuit the process of examination, bringing it to an earlier conclusion. This was not something sought by the abused themselves. They spent the first four years of the nine-year period of investigation watching the State, through the Department of Education, delaying the Commission's work under Ms Justice Mary Lafoy and had already lost patience when Seán Ryan took over.

A further 400 pages in the third volume, detailing the work of the Commission's Confidential Committee, gives harrowing personal data, not specifically related to places but presented on a thematic basis. Chapters define the family backgrounds of those incarcerated. The forms of abuse used on male victims are separated into one chapter. What happened to females is contained in another. There is some detail given of positive experiences. The Commission's remit covered a range of institutions beyond the industrial school system itself, recounting abuse experiences in special needs schools, children's homes, foster care, hospitals, primary and secondary schools, and residential laundries.

It is in this volume that the thorny issue of committal is addressed, though only in a technical sense, under the heading 'Pathways to Industrial and Reformatory Schools'. It was a massive process masquerading as 'care' but in fact it was what Frank Duff, the founder of the Legion of Mary, described to Archbishop John Charles McQuaid—both men were opponents of the industrial school system—as the 'shovelling in' of children to these iniquitous places. The committal issue—seen in the eyes of many victims of the system as by far the most violent abuse of their liberty and rights—is not analysed from this point of view. It is treated as a factual matter, one of the contributory 'pathways' into the system.

Public attention, since the publication of the report, has understandably focused on this harrowing testimony which has shocked the country all over again and probably more comprehensively than ever before, notwithstanding the fact that the story, or stories, of industrial school abuse have been matters of public concern for well over 10 years.

What has been more difficult to grapple with are the issues of blame and the fundamental question facing the Irish public: in whose interest has this commission been working? Mr Justice Seán Ryan set out to work on behalf of the Government. He was requested to do so in 'the interests of the abused'.

To this entirely acceptable objective the Government added a second. This was to complete the Commission's work 'within a reasonable period and not incur exorbitant costs'.

The conditions were contradictory. The position of the Government, in setting them, was dishonest. For the previous four years, through the actions of the Department of Education, the Government had consistently *delayed* the workings of the Commission, limiting it to the completion of just *one* industrial school survey, that of the Baltimore Fisheries School. There were no demands from the organisations acting on behalf of the victims for 'a reasonable timeframe', or for consistency between a 'proper investigation', however that is defined, and the avoidance of 'exorbitant costs'. The victims had been frustrated on the issue of a speeding up of the procedure, not because of timeframes or methodology but simply because the Government had failed to think through its operation of the Commission, fund it properly and answer simple queries coming from Ms Justice Mary Lafoy.

Four years had been largely wasted as a result of Government inaction and Department of Education frustration of the processes established by law to further the aims of the Commission. Ms Justice Mary Lafoy confronted this inexcusable blocking of due process and resigned. Mr Justice Seán Ryan set the process on a new path, claiming that the amended legislation would 'focus the Investigation on its core function'. This was to inquire into abuse of children in institutions. But this is what had been going on all along, only delayed by the refusal of the Department of Education to co-operate with the first chairperson of the Commission.

The abused are not, and were not, fools. They had reacted strongly to the delays under Ms Justice Mary Lafoy. Not knowing the background until she published the full details of the Department of Education's frustration of her work, which she did in her Third Interim Report in December 2003, the victims blamed her for prevarication and worse. When the truth came out, they lost confidence in the Commission. The avoidance of 'exorbitant costs' in the light of other tribunals was a piece of nonsense. The idea that this new Seán Ryan Commission was dedicated to 'the interests of the abused' seemed to them perverse. The introduction of 'Modules', described as 'logical units for hearings', was also scoffed at by the victims. Mr Justice Ryan promised the 'publication of interim reports as the work proceeded'. This did not happen. He also promised to establish '"trust" between the parties as to the fairness of the hearings'. In all my dealings with the victims of abuse since 2003, I can honestly say that I have never heard the word 'trust' applied to the relationship—such as it is—between the victims and the Commission.

The Ryan Report is flawed because of this. Mr Justice Seán Ryan started out on his revised operation of the Commission on the basis that he was responding to the Government's attempts to paper over the collapse of integrity and trust between the State and the previous chairperson of the Commission, Ms Justice Mary Lafoy. In her long letter of resignation, dealt with in detail in two chapters of *The Irish Gulag*, Mary Lafoy raises the spectre of this possibility. It is not something that can be definitively argued or resolved, but the evidence of a built-in malfunction of the Commission can be adduced from other more tangible shortcomings.

These include the defective historical analysis by the Commission of how the appalling circumstances in the industrial schools were allowed to develop. They also include the seriously flawed examination of the evidence of the Taoiseach, Bertie Ahern, and several of his ministers and public servants over how the process of reconciliation and recompense started. Full Cabinet and Cabinet subcommittee papers were neither sought nor analysed. Testimony that was faulty or questionable was not subjected to forensic examination. Much of the evidence published on this in the early pages of volume I of the report appears to be selective, based on recollections of different key figures unsupported by the necessary memoranda and agendas of meetings. Some of this has been in the public domain—since I put it there—for the last six years. Yet a very imperfect account is given in the Ryan Report.

The full details of the Indemnity Agreement and of the emergence of a compensation scheme for victims is also flawed. There is evidence in the Ryan Report of how this came about. It is in conflict with evidence that Ms Justice Mary Lafoy refers to in her letter of resignation in 2003. We do not know where the idea came from or from whom and this bears heavily on another issue, that of the so-called Secret Deal, the indemnifying of the religious orders by the State and the creation of a huge imbalance between the State and the religious orders in terms of who would pay the cost of recompense. The final set of circumstances was that the State, in a ratio of 10:1, would bear the cost of claims by victims.

The full details of this seriously misguided deal were published by the *Irish Independent* in 2003. The newspaper estimated at the time a cost of €1 billion which has proved reasonably accurate. It was also crystal clear at the time that the religious were not going to budge on their indemnity provisions. The State covered up embarrassment at its foolishness as best it could. While the report attempts a rather loose and uncertain survey of this lamentable exposure of the taxpayer to enormous costs, it does not make clear and appropriate judgments about what was done.

There is cursory and inaccurate attention in the Ryan Report to matters that have a historic importance. Much of this will come to light as the extensive document is more fully analysed. At this stage, it worth identifying the inexcusable examples.

One of these concerns the Kennedy Report. This report, published in 1970 and chaired by District Justice Eileen Kennedy, president of the District Court, failed to tackle any of the key problems in the industrial school system and excluded from consideration the most serious problem faced by the children: corporal punishment. Though members of the Kennedy Commission knew a good deal about this and are on record discussing the punishment circumstances in Daingean reformatory, their recollections are not recorded in the report. The closure of Daingean is recommended, but mainly because of antiquated plumbing and other physical defects. The fact that the children were flogged mercilessly is not recorded.

Furthermore, the Kennedy Report published the Rules and Regulations for the Certified Industrial Schools in Ireland but excised—and it can only have been deliberate—the key rule covering corporal punishment. This was a disgraceful abuse of public power and a suppression of the true facts. The unthinkable happened: a State regulation was included as an appendix in the Kennedy Report without the most important paragraph, on corporal punishment, in it. Corporal punishment was not discussed in the report either.

None of this is corrected, rectified or challenged. The Commission seems not to have noticed. Its members' comments refer mainly to future prognostications rather than the non-findings of criminality, abuse and deprivation that existed in the industrial schools the Kennedy Commission members visited.

The Commission to Inquire into Child Abuse sees the Kennedy Commission quite differently, admiring it and using words like 'pivotal' when in fact it achieved nothing significant beyond proposing an enhancement of the deception about the nature of the institutions by renaming them! 'Industrial Schools' were to be called 'National Boarding Schools' and the 'Detention Order' was to be called an 'Admission Order'. This was not done by the Cussen Report of 1936 and 30 years later the Kennedy Commission followed the same course. It did recommend closures, but they were slow to be implemented.

The Commission is categorically wrong in saying that the Rules and Regulations were 'unambiguous in the restrictions placed on corporal punishment'. From first to last they *were* ambiguous; they did allow extremes of punishment within the rules quite apart from the fact that the rules were widely ignored. At one level this was a departmental failure to inspect and change punishment regulations, as happened in the UK system, ironically under Winston Churchill when he was at the British Home Office!

So much for history, one might say. But in fact living history is what the Commission was engaged in throughout its nine years and its record will no more satisfy the abused than it will the general public.

All the known conclusions to be found or drawn from testimony given to the Commission are listed in the report, as are the same dismal points that have been made over the past decade, and earlier, in the pioneering documentaries on life in the industrial school system. Yes, there was abuse. Seán Ryan, at the outset of his chairmanship, said we had to ascertain this and it was done. Yes, the Department of Education behaved badly, was deferential and submissive toward the religious congregations and failed to regulate or protect the children's lives.

The Irish industrial school system flourished because the religious orders wanted it to flourish and the State ignored the alternative approaches which had been steadily developed in the United Kingdom but were notably ignored by Tomás Derrig, Fianna Fáil Minister for Education, who presided over many of the most terrible events in the system. This divergence between an old-fashioned and pernicious religious control in the Irish system and a more secular and but caring approach in the United Kingdom is not properly examined in the report.

The Commission confronts the issue of sexual abuse and gives a comprehensive account of the extent and depravity of what remains—for most of those who suffered—the worst aspect of their lives, resulting in lifelong psychological damage and inhibiting permanently their capacity to adjust and lead a fully normal life. But this confrontation is far from complete in its analysis and in its facing of difficult general areas of judgment and conclusive findings.

I have engaged with many tribunal findings at the highest level in Irish society and there is variation of competence and courage. Mr Justice Brian McCracken, for example, did more in a single page of his report on Haughey and money than Mr Justice Ryan has done in 2,500 pages.

Despite this high level of findings, Mr Justice Seán Ryan fails to confront the State on its most blatant lack of transparency and where it has been most vulnerable because of misleading and dishonest presentation of its purposes and intents. The examples are in respect of the questionable sequence of State initiatives, including departmental and Cabinet procedures leading up to the 1999 Apology, the pieces of legislation setting up and then amending the Commission and the Residential Institutions Redress Board, and the contemptible Secret Deal, negotiated and signed outside of Cabinet control and without Cabinet approval.

Mr Justice Ryan has also failed to confront the Roman Catholic Church at the highest level, where it not only allowed this truly inhuman situation to exist in the industrial schools, but actively protected the abusers. It did so through a papal policy of secrecy, whose very existence was a secret. Only by knowing a good deal about this are the enormities committed in the industrial schools to be understood.

In making these points, which are critical of the Commission, it is necessary to bear in mind the scale of the cruelty, the physical and sexual abuse, the neglect and the poverty of education offered in what were euphemistically known as 'schools'. As the Ferns Report showed, the clerical abusers in Wexford were equal in number to 1 in 4 of the total clergy strength there. The mention of about 800 abusers in orphanages suggests an even higher ratio, since we have to bear in mind that the number of nuns and brothers staffing the industrial schools was quite small. In Ferryhouse, for example, there was an average intake of children that fluctuated between a maximum of 200 but was mostly around 150. With a total staff number of around 12, and given the scale and frequency of abuse allegations, it would be difficult for the religious staff to have fulfilled their work as well as carrying out the widespread abuse. The burden of abusing was a non-stop operation.

If we extrapolate from this that the national staffing complement for the industrial schools might have been about 1,800 at its lowest, possibly rising to as many as 2,400, that would mean that the ratio of abusers—perhaps as many as 800—was worse even than in Ferns. We are possibly looking at a 1 in 3 ratio. A hospital where 1 in 3 of the staff tortured patients would be decommissioned at once. This never happened with the religious orders.

One of the more significant undertakings the chairperson, Mr Justice Seán Ryan, gave about his investigation involved the committal of the children by the courts. He said that it was important 'not to ignore the methods by which children came to be placed in institutions'. This issue of committal was never meant to be part of the process. It came far too close to the derelictions of the

State—its betrayal of the innocent children—than was comfortable.

Ms Justice Mary Lafoy covered it, but only in a detailed listing of the various legislative provisions by which children were committed and how they operated. Since this was already in the public domain, what Seán Ryan said was seen at the time, and now appears, in the words 'not to ignore the methods', to be an extension of what she had done.

It has not proved to be so in the Final Report. Setting aside everything done to the children during their incarceration, nothing was as terrible or alarming as the events which led so many of them to lose their liberty by being placed in the hands of the guards and taken away to what were child prisons, there to serve terms of up to 14 years.

The children were not represented in the courts. Their circumstances were not properly investigated. They were, as the founder of the Legion of Mary, Frank Duff, asserted in a letter to Archbishop John Charles McQuaid, 'shovelled into the industrial schools'.

This matter remains obscure and inadequately dealt with. Answers as to how it happened, and why, remain in the future. Mr Justice Ryan himself said that the importance of the issue was hard to exaggerate and that it would be unsatisfactory to ignore it. He was to seek an amendment to the Act. It was not made.

It is so central and so significant to those who have survived the abuse that it merits further consideration. It is a far more important question than the one that gained considerable public attention after the publication of the report, namely the Secret Deal.

We have to focus on the fact that, among all the terrible things that happened to thousands of boys and girls on their way into the juvenile prisons in Ireland—those places that masqueraded as industrial 'schools'—probably the worst of all was the committal of those children in the District Courts. Not all went that way but a substantial number of those recorded in the Ryan Report did. In the august atmosphere of a courtroom, with guards, priests, supposed social workers and guardians of good Catholic family life looking on, the child, alone or with siblings but without proper legal defence, was removed from the limited life they had led up to that point, and sent for years to a prison in all but name, inadequate and cruel in almost every aspect. Many of them simply became slave labour.

It was not open to the Commission to examine this terrible court event, despite the fact that it overshadowed the lives of the victims. The court process was never satisfactorily sorted out in terms of its criminal implications and whether or not the long incarceration stained the children with a criminal record.

Michael Woods, in the drafting of the Commission legislation, said in the Dáil that a legal or constitutional *review* of these court findings was 'unacceptable'. This was obvious to everyone. The court judgments may have been wrong, but they were final. What Woods did was to use a tenuous constitutional doubt quite improperly to frustrate the entirely legitimate role of the Commission, which would have been to examine whether or not the process had been wrong. But on the basis of a spurious representation of some kind of constitutional 'doubt', the issue of committals was excised from the legislation and placed outside the remit of the two judges, Mary Lafoy and Seán Ryan.

Mary Lafoy tried to put it back in again, and did publish some detail about how the committals worked in her Third Interim Report. Seán Ryan said the issue needed to be examined in greater depth, but did not do so in any comprehensive or meaningful way.

Thus Michael Woods was able, on a false representation of the facts, to block off perhaps the most significant area of State impropriety and possibly human rights abuse, together with misuse of the existing laws on child imprisonment.

On every other issue covered by the vast Final Report, there exists a scale of balances between the Roman Catholic Church and the Irish State, with the two hugely powerful institutions flipping and flopping this way and that in terms of who was most to blame. Inevitably, from any reading of the account that is published, the Church carries the greater share of blame. In fact, this is wrong and misguided.

It was the duty of the Commission to investigate and make public the inescapable reservations about the political dimension of what happened. It has failed to do so. The political analysis in the report is flaccid and ambivalent. There is no reliable examination of Bertie Ahern and the ministers in his first administration, from 1997 to 2002, undertaken by the report. Instead, it relies on opinion and speculation, with one witness giving his view, another witness giving a slightly different point of view. And we are talking about the highest officers in the State: the Taoiseach, his ministers and senior civil servants.

The Commission does not challenge such testimony. The section headed 'State Evidence' is unreliable, selective and flawed. Evidence critical of Government and published by myself in the *Irish Independent* during the nine-year period covered by the Commission in its work is reflected, when reflected at all, by imprecise and flabby presentation of data and selective use of statements given to the Commission by the key political people responsible for what was being done. The truth is not tested, the factual justification not examined.

The inexcusable line adopted by Michael Woods is neither investigated as it should be nor challenged or confronted. Within the wider terms of reference thought out by Mr Justice Seán Ryan and put into the amending legislation, which changed the remit and direction of the Commission, he created greater freedom to act than had been available to Mary Lafoy. He did not use it properly or effectively.

The report contains nothing about the steady flow of reform in the British system of child care, begun by Winston Churchill when he was Home Secretary—and this was before Ireland's independence—and continued throughout the grim period in which Tomás Derrig was Minister for Education. From 1932 Derrig placed an iron fist on top of the smouldering dustbin of industrial school illegality and did nothing at all. Irregularly, cases came up in the courts, the press and the Dáil that cried out for investigation. It was always refused by him. It was generally refused by other ministers. Nothing is said of this in the report.

Once again, we are rerunning clerical abuse and letting the State off the hook—and not just the State in the period covered by the Commission, beginning in 1936, but also the iniquities of the State during the last nine years, allowing the Department of Education to control and monitor the investigation of its own shortcomings, delaying the workings of the Commission for three years, changing direction with amending legislation and without the approval of the victims, and now, since publication of the report, demonstrating that no one in the Government knows which set of responses they should be using. The report is lame and ambivalent on this area of criticism.

No matter what we have lived through, in terms of revelation about what the victims suffered in this territory of abuse and cruelty, neglect and indifference, over many years now, it still comes back to haunt and worry us. But in asking: *how did Ireland permit this regime and why did no one stop it?* we need to confront the glaring fact that the story has not been properly told and the evidence not analysed adequately.

In the face of this, the present public outrage—greater than it was before we set out on this path of supposed reconciliation and healing—is entirely legitimate and justified. Unhappily, it is also largely futile.

The real culprit was and is the State, which is still floundering over child protection. The State approved, backed and used, intemperately and without consideration of the lives of victims, our legal system to incarcerate vast numbers of children. It was done for largely trivial, superficial and unresearched reasons and on the entirely meretricious excuse that it was for the good of the children. It was not; and the people responsible, from the Department of Education, from within successive governments, also within the judiciary and the police and the Christian aid societies and organisations, knew this. How well they knew it. Everyone in the country had a whiff in their nostrils of the fear emanating from behind the high walls of the industrial schools.

The report will bring no closure for the victims. They have read it all before. They distrust almost everyone involved. They will go to their graves carrying the sentences passed on them as children, part of a burden of guilt and inadequacy that has been deeply embedded in their lives and has run like tainted blood through their veins. It will do so until their hearts stop beating.

I was with John Kelly in Daingean to hear him describe the awful beatings he suffered there on the fake marble staircases from which his screams of fear and pain echoed up into the dormitories so that every inmate knew what they might expect for trivial misdemeanours.

For many people, John Kelly has become the living and outspoken embodiment of the ghostly screams and unending tears that are now part of the Ryan Report. The bulk of its achievement is this record.

On that occasion, which I will never forget, there was a third person present, Tommy O'Reilly, from Enniscorthy. After the visit, he wrote to tell me of his acute distress on his way home when he stopped at the roadside to shed tears over what had happened to him. He has since died of cancer. He was a gentle person, puzzled to the end by the levels of cruelty that so damaged his life. His main feeling was one of incomprehension at the failure of the Oblates of Mary to give him any kind of respect or help towards his future life. The final challenge to his human rights was when a brother brought in to him, at the time of his departure from Daingean, an Irish Army uniform and told him to put it on. He was to be drafted, against his will, into the Defence Forces. This conscription into one of the State's arms of law and order was a last, ironic humiliation not envisaged or covered by the Ryan Report. It was an abuse, as had been the court appearance that started his Daingean sentence. He remembered until his death the shame he felt at this ultimate arbitrary act.

EPILOGUE: KATHY'S STORY

Kathy Ferguson's life has been dominated by her search for identity. The trail she has followed is not unlike the account by Henry Fielding of Tom Jones, the foundling. But in Kathy's case the ending is not a happy one and most of the doubts and questions she has faced all her life still remain. She believes that she was born on 2 March 1945 but has never been able to find her birth certificate. The only reference she has to her birth and the date is contained in an order for maintenance filed by Ellen Power on behalf of 'a Bastard Child' and served on her father, Thomas Stanger, by the Coventry magistrates. This order, for 10s, was served on 6 September 1945; it continued to be paid by Thomas Stanger, a soldier who had been in Special Operations Executive, the task force established by Winston Churchill from hand-picked men, whose life expectancy in the chosen operations was short, to the mother, as was required, until Kathy was 16.

Later evidence of the date of birth is contained in the records of the District Court of Killaloe, County Clare, where she appeared as the sole defendant in her own case at the age of three years and nine months. She was brought before the court by John Foley, the local inspector of the NSPCC. She is named in the charge sheet as 'Kathleen Power'. The written citation in the appropriate space reads as follows:

Kathleen Power who appears to the Court to be a child under the age of 15 years having been born so far as has been ascertained on the 2nd day of March 1945 and who resides at New street Killaloe County of Clare has been found destitute and is not an orphan and her mother Ellen Power is unable to support the said child and the mother of the said Kathleen Power consenting to such order being made (whereas the said child is illegitimate) [at this point the hand-written preamble in the case gives way to printed text with detail inserted] And whereas the Council of the said county has been given an opportunity of being heard. And whereas the Court is satisfied that it is expedient to deal with the said child by sending her to a Certified Industrial School. And whereas the religious persuasion of the said child appears to be Catholic. It is hereby ordered that the said child shall be sent to the Certified Industrial School at Convent of Mary Ennis Clare being a school conducted in accordance with the doctrines of the Catholic Church, the managers whereof are willing to receive her to be there detained until, but not including the 2nd day of March 1961.

The signature at the foot of this sheet is not legible beyond the Christian name, Seán, but the date, 20 December 1948, is clear. Kathy did not serve the full sentence of more than 12 years when she would have been 16. Instead she was discharged at the age of ten years and nine months.

She suffered extensive and sustained abuse while in the care of the nuns at Our Lady's Industrial School in Ennis. The Sisters of Mercy ran this institution. It had been founded as an orphanage, opening in 1875 with places for 100 children. Like many such establishments, it applied for industrial school certification, which was granted in 1880, though for only 40 children. Five years before Kathy arrived there, the school was inspected by the Department of Health. Their inspectors found it overcrowded, with an unsatisfactory water supply and inadequate sanitary and bathing facilities. This did not interfere with Department of Education's registration of the school as fully fit. It contained over 100 children at the time, 60 more than it was certified for.

Kathy suffered the usual abuses, affecting her general health, education, diet and the rest, but additionally she received brutal beatings around the head, in one of which her left eye was injured, causing her chronic trouble thereafter. Medical examination of her eye injury in November 1953 is recorded but the cause by then could not be related in any provable way to the original beating. She was, in common with other inmates, made to do physical work which was inappropriate to her years. Of course she gained no meaningful skill from it. Like the other girls, she was constantly hungry, so much so that she took pig food from the pig bins on occasion and fed on berries. She had only one visit while she was there. From a very early age the girls had to learn darning and knitting, and scrub floors. One day, coming back from school at noon past the convent and limping, a nun shouted at her, asking her why was she not walking properly. The nun pulled down Kathy's sock and found her right leg badly swollen and red. She looked at it in amazement and tried to take hold of Kathy, but the young girl passed out. Kathy awoke in bed in the dormitory where she remained for three weeks before any doctor was called. When he came, he took out a knife and opened up Kathy's leg; no painkillers were used.

Her discharge from Our Lady's Industrial School in Ennis was a murky affair. It was sought and obtained by a Mrs Boqusz who was not, in Kathy's earliest opinion, her mother. In fact, she was discharged into the wrong family. It was most unusual for a mid-term discharge to be allowed, even when the inmate of the school was there by maternal consent. Given that the applicant was living in the United Kingdom, and that business of this kind was rarely if every conducted by telephone, there should have been written records. Before addressing this point, it is relevant to explain something of the first identity trauma that faced Kathy when she began to sort out who she was.

Kathy's mother, whose name was Ellen Power, had been married to David Power. They had separated two years before Kathy's birth and she learnt later that her father was a man called Thomas Stanger. Ellen Power gave Kathy the name of her former husband rather than the name of the child's father, while at the same time accepting that the child was illegitimate. It appears to be the case that the Sisters of Mercy in Ennis knew the true identity of the father, a member of the British Army, but this information was withheld from Kathy.

It is typical of Kathy's dogged determination that subsequently, working from the archive files in Coventry which she obtained in November 1999, she located and met her half-brother David Power, who had been born in June 1939, as well as his elder sister, Mary. They knew of Kathy's mother's meeting with Boqusz but had never heard of Kathy. According to the records, someone paid something towards Kathy's industrial school costs, possibly her grandparents or her uncle or possibly Stanger. The woman she knew finally as Ellen Boqusz, and eventually accepted as her mother, perhaps for want of someone better, was born in 1920 and had married David Power in 1937. She came originally from Tipperary where *her* mother had died at the age of just 18. Mr Boqusz did not come into the picture until 1948. He was one of the 7,000 or so Polish soldiers, many of them from the Polish Brigade, who had fought up through Italy and had shown greater bravery at the protracted Battle of Monte Cassino. They arrived back in England in 1947 and were housed in numerous camps throughout England, Scotland and Wales.

When Mrs Boqusz sought the discharge of her supposed daughter from Our Lady's in Ennis she was in a position to rely on her own identity and on the consensual aspect of the committal to obtain Kathy's release. It was most unusual in the 1950s for industrial schools to agree to the discharge of children even where they had been committed by consent. And it would have been virtually without precedent to do this without some form of initial communication between the institution's resident manager and the Department of Education. After all, the child had been in care for seven years, since the age of three.

Of much greater importance was the question of whether or not the Department inquired into the circumstances of the family. It had every reason to do so, given the original committal circumstances in which the child had been judged by the District Court to have been destitute and illegitimate. In addition, there is evidence that the State knew that the mother had been married, had then had a liaison with Kathy's father, and was now apparently married to another man and living in or near the city of Coventry.

There was a further duty incumbent on the Irish State before granting Kathy's release. This was to look into any reports or investigations by the United Kingdom Social Services. This, it seems, was overlooked at a time when Kathy's continued internment in the Ennis industrial school had a further five years at least to run.

There is no extant written record showing that the Department of Education looked into the living conditions of the Boqusz family before discharging Kathy into their care. The inference from the documents, which were held by the UK authorities, is that they did so. There are no Irish records to this effect. As has already been said, there should have been a paper trail and it should have been preserved. No such paper trail appears to exist.

Ellen Boqusz's decision to recover Kathy from Ennis seems to have been prompted by the death of the child's Irish grandparents, or so it was claimed by Ellen Boqusz. An uncle remained of her family in Ireland but he apparently intended to marry a widow with children. He did not want to have Kathy in addition to this family. The application by Mrs Boqusz for the discharge of Kathy from the Ennis institution appears to have come out of the blue. It escaped the attention of the UK authorities that Mrs Boqusz's motivation may have been questionable. It is possible it was connected with her need to get better housing than a caravan.

The Department of Education at first refused release, but Mrs Boqusz persisted and was eventually successful. Given the infrequency of such discharges from the industrial school system as a whole, together with the fact that the Irish authorities initially challenged the application—for which there must have been reason—it is surprising that the Department then released Kathy.

As it turned out, they were correct to have had reservations. What is a continuing puzzle is the absence of any record about how their ultimate decision to approve the discharge was made.

The story gets worse rather than better. For six months preceding the Department of Education's ministerial order for Kathy's release, which was in December 1955, United Kingdom Social Services had been visiting the Bosqusz household because of concerns about two other children, Joseph and Maria. Kathy came into this cramped environment briefly in December, joining the other four inhabitants of the caravan which was an 18-foot 'Bluebird'. She had no bed to sleep in but had to lie on a bench, without sheets and with just a blanket over her. This was in the sitting room part of the caravan, with other people coming in at night. Shortly after Kathy's arrival at the caravan home, the Bosqusz family was promised a council house. The application for this was long-standing. Though the original prediction was that it would be six months before a house might be available, the family was housed within weeks of Kathy's arrival. Events now took a new and dismal turn.

Kathy's response to her new life is recorded in Social Services reports which give a depressing account of new forms of abuse in her life, by both her supposed mother and her stepfather. Mrs Boqusz complained that Kathy had attempted to burn down the caravan in which the family was residing soon after her arrival in the United Kingdom. In February 1956 Kathy was accused of stealing £5 from her 'step-father's' wallet. She ran away. She arrived at the local Coventry children's department offices on the afternoon of 9 February 1956 to report that she had run away, had not been to school and had received a bad beating from her father, who hit her with a poker and broke a tooth. She was immediately examined and found to have bruising and laceration, both old and new, to her head and body. Four different recent periods of abuse were detected by the doctor's examination. Mrs Boqusz gave a false account to Social Services that Kathy had fallen down the stairs of the new home the day before Kathy reported the theft. Within six weeks Kathy was wetting and soiling her underwear.

Kathy was taken into care and put into The Grange, a home under council supervision. She remained there during attempts at rehabilitation within the family and at a time when her influence on the other Grange children was judged to be disruptive. A series of reports followed. Kathy's arrival had speeded up the provision of a house to replace the caravan but Kathy herself never got to see or live in the house. She was in care before the move took place. Two weeks after the family moved into the new council house, Mrs Boqusz indicated to a social worker that she would not mind if Kathy were to be taken from her altogether. Mrs Boqusz revealed to the Social Services visitor that her own mother had died in a mental hospital and that she feared that Kathy had inherited her grandmother's mental condition. On 3 March 1956 Kathy was made a ward of court until her eighteenth birthday.

In so far as it can be established, the behaviour of the Department of Education is puzzling and inconsistent in its responsibilities towards Kathy. The Department obtained possession of reports on the Boqusz family dealing with the period before Kathy's discharge, but obtained them *after the events described here*. There is certainly no evidence that those reports concerning the other children were seen before. Had they been seen, their nature and content would have precluded any release of Kathy into Mrs Boqusz's care, so one wonders, how and why were they obtained and kept? Certainly they were not available to the Minister, who made the discharge order prior to the actual discharge. Though this can be seen as a modest vindication what it really indicates is that there was no proper examination of the child's prospects on release.

The whole process by which Kathy was released and moved to Coventry therefore remains a mystery. It is by no means clear from the records on what grounds and by whose decision it was deemed necessary that the Boqusz home in Coventry be visited and a report on the home conditions be sent to the Department of Education in Dublin. There is no apparent evidence on the part of the Irish authorities at ministerial, departmental or institutional level as to any investigation of the living conditions where Kathy was to live on her discharge from the Ennis industrial school. So here was a child, bounced unceremoniously out of the only environment she had known and placed in the care of a woman clearly unsuited to have the child in her charge.

From the point of view of this book, the events reflect very poorly on the Irish side. From well before Kathy's discharge, if evidence had been sought, it would have been readily apparent that any discharge from Ennis was unsound and even dangerous. Mrs Boqusz was allowed to take on an almost 11-year old child, effectively unknown to her, at a time when the family—already the subject of Social Services supervision—was in need of housing. It appears that the Coventry authorities were incompetent; it appears that the Irish authorities were both silent and incompetent as well, letting down the child in their care very badly.

Many years later, as the result of a visit from Joseph Boqusz, the son of her mother and Polish stepfather, who tried to persuade Kathy to be photographed and told her that her birth certificate given to her in 1969 did not belong to her and tried to prevent her from going to Coventry Social Services to see what documents they had, she discovered an extensive file on her which she was allowed to see but not remove or copy. 'It seems that I had been an NSPCC child, and that my files had to be kept for 75 years, and must not be destroyed.' She asked the clerk if her birth or baptismal certificates were on file but this was not the case. She found her court and NSPCC records and the reason why she had been put into care by the court in Coventry in 1956. She found the doctor's report on her injuries.

When Kathy was 18 she left her last school, St John's in Birmingham run by the St Vincent De Paul Society, in August 1962. By 17 November she was married. She gave birth to four sons, but was divorced in 1973. She was in a car crash in 1979 and found it difficult to manage with no family to turn to, going out to work in any job she could find to put food and a roof over their heads.

> I found a nice man and we are now living happily together. I have survived. I seem to have come into my own in the last ten years. I get angry at what was done to me as a child, and I ask: How could a child with two NSPCC records, one in Ireland and the other in England, have had such a childhood? Did nobody care? On my English passport it states that I am a foundling born somewhere in the west of Ireland. Ireland gave me a criminal record. It is still with me today.

Kathy has spent much of her life trying to piece together the truth of her story. She has been frustrated by the widespread destruction or disappearance of documents relating to her case and her search has been a poignant and painful one. But she is a defiant and determined woman and in the last decade she has become a quite extraordinary authority on the legislation and documentation surrounding industrial school life, the religious communities who ran the institutions in the Irish Gulag, the politicians and public servants, and many of her fellow-abused.

Kathy has been a passionate and intrepid fighter on behalf of the abused, taking up many issues, pursuing public officials, criticising the institutions of State and both the Commission to Inquire into Child Abuse and the Redress Board. Among other points she has raised is the omission of some 37 industrial schools for girls from investigation, coming to the personal conclusion that this is discrimination against women. The weight of evidence clearly indicates many questions that needed to be asked about the appalling ignorance in the treatment of the girls.

She asks: how can you get answers if you do not call the nuns to account for what happened in the industrial schools and in the Magdalen laundries, to which many inmates were sent illegally? And what about those who have spent all their lives in the same Magdalen laundries? She also asks: how many girls were sent to mental institutions? How many girls died in the industrials schools? Where are their death certificates? Have such documents been sought? Why have all the religious orders that were signatories to the Indemnity Deal not appeared before any public hearing in that capacity? There were 18 signatories from religious orders yet only six religious orders gave evidence to the Commission.

Kathy described accurately her own experiences before the Investigation Committee where she had an interview, with two Senior Counsels. Nothing was written down or recorded. I was present for that encounter and was struck by the apparent indifference shown towards Kathy. She took up the offer of a hearing before the Commission in 2000 but she was not seen until 19 September 2005.

Kathy Ferguson has applied for, appealed and rejected all offers of Redress Board compensation.

APPENDICES

APPENDIX 1

INDUSTRIAL SCHOOL RULES

Rule 11 (of 1870, 1912), 'Spirit of Industry' was removed in 1933. Tomás Derrig's rules, as quoted in Cussen, are therefore 29 in number and not 30.

In publishing the Kennedy Report, the Department of Education excised, without explanation, two rules. One of these was Rule 17, 'State Grants'. This rule, rendered obsolete by the 1941 Act (which allowed for the payment of capitation grants for children under the age of six), was correctly excised. Rule 13, however, remained in force long after the Kennedy Report of 1970 and its removal was an extraordinary act of deception. It dealt with the key problem within the industrial schools, punishment. It was the most controversial of all the rules, abused and broken on a daily basis throughout the industrial school system.

The breach of the rules generally was widespread and countless internees of the industrial school system have given testimony of this. Had the rules been followed strictly in accordance with the legislation, an entirely different story of Irish industrial school life would have emerged.

The actual copy of the rules, given below and universal in its form, applied to Artane Industrial School and is so designated:

RULES AND REGULATIONS
FOR THE CERTIFIED INDUSTRIAL SCHOOLS IN
SAORSTÁT ÉIREANN
APPROVED BY THE MINISTER FOR EDUCATION, UNDER THE 54th
SECTION OF THE ACT, 8 EDW. vii., Ch.67

NAME AND OBJECT OF SCHOOL	THE ARTANE INDUSTRIAL SCHOOL, CO. DUBLIN, FOR ROMAN CATHOLIC BOYS.
DATE OF CERTIFICATE	9th JULY, 1870.
NUMBER FOR WHICH CERTIFIED	Accommodation is provided in this school for only 825 children This Number shall not be exceeded at any one time. No child under the age of six years is chargeable to the State Grant, and of the children of the age of six years and upwards not more than 825 are chargeable to that Grant.

CONSTITUTION AND MANAGEMENT	A Staff of Christian Brothers under a Committee.
CONDITIONS OF ADMISSION	Roman Catholic Boys sent under the provisions of the Children Act, 1908, or the School Attendance Act, 1926, or the Children Act, 1929, or otherwise as the Management may determine.
LODGING	The children lodged in the School shall have separate beds. Every decision to board out a Child, under the 53rd Section of the Children Act 1908 shall have received previous sanction from the Minister for Education, through the Inspector of Industrial Schools.
CLOTHING	The children shall be supplied with neat, comfortable clothing in good repair, suitable to the season of the year, not necessarily uniform either in material or colour.
DIETARY	The children shall be supplied with plain wholesome food, according to a Scale of Dietary to be drawn up by the Medical Officer of the School and approved by the Inspector. Such food shall be suitable in every respect for growing children actively employed and supplemented in the case of delicate or physically under-developed children with such special food as individual needs require. No substantial alterations in the Dietary shall be made without previous notice to the Inspector. A copy of the Dietary shall be given to the Cook and a further copy kept in the Manager's Office.
LITERARY INSTRUCTION	Subject to Rule 8, all children shall be instructed in accordance with the programme prescribed for National Schools. Juniors (that is, children under 14 years of age) shall have for the same purpose not less than three hours, five days a week, at least two-thirds of the periods mentioned to be at suitable hours between breakfast and dinner, when the most beneficial results are likely to be obtained. Religious Instruction may be included

in those periods, and, in the case of Seniors, reasonable time may be allotted to approved general reading. Should the case of any individual pupil call for the modification of this Rule it is to be submitted to the Inspector for approval. Senior boys shall receive lessons in Manual Instruction which may be interpreted to mean training in the use of Carpenter's tools.

SCHOOLS

The Manager may arrange for children to attend conveniently situated schools, whether Primary, Continuation, Secondary or Technical, but always subject to (a) the sanction of the Inspector in each case, and (b) the condition that no increased cost is incurred by the State.

INDUSTRIAL TRAINING

Industrial employment shall not exceed three and a half hours daily for Juniors or six hours daily for Seniors. The training shall, in the case of boys, be directed towards the acquisition of skill in and knowledge of farm and garden work or such handicraft as can be taught. Due regard being given to fitting the boys for the most advantageous employment procurable. The training for girls shall in all cases be in accordance with the Domestic Economy Syllabus, and shall also include, where practicable, the milking of cows, care of poultry and cottage gardening. Each school shall submit for approval by the Inspector a list setting forth the occupations which constitute the industrial training of the children and the qualifications of the Instructors employed to direct the work. Should additional subjects be added or any subject be withdrawn or suspended, notification shall be made to the Inspector without delay.

INSPECTION

The progress of the children in the Literary Classes of the Schools and their proficiency in Industrial Training will be tested from time to time by Examination and Inspection.

[FORMER RULE 11 (REMOVED BY T. DERRIG)]:

A SPIRIT OF INDUSTRY TO BE CHERISHED	*The Manager shall see that the children are constantly employed, and that they are taught to consider labour as a duty, to take kindly to it, to persevere in it, and to feel a pride in their work.*
RELIGIOUS EXERCISES AND WORSHIP	Each day shall be begun and ended with Prayer. On Sundays and Holidays the Children shall attend Public Worship at some convenient Church or Chapel.
DISCIPLINE	The Manager or his Deputy shall be authorised to punish the Children detained in the School in case of misconduct. All serious misconduct, and the Punishments inflicted for it, shall be entered in a book to be kept for that purpose, which shall be laid before the Inspector when he visits. The Manager must, however, remember that the more closely the School is modelled on a principle of judicious family government the more salutary will be its discipline, and the fewer occasions will arise for resort to punishment.
PUNISHMENTS	Punishments shall consist of:- (a) Forfeiture of rewards and privileges, or degradation from rank, previously attained by good conduct. (b) Moderate childish punishment with the hand. (c) Chastisement with the cane, strap, or birch. Referring to (c) personal chastisement may be inflicted by the Manager, or, in his presence, by an Officer specially authorised by him, and in no case may it be inflicted upon girls over 15 years of age. In the case of girls under 15, it shall not be inflicted except in cases of urgent necessity, each of which must be at once fully reported to the Inspector. Caning on the hand is forbidden. No punishment not mentioned above shall be inflicted. [Rule 13 is simply removed, without explanation, from the set of rules published as an appendix to the Kennedy Report.]

RECREATION

Seniors shall be allowed at least two hours daily, and Juniors at least three hours daily, for recreation and shall be taken out occasionally for exercise beyond the boundaries of the school, but shall be forbidden to pass the limits assigned to them without permission. Games, both indoor and outdoor, shall be encouraged; the required equipment shall be provided; and supervision shall be exercised to secure that all children shall take part in the Games. Fire Drill shall be held once at the least in every three months, and each alternate. Drill shall take place at night after the children have retired to the dormitories. A record of the date and hour of each Drill shall be kept in the School Diary.

VISITS (Relatives and friends)

Parents, other Relations, or intimate Friends, shall be allowed to visit the children at convenient times, to be regulated by the Committee or Manager.

Such privilege is liable to be forfeited by misconduct or interference with the discipline of the School by the Parents, Relative, or Friends. The Manager is authorised to read all Letters which pass to or from the Children in the School, and to withhold any which are objectionable.

Subject to the approval of the Inspector, holiday leave to parents or friends may be allowed to every well conducted child who has been under detention for at least one year, provided the home conditions are found on investigation to be satisfactory. Such leave shall be limited to seven days annually.

In a very special or urgent case, such as the serious illness or death of a parent, the Manager may also, at his discretion, if applied to grant to any child such brief leave of absence as will enable the child to spend not more than one night at home: the circumstances to be reported forthwith to the Inspector's Office.

CHILDREN PLACED OUT ON
LICENCE OR APPRENTICED

Should the Manager of a School permit a Child, by Licence under the 67th Section of the Children Act of 1908, to live with a trustworthy and respectable person, or apprentice the Child to any trade or calling under the 70th Section of the Act, notice of such placing out on Licence, or apprenticeship of the Child accompanied by a clear account of the conditions attaching thereto, shall be sent, without delay, to the Office of the Inspector.

STATE GRANT

Under the present financial arrangement no Child will be paid for out of the Funds voted by the Oireachtas until it has reached the age of Six Years. A Child, however, under the age of Six Years may be sent to the School under an Order of Detention signed by a District Justice: but in such case the State allowance for maintenance will not be made until it shall appear from the Order of Detention that the Child is Six Years old—from that only will it be regularly paid for.

[Rule 17 was made redundant by the Children Act 1941 and is excluded from the set of rules published as an appendix in the Kennedy Report.]

PROVISION ON DISCHARGE

On the discharge of a Child from the School, at the expiration of the period of Detention, or when Apprenticed, he (or she) shall be provided, at the cost of the Institution, with a sufficient outfit, according to the circumstances of the discharge. Children when discharged shall be placed, as far as practicable, in some employment or service. If returned to relatives or friends, the travelling expenses shall be defrayed by the Manager, unless the relatives or friends are willing to do so. A Licence Form shall be issued in every case and the Manager shall maintain communication with discharged children for the full period of supervision prescribed in Section 68 (2) of the Children Act, 1908. The Manager shall recall from the home or from employment any child whose occupation or circumstances are unsatisfactory, and he shall in due course make more suitable disposal.

VISITORS

The school shall be open to Visitors at convenient times, to be regulated by the Committee (or Manager), and a Visitors' Book shall be kept. The term 'visitors' means members of the Public interested in the school.

TIME TABLE

A Time Table, showing the Hours of Rising, Work, School Instruction, Meals, Recreation, Retiring, etc., shall be drawn up, shall be approved by the Inspector of Industrial Schools, and shall be fixed in the Schoolroom, and carefully adhered to on all occasions. All important deviations from it shall be recorded in the School Diary.

JOURNALS, etc.

The Manager (or Master or Matron) shall keep a Journal or Diary of everything important or exceptional that passes in the School. All admissions, discharges, licences and escapes shall be recorded therein, and all Record Books shall be laid before the Inspector when he visits the School.

MEDICAL OFFICER
I.

A Medical Officer shall be appointed who shall visit the school periodically, a record of his visits being kept in a book to be provided for the purpose.

II.

Each child shall be medically examined on admission to the School, and the M.O.'s written report on the physical condition of the Child should be carefully preserved.

III.

A record of all admissions to the School Infirmary shall be kept, giving information as to ailment, treatment, and dates of admission and discharge in each case. Infirmary cases of a serious nature and cases of more than three days' duration shall be notified to the Inspector's Office.

IV.   The M.O. shall make a quarterly examination of each child individually, and give a quarterly report, as to the fitness of the children for the training of the school, their general health, and the sanitary state of the school. The quarterly report shall be in such form as may be prescribed from time to time by the Minister for Education. Application shall be made to the Minister for the discharge of any child certified by the M.O. as medically unfit for detention.

V.   Dental treatment and periodic visits by a Dentist shall be provided and records of such visits shall be kept. In the event of the serious illness of any child, notice shall be sent to the nearest relatives or guardian and special visits allowed.

INQUESTS   In the case of violent death, or of sudden death, not arising in the course of an illness while the child is under treatment by the M.O., a report of the circumstances shall be at once made to the local Gardaí for the information of the Coroner, a similar report being at the same time sent to the Inspector.

RETURNS, etc.   The Manager (or Secretary) shall keep a Register of admissions and discharges, with particulars of the parentage, previous circumstances, etc., of each child admitted, and of the disposal of each Child discharged, and such information as may afterwards be obtained regarding him, and shall regularly send to the Office of the Inspector the Returns of Admission and Discharge, the Quarterly List of Children under detention, and the Quarterly Accounts for their maintenance, and any other returns that may be required by the Inspected. All Orders of Detention shall be carefully kept amongst the Records of the School.

INSPECTOR   All Books and Journals of the School shall be open to the Inspector for examination. Any teacher employed in the school who does not hold recognised qualifications may be examined by the Inspector, if he thinks it necessary, and he shall be informed of the qualifications of new teachers on their appointment. Immediate notice shall be given to him of the appointment, death, resignation, or dismissal of the Manager and Members of the School Staff.

GENERAL REGULATIONS

Whenever a child is sent to a Reformatory School, under the provisions of the 71st or 72nd Sections of the Children Act of 1908, the Manager shall, without delay, report the case to the Inspector.

REMOVAL TO A REFORMATORY

Whenever a Child is sent to a Reformatory School, under the provisions of the 71st or 72nd Sections of the Children Act of 1908, the Manager shall, without delay, report the case to the Inspector.

CHILD NOT PROFESSING RELIGIOUS PERSUASION OF THE MANAGER TO BE REMOVED FROM THE SCHOOL.

In order to ensure a strict and effectual observance of the provisions of the 66th Section of the Children Act of 1908, in every case in which a Child shall be ordered to be detained in a School managed by Persons of a different Religious Persuasion from that professed by the Parents, or surviving Parent, or (should that be unknown), by the Guardians or Guardian of such Child, (or should that be unknown) different from that in which the Child appears to have been baptised or (that not appearing), different from that professed by the Child the Manager or Teachers of such School shall, upon becoming acquainted with the fact, or having reason to believe that such is the fact, give notice in writing, without delay, to the Inspector, who will thereupon immediately take any necessary steps in the matter.

ESCAPES

Should any Escape from the School occur, the Manager shall, with as little delay as possible, notify the particulars to the nearest Gardaí Station, to the Gardaí Superintendents of the County and adjoining Counties, and to the Inspector's Office.

These Rules have been adopted by the Managers of Artane Industrial School. Co. Dublin.

Approved under the 54th Section of the Children Act of 1908.

T. O'Deirg, Minister for Education, 4 Feb, 1933.

In the case of Artane Industrial School, Co. Dublin, the foregoing Rules may be modified in accordance with Time Table attached hereto.

APPENDIX 2

KENNEDY REPORT SUBMISSIONS
The following made submissions to the Kennedy Report:

Mr Michael McGrath, 12 McDonagh Street, Nenagh
Miss Rebecca M. Ryan, 'Roseville', The Grove, New Line, Dungarvan
Mr Richard Power, 41 Rockenham, Ferrybank, Waterford
Miss M.C. Prendergast, St Patrick's Hospital, James's Street, Dublin
Mrs Alys Goodbody, Clara, Offaly
Mr Brendan O'Donoghue, 87 Silchester Park, Glenageary, Dublin
Los Angeles Society, 26 Arran Quay, Dublin
Galway Health Authority
Knights of St Columbanus, Ely House
Society of St Vincent de Paul
St Mary's Adoption Society, Killarney
Church of Ireland Social Service, 39 Molesworth Street, Dublin
Civics Institute of Ireland, 20 North Frederick Street, Dublin
St Joseph's School, Mercy Convent, Mallow
Irish Medical Association, 10 Fitzwilliam Place, Dublin
Nazareth House, Sligo
St Colman's School, Rushbrooke, Cork
St Michael's Industrial School, Convent of Mercy, Wexford
Irish Association of Social Workers
Knights of St Columbanus (Supplementary Report)
A Group of North Dublin City Youth Clubs
Mr Ian Hart, Economic and Social Research Institute.
Bardas Atha Cliath (Roinn Freastail Scoile)
Mr Brian Doolan, 26 Glenabbey Road, Mount Merrion, Dublin
William A. Tormey, District Justice, Athlone
Galway God-Parents' Association
T.G.A. Burke, District Justice, Galway
Industrial and Reformatory Schools Resident Managers' Association
Society of St Vincent de Paul (Probation and Aftercare Association), Cork
Irish Society for the Prevention of Cruelty to Children
Voluntary Advisory Body, St Joseph's, Killarney
M/S Donohoe and Doyle, Welfare Services Department, Dublin Health Authority
Dublin Institute for Adult Education
Incorporated Law Society of Ireland

F. Leo McCormack O.P., Dominican Boys Home, 20 Lower Dominick Street, Dublin
Very Rev. William O'Brien, Provincial, Oblates of Mary Immaculate
Association for Child Psychology and Psychiatry (Irish Branch)
Dr R.A. McCarthy, Medical Superintendent, Our Lady's Hospital, Cork
Mr John McLoughlin, Chief Clerk, Dublin Metropolitan Children's Court
Mr James McLoone, Diagnostic and Assessment Clinic, Renmore, Co. Galway
Institute of Professional Civil Servants, Welfare Officers' Branch, 64 Adelaide Road, Dublin

ORAL SUBMISSIONS
Mr G. Lamb, Information Officer, Department of Social Welfare
Miss E. Murray, Children's Section, Department of Health
Officers and Members of the Adoption Board
Rev. Fr O'Doherty, Professor of Logic and Psychology, University College, Dublin
Mrs Alys Goodbody and Mrs Dunne, Offaly Irish Countrywoman's Association
M/S F.J. Donohoe and J.J. Doyle, Welfare Services Department, Dublin Health Authority
M. Brian Callinan, Secretary, and Mrs McPartland, ISPCC
Mr Noel Clear, Welfare Officer, St Patrick's Institution
Mr Martin Tansey, Welfare Officer, Mountjoy Prison
Very Rev. Fr Pierce, PP, Chairman, Catholic Youth Clubs Guild Association
Rev. Fr Carey, Secretary, Catholic Youth Clubs Guild Association
Representatives, Irish Congress of Trade Unions
Messrs Sweeney, Farley and Officials, National Rehabilitation Board
Messrs O'Neill, Farley, and Leonard, Department of Labour

GROUPS OR ORGANISATIONS TO WHOM THE COMMITTEE WROTE SEEKING INFORMATION
Adoption Societies, Industrial Schools and Reformatories
Association of Managers of Reformatory and Industrial Schools
Association of Secondary Teachers
Association of Social Workers
Catholic Protection and Rescue Society
Catholic Social Welfare Bureau
Children's Department, Cork Health Authority
   —Dublin Health Authority
   —Limerick Health Authority
   —Waterford Health Authority
   —Galway County Council
Church of Ireland Representative Body
Church of Ireland Social Service
Civics Institute of Ireland, Ltd

Concilium, Legion of Mary, North Brunswick Street, Dublin
Council for All Ireland, Society of St Vincent de Paul
District Court Clerks' Association
District Justices
Dr R.A. McCarthy, Medical Superintendent, Our Lady's Hospital, Cork
Dublin Institute of Adult Education
Dublin Solicitors' Bar Association
Government Departments
Harding Boys Home, Dublin
Housing Welfare Section, Bardas Atha Cliath
International Children's Centre, Bois de Boulogne, Paris
Irish Countrywomen's Association
Irish Medical Association
Irish National Teachers' Organisation
ISPCC, 20 Molesworth Street, Dublin
Knights of Columbanus
Local Authorities
Los Angeles Society
Members of Roman Catholic and Church of Ireland Hierarchy
Metropolitan District Court Clerks' Association
Mrs Smyly's Homes, Grattan Street, Dublin
Place of Detention, Marlborough House, Dublin
Probation Administration Officer, 3 Lower Ormond Quay, Dublin
Protestant Child Care Association
Rev. Patrick Simpson, S.J., Milltown Park, Dublin
St Patrick's Guild, Haddington Road, Dublin
St Saviour's Orphanage, 20 Lower Dominick Street, Dublin
St Stanislaus Youth Club
Vocational Teachers' Association
Voluntary Homes
Youth Council, Catholic Social Service Council

APPENDIX 3

Full text of the article by the Minister for Education, Noel Dempsey TD, in which he replied to the series of articles published by the author in the Irish Independent *in January 2003.*

Mr Bruce Arnold has recently written a series of articles on the redress scheme which contained very significant factual errors. In addition Mr Arnold, in criticising elements of the agreement made between the congregations and the State, appears to have misunderstood significant aspects of that agreement. Here are the key errors:-

The Residential Institutions Redress Board has never operated illegally and the legal defects identified never existed.

Mr Arnold is entirely wrong in implying that I waited until I knew the number of applications to the Redress Board before making regulations, so as to give me some unspecified advantage. Neither my Department nor I have any knowledge of the number of applications which the Board has received.

A lodgement into court made by the State in those cases which are heard in the courts will not deny a plaintiff his award of damages. Its effect is to limit legal costs in certain circumstances.

The redress scheme has not been 'taken from the British Criminal Injuries Compensation Board system'. The scheme is unique and was devised by an independent body of legal and medical experts under the chairmanship of a Senior Counsel. It met with widespread approval from victims.

Disclosure of psychiatric or other medical reports of applicants for compensation to people accused of abuse will occur only in exceptional circumstances.

The agreement between the congregations and the State was not 'secret'. Full details were announced by press release on 30 January and 5 June 2002. A copy of the agreement has, since June, been available to anyone who wants it.

Far from the State being obliged to defend the congregations in cases which are heard in the courts, it is the case that if a congregation wants to defend its position or that of a member then the indemnity will be withdrawn.

The Redress Act is not in any way affected by the agreement with the congregations.

Inaccurate information on the scheme and its objectives does no service to victims of abuse in childhood.

Mr Arnold returned to the issue of the agreement with the congregations on 25 January and on the basis, I assume, that the facts should not get in the way of a good story again repeatedly refers to the 'secret' agreement which he now knows is not secret. The innuendo in this article that my Department may be involved in 'burning' records is outrageous, utterly unfounded and goes well beyond what might be regarded as fair comment. The significance he attaches to the 'four folders' is also the stuff of fantasy. The folders, which are appendices to the agreement, contain only a list of names (in the case of cases going to the Commission only reference numbers for reasons of confidentiality of the Commission process) of people who have already in one way or another indicated that they were victims of abuse and likely applicants for compensation. Their purpose was to establish as near as possible as on the date of the agreement how many potential claimants there would be for compensation. The folders contain no other records whatever and as for the claim that somehow they 'paralleled the work of the Commission' I have to say, with all respect to Mr Arnold, that this is utter nonsense.

In providing for financial redress to people who as children suffered abuse while in residential care, the focus must primarily be on *their* needs. Arguments about apportioning of responsibility between the State and its agencies and the religious congregations which owned and managed the institutions should never override that aim. What is important is what Irish society now wants to do for people who, as children, were abused and damaged while in the care of public authorities.

At no time was the setting up of the compensation scheme dependent upon the participation of the religious congregations. Regardless of that participation, the Government considered that the scheme was the right thing to do for the victims of childhood abuse. Arguments about apportionment of responsibility could only have delayed, indefinitely, the payment of compensation to victims, many of whom are now elderly and infirm and all of whom have waited far too long. The Government was not prepared to countenance any further delays.

The participation of the congregations in the scheme, however, was a policy goal of the Government. It gave the best opportunity to bring closure to the issue of past abuse for Irish society as a whole and it provided a basis for healing for victims. It also clearly had financial implications. An agreement was concluded last year in which the congregations agreed to contribute €128 million (in cash and property) and in which the State agreed to indemnify the congregations for cases which could be dealt with under the scheme.

Through the compensation scheme, the Government sought to put in place quick and effective access to financial redress for victims of abuse in childhood. Throughout the development of the scheme, victim support groups and lawyers for potential applicants were consulted and a substantial level of agreement achieved on the key provisions.

There are still important issues to tease out about responsibility for abuse and how we can prevent the conditions which caused it from ever being repeated. The Commission to Inquire into Child Abuse will carry out that valuable service. In the meantime, however, the redress scheme offers a sound basis for victims of abuse to get some financial security in their lives and, hopefully, a measure of healing from the trauma of the past. It is also a basis for Irish society to face up to its responsibilities, at last.

The Government's focus on the needs of victims of childhood abuse was paramount in devising the redress scheme. It is disappointing to see such inaccuracy from such a reputable journalist on such a sensitive matter.

APPENDIX 4

Daingean Reformatory

Boys were incarcerated in Daingean
For small crimes and sometimes none.
The prison walls were high in Daingean
They blotted out the sun.

We were neglected and brutalized in Daingean
By the Rev. Brothers and Fathers every one.
They raped, flogged and starved us
Every day, till our time was done.

From morning till night
They enslaved us in that oppressive regime.
And we never had hot water
To keep our tired limbs clean.

No compassion or understanding given
No consideration or words of praise
From the Oblate Fathers or Fathers
Who imprisoned us in that cage.

They took away our self-esteem
They even took away our soul.
The time in that fearsome place
On our future life took its toll.

No humanity was shown there
Only the five foot leather strap.
Floggings were received there
For even the slightest mishap.

Hell on earth I suffered in Daingean:
The Oblate Order was to blame.
Why don't they confess and clear their souls?
Say they're sorry, take their share of the shame?

The high walls were thick in Daingean
They muffled the flogging screams.
Why did it take so long? To stop this suffering?
By the people who knew, and had the means?

Will there be a Nuremburg for the Oblate Fathers?
To reveal the oppressive regime they had run?
To let the world outside Daingean walls
See the terrible deeds that were done.

The Oblate Fathers when outside,
To the local people were ever so sweet.
But inside the walls of Daingean,
We experienced their inhuman deceit.

The Oblate Fathers were street angels
And behind the walls were house devils.
They must have been all psychopaths
With their evil minds dishevelled.

My body was released from Daingean
With my mind and soul they had toyed.
They have taken away my future
My very seed they have destroyed.

Daingean, I could have absorbed
Your fearful oppressive regime.
Even my body to be burned
But without love I was spurned.

A regime of terror reigned there
No kindness ever shown.
You could not report the brutality
Because behind the walls of Daingean,
You were on your own.

THOMAS O'REILLY

3 MARCH 2003

APPENDIX 5

BERTIE AHERN'S SPEECH OF APOLOGY

Speech by An Taoiseach, Mr Bertie Ahern, TD announcing Government measures relating to childhood abuse on 11 May 1999 at 5.00 p.m. The press release issued with the speech is given under the heading 'Government Measures'.

Ministers, Deputies, Ladies and Gentlemen, distinguished guests:

How children are treated is one of the key elements which defines any society. Over recent years, more and more attention has been paid to the many failures of our society in the treatment of children. Unfortunately, this has been a piecemeal approach driven by the bravery of individual victims determined to tell their stories and seek justice. A light has been shone into the dark corners of both our past and present, and these victims have performed an immense service in challenging our collective complacency. They have shown us that we cannot put the past behind us by ignoring it. We must confront it and learn its lessons. That is the least we can do to address the injustices of the past and the dangers of the present.

The time has long since arrived when we must take up the challenge put to us all by the victims of childhood abuse.

The starting point for this is simple, but fundamental. We must start by apologising.

On behalf of the State and of all citizens of the State, the Government wishes to make a sincere and long overdue apology to the victims of childhood abuse for our collective failure to intervene, to detect their pain, to come to their rescue.

The short preface to the 1970 Report on Industrial Schools put it very simply: 'All children need love, care and security.' Too many of our children were denied this love, care and security. Abuse ruined their childhoods and has been an ever present part of their adult lives, reminding them of a time when they were helpless. I want to say to them that we believe that they were gravely wronged, and that we must do all we can now to overcome the lasting effects of their ordeals.

A new, comprehensive approach is required to deal with the effects of previous abuse, to detect the children caught in frightful isolation, and to put proper structures in place.

In March 1998 the Government first discussed the need for a formal response to the needs of victims of childhood abuse. Following ongoing discussions, a sub-committee of the Cabinet was established last December, with the remit of reporting with comprehensive proposals to address this issue. Chaired by the Minister for Education & Science, Micheál Martin, TD, the sub-committee includes the Tánaiste, and has eight members in total. They have considered best international practice and a range of different aspects to past and present instances of abuse, including how abuse cases should be handled in the future.

In all of its work the sub-committee sought to bring forward a comprehensive package, appropriate to the concerns of victims. The sub-committee's recommendations were endorsed at today's Cabinet meeting.

Commission to Inquire into Childhood Abuse
One of the responses to childhood abuse which older victims have sought is a forum, where they can tell their story. This would give them assurance that the wrongs which have been done to them are recognised publicly in a responsible manner, and that lessons are properly learned.

The Government considers that the interests of justice and the common good require the provision of such a forum, and to that end it has decided to establish a Commission to Inquire into Childhood Abuse. The Commission's terms of reference have deliberately been drawn quite broadly, and have a number of different elements.

The primary focus of the Commission will be to provide victims with an opportunity to tell of the abuse they suffered, in a sympathetic and experienced forum. In addition the Commission will establish as complete a picture as possible of the causes, nature and extent of physical and sexual abuse of children in institutions and other places. It will make such recommendations as it sees fit.

The Commission will consist of three persons, who will be appointed during the coming week.

In the first instance the Commission will be established on a non-statutory basis, with the broad terms of reference I have mentioned. Its initial task will be to decide on matters such as precisely how it will operate, whether its terms of reference need to be altered, and what powers and protections it requires to carry out its work.

It will be asked to make recommendations on these matters within three months. The Government will then seek to enact any necessary legislation without delay. This approach is one which we believe is best suited to ensure that the Commission meets the needs of victims, and achieves its objectives in an efficient and effective way.

The Government's approach to the Commission is that it will be able to carry out its work in an independent manner, without fear or favour. We hope that it will be a forum that will inspire the confidence of victims, whose co-operation is essential to its success.

Counselling Services

The victims of childhood abuse also need counselling to help them to overcome the effect of the abuse. The Government has decided to allocate an additional £4 million per annum to establish a dedicated professional counselling service in all regions. Due to likely initial difficulties in establishing such a service, particularly in relation to the availability of qualified staff, the new service may have to be phased in. In the meantime, other initiatives will be funded, and details will be announced very shortly by the Department of Health and Children.

Combined with the creation of a national counselling service, there will be co-ordination between health boards, to ensure the implementation of best practice and the effective use of resources. As part of this, specific steps will be taken to promote widespread knowledge of the availability of the service.

Statute of Limitations

Under the Statute of Limitations, claims for personal injuries arising out of negligence, nuisance, or breach of duty must be brought within three years. The Cabinet sub-committee spent some time considering the full range of issues concerning the application of the Statute to childhood abuse cases.

Particularly in light of the extensive international experience available, the Government has decided to legislate during this Dáil session to extend the concept of disability under the Statute, to victims of childhood sexual abuse, who because of that abuse have been unable to bring claims within the normal limitation period.

In addition, the Government has decided to refer the issue of limitation periods, as they apply to claims based on non-sexual childhood abuse, to the Law Reform Commission for their recommendations. This will help address issues such as the handling of evidence of the effects of such abuse, and how other jurisdictions have dealt with this area.

Mandatory Reporting

The Government is conscious of the need to ensure that we do all we can to tackle child abuse when it occurs today, and has approved a number of measures in this regard. Proposals on the mandatory reporting of instances of the sexual abuse of children will be published by the Department of Health and Children in a White Paper as soon as possible, and acted upon without delay.

Register of Sex Offenders

Legislation for the introduction of a Register of sex offenders is at an advanced stage of preparation. This legislation will be enacted and the Register will be operational by the end of this year.

Other Measures

At the same time, the Government will proceed with a number of other initiatives which are of great importance to this area.

The Child Care Act will be amended to extend the provisions relating to residential centres for children and to centres for children with physical and mental disabilities. The effect of this will be to bring these homes under the scope of the Child Care Act, including registration and inspection. In addition, work is in progress on the drafting of the Children Bill, 1999, which will provide a statutory framework, in which a new juvenile justice system can develop, replacing the system established by the Children Act 1908.

The recently-established Social Services Inspectorate, in the Department of Health and Children, will be brought to a fully operational status. As already announced, its remit over the next three years will be to concentrate on child care.

The Department of Education and Science will proceed with the modernisation of facilities and services for young offenders. This will include a £4 million project to replace the Young Offenders' Centre in Finglas which has fallen far below acceptable standards.

I am determined that it will be under this Government that we will as a society confront the realities of the abuse of children up to the present day. As I have said, this is an area which we have been considering in depth for much of our time in office. Work has been proceeding in a number of Departments and important initiatives have already been launched. What we are doing today is bringing the different elements together into what we believe is a comprehensive and appropriate response to the stories of the far too many people whose childhood was shattered by abuse.

What the Government has decided on today is not a break with the past; it is a facing up to the past and all that this involves. This may well be a painful process; but it cannot and should not be avoided.

This country has a lot to be proud of. We are developing in many ways and for the first time we are seeing movement on a range of serious problems.

But we cannot truly advance unless we acknowledge and deal with the more uncomfortable elements of our past. Only when we do this will we have matured as a self-confident and inclusive society.

The measures which I have just announced will, the Government intends, make a major contribution to this process.

PRESS SUMMARY OF GOVERNMENT MEASURES:
Package of Measures on Childhood Abuse

The Taoiseach has announced a wide package of measures relating to childhood abuse up to the present day to include a Commission to Inquire into Abuse of Children, the establishment of a £4 million professional counselling service for the victims of abuse and a number of legal changes. At the same time, the Taoiseach gave an apology on behalf of the State and the Citizens of the State to the victims of childhood abuse.

The Taoiseach was announcing the outcome of the Government's consideration of the issue of abuse. He explained that the Government has been discussing the issue for much of its time in office and that a full sub-committee of the Cabinet chaired by the Minister for Education & Science has been developing proposals since last December. He said: 'The time has long since arrived when we must take up the challenge which the victims of childhood abuse have given us all. A new, comprehensive approach is required to dealing with both the effects and prevention of this abuse.'

The details of the package are:

- The establishment of a Commission to Inquire into Childhood Abuse to be charged with establishing as clear a picture as possible of the causes, nature and extent of the physical and sexual abuse of children up to the present day.

- The establishment of a nationwide professional counselling service for the victims of abuse at an estimated cost of £4 million per annum.

- Legal changes relating to the taking of cases involving abuse.

- The publication of proposals concerning the mandatory reporting of abuse.

- The creation of a register of sex offenders.

- The implementation of a range of other measures designed to protect children at risk.

The Taoiseach, who announced the measures with the Tánaiste and the Minister for Education & Science, addressed the victims of childhood abuse saying 'On behalf of the State and of all citizens of the State, the Government wishes to make a sincere and long overdue apology to the victims. Abuse ruined their childhoods and has been an ever present part of their adult lives, reminding them of a time when they were helpless. I want to say to them that we believe that they were gravely wronged and that we must do all we can to overcome the lasting effects of their ordeals.'

'What the Government has decided on today is not a break with the past; it is a facing up to the past and all that this involves. This may well be a painful process; but it can not and should not be avoided.

'This country has a lot to be proud of. We are developing in many ways and for the first time we are seeing movement on a range of serious problems. But we cannot truly advance unless we acknowledge and deal with the more uncomfortable elements of our past. Only when we do this will we have matured as a self-confident and inclusive society.'

Ends

Terms of Reference for Commission to Inquire into Childhood Abuse

- To afford victims of abuse in childhood an opportunity to tell of the abuse they suffered to a sympathetic and experienced forum;

- To establish as complete a picture as possible of the causes, nature and extent of physical and sexual abuse of children in institutions and in other places during the period from 1940, or such earlier date as the Commission considers appropriate, to the present, including the antecedents, circumstances, factors and context of such abuse, the perspectives of the victims and the motives and perspectives of the persons responsible for committing abuse;

- To compile a report and publish it to the general public, on the activities and findings of the Commission, containing such recommendations as the Commission considers appropriate including actions which should be taken to address the continuing effects of the abuse examined by the Commission and actions to be taken to safeguard children against abuse for the future;

- To appoint specialist advisers to supply information or elucidate areas of complexity, to conduct investigations, hold hearings, both private and public and conduct or commission research for the purposes of carrying out these terms of reference.

APPENDIX 6

THE MOORE REPORT

Father Moore's letter to the Archbishop of Dublin, John Charles McQuaid, submitting his report on Artane:

38 Harmondstown Avenue,
ARTANE,
DUBLIN, 5.
7th July, 1962.

My Lord Archbishop,

In a letter of 18th May Your Grace requested me to submit a report on Artane Industrial School. I have pleasure in presenting herewith the findings of my enquiry.

Due to the confidential nature of my task and the wide terms of reference I was obliged to restrict my observations to personal experience. The details are none the less factual and complete.

I am, My Lord Archbishop,

Your Grace's Obedient Servant,
Henry Moore [signed]

Chaplain.

The Most Reverend John C. McQuaid, D.D.,
Lord Archbishop of Dublin,
Primate of Ireland

PRIVATE REPORT ON ARTANE INDUSTRIAL SCHOOL

INTRODUCTION

In this report I have attempted to describe and discuss the existing situation as the Industrial School system operates in Artane. It is not a complete examination of all aspects of the system. I have, however, studied the Report of the Commission of Inquiry into the Industrial School system of 1936 and the Report on Youth Unemployment of 1951.

In relation to the contemporary scene, and considering the advance in educational requirements, particularly as envisaged by the recent Apprenticeship Act, it seems to me that Artane is in need of drastic revision. Government policy as it affects the financial position of the school would indicate the urgent need of an enlightened approach to the problem. A serious decline in the number of committals reacts adversely on the school's financial position, since overhead expenses do not decrease pari passu with a reduction in direct maintenance charges. Despite this hardship certain improvements have been made, notably by the installation of a fine modern kitchen and the construction, now in progress, of twelve class halls in the old building.

The management of the school is the subject of this report. As I shall indicate, the methods employed are obsolete, proper training is neglected, and there is no attempt at adequate rehabilitation.

CONSTITUTION

The early association in the public mind of Artane with the Prison system is responsible for a misconception that persists regarding Artane and the boys in it. By agreement with the Department of Justice the authorities at Artane will not accept committals with a criminal charge. This means that the inmates are either school non-attendance cases—about one-third of the total—the majority being orphans or children in special circumstances. Many of these are transferred from Junior Industrial Convent Schools at Rathdrum, Drogheda, and Kilkenny; and so, the situation frequently arises where boys, on leaving Artane, have already spent 10 to 14 years in an institutional environment. It is readily acknowledged that all of these require specialised treatment.

GENERAL CARE OF THE BOYS

About 450 boys are resident at the school. For any measure of success it is necessary that this number should be divided into small units. Considering that the buildings were originally designed to accommodate 800 boys, proper planning might ensure the possibility of this. A fundamental defect is the manner in which the boys are admitted indiscriminately, without regard to their background, medical history, antecedents or suitability for the training which they are to receive. The very structure of the school is in dilapidated condition, colourless and uninspiring, and reflects the interior spirit. 'Tibi saxa loquuntur.' The atmosphere is somewhat unreal, particularly in regard to lack of contact with the opposite sex, and this unnatural situation in a group of 450 boys plus a staff of 40 men invariably leads to a degree of sexual maladjustment in the boys.

Indeed in this respect Artane is a modern Mount Athos. The boys seem to be denied the opportunity of developing friendly and spontaneous characters; their impulses become suffocated and when they are suddenly liberated their reactions are often violent and irresponsible.

DIET: The boys are reasonably well fed. There is fair variety but obvious essential requirements such as butter and fruit are never used. Milk puddings are served but these are of poor quality and without relish. In general I feel that the boys are undernourished and lacking calcium and other components. At table I have observed the unruly indelicate manner of the boys. The services of a dietician and supervision under a female staff would considerably enhance the standards. In addition to the three meals the boys are given a light refreshment which takes the form of a slice of bread and jam. The method of serving this is crude and unhealthy. The bread is transported to the yard in a large sized wooden box and the boys are paraded to receive their portion.

APPAREL: It seems to me that this aspect of the general care is grossly neglected. The boys' clothing is uncomfortable, unhygienic, and of a displeasing sameness. They are constantly dirty, both themselves and their clothes. The quality of the material is poor due to the fact that it is manufactured on the premises. Overcoats are not supplied except where a boy can pay £3 to £4 in advance, which must come from his own pocket. It is pathetic to observe hundreds of boys walking the roads of the district on Sunday mornings even in deep winter without overcoats. Moreover, on returning from their walk they are compelled to change again into their ordinary work-a-day suit. This has the effect on the boys' morale and their association of the Sunday is easily obscured. In the matter of the clothing, likewise, there is no individuality. A boy's personal clothing is as much the property of his neighbour. Shirts, underwear (vests are not worn), stockings, footwear, nightshirts (no pyjamas) are all common property and are handed down from generations. When these articles are laundered they are distributed at random, sometimes without regard to size. The laundry arrangements leave much to be desired. The boys' stockings and shirts are renewed once a week and underwear once a fortnight. Handkerchiefs are not used. This fundamental disregard for personal attention inevitably generates insecurity, instability and an amoral concern for the private property of others. This I consider to be a causative factor in the habits of stealing frequently encountered among ex-pupils. In summer the boys do not receive a change of clothing. When I visited the Industrial School at Salthill I was impressed by the way in which the boys were attired appropriately and inexpensively for the summer season. In Artane the hob-nail boots, [and] the heavy burdensome material are as much a feature of summer attire as of winter.

MEDICAL ATTENTION: I fail to understand the indifference of Departmental Inspectors to the seriously inadequate medical facilities in the school. Apart from the twice-weekly visit of the Doctor there is no matron or nurse in attendance. A Brother without qualifications and who was transferred from the care of the poultry farm is now in charge of all medical requirements. A surgical dressing room is located adjacent to the dining hall. This dreary stone flagged and depressing room resembles a vacated dairy house. Many boys, even the older ones, suffer from enuresis and nothing is done to remedy their condition.

DISCIPLINE: In a school of over 400 boys, discipline must necessarily be firmly maintained. In Artane, it seems to me that the discipline is rigid and severe and frequently approaches pure regimentation. Every group activity is martialled, even the most elementary such as the recitation of the Angelus during recreation. The administration of punishment is in charge of a disciplinarian, but in practice is not confined to him. There seems to be no proportion between punishment and offence. In my presence a boy was severely beaten on the face for an insignificant misdemeanour. Recently, a boy was punished so excessively and for so long a period that he broke away from the Brother and came to my house a mile away for assistance. The time was 10.45 p.m., almost two hours after the boys retired to bed. For coming to me in those circumstances he was again punished with equal severity. Some time ago, a hurley stick was used to inflict punishment on a small boy. The offence was negligible.

Constant recourse to physical punishment breeds undue fear and anxiety. The personality of the boy is inevitably repressed, maladjusted, and in some cases, abnormal. Their liberty is so restricted that all initiative and self esteem suffers. This is particularly evident when they leave the school. The boys find it difficult to establish ordinary human relationships and not infrequently are very difficult to manage. I recommend a more liberal approach in the matter of outings, holidays etc. This year 150 boys will be away for August. Some to their families, others to god-parents and friends. The remaining 250 will stay on in Artane. The trade shops close for two weeks but the boys are transferred to work on the farm. This naturally breeds discontent and frustration. Some effort should be made to provide a holiday, however brief, for the unlucky ones.

The introduction of interested parties and voluntary groups would lend a welcome change to the drabness and monotony of the Institute. The more winds of change that blow through Artane the less stagnation and ugliness there will be. Here I am thinking of possible work for the Volunteer Corps or its counterpart, which some day I trust will be available for girls. Greater co-operation could be obtained from the Brothers with regard to the God-parents Guild which does invaluable work in befriending destitute children. The Guild often complains to me of the difficulty in making contacts with Artane. The question of God-parents needs to be looked into, and full use of its potential obtained.

THE BAND: In my opinion the band is the only worthwhile achievement of the school. About 80 boys are involved, but this number is only a fraction of the total. The time used, the money spent, the number of engagements annually met are, I fear, out of all proportion to the results obtained. The maintenance of the band, although approximating £2,000 annually, is a continual strain on financial resources. Further, a serious gap in the boys' education follows from prolonged hours of practice and days missed from school. There is no evidence that even a small number continue their musical career on leaving the school. Instruments are costly and encouragement is lacking. Indeed, the Brother in charge could be most helpful in placing the boys in suitable positions. Unfortunately, he is unwilling. I feel obliged to refer to the interest taken in the band boys by a Protestant layman whose constant practice it is to accompany the boys on each and every engagement. He renders no service to the school, and in my opinion should not be present. On one occasion when I questioned the Brother concerning this matter I found him not only discourteous but impertinent.

The band is good publicity but its prestige revolves around itself. It is unrelated to the true conditions obtaining in the school.

RELIGIOUS OBSERVANCE

A great deal of discussion has taken place between the authorities at Artane and previous Chaplains about the problems arising in the matter of religious observance. In my experience these problems are very real. Religion seems to make little impression on the majority of the boys. With many ex-pupils the practice of their Faith is a burden to be shunned, and they associate their religious training with repression. Indeed, many of the problems I encounter are quite alarming. I suggest that much of the trouble arises from the regimentation attached to the various religious exercises.

Up to three years ago daily Mass was obligatory for the boys. It was the opinion of the Chaplains that this excellent practice was proving too much for the boys. It was decided that the boys' attendance at Mass be voluntary, as the early rising for 7 o'clock Mass was unreasonable. The result of this decision was that only a handful of boys attended Mass regularly. Last year the Superior decided to go back on this decision and oblige the boys to attend Mass on two mornings each week. It seems to me a great spiritual loss that attendance at daily Mass should be relegated to the voluntary whims of adolescent minds. The obvious solution would be to put forward the hour of the Mass by one hour, but at this suggestion the Superior was unwilling to change the programme.

The Rosary is recited daily in Chapel. Many of the boys complain to me of the weariness they have in attending the Rosary. This is quite natural, but I would like to see a change in the practice to give the boys an opportunity of appreciating the value of praying in small groups or even alone. Too often the Christian Doctrine classes are without enthusiasm, and lacking incentive. I altogether repudiate the use of physical punishment for failure at these lessons. At times it is excessive.

CHAPEL: The Chapel at Artane does not inspire devotion, or indeed little reverence. It is stone-flagged and untidy, the furnishings are rough, uncomfortable and unattractive. It is greatly in need of decoration. The brass ware is inferior, stained and damaged; the sacred linen is carelessly handled and arranged. Some time ago mice were discovered in the Sacristy and on opening the Corporal before Mass I noticed it to be soiled by animal excretion. A few days later the Chasuble was in a similar condition. These isolated incidences merely indicate the general tone of the Chapel. The care of the Sacristy should be entrusted to females, preferably nuns.

EDUCATION

PRIMARY: It is difficult to assess with satisfaction the extent of the problems attending the education, literary and technical, of the boys. To my mind the standard is extremely low. Constantly I receive letters from ex-pupils and at times I am amazed by their illegible form and unintelligible content. The majority of the boys are lacking in verbal ability. Last year a friend of mine took 22 boys on a camping holiday. He informed me that that although their ages ranged from 10 to 14 years, only 7 could write, and these had to be assisted. There seems to be an urgent need for some psychological assessment of the boys before grading them in classes. I believe that some of these boys are mentally handicapped and require psychiatric treatment. Unfortunately the Brothers are obliged to grade these boys as best they can. This is an undue hardship on teacher and pupil. I strongly recommend that the services of a competent psychiatrist should be sought.

TECHNICAL: It is, perhaps, in this department that the most glaring defect is noticed. At 14 the boy is admitted to the Trade shop. This year there are 150 boys in that department, but of these only 12 were eligible for the Vocational

School examination. Last year, out of 18 who sat for the examination only 5 were successful. In view of the requirements of Technical education, the situation in Artane is obsolete. There seems to be no effort to train the boys satisfactorily at their trades. They might be described as juvenile labourer, uneducated and unskilled. This is evident from the variety of tasks to be done by individual boys. Vocational guidance is unknown. Boys are allotted to various trades without reference to their suitability or preference. This unhappy position inevitably engenders frustration. A factual proof of this is the way in which the boys are placed on leaving the school. In the past two years 140 boys or so were discharged. Approximately 75% of these were placed at employment for which they were never trained. The purpose of the school is therefore defeated. The lay instructors are all of long standing in the school—some with service varying from 29 to 30 years. They are not acquainted with modern teaching methods and practice. Little encouragement is given them towards fostering an enthusiastic and progressive attitude towards the boys. Many of them that are competent are underpaid and unappreciated.

PERSONNEL: There are 26 Brothers in the Community. An analysis of their function reveals the shortage of specialised teachers who are kind and dedicated. Only 10 Brothers are directly involved in teaching; three of these in addition are attending the University. It seems to me that these men are overworked, for apart from the multitude of tasks attending the daily schedule and the prescriptions of their own religious life, they have in addition the supervision and care of a large dormitory and the supervision of recreation. Six Brothers are at the school from 15 to 35 years, and to these are entrusted authoritative and administrative positions. Clearly, a more enlightened and efficient staff is required, but in this connection the Provincial once complained to me of the difficulty in finding dedicated men. To me this is a startling revelation of the incompetency of the Brothers to conduct the school without the assistance of trained lay personnel.

AFTERCARE

The Report of the Commission in 1936 made specific mention of the lack of appreciation and responsibility in exercising aftercare by the authorities at Artane. Twenty six years does not seem to have brought about any change in this matter. The Children's Act 1908 obliges the Brothers to exercise aftercare for two years on a boy's discharge. This task is performed at Artane by an elderly Brother who is preoccupied in seeking employment for the boys. Within six months of my appointment I requested your Grace's permission to use a car for this purpose. I intimated that my work was increasing in this field. I am happy to acknowledge Your Grace's spontaneous and generous permission, and my work has been facilitated by Your Grace's constant support and encouragement. I work in conjunction with a Praesidium established by the past pupils of St Mary's College, Rathmines, which was requested by Father John Pierce, CC, to undertake the running of a club for Artane ex-pupils. I am obliged to say that the Brothers' attitude towards a Chaplain's work in this field is uncooperative and even resentful. I am confident that your Grace appreciates the necessity of this work. The Praesidium informs me that in the past five years 80% of these boys have emigrated. It is my experience that many of these boys whom I know personally have lapsed entirely from the Faith. In Dublin I find these boys in dead-end jobs without any opportunity of advancing themselves. For some, the working conditions, especially in the country, are primitive; others are exploited for less than a living wage. Emigration in their case is a blessing. My remarks heretofore, refer to boys discharged at 16 years of age, but at least 70 boys between 12 and 14, school non-attendance cases, have left the school in the past two years. For these latter, the Brothers relinquish all responsibility in aftercare. The Superior in Salthill Industrial School is most attentive to this aspect of the boys' training. By elaborate means and by painstaking methods he has shown what an efficient management can achieve.

CONCLUSION

In this Report I have endeavoured to illustrate, by factual information, the deficiencies in the Management of Artane. No doubt there are reasonable explanations for many of the inadequacies. It is my opinion, however, that a reappraisal of the system at Government level is necessary and a major reform of the management of Artane is desired.

I strongly recommend the introduction of female personnel, preferably nuns, who would take care of the domestic arrangements and the charge of the small boys. The school should have a patron saint by name, and the stigma of the present system should be removed from the public mind.

This Report would be incomplete without a special mention of the personal interest which Your Grace has taken in the welfare of these boys. I have been singularly impressed and I am deeply grateful for the assistance Your Grace has given me and which continues to hearten me no end.

APPENDIX 7

MS JUSTICE MARY LAFOY'S LETTER OF RESIGNATION

2nd September 2003

Mr Dermot McCarthy
Secretary General to the Government
Government Buildings
Upper Merrion Street
Dublin 2

Dear Mr McCarthy,

I am the Chairperson of the Commission to Inquire into Child Abuse, appointed by the Government pursuant to section 6 of the Commission to Inquire into Child Abuse Act, 2000. In that capacity, I request that you put this letter before the Government.

I refer to a Press release of 1st September 2003 from the Department of Education and Science announcing the decision of the Government to engage in a second phase of a review relating to the Commission. The Commission responded to that announcement in a statement posted on the Commission's website today. It its statement, the Commission explained that, for legal, practical and financial reasons, it is effectively constrained to put the substantive work of the Investigation Committee (the gathering and assessment of evidence) on hold pending the announcement of the results of the review. The Commission also announced its intention to issue an Interim Report in November of 2003.

This prolongation of the duration of the Government review is merely the latest in a series of events which have, since the inception of the statutory Commission over three years ago, impeded the completion by the Commission of its statutory mandate as set out in the Act of 2000 in a timely fashion. A range of factors over which the Commission has had no control have together produced a real and pervasive sense of powerlessness. In retrospect, it appears to me that since its establishment, the Commission has never been properly enabled by the Government to fulfil satisfactorily the functions conferred on it by the Oireachtas.

The factors which have brought about this situation include the following:
(1) the issue of compensation for survivors of abuse, first raised in July 2000 by a group of solicitors acting for a substantial number of survivors, which

was eventually dealt with in the Residential Institutions Redress Act 2002, which was enacted in April 2002;

(2) on the issue of the payment of legal costs of persons involved in the process of the Investigation Committee, first raised by solicitors on behalf of persons making allegations and solicitors on behalf of persons and bodies against whom allegations were made as early as July 2000, which also was eventually dealt with in the Act of 2002;

(3) the Government's handling of requests for the provision of adequate resources to enable the Investigation Committee to carry out its remit with reasonable expedition, when the volume of allegations which were the subject of formal statements to the Investigation Committee became known, which requests commenced in early June 2002;

(4) the Government decision of 3 December, 2002 to review the Commission's mandate, which was to be completed by mid-February, 2003, the outcome of which review has not been published yet; and,

(5) the Government decision of 3 December, 2002, to agree in principle to the provision of additional resources as requested, which in the events has proved meaningless, because it was made contingent on the outcome of the review, which still has not been published.

As Chairperson of the Commission I have always recognised that the foregoing matters and their resolution were matters of policy for the Government and that my role was to preserve intact the process put in place by the Oireachtas in the Act of 2002. However, I believe that the cumulative effect of those factors, each of which has been characterised by long periods of uncertainty for the Commission, has effectively negatived the guarantee of independence in the performance of its functions conferred on the Commission by section 3(3) of the Act of 2000 and has militated against the Commission being able to perform its statutory functions as envisaged by the Oireachtas with reasonable expedition.

Recent events, the communication to the Commission of July 2003 of a Government decision that there is to be a further phase of the review of the Commission's mandate and the publication of information in relation to that decision in the Press Release yesterday, have compounded the sense of powerlessness. On the basis of current knowledge, it is not possible—(a) to deduce the nature of the functions which are likely to be conferred on the Commission post review, save that they will be substantially different from its current functions, (b) to predict whether, as current Chairperson, I might be precluded from continued participation in the work of the Investigation Committee post review on account of involvement in the work of the Investigation Committee to date, or (c) to predict the duration of the review, which is open-ended.

As has been pointed out in recent correspondence from the Commission to the Department of Education and Science, the only clear inference to be drawn from the recent communications from the Department to the Commission is that the Government has decided that the Commission will not implement its current statutory mandate. The Government having chosen not to adopt the suggestion made by the Commission immediately following the communication to it of the decision of the 3 December 2002—that legislation be enacted to enable the Investigation Committee to suspend the operation of its current procedure pending completion of the review and the enactment of any necessary legislation to give effect to the outcome of the review—the Commission has been faced with the following fundamental difficulties.

From a formal legal point of view, the Commission is still fixed with an unqualified mandate from the Oireachtas as set out in the Act of 2000, as amended by the Act of 2002. From a practical point of view, however, although the statutory mandate remains unqualified, all participations in the process (persons making allegations and persons and bodies against whom allegations have been made), the members of the Commission and Commission personnel are now aware from Government announcements that the Commission's mandate is to be altered and that the Commission will end up working and reporting to a mandate potentially radically differently from that currently in force. It follows that the procedures under which the Commission has operated and the investigations which it has conducted up to now may transpire to be redundant or incorrectly focused in the light of some future, but as yet unknown, mandate.

That these uncertainties would impact on the Commission's work in many respects, legal, practical and financial, has been brought to the attention of the Department since the decision to radically alter the Commission's mandate was communicated to the Commission on the 4 July last. The current mandate, while still on the statute book, has, in effect, become inoperable and the Commission has in a practical sense been rendered powerless. It is clearly not possible to predict which parts of its existing functions and powers will survive the review.

The consequence of the most recent decision of the Government is that an independent statutory Commission has been put in the position that it has had to decide, following legal advice, that it cannot continue to engage in the work which it considers it should be engaged in to advance its mandate and, further, of having to publish that decision. The public now knows that the Commission is, in effect, stymied in relation to its statutory function, albeit with a proposal in the background that at some indeterminate date in the future alternative functions are to be conferred on it by statute.

Following the announcement of the Government's review last December and having been advised by the Department that the Investigation Committee should continue to operate in accordance with its existing mandate, I, in conjunction with my colleagues, consulted with the Attorney General, who led the review, in the belief, in the short term, it would bring about a situation in which the Commission would be in a position to discharge its remit in a speedier, more effective and cost effective manner. I had hoped that the outcome of the review and any legislation necessary to give effect to it would have been published around Easter last. Instead, the process had already dragged on for seven months by the time the Commission was notified of the most recent Government decision. I have come to the conclusion to abide, without protest, the outcome of the future radical review now proposed, whenever it may be concluded, would be a complete abrogation of the independence which the Oireachtas intended the Commission to enjoy and would seriously undermine my credibility as Chairperson of the Commission.

On the 29 November 2002, in a response to a request from the Department of Education and Science, to justify the Commission's request for sufficient resources to enable the Investigation Committee to work in four divisions with the objective of completing Phase 1 of its work by the end of July, 2005, on behalf of the Commission, I stated as follows:

'Apart from the possible legal consequences of the fulfilment of the Investigation Committee's remit being unduly protracted, it is not in the interests of any of the parties involved in the process that the Investigation Committee should not be in a position to complete Phase 1 of its work within a reasonable timeframe. Of particular concern are the following considerations:

- the need to bring closure for the Complainants and for other victims of abuse in childhood, many of whom are old and in bad health.
- the avoidance of unfairness to individuals against whom allegations have been made, which may not stand up following investigation. Many of the individual respondents are very old. Some are in bad health. It may be that in certain cases, the end of their lives are being unfairly blighted by the stress of a prolonged investigation. Issues of fairness also arise in relation to individuals against whom allegations have been made, who are still of working age, whose capacity to work in institutions may be affected.'

The Government's decision to review the mandate was made the following week. Nine months have elapsed since then, during which time I have repeatedly reminded the Department of my concern for the persons concerned by the process. I believe that the further indefinite protraction of the uncertainty as to the task which the Commission will ultimately be mandated to carry out announced in the Press Release is detrimental to the interests of the persons for whose benefit the Commission was established— the men and women, many of whom are now elderly, who allege that they suffered abuse in institutions in the State during childhood, who, at not inconsiderable cost, have indicated a willingness to assist the inquiry. They deserve to see the inquiry, which they were promised over four years ago, concluded within a reasonable timeframe. More-over, I believe that the inevitable future delay has the potential to give rise to unfairness and injustice to individuals against whom allegations have been made and persons with management or regulatory responsibility for institutions in which abuse is alleged to have occurred. They are entitled to expect that such allegations will be dealt with within a reasonable timeframe.

It is with great regret that I now notify the Government that I have decided to resign chairmanship of the Commission as soon as the Interim Report on the work of the Commission under its current mandate, announced in the Commission's statement is published. This report will account for the Commission's work to date and hopefully it will be of assistance to whoever takes up this work under the revised mandate. It will also outline in detail the factual circumstances which have given rise to the members of the Commission being in the wholly invidious situation in which they now find themselves. My principal reason for resolving on this course is because the Commission has, in effect, being rendered powerless by reason of the matters set out above. As subsidiary consideration which has weighed with me in reaching the decision is that there appears to be some risk that a Commission which works first to a mandate, and then to a substantially different mandate, would leave itself open to legal challenge on the ground that, in the course of exercising its first mandate, it obtained information or formed impressions which would effect its capacity to exercise the second mandate with a fully open mind. While, on the basis of independent legal advice which I have obtained, I believe that this risk is a slight one, nonetheless, even a slight risk may be unacceptable in a matter of this importance.

The extensive correspondence between the Commission and the Department sets out in greater detail the issues dealt with in this letter. For convenience of reference, I am appending copies of the Department's Press Release, the Commission's statements, the correspondence in December 2002 referred to earlier and the letter dated 4 July 2003 and subsequent correspondence between the Commission and the Department, as listed in the attached schedule.

A statement of my intention to resign will be posted on the Commission's website today, which will indicate that the reasons for my decision are set out in a letter to the Government.

Finally, the Government may be assured that, in relation to my departure from the Commission, I will take all necessary steps to ensure that the public interest is protected.

Yours sincerely
Mary Lafoy (signed)

ACKNOWLEDGMENTS

The Irish Gulag is based on writing that stretches back a number of years and includes articles written for the *Irish Independent* and for the *Sunday Independent* from the time of Bertie Ahern's Apology in May 1999 to the present. I am first of all grateful to these newspapers, for which I have worked for many years, and to their editors and staff for the support always given for columns and news stories on this subject. The writing was inherently abrasive and difficult but it provided me with much material that is used in this book.

The articles attracted support and encouragement from men and women who had passed through the industrial school and reformatory school system about which I wrote. I am grateful to all of them for their trust and confidence and for the archive material they gave and lent me, strengthening the force of much that I wrote.

In particular I was helped by the leading members of Irish SOCA (Survivors of Child Abuse). Alone, I think, among the organisations supporting and representing those who had suffered within the schools, Irish SOCA maintained its independence and received no funding, either from the State or from the Roman Catholic Church. The research work they did was of enormous value, as was their support.

I was given enormous help in the later stages of the book by Kathy Ferguson. She researched a great number of difficult questions, taking on many abstruse queries and coming up with prodigious material. Her own complicated industrial school experiences are the subject of the Epilogue.

Paddy Doyle was a great support, both personally and through his website, carrying stories of mine and reporting on issues he thought might be of help. He became an agreeable friend and has always been a tireless defender of the abused men and women.

Father Henry Moore met me on three occasions for discussions about Artane at the beginning of the 1960s, the report on conditions at Artane Industrial School which he made at the request of Archbishop John Charles McQuaid, and the Archbishop's views on industrial schools generally. I am much in his debt.

Mary Raftery's role on behalf of the abused is already acknowledged in this book as it is more widely. She had an enormous impact through her televised and written work. She was also a good working colleague and friend, encouraging a view that is not quite the same as the one she took in *States of Fear* and *Suffer the Little Children*. She was aided in this by Eoin O'Sullivan, of Trinity College, Dublin.

The following helped in many different ways:

George Bell, Jim Beresford, Eddie Birmingham, Tom Boland, Kevin Brady of the National Office for Victims of Abuse (NOVA), John Brendan, Noel Brennan, Paul Breslin, Christine Buckley, Joan Burton TD, Kevin Byrne, also of NOVA, and Loreto Byrne. Margaret Campbell and Mary Teresa Barry, Michael Collins, Liam Connolly, Bernadette Cook, Jody Corcoran, Joe Costello TD (Labour Party justice spokesperson), Sean Costello, Annie Cowen, Ciaran Craven, Brenda Crawford, Val Croagh (Galway Representative of Right of Place), Paul Cronin, Tom Cronin, Muriel Cuffe, Dolores Curley and Mary Curran.

Colin Daly (North Side Community Law Centre), Thomas Daly, Daisy Day, William Delahunty, Patricia Dervan and Joe Duffy. Bernadette El Amiri. Patrick Fahy, Mannix Flynn, Raymond Foley and Pauline Ford. Sister Teresa Gallagher, Michael Galvin and Therese Gaynor.

Victor Hackett, Mary Harte (BBC Northern Ireland), Maureen Hatton, Tom Hayes (Alliance for Healing of Institutional Abuse Northern Ireland), May Henderson, Michael Hession, Joe Higgins, former TD, Florence Horsman-Hogan of LOVE (Let Our Voices Emerge), Bruno Hrela and Martin Hynes (Irish Embassy London) along with Ambassador Daíthí Ó Ceallaigh and Anne Byrne (Irish Community Officer).

Owen Keenan and Deirdre Mortell of Barnardos, John Kelly (Irish SOCA), Norman Kelly and Albert and Mary King. Thomas Lane, Michael Lanigan, Breda Leake, Sean Leonard, Maeve Lewis, Susan Lohan (Adopted Peoples Association) with Paul Bolger and Anton Sweeney, John Lynch and Matt Lynch.

Ron and Mary McCartan, Patrick McCarthy, Margaret McCormack, Mary McCormack, Patricia McDonald, Peter McDonald, Colm McGlinn, James McGuill, Anne McLoon (Communications, North West Health Board), Eileen McMahon and Brenda McVeigh (Secretary of Commission to Inquire into Child Abuse and the Lafoy Commission).

Mike Mansfield, Jeremy Massey, Annie Matsuoka, Paul Moloney (Outreach Officer, Right of Place, Cork), Billie Morony, Billie Morton, Margaret Murnane, Denis Murphy and Eugene Murphy. Hugh O'Brien, Michael O'Brien (Chairman, Right to Peace, Clonmel), Rosaleen O'Brien, Ciaran O'Donoghue, Colm O'Gorman (One in Four), John O'Grady, Gerry O'Halloran, Kate Warrin O'Malley, Thomas O'Reilly, Timothy O'Rourke and Jan O'Sullivan.

Ruairi Quinn, Martin Reynolds and Kathleen Ruddy. Alan Shatter TD, Paul Shield, Roisin Shortall TD, Mary Slattery, Mary Smith, Eugene Sweeney. Joe Sweeney and Tom Sweeney, John Thompson. Patrick Walsh, Michael Waters and Kathleen Wrafter.

INDEX